An illustrated survey of

Ceramics Prices
at Auction

2004-2007

2008 Edition

Editor: John Ainsley B.A., B.Ed., M.I.E.E.

An illustrated survey of

Ceramics Prices
at Auction

2004-2007

2008 Edition

Editor: John Ainsley

First published in Great Britain in 2007 by
Antiques Information Services Ltd. Wallsend House,
P O Box 93, Broadstairs, Kent CT10 3YR
Telephone: 01843 862069
Fax: 01843 862014
E-mail: enquiries@antiques-info.co.uk

Further details about the Publishers may be found on our website at
www.antiques-info.co.uk

ISBN: 978-0-9546479-4-0
Whilst every care has been exercised in the compilation of this guide,
neither the Editor nor Publishers accept any liability for any financial
or other loss incurred by reliance placed on the information contained
in *Ceramics Prices at Auction*.

Printed in the United Kingdom
by The Cromwell Press, Trowbridge, Wiltshire

Contents

Introduction

The Series

We now present *Ceramics Prices at Auction* 2008 Edition. Currently in print are *Furniture Prices at Auction* published in 2004, *Silver & Jewellery Prices at Auction* and *Picture Prices at Auction*, both published in 2005. The *Series* will continue. *Glass Prices at Auction* will publish in the Spring of 2008.

Price Guides in General

Price guides have usually followed the A-Z format, values being controlled by publishers and/or editors. Many, not all, fulfil more of an information role than function as price guides! The reasons are clear. The estimates they contain are bound to be influenced to some extent by the commercial considerations of their publishers, although some now are basing their contents on actual sales following the success of this Series. In some cases it can be argued that it is the price guides which are leading the market rather than the market leading the price guides! Values quoted are often or completely lacking an essential market context which of course is always present in a real sale and are therefore prone to misrepresentation and hence reader confusion, perceptions which we at *Antiques Information Services* are involved in frequently having to correct. Nor do many understand that secondhand objects are unique and values subject to a measurable set of criteria.

It is therefore evident that estimates can never represent actual values. Using results from real sales, accompanied by the qualifications contained within the actual catalogue descriptions is a unique and ground-breaking development in the history of price guides. Readers of our new Series, even experts, dealers and auctioneers are now frequently referring to our books.

A New Rationale

Here are actual prices at auction from a mass of defined market situations representing the sales of 3,091 lots. These have been placed in 8 price bands and in actual price order in the price range £2,600,000 to £10. The price bands are arbitrary but provide a means of dividing the work into Sections which not only aid the analyses but provide a format to help the reader keep their bearings. These images have not only been chosen to represent the various price ranges but also to represent ceramic types, categories and manufacturers from mainly the last 400 years. The lots have been taken from sales occurring between 2004 and 2007, a credible four years. In this period fashions and even prices have changed and the book represents these changes.

The rationale is the rationale of the market. If you have used other price guides you will be aware of the difficulties. Their A-Z format is a weakness in itself, bearing no relationship to sales which is a straightforward matter of when an item was sold, where it sold and what it sold for! Here, the actual numeric price order, overseeing the price bands, representing the top to the bottom *is* the essential ingredient which aids a grasp of the fundamental elements which *are* the market. Here one can analyse the market in many ways. The reader can browse any price range, or, using the *Index*, it is possible to make a market study of a manufacturer, category or type of ceramic. Each Section is preceded by an Editor's analysis. It is recommended this be studied with the images and the captions themselves. The analysis is not definitive and is unobtrusive: the subject is not a science. Analyses may follow numerous paths at various levels. Hence, the Editor's analysis is personalised around the Editor's interests and level of knowledge. Each reader will seek their own analyses based on their own knowledge and interests. For example, a ceramics dealer may take a broad interest in prices or study a particular century and particular price range. Alternatively collectors may concentrate on a particular manufacturer or ceramic type.

Auction Arithmetic

Buying at auction

Most auctions in the UK publish only their hammer prices. The final price paid by the buyer is a matter of a private invoice not usually disclosed to the press.

Auctions add on a buyer's premium dependent on the hammer price. You may pay 15% on top of a hammer price of say £1,000 but only 10% on a hammer price of £30,000. In addition there is VAT on the premium and in some cases VAT may be due on the hammer price as well, depending on the age and origin of the lot. We have added to each lot description both the hammer price and the approximate buyer's price (APB) which includes a 15% buyer's premium plus VAT, i.e. 17.625%. Auction catalogues will include the buyer's and vendor's terms and conditions and there are variations.

Selling at auction

The final cost to the vendor is again outside the public domain. There is a premium to pay which on average will be at least 10-15% or more of the hammer price. Then there is the VAT and there may be charges related to photographs, storage and even insurance. We suggest that if you use this price guide to gauge how much you would receive if you were to sell an item, that you subtract from the hammer price the amount added to give the APB. This is an important market statement. The real buying price and the real selling price will usually vary by at least 35%. Again the auction catalogue will explain the terms and conditions relating to selling at auction. If the reader is in any doubt, auctions are always willing to explain their operations. And on viewing days, staff are usually on hand to offer information or advice on the lots themselves.

Ceramics Prices and the Market

Twenty five years ago, back in the early 1980s, fairs and antiques centres were rather thin on the ground and queues were commonplace. Prices were affordable and dealers' stock turned over more quickly than nowadays. But the market was expanding rapidly. *Going for a Song* failed to satisfy a growing consumer demand and the up-and-coming *Antiques Roadshow* began to attract soap-sized audiences. *The Shops Act, 1951* still held sway but councils turned a blind eye. Fairs had Sundays to themselves and a burgeoning industry emerged. Shops and the new multi-dealer antique centres proliferated and the expansion embraced high streets, town halls and green spaces throughout the country. Boot fairs spread their influence across the empty car parks of giant super-markets on Sundays, a naive public preened themselves at their enterprise and the Trade made off with Georgian coffee cans or Georgian rummers at 10 or 20 pence each, bought Clarice Cliff for a song and fished or even filched solid silver for next to nothing. In general prices were affordable. Coffee cans were actually about £5 although a rarer Pinxton cup and saucer could be bought for £20 to £40. Today the same may cost you £800! Nobody could pronounce Nantgarw and many thought majolica came from Majorca. Pieces swapped hands for tens of pounds that today fetch thousands. Clarice Cliff and perhaps Moorcroft apart, no one cared much about the twentieth century but this was to change. Evolution may be sustained but revolution cannot. Every Tom and Dick got involved and spoiled it for Harry. Standards plummeted. Many fairs were a travesty, and could have been prosecuted under the *Trades Description Act*! By the closing decade of the twentieth century the public were already voting with their feet. In any event there were just too many events.

The buying spree had already spawned reproductions and fakes on a massive scale and as everyone is aware these were to affect values in the real market. Displaying reproductions in shops or in fairs in situations and in circumstances that were likely to confuse the novice or trap the unwary is unprofessional and a further turn off for the serious collector. It is still going on today and represents the lack of any governing control that is always applied through professional bodies such as BADA or LAPADA and through fairs organisers who practice vetting or self-vetting procedures.

Nor did the invasion of television, so promising in the early days, match up to earlier standards. Most profes-sionals across the industry agree that television programmes in general have had an adverse effect on trade. Their misleading manipulation of the real market in the interests of their game show formats has done little to serve the interests of the industry, who at first welcomed them with open arms, and at its worst blatantly compromises the truth about how the real market works. The public are fed hyperbole. The manip-ulation of the real market in the interests of enter-tainment are reprehensible and invidious. Television has been mauled recently for its phone-in competition practices, but misleading the public is in my judgement endemic throughout the industry. This however is not to suggest that there are no worthwhile programmes. Television does have a part to play in promoting the antiques and collecting arena.

Much more damaging is the impact of Sunday Trading which commenced in 1994 when the old *Shops Act* was abolished. The fairs industry became marginalised and Sunday was never the same again. Even more damaging is the impact of Ebay which is on-going. Who could have imagined that an American Company could seriously disable the UKs retail industry by providing a buying and selling experience through a screen in our own homes. Still, change is part of life and both dealers and collectors now have a new medium in the internet, which is a huge resource for those who embrace it. Nothing of course is all gloom. The fairs industry needed a kick up the pants and the survivors, including shops and centres have improved and the future looks brighter. People will always be interested in their heritage and new collectors continue to appear. TV is improving and apart from a few poor programmes have a part to play in encouraging the participation of the collector. The industry is leaner but much fitter. The preoccupation with the twentieth century has subsided to some extent and prices have succumbed and settled at sensible levels. As the twentieth century turned around into a new millennium, the market has continued to polarise across certain manufacturers, categories and types of ceramics. The top end of the market continues to see auction records although the market has seen a bit of a dip in certain areas such as majolica, influenced no doubt by the poor exchange rate for Americans.

The early Sections of this book, covering hundreds of sales in the last four years, shows the market leaders to be Chinese ceramics, English delft, slipware, the eighteenth century soft pastes such as Chelsea, Derby and Worcester, paté-sur-paté, Martinware, majolica, Royal Doulton and the incredible rise in the prices of Swansea and Nantgarw. Perhaps surprisingly there are early entries for William de Morgan, Burmantofts, Charles Vyse, Clarice Cliff and Wemyss, as well as Iznik and maiolica. Ironstone and stone china make it into the top Section as services. As we move under £5,000 and into Section II the same categories reappear but there is perhaps more of the twentieth century with Wilkinson and Morrisware and Fairyland Lustre, Lenci and even Zsolnay. European porcelain is apparent and Satsuma has also appeared as has Beswick and George Tinworth and Hannah Barlow. Royal Dux in particular has arrived with some of their best still to come. Even Bretby and Troika are showing, Bretby at over £3,000 and Troika at

£3,400, heady prices, but can we be certain that twentieth century ceramics, and in particular Troika may not succumb to a change in fashion?

Meanwhile as our pages progress through the middle and into the lower end of the market it will become clear that the market reappraisal and adjustment has seriously affected not only twentieth century ceramics but even the traditional eighteenth and nineteenth century bodies and pastes. Even English delft is not fetching its value at the lower end of the market. Look particularly at the under £100 price range where creamware, pearlware, basalt, caneware, porcelains and faience prices now cautiously offer investment potential in the longer term. The same cannot be said of the twentieth century. I am hopeful that the days are long gone when collectors were paying more for Shelley than first period Worcester and more again for those endless twentieth century figurines than say, Chelsea-Derby, which represents the pinnacle of ceramic art and achievement. The crash in the prices paid for Nat West pigs says it all, as does a superb Minton parian figure *Dorothea* by John Bell, which reached only £150 hammer in 2006. Similarly an eighteenth century Worcester teapot (admittedly only a printed *Fence Pattern*) sold for the same price and a Worcester *Cabbage Leaf* pattern mask jug, with minor damage, fetched only £120. Or the insulting example of four early Mason's Patent Ironstone jugs, three of them graded, which fetched a dismal £70 hammer in 2005. An early blue and white cow creamer could do no better in 2006. Browse the lower Sections for more examples.

The good thing about today's auctions market, and the same applies to the retail sector, is that once more prices are keen and it is indeed a very good time to buy. And the upheavals and the turmoil of the last few years also means that we have lived through the recent experiences of market adjustments and can perhaps benefit from this knowledge and buy more wisely in the future. I sincerely hope that this volume with its 3091 examples and market analyses from the last four years will help.

Pitfalls in the market

It is certain that in most cases, investing in antiques is a safer bet than buying a car, an insurance policy, finding the cheapest railway ticket, contributing to a pension scheme or choosing your electricity, gas or telephone supplier. The marketing is rarely deliberately oblique and you will never face the onerous task of having to deal with a call centre. It is also nice to know that you are very unlikely ever to see dealers driving fast cars and living fast lifestyles: profit margins are too low.

However there are buying sources in which you cannot put your total trust. Rarely is there deliberate deception but there are reproductions and fakes about, and even genuine antiques that are misdescribed through a lack of knowledge on behalf of the dealer. Ceramics also lends itself to the either naive or deliberate concealment of restoration and repair. If you are not an expert in your subject, and even experts can be deceived or mistaken, it is wise to buy from sources which give you consumer protection. Fine art fairs and dealers and auctions that are members of Trade associations are safer. Here you will always receive a receipt and the receipt should give not only a good description of the item but also its condition and an approximate date of manufacture. If buying from an auction check for a rescission clause in their conditions related to buying. This will guarantee the auction will rescind the sale and refund your money if within a certain time you are able to prove inaccuracy in the lot description. However if you are buying in a less controlled situation, ensure you get a receipt which includes the necessary information. If the vendor won't provide a receipt don't buy, unless you are the expert.

How to use this book

This book is an ideal browsing medium but it is recommended that both the full **Introduction** and the **Section Analyses** are read at an early stage. A significant part of this work is the lot descriptions. These conclude with colour-coded market information, viz: *where the lot was sold, when the lot was sold* and *what the lot was sold for*. The prices quoted are firstly the actual hammer price and secondly the approximate buyer's price. (APB) This actually amounts to 17.625% being an average 15% buyer's premium plus the VAT on that premium. Some auctions will charge more or less than this for the buyer's premium as well as the vendor's premium. The operating rates can always be found in auction catalogues or by consulting the relevant auction.

In addition, whilst every effort has been made by the Editor to check out the attributions, there exists the unlikely possibility of error. Auction cataloguing is a difficult task and even specialists cannot know everything. However, great care is usually taken and 'labelling' is in most cases very accurate. Incidentally, many auctions will rescind a sale within a set period of the purchase if the buyer can show inaccuracies in the catalogue description. Disputes usually revolve around damaged, restored or misrepresented lots.

In some cases captions have been rationalised in order to solve editing requirements. Syntactical changes have been made and abbreviations used which did not occur in the original auction catalogue. And on occasions the Editor has used his discretion to omit descriptive detail which would be tedious and which would not materially influence the price. In all cases, the Editor has ensured that changes in meaning have not occurred and that the content of a caption remains true to the original version. Foreign spellings and name spellings also varied in the original catalogues. These have been standardised to ensure the integrity of the Indexing system.

Finally, the reader's attention is drawn to the *Glossary of Terms* and the *Index*. These are integral parts of this work. The *Index* has about 4,500 cross-references.

The Editor wishes to thank the dozens of auctions up and down the country who have supplied the sales information that appears in the main body of this book.

Section I: Over £5,000

'It is reasonable to suggest that in terms of turnover at UK auctions, Chinese ceramics dominates the market....the nearest we can get in our home market is probably English delft, spelt by the way with a small 'd'. Doulton...has eight entries commencing with the Sir Stanley Matthews character jug at 10...........'

There are eight sections to this book covering the various price ranges down to under £50. **Sections II** to **VIII** concentrate on the market since 2004 and particularly 2005 to 2007. Here, by way of an introduction, this short section shows many of the most important sales over the last ten years or so, ensuring that I am able to analyse most of the categories, manufacturers and types of ceramics fetching over £5,000.

It is reasonable to suggest that in terms of turnover at UK auctions, Chinese ceramics dominates the market. At **1** a Yuan Dynasty double gourd vase fetched over £3,000,000 at Woolley & Wallis, Salisbury in 2005, whilst two eighteenth century lots at **5** and **9** fetched over £100,000 between them. It is worth noting the price for simple brush pots. See the blue and white example at **28** and the famille rose at **33** averaging over £18,000. The pair of hawks at **31** are in the same league. Then go to **58** where a famille verte moon vase fetched over 10,000. See the famille rose Yongzheng bowls (1723-1735) and the twentieth century bowls at **67** reaching nearly £9,000 at *Canterbury Auction Galleries* in 2006. There are more Chinese ceramics at **75**, **78** and **98**.

The nearest we can get in our home market is probably English delft, spelt by the way with a small 'd'. At **2**, a marriage dish made over £280,000 in June 1994. This piece is dated 1638 and about the earliest English delft ever found dated to about 1600. One must assume the £53,000 cat at **6** (rather damaged) is English. Next is a pill slab at **27** and an early armorial plate at **47**, dated 1653, quickly followed by the Fazackerly jug at **49** (£10,000 HP) and also the Queen Caroline commemorative at **50**. Further English delft can be found at **59**, **63**, **64**, **72**, **79**, **83**, **84** and **96**. English delft is a tin-glazed earthenware, very prone to chipping, glaze loss and general damage. This is more acceptable than it would be in later bodies or pastes.

The English eighteenth century soft pastes are dominated by Chelsea, Worcester and Derby in that order, although the most expensive of these factories is actually a Royal Crown Derby suite of five vases at **4** and a twentieth century pair of Worcester plaques at **14** by Harry Davis. Probably the rarest soft paste example here is the Girl-in-a-Swing bonbonniere at **105**. I expect that if this were to appear on the market today it would fetch considerably more than the weak £6,000 it fetched in 2003. Whilst Nantgarw and Swansea have six entries in this section, the best being painted by William Billingsley at **12**, other porcelains have to give way to

the dominance of pottery. Martinware has three entries here at **8**, **23** and **37**. At any level of the market their stoneware is expensive but always a good potential investment. Their output can be followed closely throughout this book by referring to the *Index*.

Majolica, a lead-glazed earthenware, has eight entries commencing with the Minton teapot at **24**, which fetched just under £20,000 at *Canterbury Auction Galleries* in 2007. Further Minton examples can be found at **41**, **56**, **68**, **71** and **93**. Two George Jones examples can be found at **95** and **99** but all the other manufacturers appear in later pages. Doulton also has eight entries. See **10**, **25**, **45**, **48** and **55**. All are character jugs commencing with *Sir Stanley Matthews* and concluding with *George Washington*. A Titanianware vase breaks the mould at £9,174. This is probably an auction record for this type. *The Swimmer*, HN1270 follows at **85** and *The Windmill Lady* at **103**.

The rare Wedgwood & Bentley blue jasper plaques at **3** and over £70,000 are a one-off. Moorcroft can fetch astonishing prices but there are only two here over £5,000. See **21** where a pair of florian vases decorated with Japanese carp reached over £22,000 and **61** where a Claremont flambé vase, 1928 crept under £10,000. There are three examples of pâte-sur-pâte in these pages, the first two at **19** and **30**, both by Louis Solon, and the third at **40** decorated by Charles Toft Junior. Note they are all by Mintons. Clarice Cliff is down the pecking order with her first entry at **57**, being a Persian pattern wall plate fetching over £10,000. There are Lotus jugs at **70** and **90**, the first being the rarer *Tennis* pattern and the second *Blue Firs*, still expensive collector's items.

Ironstone china dinner services will always feature in this price range. See the Hicks and Meigh extensive service of 123 pieces at **43** and the two Mason's services at **88** and **100**. The reader should note the rare slipware jug at **13** and two late Italian maiolica entries at **94** and **107**. Two Iznik pieces feature at **38** and **97**. Summarising the remainder there are appearances by William de Morgan, Wemyss, Newhall and some rare Staffordshire such as the Wood type creamware at **77** and the rabbits at **82**. Note also the expensive £11,000 creamware jug at **52** but this does have cricket and horse-racing overtones. Finally, I am surprised that Burmantofts made it into this Section at **87** and Belleck at **102**. The Charles Vyse group at **89** is also unexpected. Less surprising is the pair of Minton's art pottery chargers at **42**, painted with a semi-erotic subject by W S Coleman.

Hammer: £2.6 million - £26,000

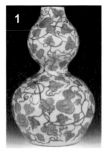

Chinese blue/white double gourd vase, Yuan Dynasty, mid 14thC, 47.5cm high. Woolley & Wallis, Salisbury. Jul 05. HP: £2,600,000. ABP: £3,058,250.

London Delftware marriage dish painted with a nativity scene, dated 1638 in 2 places, reverse with potter's initials R.I. and bride and grooms initials, 41.5cm dia. Phillips, London. Jun 94. HP: £240,000. ABP: £281,436.

Set of 6 Wedgwood & Bentley blue jasper 'Herculaneum' oval plaques, c1778, overall 12in. Sotheby's, Billingshurst. Sep 99. HP: £61,000. ABP: £71,751.

Suite of five Royal Crown Derby vases, painted with flowers by Leroy. Hy. Duke & Son, Dorchester. Sep 01. HP: £58,000. ABP: £68,222.

Chinese Imperial porcelain dish depicting five Dragons, represents the Yongzheng Emporer, dated to his reign 1723-1735, 48cm dia, two hairline cracks, small repair. Clevedon Salerooms, Bristol. Mar 06. HP: £52,000. ABP: £61,165.

Rare Delft tin glazed earthenware cat, 17thC, 5in high. Halls Fine Art, Shrewsbury. Mar 03. HP: £45,000. ABP: £52,931.

Six Limoges enamel plates, each painted with a month of the year, reverses decorated in the mannerist style, monogram 'PC', enameller Pierre Courteys (Courtois 1520-1586). Hy Duke & Son, Dorchester. Mar 06. HP: £44,000. ABP: £51,755.

Large Martin Brothers stoneware bird. Woolley & Wallis, Salisbury. Dec 04. HP: £40,000. ABP: £47,050.

Chinese Imperial wine pot, Qianlong (1736-1795), eight Buddhist Emblems interspersed with lotus flowers, scrolls and a fanged monster, 7.5in high. Hy. Duke & Son, Dorchester. Feb 07. HP: £36,000. ABP: £42,345.

Royal Doulton, Sir Stanley Matthews small character jug, A7164, No. 1 of a Ltd. Edn. of 3. Louis Taylor, Stoke on Trent. Jun 01. HP: £32,200. ABP: £37,875.

Pair Derby ice pails, painted with views, impressed 2E, painted crown, crossed batons, D, 299 and script titles in blue, exh. labels, 24cm high, c1797-1800. (2) Mellors & Kirk, Nottingham. Apr 03. HP: £32,000. ABP: £37,640.

Welsh porcelain campana vase, lavishly painted by William Billingsley, marked 'NANTGARRW' painted in red, c1813-23, 27.5cm. Woolley & Wallis, Salisbury. Nov 02. HP: £30,000. ABP: £35,287.

Important Barnstable slipware jug by Thomas Fields, dated 1757. Bonham's, Bath. Jun 03. HP: £28,000. ABP: £32,935.

Pair of Worcester porcelain plaques by H. Davies, oval form painted with sheep in a highland landscape, dated 1921, 9 x 5.5in, gilt foliate moulded frames. Andrew Hartley, Ilkley. Apr 05. HP: £27,000. ABP: £31,758.

> **Prices quoted are actual hammer prices (HP) and the Approximate Buyer's Price (ABP) includes an average premium of 15% + VAT.**

Early Worcester mug with exotic birds amongst foliage in polychrome in the Imari manner, 3.25in high. Hy. Duke & Son, Dorchester. Sep 02. HP: £26,000. ABP: £30,582.

Finely painted 19thC Nantgarw cabinet plate, The Three Graces, border gilded in raised gold, impressed NANTGARW CW, 9.25in. Philip Serrell Auctioneers, Malvern. May 04. HP: £26,000. ABP: £30,582.

First period Worcester pair of gugglets, c1753-55, blue painted in 'The Lange Lijzen' pattern, 24cm, one with rim chips. Bristol Auction Rooms, Bristol. Jul 03. HP: £24,000. ABP: £28,230.

Rare Japanese Kakiemon tankard of European form, moulded with panels of dragons and chrysanthemum on an unglazed 'fish roe' ground, karakusa scroll to the handle, c1670, 14cm. Woolley & Wallis, Salisbury. May 01. HP: £21,000. ABP: £24,701.

Pair of Mintons pate sur pate plaques, signed L. Solon (18(80), 17 x 15cm, period gilt Florentine frames. Richard Winterton, Burton on Trent, Staffs. Sep 01. HP: £20,000. ABP: £23,525.

Royal Crown Derby boat shaped vase & cover painted with panels of flowers by Desire Leroy, 5.75in high. Hy. Duke & Son, Dorchester. Sep 01. HP: £20,000. ABP: £23,525.

Pair of early Moorcroft florian vases with Japanese carp amidst underwater foliage, 11.75in. Gorringes, Lewes. Oct 99. HP: £19,000. ABP: £22,348.

Pair Derby wild boars, bases applied flowers & enamelled details, c1755, 16.5cm wide, bases with stencilled marks 'Bt. at Dr. Wake Smarts Sale, April 1895, Lot 103, Chelsea China'. Woolley & Wallis, Salisbury. May 01. HP: £19,000. ABP: £22,348.

Martinware stoneware bird jar/cover, incised 'R.W. Martin & Bros. London & Southall' dated 1-1-85, minor chips to rim of base and one flake chip, small hairline crack, 11.25in high. Canterbury Auction Galleries, Kent. Aug 05. HP: £19,000. ABP: £22,348.

Minton majolica teapot as a vulture attacking a snake, 8in high, impressed factory mark to base, No. 1851, date code for 1878, handle restuck. Canterbury Auction Galleries, Kent. Feb 07. HP: £17,000. ABP: £19,996.

Doulton. Baseball player, prototype character jug, D6624, by David Biggs, c1970, 21cm. Phillips, London. Nov 99. HP: £16,000. ABP: £18,820.

Pair of Chamberlain shell painted ice pails, covers and liners, c1810. Bonham's, Bath. Jun 03. HP: £16,000. ABP: £18,820.

London Delft pill slab, c1700. Bonham's, Bath. Jun 03. HP: £16,000. ABP: £18,820.

Chinese blue/white brush pot, well painted, no mark, Kangxi, c1680, 16cm high, 17cm wide. Woolley & Wallis, Salisbury. Nov 03. HP: £16,000. ABP: £18,820.

Nantgarw part dessert service, c1820, impressed NANTGARW CW. Dreweatt Neate, Newbury. Feb 04. HP: £15,500. ABP: £18,231.

Monumental Minton Pâte-sur-pâte vase by Louis Solon, c1899, entitled 'The Idol Seller'. Bonham's, London. Jul 02. HP: £15,000. ABP: £17,643.

Pair of 18thC Chinese figures of hawks, very af, 10.5in high. Tring Market Auctions, Herts. Jan 03. HP: £15,000. ABP: £17,643.

Rare Chelsea figure of Bajazzoo, from Commedia dell'Arte series after a Meissen original, c1755, red anchor mark, 16cm. Woolley & Wallis, Salisbury. Sep 01. HP: £15,000. ABP: £17,643.

18thC Chinese famille rose brush pot decorated with peony, prunus and magnolia, 18.5cm wide, 15.5cm high. Woolley & Wallis, Salisbury. Nov 03. HP: £15,000. ABP: £17,643.

Hammer: £14,500 - £9,500

34

Chelsea blue/white soup plate, 22.5cm, blue anchor mark, c1755. Dreweatt Neate, Newbury. Feb 04. HP: £14,500. ABP: £17,055.

35

Pair of Chelsea porcelain models of Chinese pheasants, prob. decorated in workshop of William Duesbury, red anchor marks, c1750-52, 21cm high. (damaged) Bearne's, Exeter. Jul 03. HP: £14,000. ABP: £16,467.

36

Meissen 'Tulip' tea/coffee service, late 1750s. Hy. Duke & Son, Dorchester. Jan 02. HP: £14,000. ABP: £16,467.

37

Martin Brothers grotesque, dated 1888, detachable head with grinning eyes and open mouth, his arms held together at chest, incised mark to his rear R W Martin, Southall, 1888 and to neck-rim R W Martin Bros., London + Southall, 9.75in. Gorringes, Lewes. Oct 05. HP: £13,000. ABP: £15,291.

38

Two near Eastern pottery plates decorated in 'Isnik' manner, 12.5in. Canterbury Auc. Galleries, Kent. Apr 04. HP: £12,600. ABP: £14,820.

39

Important Chelsea milk jug, c1745-49. Bonham's, Bath. Jun 03. HP: £12,500. ABP: £14,703.

40

Mintons pâte-sur-pâte vase, c1880, decorated by Charles Toft Junior, 57.5cm high. Rosebery's, London. Sep 03. HP: £12,000. ABP: £14,115.

41

Minton majolica garden seat, c1867. Sotheby's, London. Jul 02. HP: £11,500. ABP: £13,526.

42

Pair of Minton's art pottery chargers painted with semi erotic subjects, signed W S Coleman, depicting nude maidens, 17in dia. Tring Mkt Auctions, Herts. May 04. HP: £11,100. ABP: £13,056.

43

Hicks and Meigh ironstone extensive dinner service, c1815-22, comprising 123 pieces. Sotheby's, Billinghurst. Nov 00. HP: £11,000. ABP: £12,938.

44

French pâte-sur-pâte plaque by Louis Solon dated 1869. Bonham's, London. Jul 02. HP: £11,000. ABP: £12,938.

45

Doulton. George Washington by Stan Taylor, D6669, 19cm. (special certificate) Phillips, London. Nov 99. HP: £10,500. ABP: £12,350.

46

Pair of Worcester Flight, Barr & Barr candlesticks, c1820, 6.5in high. Sotheby's, Billinghurst. Jan 01. HP: £10,500. ABP: £12,350.

47

Early English Delft armorial plate dated 1653, painted in blue, yellow and ochre with the initial letters P, M & A, 1653, 22.5cm. Woolley & Wallis, Salisbury. Nov 01. HP: £10,200. ABP: £11,997.

48

Doulton. Baseball player, prototype character jug, D6624 by David Biggs, c1970, 18cm. Phillips, London. Nov 99. HP: £10,000. ABP: £11,762.

49

Delftware 'Fazackerly' palette puzzle jug, Bristol or Liverpool, c1760, 20cm. Sotheby's, Billinghurst. Nov 00. HP: £10,000. ABP: £11,762.

50

English Delft Queen Caroline commemorative plate, dated 1738. Bonham's, Bath. Jun 03. HP: £9,800. ABP: £11,527.

51

Newhall mug by Fidelle Duvivier, c1790, chip to rim, 14cm high. Trembath Welch, Great Dunmow. Jul 03. HP: £9,500. ABP: £11,174.

52

18thC creamware jug, poss. Staffs, scenes of a cricket match and a horse race. Dreweatt Neate, Donington. Sep 06. HP: £9,500. ABP: £11,174.

Pair of Nantgarw porcelain oval plates, prob. by Thomas Pardoe, 10 x 14.25in, c1820. Canterbury Auction Galleries, Kent. Aug 03. HP: £9,400. ABP: £11,056.

Early Worcester blue/white jug of the 'scratch cross' type, c1755 (minute chip), rare pattern of birds to the reverse. Woolley & Wallis, Salisbury. Dec 99. HP: £9,200. ABP: £10,821.

Doulton. George Washington by Stan Taylor, 19cm. (special certificate) Phillips, London. Nov 99. HP: £9,000. ABP: £10,586.

Mintons majolica butter dish and cover in the form of a bale of hay, field mouse handle, impressed mark and date code 1872, 9.5in. Gorringes, Lewes. Jan 04. HP: £9,000. ABP: £10,586.

Clarice Cliff Persian pattern inspiration wall plate. Hogben Auctioneers, Folkestone. Feb 01. HP: £8,900. ABP: £10,468.

Famille verte moon shaped porcelain vase, painted with landscape scenes and script to reverse, 33cm high. Eastbourne Auction Rooms, Sussex. Dec 05. HP: £8,600. ABP: £10,115.

Delftware punch bowl, poss. Liverpool, 1775, inscribed harvest verse and dated March 17th 1775, James Duke'. Sotheby's, Billingshurst. Jun 00. HP: £8,500. ABP: £9,998.

Pair of famille rose bowls from the Yongzheng period. Hamptons, Godalming. Sep 00. HP: £8,500. ABP: £9,998.

Claremont, a large Moorcroft flambe vase, 1928, blue painted signature and date, impressed 'Made in England', 12in high. Sotheby's, Billingshurst. Mar 01. HP: £8,500. ABP: £9,998.

Important early Lowestoft wash basin, c1759-60. Bonham's, Bath. Jun 03. HP: £8,500. ABP: £9,998.

Rare Bristol delftware blue dash charger, c1700, painted with a figure full portrait of Prince George, initials PG, cracks, restoration, 35.5cm, paper labels. Sworders, Stansted Mountfitchet. Jul 04. HP: £8,400. ABP: £9,880.

Rare Liverpool Delft mug, printed by Sadler, c1762. Phillips, London. Feb 01. HP: £8,200. ABP: £9,645.

The numbering system acts as a reader reference and links to the Analysis of each section.

Pair of Derby chocolate cups, covers and one stand, c1794, enamelled with oval black on moonlight titled scenes, blue crown cross batons mark and no. 231, 11.5cm high. Wintertons, Lichfield. May 03. HP: £8,000. ABP: £9,410.

Royal Doulton exhibition quality Titanianware vase, painted and signed by Harry Tittensor, impressed number 1345, 16.75in. Louis Taylor, Stoke on Trent. Mar 06. HP: £7,800. ABP: £9,174.

Pair of 20thC Chinese porcelain bowls, in 'Famille Rose' with geese and flowers, 5in dia x 2.75in, six character mark. Canterbury Auction Galleries, Kent. Feb 06. HP: £7,600. ABP: £8,939.

Large Mintons majolica flower holder, c1873, after A. Carrier Belleuse, impressed marks. Sotheby's, Billingshurst. Apr 00. HP: £7,500. ABP: £8,821.

London decorated Nantgarw plate, painted with 4 doves, 'C' scroll and foliate border, sprays of pink roses, gold seeded ground, 'Nantgarw CW' impressed, c1814-23, 25cm. Woolley & Wallis, Salisbury. Nov 01. HP: £7,500. ABP: £8,821.

Clarice Cliff 'Tennis' Bizarre Lotus Jug, 11.5in. Gardiner Houlgate, Corsham. Apr 05. HP: £7,200. ABP: £8,469.

Minton majolica two handled tureen/cover, dates from June 1870, 13.5in overall. Canterbury Auction Galleries, Kent. Nov 99. HP: £7,000. ABP: £8,233.

Hammer: £7,000 - £5,800

72

Lambeth Delft wet drug jar dated 1679, inscribed 'S: Ros: Sol:-Cv: Ag', 28cm. Woolley & Wallis, Salisbury. Feb 03. HP: £7,000. ABP: £8,233.

73

Chelsea figure, Scaramouche, from the Commedia dell'Arte series after a Meissen original, c1755, red anchor mark, 14.5cm. Woolley & Wallis, Salisbury. Sep 01. HP: £6,800. ABP: £7,998.

74

Chelsea red anchor plate measuring only 7.5in dia sold to the London Trade. Sworders, Stansted Mountfitchet. Jan 99. HP: £6,600. ABP: £7,763.

75

Pair of Canton porcelain garden seats. Bearne's, Exeter. Jun 05. HP: £6,600. ABP: £7,763.

76

Wedgwood majolica oval game pie dish cover, c1882. Sotheby's, London. Jul 02. HP: £6,500. ABP: £7,645.

77

Staffordshire creamware, Wood type 'Prince Hal' Toby jug, early 19thC, 39.5cm. Sotheby's, Billingshurst. Nov 00. HP: £6,500. ABP: £7,645.

78

Chinese blue/white porcelain brush pot, Kang Hsi period, 15cm. (3cm hairline crack) Stride & Son, Chichester. Jan 04. HP: £6,500. ABP: £7,645.

79

Mid 18thC Delft plate, 'Success to the John & Mary, John Spencer', 23cm dia. Cheffins, Cambridge. Apr 03. HP: £6,400. ABP: £7,528.

80

18thC Caughley miniature tea/coffee service, chinoiserie scenes in under glaze blue, 'S' mark. Hy. Duke & Son, Dorchester. Sep 02. HP: £6,400. ABP: £7,528.

81

Pair Staffs recumbent lions, bases with Pratt colours, late 18thC, 21.5cm, one with chip and fire cracks. Woolley & Wallis, Salisbury. Nov 02. HP: £6,400. ABP: £7,528.

82

Pair of Staffordshire pottery rabbits, c1870, modelled munching at green lettuce leaves. Sotheby's, Billingshurst. Jun 00. HP: £6,200. ABP: £7,292.

83

Delftware polychrome sparrow beak jug, probably London, c1765. Sotheby's, Billingshurst. Sep 00. HP: £6,200. ABP: £7,292.

> The illustrations are in descending price order. The price range is indicated at the top of each page.

84

Delftware blue and white two handled vase, painted with cattle, houses and haystacks, mid 18thC, 21cm high. (rim chip, scroll to one handle lacking and 11cm hairline) Woolley & Wallis, Salisbury. May 03. HP: £6,200. ABP: £7,292.

85

Royal Doulton. The swimmer HN 1270, designer L. H., intro 1928, withdrawn 1938. Louis Taylor, Stoke on Trent. Dec 00. HP: £6,000. ABP: £7,057.

86

William de Morgan vase, by Frederick Passenger, c1890, painted/impressed marks, 39.5cm. (chip to rim, glaze chips and cracks) Sworders, Stansted Mountfitchet. Feb 04. HP: £6,000. ABP: £7,057.

87

Burmantofts faience anglo Persian vase by Louis Kramer, with band of fish in green/turquoise, ivory ground, signed monogram to base, impressed marks, 16.25in. Andrew Hartley, Ilkley. Dec 04. HP: £6,000. ABP: £7,057.

88

Mason's ironstone dinner service, c1820. Sotheby's, Billingshurst. Nov 99. HP: £5,800. ABP: £6,822.

89

Charles Vyse pottery group, c1929, incised c.Vyse Chelsea 1929, 12.25in high, ebonised wood base. Sotheby's, Billingshurst. Mar 00. HP: £5,800. ABP: £6,822.

Clarice Cliff 'Blue Firs' Lotus jug. D M Nesbit & Company, Southsea. Jul 00. HP: £5,800. ABP: £6,822.

Swansea porcelain 'London' shape part tea service, pattern No. 411, printed iron-red mark, c1818. (slight damage) (54) Dreweatt Neate, Newbury. Nov 01. HP: £5,800. ABP: £6,822.

Chelsea figure of Mezzetino, from the Commedia dell' Arte series after Meissen original, c1755, 15.2cm. Woolley & Wallis, Salisbury. Sep 01. HP: £5,600. ABP: £6,587.

Mintons majolica dove tureen. Some damage. Eastbourne Auction Rooms, Sussex. Feb 04. HP: £5,600. ABP: £6,587.

Four late 16th/Early 17thC Venetian albarelli, blue/white decoration and enamel coats of arms, 7.25in high. substantial chips. Sworders, Stansted Mountfitchet. Feb 02. HP: £5,500. ABP: £6,469.

George Jones majolica 'Punch' bowl, c1875. Sotheby's, London. Jul 02. HP: £5,500. ABP: £6,469.

Set of ten dated Delft blue & white plates, each initialled W over IE and 1700, crowned cartouches supported by griffins, 22.5cm. (2 damaged) Cheffins, Cambridge. Apr 03. HP: £5,500. ABP: £6,469.

Iznik glazed pottery tankard, 20cm high. Rosebery's, London. Apr 05. HP: £5,500. ABP: £6,469.

Three 19thC Chinese bowls bearing seal marks of Daoguang, painted in famille verte with dragons and phoenix, 16cm dia. (R) (3) Cheffins, Cambridge. Apr 05. HP: £5,500. ABP: £6,469.

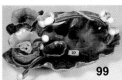

George Jones & Son Ltd, majolica strawberry dish in the form of a lily leaf, fitted with cream jug and sugar basin with sifter spoon, leaf serving spoon to dish. Thos Mawer & Son, Lincoln. Apr 02. HP: £5,400. ABP: £6,351.

Hammer: £5,800 - £5,200

Extensive 19thC Masons Ironstone service with panels of Oriental figures in gardens, 118 items. Ewbank, Send, Surrey. Oct 05. HP: £5,400. ABP: £6,351.

Creamware jug, printed with a view of a cricket match and a view of the Oatland Stakes at Ascot, makers Fletcher & Co. Shelton, c1795, 17.7cm. (staining and old restoration) Woolley & Wallis, Salisbury. Sep 02. HP: £5,200. ABP: £6,116.

Belleek armorial tea service of 'Echinus' design, forms as sea urchins and coral, tray with crest and the motto 'Per Mare Per Teras', Alexander family of Co. Armagh, first period marks. (10) Woolley & Wallis, Salisbury. Sep 02. HP: £5,200. ABP: £6,116.

Royal Doulton. The windmill lady, no number - should be HN 1400, designer L.H., intro 1930, withdrawn 1937. Louis Taylor, Stoke. Dec 00. HP: £5,200. ABP: £6,116.

Wemyss iris bulb vase, baluster shape painted with irises and leafage in natural colours, shoulder perforated, Goode retailer mark, impressed maker's mark, 14.5in. Gorringes, Lewes. Jul 06. HP: £5,200. ABP: £6,116.

'Girl in a Swing' gilt metal mounted bonbonniere with hinged cover, French hen on brood, 5cm high, 1749-54. Dreweatt Neate, Newbury. Jun 03. HP: £5,200. ABP: £6,116.

Pair of very large Meissen figures of a gallant and his lady, mid 19thC. Hamptons, Godalming. Jul 00. HP: £5,200. ABP: £6,116.

Italian maiolica wet drug jar of Orsini Colonna type, 18thC, (poss. earlier) 9in high. Andrew Hartley, Ilkley. Feb 04. HP: £5,200. ABP: £6,116.

Section II: £5,000-£2,000

'Pottery is always more highly prized and more prolific in this price range.....*Duchess with flowers* fetched £3,411 with premium.....in other words the buyer paid over two and a half times the market value...Lenci's 'fashionable young women' are averaging £4,000 including premium.'

This larger 172 lot section is studded with Chinese porcelain. At **18** in **Section I** there was only one Japanese entry fetching almost £25,000. This fine porcelain Kakiemon tankard was early and its distinctive palette and design quite unique. Appearing for the first time is early pottery from the Tang Dynasty. See **208** and **245**. Also we have our first Japanese pottery. These are all Satsuma. Check out **155**, **164**, **181-183**, **196**, **217** and **238**. Most will have been made at Kyoto during the Meiji period. (1868-1912) Satsuma decoration usually includes dragon and storytelling figurines in colour, mellowed by pencilled gold. There are some exceptional Chinese porcelain examples ranging from the late nineteenth century bowl at **111** and the seventeenth century Wucai vase at **119** through to two fine blue and white lots at **251** and **256**.

There are a similar number of English and European porcelain examples. Many are of exceptional quality and decoration such as the Royal Worcester at **109** or the Vienna porcelain at **124**. At **129** is a Lowestoft soft paste wall pocket, which at £4,000 hammer indicates its rarity and desirability. Similarly it is worth looking at **201** and **240**. William Cookworthy invented English hard paste porcelain at Plymouth in the 1760s and the type was manufactured by about a dozen other manufacturers up to about 1813 when it gave way to bone china, invented by Spode c1800. Cookworthy is rare and desirable. See also the rare Derby soft paste eye bath at **235** which will surprise many at about £3,000 including premium.

Pottery is always more highly prized and more prolific in this price range. There is very little English delft here. If I include European delft, faience and maiolica there are only nine examples in this Section. These can be found at **112**, **127**, **172**, **177**, **186**, **190**, **220**, **250** and **261**. The pick is the exceedingly rare English delftware ladies shoes at **112** and the Brislington dish at **261**, certainly mid-seventeenth and not mid-sixteenth century.

Moving from tin to lead-glazed earthenwares, there are 15 examples of majolica. Most are by George Jones with several Minton examples, but Brown, Westhead, Moore & Co. make their first appearance at **113** for an astonishing £5,646 including premium. Earlier pottery is represented by the Thomas Toft slipware charger at **185**. It seems unimaginable that a piece in such terrible condition could reach £3,000 hammer. See also the Creamware coffee pot at **210**, the Obadiah Sherratt figure group at **202** and the Walton spill vase at **222**. It remains now to discuss the nineteenth and mainly twentieth century potteries which dominate this Section, outnumbering by far all of the Oriental, European and English porcelains put together.

William de Morgan had only one entry for a Persian vase in **Section I**. (see **86**) Here are two lustre chargers at **114** and **169** and tiles at **200**, **226** and **258**. Can there be any more valuable tiles in ceramics than these? Five Wedgwood Fairyland lustre now enters the frame. See **115**, **152**, **157**, **170** and **252** with a further lustre bowl at **146**. Moorcroft makes an even bigger impression with eleven entries. See **110**, **126**, **135**, **161**, **166**, **198** etc. Note that all of the higher priced lots are pairs, always more prized than singles. Remember the Moorcroft pair of Florian vases at **21** which fetched over £22,000? Moorcroft is matched by Doulton entries commencing with a simple Lambeth stoneware tobacco jar at **132**, boosted by its cricketing figures. A *Shepherd* leads the figures, at **136** and one of Royal Doulton's most desirable figures *Mamselle*, HN659, appears at **171**. Hannah Barlow makes her first appearance at **207** and again at **272** and George Tinworth at **239** and £2,400 hammer with *Quack Doctor*. Four Beswick entries commence with a huntsman and horse MN1501, by Arthur Gredington. See **153** and also **194**, **209** and **255**. Check out **194** more closely. At Brettells, Newport in July 2005, following a bidding war, Beatrice Potter's *Duchess with flowers* fetched £3,411 with premium. Analysing the sales of BP-2a over the last seven years, the auction average works out at £1,332 including premium. In other words the buyer paid over two and a half times the market value and the underbidder had a very fortunate escape!

There are three Martinware lots at **195**, **203** and **212** and only three Clarice Cliff entries at **216**, **260** and **275**, two being services. Charles Vyse makes a second appearance at **118** as does Burmantofts at **277**, this another Anglo-Persian vase. The first Morriswafe is at **121** but this is a very special pair of biscuit jars and well over the usual price range. Goldscheider appears at **143** with a superb terracotta table lamp as an Art Nouveau maiden, and Royal Dux at **199** with a pair of water carriers at £2,800 hammer. The buyer didn't overpay. See also **278**. Troika enters at **191**, **269** and **206**. Will these prices be maintained? Bretby appears for the first time at **224**. Take note of Lenci at **131**, **140** and **174**. Over the last several years their 'fashionable young women' have averaged over £4,000 including premium. I cannot think of any other output to compare and I do not see prices falling.

108

George Jones majolica camel, saddle hung with a turquoise basket on each side on palm leaf decorated oval base, Registration mark for 1871, (part of tail broken off), 9in. Gorringes, Lewes. Oct 04. HP: £5,000. ABP: £5,881.

109

Pair Royal Worcester porcelain vases by Harry Davis of bottle form, flared gilded rim moulded with stiff leaf banding, painted with sheep, dated 1914, 9.25in high. Andrew Hartley, Ilkley. Oct 05. HP: £5,000. ABP: £5,881.

110

Pair Moorcroft vases, 11.75in. Louis Taylor, Stoke. Mar 04. HP: £5,000. ABP: £5,881.

111

Late 19thC Chinese Mandarin palette porcelain bowl. Henry Adams, Chichester. Dec 05. HP: £5,000. ABP: £5,881.

112

Pair of English delftware lady's shoes, dated 1729, London or Bristol, highheeled, painted with flowers in blue, painted date with initials W.I.M. 5.5in long. Gorringes, Lewes. Jun 06. HP: £5,000. ABP: £5,881.

113

Majolica jardiniere by T C Brown, Westhead, Moore & Co, hen and chicks, mould No. 1245.31, 12in wide. Andrew Hartley, Ilkley. Apr 04. HP: £4,800. ABP: £5,646.

114

William De Morgan lustre charger by Charles Passenger, patt. 1208, painted initials, CP to reverse, 14.75in. Gorringes, Lewes. Apr 04. HP: £4,600. ABP: £5,410.

> Categories or themes can be followed through the colour coded Index which contains 1000s of cross references.

115

Pair of Wedgwood pottery Fairyland lustre candlemass pattern baluster vases, blue/purple ground with gilt pixie and female figure decoration, 9in high. Clarke Gammon Wellers, Guildford. Apr 05. HP: £4,600. ABP: £5,410.

116

Pair early 19thC Schoelcher, Paris porcelain campana vases, painted with named views, gilt handles with mask terminals, gilded royal blue ground, printed mark, 12.75in. Gorringes, Lewes. Sep 05. HP: £4,600. ABP: £5,410.

Hammer: £5,000 - £4,000

117

Eleven Wilkinson Toby jugs of allied war leaders, 1915-1919, by Sir F Carruthers Gould (1844-1925), facsimile signatures, Soane and Smith backstamp, certificates, 9.5in to 12.25in high. Diamond Mills & Co, Felixstowe. Dec 04. HP: £4,500. ABP: £5,293.

118

Charles Vyse figure of Scarecrow, introduced in 1934. Halls Fine Art, Shrewsbury. Dec 05. HP: £4,500. ABP: £5,293.

119

Transitional Wucai vase/cover, mid 17thC, in underglaze enamels with a scene of Ma Gu, ladies playing instruments and hare in the moon pounding the elixir of life, 47cm, neck repaired. Sworders, Stansted Mountfitchet. Nov 04. HP: £4,400. ABP: £5,175.

120

Garniture of Chinese vases, Qianlong period, mandarin cell-pattern ground, 11.5in. Gorringes, Lewes. Jun 05. HP: £4,400. ABP: £5,175.

121

Pair of Morrisware biscuit jars by G W Cartlidge, fax signature, numbered C62-28, printed mark for Hancock & Sons, one restuck chip to lid, 19.5cm. Sworders, Stansted Mountfitchet. Apr 05. HP: £4,200. ABP: £4,940.

122

Royal Worcester part dessert service, 1918-1919, panels of fruit by R Sebright, signed, printed marks, date codes, painted No. W8346, plate 22.5cm. (8) Sworders, Stansted Mountfitchet. Jul 05. HP: £4,200. ABP: £4,940.

123

Pair of Amstel porcelain two-handled urns and covers, c1800. Dreweatt Neate, Donnington. Feb 07. HP: £4,200. ABP: £4,940.

124

Vienna porcelain dessert service, 12 settings, depicting classical maidens, signed, inscribed verso, incl. six comports, 19thC, 9in wide. (18) Hartleys, Ilkley. Oct 06. HP: £4,100. ABP: £4,822.

125

Pair Chinese yellow ground bowls, seal mark, Jiaqing, four iron red shou roundels on scrolling lotus ground, five wufu and central shou character, 14.5cm dia. Cheffins, Cambridge. Nov 04. HP: £4,000. ABP: £4,705.

Hammer: £4,000 - £3,700

Pair Moorcroft Florian ware vases, c1905, daisy design, signed W Moorcroft, 8.25in. rim repaired. Halls Fine Art, Shrewsbury. Mar 04. HP: £4,000. ABP: £4,705.

English delftware barrel, initialled B:P dated Oct. 20, Deal, 1793, grapes, vines and a view inscribed 'the Best under the Sun', pedestal stem re-attached, 6.25in. Gorringes, Lewes. Dec 04. HP: £4,000. ABP: £4,705.

Early 19thC Spode 221-piece part dinner service, Japan pattern with gilt highlights, pattern no. 2963, c1805/6. Gorringes, Lewes. Sep 04. HP: £4,000. ABP: £4,705.

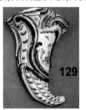

Lowestoft blue/white moulded wall pocket, relief decoration, painters no. 5, c1760, 8.5in. Gorringes, Lewes. Sep 04. HP: £4,000. ABP: £4,705.

18thC Chinese blue/white Kraak type charger, 21.5in. Gorringes, Lewes. Dec 06. HP: £4,000. ABP: £4,705.

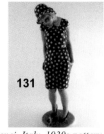

Lenci, Italy, 1930s pottery figure of a young woman wearing white polka dot hat and dress, with song bird, 41cm. Locke & England, Leamington Spa. Feb 06. HP: £4,000. ABP: £4,705.

Doulton Lambeth stoneware tobacco jar, decorated in relief with figures of cricketers. Dreweatt Neate, Donington. Sep 06. HP: £4,000. ABP: £4,705.

Prices quoted are actual hammer prices (HP) and the Approximate Buyer's Price (ABP) includes an average premium of 15% + VAT.

Late 19thC Chinese vase, painted with landscape decoration, 7in. Gorringes, Lewes. Feb 07. HP: £4,000. ABP: £4,705.

Pair Royal Worcester vases by John Stinton decorated with Highland cattle, puce marks no 2337, signed. (One base damaged and pinned). 30cm. Boldon Auction Galleries, Tyne & Wear. Sep 04. HP: £3,900. ABP: £4,587.

Pair of Moorcroft Hazeldene vases, c1910, signature, 12cm. Sworders, Stansted Mountfitchet. Nov 04. HP: £3,900. ABP: £4,587.

Royal Doulton, 'A Shepherd', impressed date 1925. Louis Taylor, Stoke on Trent. Jun 05. HP: £3,900. ABP: £4,587.

Van Der Velde stoneware vase, impressed to underside, model number, 19cm high. Rosebery's, London. Mar 04. HP: £3,800. ABP: £4,469.

Cased set of 6 R. Worcester coffee cans/saucers. Stinton. Humberts inc Tayler & Fletcher, Andoversford. Jun 04. HP: £3,800. ABP: £4,469.

Royal Worcester Aesthetic teapot, c1882, prob. by R. W. Binns, modelled by James Hadley, 15cm high. Rosebery's, London. Sep 04. HP: £3,800. ABP: £4,469.

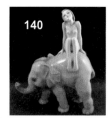

Lenci, nude girl on elephant, painted mark Lenci, Made In Italy, 1-38, 16in high. Gorringes, Lewes. Oct 05. HP: £3,800. ABP: £4,469.

Zsolnay lustre bowl, c1900, impressed Zsolnay Pecs, 4669 and printed five spires mark, cracked 20cm. Sworders, Stansted Mountfitchet. Feb 06. HP: £3,800. ABP: £4,469.

Pair of Flight, Barr & Barr ice pails, c1813-40, named botanical studies, 28cm. (6) Sworders, Stansted Mountfitchet. Feb 05. HP: £3,700. ABP: £4,352.

Goldscheider terracotta table lamp after F Gross, Art Nouveau maiden, Greek figure mark, 33in high. Andrew Hartley, Ilkley. Aug 05. HP: £3,700. ABP: £4,352.

Chinese Doucai bowl, mark & period Daoguang, (1821-1850) 15cm. Sworders, Stansted Mountfitchet. Nov 05. HP: £3,700. ABP: £4,352.

145

Royal Doulton Prestige figure group 'The Charge of the Light Brigade' HN3718, designer A.M. introduced 1995, 17in high. Louis Taylor, Stoke on Trent. Sep 06. HP: £3,700. ABP: £4,352.

146

Wedgwood lustre bowl in irridescent enamels and gilt with a Middle Eastern figure in garden landscape, Portland Vase mark & Z5494 to base, 6.25in dia. Louis Taylor, Stoke on Trent. Dec 06. HP: £3,700. ABP: £4,352.

147

George Jones majolica rooster teapot, c1870, painted in black (3203) and impressed 'G J' (1861-73) damaged, 6.25in high. Halls Fine Art, Shrewsbury. Dec 04. HP: £3,600. ABP: £4,234.

148

Group of four porcelain jazz musician figures, c1930, tallest 25cm high, painted marks 'Robj' Paris, made in France, af. Rosebery's, London. Mar 05. HP: £3,600. ABP: £4,234.

149

Pair of Chinese porcelain dogs, late 18th/early 19thC, chips to tail and paws, 9.8cm. Sworders, Stansted Mountfitchet. Nov 05. HP: £3,600. ABP: £4,234.

150

Pair ormolu-mounted Chinese porcelain vases, 'famille verte' enamels, ormolu cast in rococo style, 18.5in. Gorringes, Lewes. Apr 05. HP: £3,600. ABP: £4,234.

151

19thC Ridgways porcelain dessert service, shaped and moulded borders, enamelled in colours, 20 pieces, pattern No 1177 in red. Canterbury Auction Galleries, Kent. Apr 04. HP: £3,500. ABP: £4,116.

152

Wedgwood Flame Fairyland lustre punch bowl, by Daisy Makeig-Jones, Woodland Bridge pattern inside, Z5360, Poplar Trees pattern outside, Z4968, 4 gilded monograms 'MJ', painted/printed marks, 28.5cm dia. Cheffins, Cambridge. Apr 05. HP: £3,500. ABP: £4,116.

153

Beswick huntsman, rocking horse grey/white gloss horse, by Arthur Gredington MN 1501, issued 1957-1995. Batemans, Stamford. Mar 06. HP: £3,500. ABP: £4,116.

154

Large Royal Worcester pot pourri ja and cover, signed Freeman. Henry Adams, Chichester. Jul 06. HP: £3,500. ABP: £4,116.

155

Satsuma earthenware box & cover, Meiji period, (1868-1912) enamelled in colours and gilded, procession of figures carrying a dignitary, black and gilt seal mark, Kaizan Sei (Kaizan Made), 5.25in wide. Halls Fine Art, Shrewsbury. Jul 04. HP: £3,400. ABP: £3,999.

156

Samuel Alcock Staffordshire earthenware Leech jar and cover, mid 19thC, inscribed on a label 'LEECHES', chips, discoloured, 31cm, moulded mark. Sworders, Stansted Mountfitchet. Jul 04. HP: £3,400. ABP: £3,999.

157

Wedgwood Fairyland lustre vase, by Daisy Makeig-Jones, Candlemas pattern, 22cm high. Cheffins, Cambridge. Sep 04. HP: £3,400. ABP: £3,999.

158

KPM porcelain plaque, with a semi-clad winged female greeting a butterfly, 9.5 x 6.5in, gilt frame. Gorringes, Lewes. Dec 06. HP: £3,400. ABP: £3,999.

159

Pair Meissen porcelain figures of horse tamers modelled by J.J. Kaendler, 9.75in and 10.25in high, overglazed crossed swords mark to base, one with incised No. 136. Canterbury Auction Galleries, Kent. Feb 07. HP: £3,400. ABP: £3,999.

160

Pair Theodore Deck faience vases, c1880, scenes of birds amongst blossoming branches, dragon handles, imp'd T H Deck, faults, 56cm. Sworders, Stansted Mountfitchet. Jul 05. HP: £3,300. ABP: £3,881.

161

Pair of William Moorcroft pottery vases, tube lined in Cornflower design, 8.25in high. Hartleys, Ilkley. Oct 06. HP: £3,300. ABP: £3,881.

162

Cased Royal Worcester set of six Harry Stinton cups and saucers. Wintertons Ltd, Lichfield. Nov 04. HP: £3,200. ABP: £3,764.

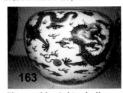

163

Chinese blue/white bulbous jardiniere, H 28cm Dia 39cm Gorringes, Bexhill. Sep 04. HP: £3,200. ABP: £3,764.

Hammer: £3,200 - £3,000

Satsuma vase, bands of chrysanthemums, signed, 18.5in. Gorringes, Lewes. Oct 04. HP: £3,200. ABP: £3,764.

19thC majolica figural centrepiece, floral decorated basketwork bowl, damaged, 16in. Gorringes, Lewes. Oct 04. HP: £3,200. ABP: £3,764.

Pair of Moorcroft Macintyre vases, with Alhambra version of the green and gold Florian design in pink, 24.5cm high. Cheffins, Cambridge. Sep 04. HP: £3,200. ABP: £3,764.

Chamberlain's Worcester Regent dinner service, 53 pieces, c1811-20, chrysanthemum pattern, printed marks, soup tureen 10in. Gorringes, Lewes. Sep 04. HP: £3,200. ABP: £3,764.

Chinese blue/white jardiniere, panels of domestic scenes, 19.5in. Gorringes, Lewes. Sep 05. HP: £3,200. ABP: £3,764.

William de Morgan Lustre charger, with a peacock standing on a brick wall, reverse with star centre, 14ins. Gorringes, Lewes. Jan 05. HP: £3,200. ABP: £3,764.

Wedgwood Flame Fairyland lustre punch bowl, by D. Makeig-Jones, Woodland Bridge pattern, Z5360, Poplar Trees pattern exterior, Z4968, 4 gilded monograms MJ to interior, 9.25in. Gorringes, Lewes. Mar 05. HP: £3,200. ABP: £3,764.

Royal Doulton figure, Mamselle, HN 659. Louis Taylor, Stoke. Sep 04. HP: £3,200. ABP: £3,764.

19th/20thC Quimper faience 2-handled urn shaped vase, classical woman to represent 'Peace' in vignette, musical trophies to reverse, 26in, Quimper mark to base. Canterbury Auc. Galleries, Kent. Dec 05. HP: £3,200. ABP: £3,764.

Chinese porcelain vase, with a reindeer and storks in a peony garden, 14in. Gorringes, Lewes. Mar 06. HP: £3,200. ABP: £3,764.

Lenci pottery figure from a model by Helen König Scavini, painted marks, dated 7-4-32, 24cm high. Lyon and Turnbull, Edinburgh. Nov 06. HP: £3,200. ABP: £3,764.

Royal Doulton, Henry V at Agincourt HN3947, designer A.M. introduced 1997, 18.5in high. Louis Taylor, Stoke. Sep 06. HP: £3,100. ABP: £3,646.

Chinese ginger jar & 2 vases, enamelled decoration, tallest 8in. Gorringes, Lewes. Feb 07. HP: £3,100. ABP: £3,646.

Pair Dutch Delft tulipieres, 18thC, 5 graduated trumpets and 3 holes, lizard handles, heads missing and other damage, 30cm. Sworders, Stansted Mountfitchet. Feb 06. HP: £3,100. ABP: £3,646.

Late 19thC Chinese vase, famille rose patterns with sinuous dragons and fans, six character mark of Yong Cheng, 39cm. Sworders, Stansted Mountfitchet. Feb 06. HP: £3,100. ABP: £3,646.

Royal Doulton porcelain figure 'Princess Badoura', HN 2081, by H. Tettensor, Harry E. Stanton and F. Van Allen Phillips, 21.5in high, printed mark, signed P. Smith, dated 13/3/90. Canterbury Auction Galleries, Kent. Feb 04. HP: £3,000. ABP: £3,528.

Derby emerald green ground teacup & saucer, c1797, views of Wootton Park, Staffs and Cotton Mill, Nr Matlock, crown cross batons mark and number 315 in blue, gilded number 1, titled view in blue. Wintertons, Lichfield. Mar 04. HP: £3,000. ABP: £3,528.

Satsuma earthenware bowl, Meiji period (1868-1912), with a procession of figures and a dignitary in a sedan chair, black and gilt seal mark, Kaizan Sei (Kaizan Made), 6in. Halls Fine Art, Shrewsbury. Jul 04. HP: £3,000. ABP: £3,528.

182

Meiji period Satsuma charger. Gorringes, Bexhill. Sep 04. HP: £3,000. ABP: £3,528.

183

Meiji period Satsuma square baluster vase. Gorringes, Bexhill. Sep 04. HP: £3,000. ABP: £3,528.

184

Worcester Flight & Barr jardiniere. Dreweatt Neate, Godalming. Mar 06. HP: £3,000. ABP: £3,528.

185

Late 17thC Thomas Toft slipware charger, decorated the Royal Arms, lion and unicorn supporters. (broken into 3 pieces, lacking much glaze, 43 cm. Charterhouse Auctioneers, Sherborne. Oct 06. HP: £3,000. ABP: £3,528.

186

16thC Deruta maiolica wet drug jar, 'Lalocretia', with a Romayne portrait bust of a lady, arabesques and flower border, spout with entwined support, 9in, base re-attached. Gorringes, Lewes. Dec 06. HP: £3,000. ABP: £3,528.

187

Doulton Burslem Luscian ware vase, 'The Merchant of Venice - Lorenzo and Jessica - in Such a Night', lovers in panoramic landscape, signed by William Nunn, gilt embellished, 19.5in. Louis Taylor, Stoke on Trent. Dec 06. HP: £3,000. ABP: £3,528.

188

Pair of Chinese saucers, Guangxu, 1875-1908, with Buddhistic emblems against a yellow ground, character marks, 6in. Gorringes, Lewes. Feb 07. HP: £3,000. ABP: £3,528.

> The numbering system acts as a reader reference and links to the Analysis of each section.

189

George Jones Majolica dish, kingfisher perched above aquatic leaves, impressed marks include Patent Office registration for 10 December 1873 and GJ monogram, model No. 3369/T. Ewbank, Send, Surrey. Mar 04. HP: £2,900. ABP: £3,411.

190

Savona, blue/white vase, prob. 18thC maiolica, 'Ag Acettose', handles broken. Stride & Son, Chichester. Mar 04. HP: £2,900. ABP: £3,411.

191

Troika pottery wall plaque by Benny Sirota, c1964, Sirota's finger prints each end, 15.5in. Burstow & Hewett, Battle. Mar 04. HP: £2,900. ABP: £3,411.

192

Minton majolica teapot and cover, 5in, c1870s. Louis Taylor, Stoke. Jun 04. HP: £2,900. ABP: £3,411.

193

Pair of Canton polychrome jardinieres/covers, c1900, figures & chickens in panels, 21.5cm. Sworders, Stansted Mountfitchet. Feb 05. HP: £2,900. ABP: £3,411.

194

Beswick, Beatrix Potter's Duchess with Flowers. Brettells, Newport. Jul 05. HP: £2,900. ABP: £3,411.

195

Martin Brothers jug, reptile handle, pouring lip with hand-pierced filter, incised mark Martin, London + Southall, 5.5in high. Gorringes, Lewes. Oct 05. HP: £2,900. ABP: £3,411.

196

Satsuma vase, c1875, 47cm. Sworders, Stansted Mountfitchet. Nov 05. HP: £2,900. ABP: £3,411.

197

Pr. R. Worcester vases, highland cattle in landscape, H Stinton, 5.75in, No G42. Brightwells, Leominster. Jan 06. HP: £2,900. ABP: £3,411.

198

Moorcroft pottery vase, tube lined in the Pansy design, 9.25in. Hartleys, Ilkley. Aug 06. HP: £2,900. ABP: £3,411.

199

Pair of Royal Dux porcelain water carriers, mould no. 614, pink triangle, 28in. Andrew Hartley, Ilkley. Dec 04. HP: £2,800. ABP: £3,293.

200

Eleven William de Morgan floral tiles, 6 with Sands End Pottery backstamp, 5 with Merton Abbey mark, 6in. Gorringes, Lewes. Jun 05. HP: £2,800. ABP: £3,293.

Hammer: £2,800 - £2,600

201

Plymouth (W. Cookworthy) porcelain mug dating from 1768, decorated with exotic birds. Bearne's, Exeter. Jun 05. HP: £2,800. ABP: £3,293.

202

Figure group by Obadiah Sherratt, some damage, 11in high. Tring Market Auctions, Herts. Mar 04. HP: £2,800. ABP: £3,293.

203

Martin Brothers stoneware bird jar, incised 'Martin:- London & Southall', dated 1902 to base, 3.5in high. Andrew Hartley, Ilkley. Feb 04. HP: £2,700. ABP: £3,175.

204

Late 19thC European majolica deer, impressed fish marks, 29.5cm high. Cheffins, Cambridge. Feb 04. HP: £2,700. ABP: £3,175.

205

Large 19thC George Jones majolica salmon tureen. Humberts inc Tayler & Fletcher, Andoversford. Oct 04. HP: £2,700. ABP: £3,175.

20 *Ceramics Prices*

206

Troika Newlyn pottery mask, double sided, Simone Kilburn, 10in high. Burstow & Hewett, Battle. Mar 04. HP: £2,700. ABP: £3,175.

207

Pair of Doulton Lambeth stoneware vases, by Hannah Barlow. Wintertons Ltd, Bakewell. Dec 04. HP: £2,700. ABP: £3,175.

208

Pottery Sancai glazed camel, Tang dynasty (7th-10thC AD) neck restored. Sworders, Stansted Mountfitchet. Nov 04. HP: £2,700. ABP: £3,175.

209

Beswick figure of a huntsman, mounted on a rearing dapple grey horse, 9.5in. Gorringes, Lewes. Mar 04. HP: £2,700. ABP: £3,175.

210

18thC creamware coffee pot, floral design, 9.75in. Gorringes, Lewes. Apr 05. HP: £2,700. ABP: £3,175.

211

Famille verte fish bowl, late 19thC, audience scenes, interior with Shibumkin, 46.5cm. Sworders, Stansted Mountfitchet. Feb 06. HP: £2,700. ABP: £3,175.

212

Early 20thC Martinware double sided face jug, incised to base 'RW Martin & Bros, London Southall', 5.25in high. Halls Fine Art, Shrewsbury. Sep 06. HP: £2,700. ABP: £3,175.

> The illustrations are in descending price order. The price range is indicated at the top of each page.

213

Pair of Sevres style vases and covers. Gorringes, Bexhill. Sep 04. HP: £2,600. ABP: £3,058.

214

Pair of mid 19thC English porcelain twin handled pedestal urns, painted with floral sprays, 13in. Gorringes, Lewes. Sep 04. HP: £2,600. ABP: £3,058.

215

Pair of 19thC Chinese earthenware jardinieres, famille rose enamel, (faults), 20.5in. Gorringes, Lewes. Jan 05. HP: £2,600. ABP: £3,058.

216

Clarice Cliff coffee set, Pastel Autumn, design, cup cracked, plates worn, pot 7in. (16) Gorringes, Lewes. Mar 05. HP: £2,600. ABP: £3,058.

217

Satsuma vase, Japanese 19th/20thC, painted with 3 panels, square 9 character black seal mark to base, 17cm. Rosebery's, London. Jun 05. HP: £2,600. ABP: £3,058.

218

Chinese baluster vase, with figures on a garden terrace in 'famille verte' enamels, 18in. Gorringes, Lewes. Feb 06. HP: £2,600. ABP: £3,058.

219

Chinese Qing Dynasty blue/white moon flask, raised reserve of pomegranates, seal mark, 25cm high. Rosebery's, London. Mar 06. HP: £2,600. ABP: £3,058.

220

Late 18th/early 19thC Urbino style Istoriato maiolica dish, (restored), 9.25in. Gorringes, Lewes. Dec 06. HP: £2,600. ABP: £3,058.

221

Pair of 19thC Chinese moon flasks, with sages, musicians, other figures, clouds & flora, 29cm. Locke & England, Leamington Spa. Mar 06. HP: £2,600. ABP: £3,058.

222

Early 19thC Walton pottery spill vase as the royal coat of arms, marbled base, 6in high, impressed mark on scroll to reverse, damage. Canterbury Auc. Galleries, Kent. Apr 06. HP: £2,600. ABP: £3,058.

223

George Jones majolica garden seat, top and base moulded as wicker bound, birds, dragonfly within bull rushes & lillies in relief, 18in high. Hartleys, Ilkley. Jun 06. HP: £2,600. ABP: £3,058.

224

Pair of Bretby cold painted earthenware figures of Bavarian children, 29in. Gorringes, Lewes. Oct 06. HP: £2,600. ABP: £3,058.

225

19thC blue/white Davenport dinner service. Kidson Trigg Auctions, Swindon. May 04. HP: £2,500. ABP: £2,940.

226

Tile from 'P & O ship India', built at Greenock in 1896 by Caird & Co, one of 12 for which De Morgan supplied the tiles. Sworders, Stansted Mountfitchet. Feb 05. HP: £2,500. ABP: £2,940.

227

Pair Moorcroft Florian twin handled vases, with tulips & forget-me-nots, c1916/18, 8in. Gorringes, Lewes. Mar 05. HP: £2,500. ABP: £2,940.

228

R. Worcester porcelain tyg, shape No. 2217, by Chivers, fruit panels within gilded borders, 9in high, dated 1903. Andrew Hartley, Ilkley. Apr 05. HP: £2,500. ABP: £2,940.

229

Moorcroft pottery fruit bowl, deep sides, Pomegranate pattern, 12in dia x 7in high, full signature in green, 'Made for Liberty & Co' in brown, c1910. Canterbury Auction Galleries, Kent. Jun 05. HP: £2,500. ABP: £2,940.

230

Early 18thC Chinese famille verte bowl, garden panels below diaper and overglaze blue framed vignettes, 33.5cm dia. (D) Cheffins, Cambridge. Apr 05. HP: £2,500. ABP: £2,940.

Hammer: £2,600 - £2,400

231

Moorcroft Parramore. Stroud Auctions, Stroud. May 05. HP: £2,500. ABP: £2,940.

232

Four Chinese yellow porcelain bowls from Kang Hsiu (1875-1908) painted with green dragons. Stride & Son, Chichester. Aug 05. HP: £2,500. ABP: £2,940.

233

Minton majolica monkey teapot. Kent Auction Galleries, Folkestone. Nov 05. HP: £2,500. ABP: £2,940.

234

Set of four Russian porcelain sauce boats/stands from the Grand Duke Alexander Alexandrovich Service, Imperial Porcelain Manufactory, Period of Alexander II, 1855-1881, 20cm long. Rosebery's, London. Mar 06. HP: £2,500. ABP: £2,940.

235

Derby eye bath c1775-80, shell moulded form, scroll moulded pedestal stem, 5.5cm high. Halls Fine Art, Shrewsbury. Dec 06. HP: £2,500. ABP: £2,940.

236

W. Moorcroft 3 piece teaset, Florian design, damage. Louis Taylor, Stoke. Sep 04. HP: £2,450. ABP: £2,881.

237

Majolica teapot, prob. George Jones, form of a citrus fruit with green leaves and white buds, cover modelled as a mushroom, indistinct impressed marks, 4.5in. high Gorringes, Lewes. Dec 04. HP: £2,450. ABP: £2,881.

238

Japanese Satsuma bowl, with procession of dignatry, Meiji period, seal mark to base - Yama Fuji Seikozen, 7in dia x 2.5in high. Louis Taylor, Stoke on Trent. Sep 06. HP: £2,450. ABP: £2,881.

239

Doulton Lambeth stoneware menu holder 'Quack Doctor', by George Tinworth, 3.75in high, impressed mark, dated 1885, incised GT to rear. Canterbury Auction Galleries, Kent. Feb 04. HP: £2,400. ABP: £2,823.

240

Plymouth, William Cookworthy porcelain mug, ribbed strap handle, Chinese landscape, 9.5cm high, c1768-1770, paper label to base. Bearne's, Exeter. Mar 04. HP: £2,400. ABP: £2,823.

Hammer: £2,400 - £2,300

Pair of large enamel vases, probably early 19thC. Richard Winterton, Burton on Trent, Staffs. Aug 04. HP: £2,400. ABP: £2,823.

Portuguese majolica charger, c1880. Brettells, Newport, Shropshire. Sep 04. HP: £2,400. ABP: £2,823.

Pr. large earthenware figures, Gladstone and Disraeli, Wittmann & Roth, Reg mark 1876, marked copyright & W & R L mark, both damaged. Boldon Auction Galleries, Tyne & Wear. Sep 04. HP: £2,400. ABP: £2,823.

Paris porcelain pill box as a white mouse, 18thC, silver mounted lid, painted rats, interior with weasel, chicken, London 1797, hair crack to body, 6cm high. Sworders, Stansted Mountfitchet. Nov 04. HP: £2,400. ABP: £2,823.

Unglazed pottery horse, Tang dynasty (7th-10thC), later base and restoration, 60cm. Sworders, Stansted Mountfitchet. Nov 04. HP: £2,400. ABP: £2,823.

Pair of Feuillet, Paris, mid 19thC, ice pails/covers/ liners, with flowers, insects & fruit, 26cm, chips. Sworders, Stansted Mountfitchet. Feb 05. HP: £2,400. ABP: £2,823.

Mason's Ironstone dinner service, c1840, 77 pieces. Sworders, Stansted Mountfitchet. Feb 05. HP: £2,400. ABP: £2,823.

Minton majolica oyster stand, as tiers of oyster shells, brown undersides encrusted with green seaweed, finial as pink fish and eel, revolving foot impressed Minton, No. 636, c1865, rim chips, 12in wide. Gorringes, Lewes. Jan 05. HP: £2,400. ABP: £2,823.

Pair Cantonese candlesticks as saddled & caparisoned elephant, famille rose decoration, 17cm long, 19thC, glue repair. Bearne's, Exeter. Jun 05. HP: £2,400. ABP: £2,823.

Bristol Delft 'Farmyard' plate in blue with a peacock stood before sponged trees, 22cm dia, c1740, rim chips. Bearne's, Exeter. Jun 05. HP: £2,400. ABP: £2,823.

16/17thC, Chinese blue/white vase, misty underglaze blue with panels of figures on a ground of scrolling flowers, opened firing crack, 37cm. Sworders, Stansted Mountfitchet. Nov 05. HP: £2,400. ABP: £2,823.

Wedgwood Fairyland lustre bowl, night time scene with trees, birds & fairies, interior with trees, spiders web, goblins by pool, 8.75in dia, 'Daisey' Makeig-Jones, c1919. Ibbett Mosely, Sevenoaks. Nov 05. HP: £2,400. ABP: £2,823.

1920s Russian figure of a girl, in head scarf, green coat and boots, snowy oval base, dated 1924, Volkhov & Morjantseva, 8in. Gorringes, Lewes. Feb 06. HP: £2,400. ABP: £2,823.

Moorcroft for Macintyre vase, landscape design, Florian Ware range, printed marks and green signature to base, c1903, 11.75in. Gorringes, Lewes. Jul 06. HP: £2,400. ABP: £2,823.

Beswick: girl on dapple grey pony, gloss MN 1499. Batemans, Stamford. Mar 06. HP: £2,400. ABP: £2,823.

Pair Chinese porcelain vases & covers, 18thC, 54cm high. (faults) Rupert Toovey & Co, Washington, Sussex. Jan 04. HP: £2,300. ABP: £2,705.

Categories or themes can be followed through the colour coded Index which contains 1000s of cross references.

Spode porcelain campana shaped pastel burner, c1820, iron red mark and pattern number 1166. Dreweatt Neate, Newbury. Feb 04. HP: £2,300. ABP: £2,705.

Four William De Morgan 'India' tiles, impressed Sands End, Fulham Pottery rose mark, c1896, 9in sq. Sworders, Stansted Mountfitchet. Feb 05. HP: £2,300. ABP: £2,705.

Chinese blue/white plaque, 19thC, with a traveller on a bridge in a rocky landscape, 46.3 x 33cm. Sworders, Stansted Mountfitchet. Nov 05. HP: £2,300. ABP: £2,705.

260

Clarice Cliff Sharks Teeth jar and cover, 21cm. Great Western, Glasgow. May 05. HP: £2,300. ABP: £2,705.

261

English delft, prob. Brislington, shallow dish decorated with 3 simple pomegranates about a central motif, 35cm dia, mid 16thC, cracked. Bearne's, Exeter. Jun 05. HP: £2,300. ABP: £2,705.

262

Early 19thC Spode 'New Stone' dinner service, 44 pieces, pattern no. 3875, impressed marks. Gorringes, Lewes. Apr 04. HP: £2,300. ABP: £2,705.

263

Pair E.B.Fishley Fremington Pottery twin handled vases, decorated in cream slip, dated 1882 (a.f) 16.5in. Gorringes, Lewes. Feb 06. HP: £2,300. ABP: £2,705.

264

William Moorcroft vase, Cornflower design, signature to base, 12.5in high. Louis Taylor, Stoke on Trent. Mar 06. HP: £2,300. ABP: £2,705.

265

R. Worcester vase, highland cattle in landscape, signed J Stinton, 8.75in, No G42. Brightwells, Leominster. Sep 06. HP: £2,300. ABP: £2,705.

266

Song/Ming dynasty celadon duck water dropper, one wing removable for filling chamber, beak forming the spout, 17cm high. (2) Cheffins, Cambridge. Jun 04. HP: £2,200. ABP: £2,587.

267

Early 19thC Worcester cream vase and cover. Gorringes, Bexhill. Sep 04. HP: £2,200. ABP: £2,587.

268

Majolica jardiniere with swans and bullrushes in relief, by George Jones, base cracked and minus pedestal. Stride & Son, Chichester. Sep 05. HP: £2,200. ABP: £2,587.

269

Troika sculpture as a mask. Gorringes, Bexhill. Apr 05. HP: £2,200. ABP: £2,587.

Hammer: £2,300 - £2,050

270

Early 19thC Staffs dinner service, attributed to William Mason, 1811-24, chips throughout. (74) Gorringes, Lewes. Mar 06. HP: £2,200. ABP: £2,587.

271

Minton majolica bowl, 1873. Richard Winterton, Burton on Trent. Jan 07. HP: £2,200. ABP: £2,587.

272

Doulton Lambeth stoneware jug by Hannah Barlow, silver collar, impressed Lambeth, initialled HB date stamped 1875, 14.5cm high. Rosebery's, London. Mar 04. HP: £2,100. ABP: £2,470.

273

Pair of Moorcroft Hazeldene pattern vases, c1910, printed mark 'Made For Liberty & Co', painted signature, 16cm. (2) Sworders, Stansted Mountfitchet. Nov 04. HP: £2,100. ABP: £2,470.

274

Pair Copeland Spode plates, dated 1885 and painted by C F Hurton, printed & impressed marks, 23cm dia. Cheffins, Cambridge. Feb 05. HP: £2,100. ABP: £2,470.

275

Clarice Cliff orange trees and house pattern tea set, 1931, damages. (9) Sworders, Stansted Mountfitchet. Apr 05. HP: £2,100. ABP: £2,470.

276

Pair early 19thC Derby urns, socles and square feet, marks in red, 33cm high. (R) Cheffins, Cambridge. Apr 05. HP: £2,100. ABP: £2,470.

277

Burmantofts faience 'Anglo-Persian' vase, prob. decorated by Victor Kramer, 20.5in, imp'd 'Burmantofts Faience 25' with artist's initials, rim broken in several places and restuck. Canterbury Auction Galleries, Kent. Dec 05. HP: £2,100. ABP: £2,470.

278

Pr. R. Dux porcelain vases by Hampel, 13in high, signed. Andrew Hartley, Ilkley. Apr 06. HP: £2,100. ABP: £2,470.

279

Royal Doulton Titanian ware Crucifix, by Noke, 10.25in long x 5.75in wide. Louis Taylor, Stoke. Mar 06. HP: £2,050. ABP: £2,411.

Section III: £2,000-£1000

'The Section is dominated by.....twentieth century pottery, with the ubiquitous Doulton paramount.....don't underestimate slipware. This one, combed in brown with a yellow glaze at over £2,000 including premium.....these plates were copied by Miles Mason in a 'hybrid' paste from about 1800.....'

The number of lots covered now doubles. New factories are showing for the first time. Japanese entries are increasing and Japanese porcelain makes an appearance, for example at **447** and **555**. Chinese porcelain still represents at least 15-20% of the market. There is a smattering of early tin-glazed earthenware, about ten entries, and over twenty examples of early porcelain and of other early pottery. The Section is dominated by English nineteenth century and mainly twentieth century pottery, with the ubiquitous Doulton paramount with twenty eight examples. At **280** is *The Swimmer* at £2,000 hammer. The Index is the key to research. Remember she appeared on page 12 at £6,000 hammer and the same figure appears again on page 34 at £1,300 hammer and page 53 at only £850 hammer. The highest price was paid in 2000. At **308** is *The Balloon Seller* and she appears again on page 114 at a tenth of the price.You would need to be a Doulton expert to explain these prices. Pilkingtons makes a first appearance at **284** and a Gallé faience bulldog at **29**. Royal Dux has made two earlier appearances but in my opinion the pair of Hampel figures at **287** are superb and unsurpassed. The Royal Crown Derby service at **314** works out at about £40 a piece but I doubt if it will ever get used, whilst the services at **290** and **291** probably will. Note Charlotte Rhead at **330** and follow Burleighware through the Index. Wemyss makes a second appearance at **323** with their first, rather affectionate looking pig, very simply decorated. Note the high prices for ceramic garden seats **(327)** and don't underestimate slipware dishes, **(331)** this one combed in brown with a yellow glaze at over £2,000 including premium. Thinking back to when I used to sell early pottery twenty years ago, I could never have imagined that such prices would be attained. The early Mason's Patent ironstone dessert service at **354**, where twenty five pieces fetched £2,000 is about par for the course. I expect this service to be used or at least displayed in a house of distinction. Rockingham appears at **351**, one card tray approaching nearly £2,000 at Neale's in Nottingham in 2004. This South Yorkshire factory rarely appears at auction but there is a dessert plate at **513**, with a still life by Steel. The Doncaster Racecourse Antiques Fair always has specialist dealers selling Rockingham.

Meissen always sells well and there are probably over sixty lots in these pages. The price range here is from £14,000 hammer on page 10 to a mere £30 for a plate at **2951**. See the tea/coffee service at **359**. At **369** is a set of twenty four Chinese export dinner plates. They sold for £1,600 hammer in 2006, more than £52 each including premium. These octagonal plates were copied by Miles Mason in a 'hybrid' hardpaste from about 1800. The East India Company had ceased importing Chinese porcelain as ballast in the 1790s following a dispute with the dealers (Chinamen) over 'ringing'. These Chinese plates usually fetch about £30-£40 each and I would be interested to know what happened to them next! Incidentally the large Mason's footbath at **373** fetched an astonishing price considering it was a/f, but large items of Mason's do fetch a premium. Mason's commence at nearly £7,000 (**88**) and follow through to £82 on page **149**. Note also the Spode footbath at **390** and £1,500 hammer. I hope this is an early nineteenth century example and not a modern reproduction.

Check out the only example of Doulton's *The Sunshine Girl* at **401** and the first Ruskin entry on page 29. (**367**) The first of fifty Carltonware entries appear at **457** on page 34. I didn't realise this firm could notch up £1,500. Do you remember our first Bretby at **224** and over £3,000? Their second example, another figure appears at **438** and we have to wait until **1709** on page 105 to find an extremely modest price paid for a fine table centre in the form of three swans at **1709**. Note this lot also includes a jardiniere stuck rather incongruously on top. I am interested in the £1,400 hammer paid for a Staffordshire greyhound, with a restored leg, at **431**. This is a high price but an exceptionally good figure. Other items that interest me are the £1,500 paid for an early Royal Doulton *Reggie Bunnykins* at **442** and the similar price paid for a fine pair of Copeland figural comports at **437**. I wonder which will prove the better investment? If you were to ask me to chose between the Meissen salt at **459** and the Wedgwood Ravillious lemonade set at **456**, there would be no contest. See also for about £1,500, the fine pair of Royal Dux figures at **470** and the Worcester at **486**. Staffordshire pearlware at **481** and **482** should not be overlooked. These little chapels and churches are very valuable in their Prattware colours. Follow Prattware through the Index.

At **531** is a further Royal Dux figure of an Art Deco naked female clasping a robe. The price reflects the quality. At **514** and **564** are a further two Charles Vyse figures. The lowest price for Vyse is £190 hammer paid for a bowl at **1913** on page 116. Finally check out the surprising £1,050 hammer price paid for an early Wade *Snow White and the Seven Dwarfs* at **581**.

280

Royal Doulton, The Swimmer, no HN number. Louis Taylor, Stoke. Jun 04. HP: £2,000. ABP: £2,352.

281

18thC Meissen porcelain figure, by J.J. Kaendler, 7in high, unmarked, brown enamel to apron degrading, c1748. Canterbury Auction Galleries, Kent. Apr 04. HP: £2,000. ABP: £2,352.

282

Pilkington's Lancastrian lustre moon flask by William S. Mycock, c1908, shape No. 2715, imp'd, painted marks, 10.5in. Gorringes, Lewes. Dec 04. HP: £2,000. ABP: £2,352.

283

Two 19thC mahogany framed porcelain plaques of dogs in the style of George Armfield, one signed R.T. Perling, 22cm dia inside frames. John Taylors, Louth. Apr 05. HP: £2,000. ABP: £2,352.

284

Pilkington's Royal Lancastrian lustre bottle vase by R. Joyce, c1920, young maidens holding floral ribbons, shape No. 2962, impressed and painted marks, 12.5in. Gorringes, Lewes. Dec 04. HP: £2,000. ABP: £2,352.

285

Glazed pottery horse, Tang dynasty (7th-10thC AD), the saddle in green with ochre splashes, distressed. 29cm, O.C.S. label, 1955 Exhibition No.59. Sworders, Stansted Mountfitchet. Nov 04. HP: £2,000. ABP: £2,352.

286

Wedgwood mauve Jasperware 2-handled urn/cover, 12.5in high, impressed mark, and a pair of similar 2-handled urn shaped vases/covers, 7.75in high (impressed mark, No. 64, handle restored). Canterbury Auction Galleries, Kent. Apr 05. HP: £2,000. ABP: £2,352.

287

Pair of Royal Dux porcelain figures by Hampel, moorish water carriers, pink triangle mark, stamped 1433/1434, 31.5in. A. Hartley, Ilkley. Apr 05. HP: £2,000. ABP: £2,352.

288

George IV Spode electioneering jug, printed with an Italian-type pattern in blue, overglaze wreath 'Lord Anson for Ever, Huzza. 1826', 9.75in. Gorringes, Lewes. Jun 05. HP: £2,000. ABP: £2,352.

289

Early 19thC Staffs group in style of Obadiah Sherratt, Dr Syntax playing cards with his opponent, 20cm high. (D) Cheffins, Cambridge. Feb 06. HP: £2,000. ABP: £2,352.

290

Early 20thC Meissen dinner service, second quality, with fruit/flower sprays, crossed swords marks in underglaze blue with two incisions. (76) Gorringes, Lewes. Jul 06. HP: £2,000. ABP: £2,352.

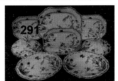

291

Chinese famille verte dinner service. Richard Winterton Auctioneers, Lichfield. Aug 06. HP: £2,000. ABP: £2,352.

292

Moorcroft vase, grape and pomegranate pattern, blue ground, 11.5in. Gorringes, Lewes. Dec 06. HP: £2,000. ABP: £2,352.

293

Royal Worcester porcelain coffee service, six settings painted with golden pheasants by Sedgley, silver enamelled teaspoons, dated 1924. Hartleys, Ilkley. Dec 06. HP: £2,000. ABP: £2,352.

294

Galle faience figure of a bulldog, c1900, painted with flowers and blue ribbons, glass eyes, signed E Gallé, Nancy, front paw damaged. Sworders, Stansted Mountfitchet. Feb 07. HP: £2,000. ABP: £2,352.

> **Prices quoted are actual hammer prices (HP) and the Approximate Buyer's Price (ABP) includes an average premium of 15% + VAT.**

295

Pair Derby baskets, c1758-60, enamelled with birds, slight restoration to back of handles, 4.3in wide. Wintertons, Lichfield. Mar 04. HP: £1,900. ABP: £2,234.

296

Garniture of 5 Chinese vases, early Qianlong period, 2 pairs of squared baluster vases, 10.5in.& 9.5in, with floral sprigs in underglaze blue and enamels, and a similar vase in underglaze blue and gilt, some restoration. Gorringes, Lewes. Oct 04. HP: £1,900. ABP: £2,234.

Hammer: £1,900 - £1,850

Large 18thC stoneware mug. Gorringes, Bexhill. Sep 04. HP: £1,900. ABP: £2,234.

18thC Lowestoft blue butter tureen/stand, fluted oval shape, with an Oriental view, bird finial, c1760-65, stand 7in. long. Gorringes, Lewes. Sep 04. HP: £1,900. ABP: £2,234.

Wedgwood fairyland lustre lily tray (2483), Firbolgs pattern, centre with a lady riding on a bird, dragon bead borders and open mouth fish, Z5200 mark below, 13in. Gorringes, Lewes. Mar 04. HP: £1,900. ABP: £2,234.

Four William De Morgan 'India' tiles, c1896, imp'd Sands End, Fulham Pottery rose mark, 9in square. From the 'P & O ship India', built at Greenock in 1896 by Caird & Co. Sworders, Stansted Mountfitchet. Apr 05. HP: £1,900. ABP: £2,234.

Mixed collection of 5 William de Morgan floral tiles on a board and 6 others. Gorringes, Lewes. Jun 05. HP: £1,900. ABP: £2,234.

Chinese vase, an elder/scribes in a garden between blue leaf-scroll borders, 16in. Gorringes, Lewes. Jun 06. HP: £1,900. ABP: £2,234.

Chinese brush pot, Kang H'si period, painted with warriors and landscape in underglaze blue, lightly incised with leaf-scroll borders, 8in. Gorringes, Lewes. Jul 06. HP: £1,900. ABP: £2,234.

Chinese famille verte vase, decorated with mountains and script, seal mark to base, 14in. Gorringes, Lewes. Jul 06. HP: £1,900. ABP: £2,234.

Meissen part monkey band, after J J Kaendler, 14cm high and smaller, post Second World War. Dreweatt Neate, Donnington. Feb 07. HP: £1,900. ABP: £2,234.

Chelsea tea bowl and saucer, Gold Anchor period, 1756-69, view of church buildings, painted mark, ex Geoffrey Phillips Collection. Gorringes, Lewes. Oct 06. HP: £1,900. ABP: £2,234.

Bernard Moore flambe figure of a monkey clutching a coconut, crimson glazed, coat in iridescent shades of green and purple, signed to reverse, 6in. Louis Taylor, Stoke on Trent. Dec 06. HP: £1,900. ABP: £2,234.

Royal Doulton figure 'The Balloon Seller', no HN number, baby in mauve hat and coat, dated 7.21, green factory mark to reverse, 9in. Louis Taylor, Stoke. Dec 06. HP: £1,900. ABP: £2,234.

> The numbering system acts as a reader reference and links to the Analysis of each section.

A further four William De Morgan 'India' tiles, c1896, back of each tile imp'd Sands End, Fulham Pottery rose mark, 9in square. From the 'P & O ship India', built at Greenock in 1896 by Caird & Co, Sworders, Stansted Mountfitchet. Apr 05. HP: £1,850. ABP: £2,176.

George Jones majolica part tea service, c1875, monkey handles, each piece moulded with blossoming briars, moulded marks incl. registration letter E for 1881, teapot 15.2cm. (8) Sworders, Stansted Mountfitchet. Apr 05. HP: £1,850. ABP: £2,176.

Vienna cabaret set, Austrian early 19thC: 11 pieces, with a view of Vienna within gilt borders, restoration, tray 24.5 x 29cm. Rosebery's, London. Jun 05. HP: £1,850. ABP: £2,176.

English blue/white dish poss. Lowestoft, c1765-70, painted with two figures on a bridge, minute chip, 17cm. Sworders, Stansted Mountfitchet. Jul 05. HP: £1,850. ABP: £2,176.

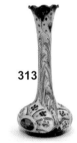

Macintyre florian ware vase, tube lined with peacock feathers, 6in high. Andrew Hartley, Ilkley, W Yorks. Feb 06. HP: £1,850. ABP: £2,176.

Royal Crown Derby part dinner service for 6 settings, Imari style panels in red, blue and gold, printed red marks. (51) Hartleys, Ilkley. Oct 06. HP: £1,850. ABP: £2,176.

Royal Doulton Prototype figure 'The Centaurs Embrace', no Doulton mark. Louis Taylor, Stoke. Mar 07. HP: £1,850. ABP: £2,176.

Minton majolica, Woodpecker Flower Holder, shape No. 1558, Reg. Diamond 1870. (restoration) John Taylors, Louth. Jan 04. HP: £1,800. ABP: £2,117.

Chinese vase, deer in landscape, Kang Hsi period. 44cm, table lamp, cracked. Stride & Son, Chichester. Mar 04. HP: £1,800. ABP: £2,117.

George Jones Majolica jar & cover, c1880, relief moulded with wheat ears and daisies, turquoise ground, painted in black '1795' and impressed 'G J & Sons', 7in high. Halls Fine Art, Shrewsbury. Dec 04. HP: £1,800. ABP: £2,117.

Square based Ming period oriental pottery bottle vase, hand painted with blue flowers, 26cm. Eastbourne Auction Rooms, Sussex. Dec 05. HP: £1,800. ABP: £2,117.

19thC Minton majolica vase, as an open lily with bud and further flowerhead on a leaf base, 17cm. Locke & England, Leamington Spa. Jan 05. HP: £1,800. ABP: £2,117.

Pair Doulton Lambeth vases, Florence Barlow, 4 pate-sur-pate panels of birds, sgraffito foliate motifs in shades of blue, green & ochre, 18.5in. Gorringes, Lewes. Apr 05. HP: £1,800. ABP: £2,117.

Royal Doulton, 'The Rocking Horse', HN 2072. Louis Taylor, Stoke. Jun 05. HP: £1,800. ABP: £2,117.

Rare Wemyss Ware pig. Thos Mawer & Son, Lincoln. Jul 05. HP: £1,800. ABP: £2,117.

Pair Chinese beaker vases, with a dragon chasing the flaming pearl in underglaze blue, 17.5in. Gorringes, Lewes. Feb 06. HP: £1,800. ABP: £2,117.

Hammer: £1,800 - £1,700

18th/early 19thC creamware Grand Platt Menage, 17.75in, prob. Leeds, restoration. Canterbury Auction Galleries, Kent. Feb 06. HP: £1,800. ABP: £2,117.

Clarice Cliff Fantasque lotus vase, 'Orange House', printed mark to base, damage, 11.5in. Gorringes, Lewes. Mar 06. HP: £1,800. ABP: £2,117.

Pair 19thC ironstone garden seats, poss. Ashworths, 20.5in. Gorringes, Lewes. Dec 06. HP: £1,800. ABP: £2,117.

Italian maiolica dish, 2nd half 19thC, in Deruta style with Annunciation, cracks, 39.5cm. Sworders, Stansted Mountfitchet. Feb 07. HP: £1,800. ABP: £2,117.

Macintyre Moorcroft two handled vase, cornflower pattern, signed, printed marks to base, made for Rigg & Son, Glasgow, 10in. Great Western Auctions, Glasgow. Nov 06. HP: £1,760. ABP: £2,070.

Burleigh ware pottery charger Charlotte Rhead, tube lined, Persian flowers, 14in, No. 4013. A Hartley, Ilkley. Apr 05. HP: £1,750. ABP: £2,058.

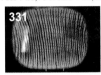

18thC slipware dish in brown and yellow glazes, 15in, hairline crack. Brightwells, Leominster. Jan 06. HP: £1,750. ABP: £2,058.

Clarice Cliff Red Roofs Bizarre pattern wall plate, printed marks, 33.5cm. Sworders, Stansted Mountfitchet. Apr 06. HP: £1,750. ABP: £2,058.

Troika pottery mask, double sided, Aztec design, Cycladic to other, restorations to base, Simone Kilburn, 10in. Burstow & Hewett, Battle. Mar 04. HP: £1,700. ABP: £1,999.

Early 19thC Sunderland or Newcastle Death of Nelson commemorative cream ware frog mug, portrait of Admiral Lord Nelson, interior with a brown frog, 5.5in high. Halls Fine Art, Shrewsbury. Sep 04. HP: £1,700. ABP: £1,999.

Ceramics Prices 27

Hammer: £1,700 - £1,650

335

Beswick dairy shorthorn bull, cow and calf. Brettells, Newport, Shropshire. Sep 04. HP: £1,700. ABP: £1,999.

336

Pilkingtons Royal Lancastrian lustre vase, by Richard Joyce, with fish and seaweed, lustre lion's head, JR monogram to base, 9in high. Maxwells, Wilmslow. Sep 04. HP: £1,700. ABP: £1,999.

337

Pilkingtons Royal Lancastrian squat vase, neck decorated with fish and scrolled weed, green lustre ground, 7.5in. Maxwells, Wilmslow. Sep 04. HP: £1,700. ABP: £1,999.

338

Pair of 18thC Chinese vases, moulded with domestic objects against a green/gilt scroll ground, 16.5in. Gorringes, Lewes. Oct 04. HP: £1,700. ABP: £1,999.

339

Late 18thC English porcelain cabinet cup/saucer cup with a river and landscape, yellow ground, blue border. Gorringes, Lewes. Mar 04. HP: £1,700. ABP: £1,999.

340

Satsuma koro/cover, Yasuda Company trademark, Meiji period, double-walled and reticulated, cover similarly reticulated, painted signature beneath and Satsuma mon, 5.5in. Gorringes, Lewes. Apr 05. HP: £1,700. ABP: £1,999.

341

Troika love plaque, decoration of an embracing couple flanked each by other figures in mottled green, blue & light brown, 13 x 39cm. Clevedon Salerooms, Bristol. Jun 05. HP: £1,700. ABP: £1,999.

342

Bristol delft shallow dish, tulip and two buds in yellow, blue, green and red enamels, stylised band, sponged flat rim, 35cm, c1720, stapled. Bearne's, Exeter. Jun 05. HP: £1,700. ABP: £1,999.

343

Pair Doulton stoneware vases, by Hannah Barlow, Florence Barlow & Emily Stormer, 32cm, imp'd, incised marks, c1880, a rim broken. Bearne's, Exeter. Jun 05. HP: £1,700. ABP: £1,999.

344

Pair of Coalport porcelain cachepots & stands, 'flower pot' form, ring handles, gilt edged yellow ground, 16cm, c1800. Bearne's, Exeter. Jun 05. HP: £1,700. ABP: £1,999.

345

Robinson & Leadbetter parian bust of Victoria, 20.5in. Gorringes, Lewes. Sep 05. HP: £1,700. ABP: £1,999.

346

Creamware tea canister, painted with vertical border design in enamels, 18thC, 4in. Gorringes, Lewes. Nov 05. HP: £1,700. ABP: £1,999.

347

Clarice Cliff / Wilkinson Ltd, Ltd. Edn. Winston Churchill toby jug, 'Going into Action and may God defend the Right, c1941, 12in. Louis Taylor, Stoke. Mar 06. HP: £1,700. ABP: £1,999.

348

Chinese 'blanc de chine' group of Dutch traders and Chinese attendants, c1770, 6.75in. Gorringes, Lewes. Mar 06. HP: £1,700. ABP: £1,999.

349

Pair of 17th/18thC Syrian tiles, blue/green with scrolling foliage & palmettes, 11.5in. Gorringes, Lewes. Dec 06. HP: £1,700. ABP: £1,999.

350

19thC Worcester dessert service, pale blue & gilt rope-twist borders, centres with ferns & wild flowers: 7 comports, and 8 plates. All 9in. Ewbank, Send, Surrey. Dec 06. HP: £1,700. ABP: £1,999.

351

Rockingham named view canted card tray, 'Suspension Bridge, Shoreham', gilt with Regency scrollwork, 28cm wide, printed griffin mark in puce, c1830. (stapled) Neales, Nottingham. Jun 04. HP: £1,650. ABP: £1,940.

352

Leeds creamware documentary teapot/cover, 1774, inscribed and dated 'Elizath. Webster Winstrope, 1774', reverse in polychrome with a Chinaman in a garden, chips, 14.5cm high. Sworders, Stansted Mountfitchet. Nov 04. HP: £1,650. ABP: £1,940.

353

19thC Majolica vase, relief decorated with bluebells and grasses on a pink ground, naturalistic pedestal foot, 26cm. Locke & England, Leamington Spa. Mar 05. HP: £1,650. ABP: £1,940.

354

Mason's ironstone part dessert service: famille verte palette with central Chinese garden scene, printed crown & ribbon marks, c1840, two plates with damage. (25) Bearne's, Exeter. Jun 05. HP: £1,650. ABP: £1,940.

355

Saltglazed stoneware bottle jug, Doulton & Watts Lambeth Pottery in London, marked 'Trafalgar 1805' & 'England Expects......', 16in high. Wallis & Wallis, Lewes. Oct 05. HP: £1,650. ABP: £1,940.

356

Shelley porcelain tea set, 12 settings, conical form, triangular handles, geometric vogue design in green, black, silver. (40) A. Hartley, Ilkley. Oct 05. HP: £1,650. ABP: £1,940.

357

Pair of Canton Famille Rose vases, late 19thC, faceted bodies with panels of figures and shou, mask/ring handles, one with chip & crack, 42cm. Sworders, Stansted Mountfitchet. Nov 05. HP: £1,650. ABP: £1,940.

358

Meissen figure of Harlequin playing the bagpipes by J.J. Kaendler, c 1738, 5in, repair to hat & pipe, imp'd OD45, Gorringes, Lewes. Jan 04. HP: £1,600. ABP: £1,882.

359

Meissen tea/coffee service, c1870, crossed swords, approx 130 pieces. Sworders, Stansted Mountfitchet. Feb 05. HP: £1,600. ABP: £1,882.

360

Doulton character jug, Drake, (hatless), number D6115, designer H Fenton 1940-41, 6in high. Dee, Atkinson & Harrison, Driffield. Mar 04. HP: £1,600. ABP: £1,882.

361

Pair R. Worcester pedestal vases/covers, painted with mixed fruit, signed Roberts, gilt handles, shape no. 2363, 8in. Gorringes, Lewes. Jan 05. HP: £1,600. ABP: £1,882.

362

Beswick hunting set, designed by Arthur Gredington & by Mr Watkin. (9) Halls Fine Art, Shrewsbury. Apr 05. HP: £1,600. ABP: £1,882.

363

19thC majolica centrepiece, floral decorated basketwork bowl supported by a putto holding tambourine, damage, 16in. Gorringes, Lewes. Apr 05. HP: £1,600. ABP: £1,882.

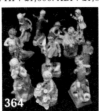

364

Set of Worcester 'Months of the Year' figures, modelled by F.G. Doughty, tallest 7in. Gorringes, Lewes. Jun 05. HP: £1,600. ABP: £1,882.

365

Royal Crown Derby vase, English 1905, 2-handled urn form, panel of flowers, gilt borders with turquoise and white jewelling, panel signed 'Leroy', No. 418/1244, 16cm. Rosebery's, London. Jun 05. HP: £1,600. ABP: £1,882.

366

Pair Chinese vases, painted with squirrels, flowers and diaper borders in iron-red enamel, 9.25in. Gorringes, Lewes. Nov 05. HP: £1,600. ABP: £1,882.

> The illustrations are in descending price order. The price range is indicated at the top of each page.

367

Ruskin high fired stoneware vase, 11.5in. Louis Taylor, Stoke. Jun 06. HP: £1,600. ABP: £1,882.

368

R. Worcester ewer by Baldwyn, swans against a powder blue ground, signed, printed marks, c1901, No. 1065, 7in. Gorringes, Lewes. Jul 06. HP: £1,600. ABP: £1,882.

369

Set 24 Chinese export dinner plates, pagoda pattern in underglaze blue, 9.5in, and three other similar plates. Gorringes, Lewes. Mar 06. HP: £1,600. ABP: £1,882.

370

Set of five Meissen senses, c1870, each modelled as a girl seated experiencing a sense, firing cracks, chips and restoration, cancelled crossed swords, 12-15cm. Sworders, Stansted Mountfitchet. Apr 06. HP: £1,600. ABP: £1,882.

371

19thC Chinese bowl, with flowering shrubs in 'famille rose' enamels, 10in, hardwood stand. Gorringes, Lewes. Jun 06. HP: £1,600. ABP: £1,882.

372

Royal Worcester two-handled vase, painted highland cattle in landscape, signed J Stinton, 6.75in, No 1969. Brightwells, Leominster. Sep 06. HP: £1,600. ABP: £1,882.

373

Masons patent ironstone footbath, 19thC, imari palette with scrolling flowers and foliage within 2 lamprey head handles, blue printed mark, a/f, 37.5cm wide. Halls Fine Art, Shrewsbury. Dec 06. HP: £1,600. ABP: £1,882.

Hammer: £1,550 - £1,500

374

Chinese famille rose 'hunting' punch bowl, Qianlong, c1770, decorated with bright enamels & gilt in Mandarin palette, 30cm dia, cracks. Hampton & Littlewood, Exeter. Apr 04. HP: £1,550. ABP: £1,823.

375

Clarice Cliff 'Secrets' Fantasque Bizarre Stamford Tea for Two, small chip to a cup rim. (8) Gardiner Houlgate, Corsham. Apr 05. HP: £1,550. ABP: £1,823.

> Categories or themes can be followed through the colour coded Index which contains 1000s of cross references.

376

George Jones Majolica game pie dish, liner, cover, moulded in relief with a fox and dead goose, applied blue pad to base with George Jones cypher and 'Stoke on Trent', damage. 10.25in wide. Halls Fine Art, Shrewsbury. Mar 06. HP: £1,550. ABP: £1,823.

377

Pair Crown Devon plaques painted by R. Hinton, each depicting setters chasing game, 23 x 17.5cm. John Taylors, Louth. Sep 04. HP: £1,520. ABP: £1,787.

378

Delftware drug jar, mid 18thC, inscribed C:LUJULÆ below a basket of flowers, 16.5cm, chip. Sworders, Stansted Mountfitchet. Jul 04. HP: £1,500. ABP: £1,764.

379

Full set Worcester 'Months of the Year' figures, modelled by F.G. Doughty, tallest 7in. Gorringes, Lewes. Dec 04. HP: £1,500. ABP: £1,764.

380

Matched set of 6 cups/saucers by Hale, Lockyer, Ricketts & Price, gilded to exterior, with silver teaspoons, 13.5in wide. A. Hartley, Ilkley. Dec 04. HP: £1,500. ABP: £1,764.

381

Beswick merino ram, grey with white face. Gorringes, Lewes. Jan 05. HP: £1,500. ABP: £1,764.

382

Troika pottery mask in grey, blue, brown & biscuit glaze, painted mark and monogram for Jane Fitzgerald, 27cm high. Clevedon Salerooms, Bristol. Feb 05. HP: £1,500. ABP: £1,764.

383

18thC Meissen porcelain figure of a seated beggar musician, by J. J. Kaendler, 5.5in high, crossed swords mark in underglaze blue to base, c1740. Canterbury Auction Galleries, Kent. Apr 04. HP: £1,500. ABP: £1,764.

384

Satsuma high shouldered vase, decorated with cage birds amongst wisteria, signed, 4.75in. Gorringes, Lewes. Mar 05. HP: £1,500. ABP: £1,764.

385

Chinese export oval dish and pair of matching plates, with figures and stately terraces in enamels against puce diaper cavettos and pierced borders, 12.5in and 9in. Gorringes, Lewes. Apr 05. HP: £1,500. ABP: £1,764.

386

Early 17thC blue/white porcelain European shape cistern, with birds and flowers, with European gilt metal figural top, hinged lid and 3 claw and ball feet, damage. 14.5in. Gorringes, Lewes. Jun 05. HP: £1,500. ABP: £1,764.

387

19thC Cantonese vase, with handles to the neck in the form of wild birds, painted with a court scene, 24in. Gorringes, Lewes. Apr 05. HP: £1,500. ABP: £1,764.

388

William de Morgan Persian design chrysanthemum tile, Sands End rose backstamp and another similar with late Fulham Period mark, 8in. Gorringes, Lewes. Jun 05. HP: £1,500. ABP: £1,764.

389

Early 20thC Chinese famille rose vase painted with a coquettish horseman and attendants, 24.5cm high. Cheffins, Cambridge. Apr 05. HP: £1,500. ABP: £1,764.

390

Spode pottery footbath, loop side handles, blue printed in Spode Italian pattern, 19.5in wide. A. Hartley, Ilkley. Apr 05. HP: £1,500. ABP: £1,764.

391

Clarice Cliff Fantasque Bizarre viking boat, Bobbins pattern, 16in long, minor chip to a foot. Dee, Atkinson & Harrison, Driffield. Jul 06. HP: £1,500. ABP: £1,764.

392

Royal Doulton figure 'Out for a Walk', HN748. Louis Taylor, Stoke on Trent. Sep 05. HP: £1,500. ABP: £1,764.

393

Royal Worcester porcelain vase, pierced and gilded lid with spire finial, painted by Sedgley with a nymph by a lake, mountainous background, dated 1929, 7.25in high. Andrew Hartley, Ilkley. Oct 05. HP: £1,500. ABP: £1,764.

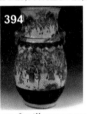

394

Chinese famille rose vase, late 19thC, applied deer handles, bronzed bands and painted with warriors, Chenghua seal mark, 43.5cm. Sworders, Stansted Mountfitchet. Nov 05. HP: £1,500. ABP: £1,764.

395

Minton majolica jardiniere stand in form of a maiden, date cipher for April 1862. 65cm high. Brettells, Newport. Nov 05. HP: £1,500. ABP: £1,764.

396

Late 17thC Swatow blue and white hexagonal vase/cover painted with Shoulao and the Daoist immortals with boy attendants in a pine grove, 31.5cm high. (D) Cheffins, Cambridge. Feb 06. HP: £1,500. ABP: £1,764.

397

Pair Minton majolica ewers, by Hughes Protat, vineous barrel form, applied with putti, date code 1871, 14.5in. Gorringes, Lewes. Nov 05. HP: £1,500. ABP: £1,764.

398

Russian porcelain plate, with half length portrait of Nicholas I, green ground rococo scroll border, portrait surmounted with an Imperial crest, 22cm dia. Rosebery's, London. Mar 06. HP: £1,500. ABP: £1,764.

399

Royal Doulton character fox with chicken, HN1102, 4.75in. Louis Taylor, Stoke. Mar 06. HP: £1,500. ABP: £1,764.

400

Pair Moorcroft earthenware vases, flambe decorated with leaf & berry on an autumnal red, green & brown ground, 23cm. Locke & England, Leamington Spa. Jul 06. HP: £1,500. ABP: £1,764.

Hammer: £1,500 - £1,450

401

Royal Doulton figure 'The Sunshine Girl', HN1348, hairlines. Louis Taylor, Stoke. Mar 06. HP: £1,500. ABP: £1,764.

402

Chinese Celadon Ware vase, bottle form moulded, painted with monkeys climbing a tree and rocks, 19thC, 16.5in high. Hartleys, Ilkley. Jun 06. HP: £1,500. ABP: £1,764.

403

Pair Royal Worcester porcelain dishes, by R Sebright, dated 1911, 11in wide, signed, mark for Townsend & Co, Newcastle-on-Tyne. Hartleys, Ilkley. Aug 06. HP: £1,500. ABP: £1,764.

404

Rockwood pottery plaque, painted by McDermott with 'Lake of the Woods', 9.25in wide, inscribed verso. Hartleys, Ilkley. Oct 06. HP: £1,500. ABP: £1,764.

405

New Hall coffee cup, painted with a tallship in a harbour, New Hall coffee can printed with a rural view and a New Hall coffee can painted with a rural view, latter cracked. Gorringes, Lewes. Feb 07. HP: £1,500. ABP: £1,764.

406

Collection Beswick hunting figures, Master No. 1501, huntswoman No. 1730, and a boy No. 1500, (1957-76) and a small pack of hounds with two foxes. (12) Halls Fine Art, Shrewsbury. Mar 04. HP: £1,450. ABP: £1,705.

407

Pair of Moorcroft Macintryre florian ware vases with gilt decoration on blue ground, pattern no. M2093, 15cm. John Taylors, Louth. Nov 04. HP: £1,450. ABP: £1,705.

408

Pair large Chinese porcelain cockerel ornaments. Henry Adams, Chichester. Apr 06. HP: £1,450. ABP: £1,705.

409

Large twin-handled Canton vase, 64cm high. Gorringes, Bexhill. Sep 04. HP: £1,450. ABP: £1,705.

410

Chinese porcelain vase in famille enamels with 4 figures in a garden pavilion, 40cm high, Shunzhi reign mark, but later. Bearne's, Exeter. Jun 05. HP: £1,450. ABP: £1,705.

Hammer: £1,450 - £1,400

Royal Worcester coffee service c1925, by various artists including F. Harper, W.H Austin, T Lockyer, M. Everett, Moseley and Ricketts, various date codes, a/f. (21). Halls Fine Art, Shrewsbury. May 06. HP: £1,450. ABP: £1,705.

Set Royal Doulton porcelain figures modelled as Henry VIII and his 6 wives, HN3232, 3233, 3349, 3356, 3449, 3450 & 3458, all with certificates. Andrew Hartley, Ilkley. Apr 06. HP: £1,450. ABP: £1,705.

Royal Worcester Temple vase, with a panel showing Venus with her attendants, signed by J Callowhill, dated 1870, chip, damage to enamel. Brightwells, Leominster. Jun 06. HP: £1,450. ABP: £1,705.

Blue/white Chinese moon flask, c1880, faces printed with a warrior on horseback, 45cm. Sworders, Stansted Mountfitchet. Feb 06. HP: £1,450. ABP: £1,705.

Pair Chinese porcelain vases, applied kylin and dragons to neck, blue painted, figural scenes, late 19th/20thC, 18in. Andrew Hartley, Ilkley. Aug 05. HP: £1,450. ABP: £1,705.

Belleek basket with mother of pearl lustre glaze, marked Belleek, Fermanagh Island incised into ceramic strip. Kent Auction Galleries, Folkestone. Aug 06. HP: £1,450. ABP: £1,705.

Pair of Royal Worcester fruit dishes by H. Ayrton, apples & blackberries under a mossy bank, signed H Ayrton, printed base mark, c1959, 11in wide. Tring Market Auctions, Herts. Mar 05. HP: £1,420. ABP: £1,670.

Doulton Lambeth stoneware menu holder, 'Potters' by George Tinworth, imp'd mark, dated 1885, incised GT, 3.75in, damage. Canterbury Auction Galleries, Kent. Feb 04. HP: £1,400. ABP: £1,646.

Clarice Cliff 'Gibraltar' Fantasque Bizarre Daffodil bowl, shape 475, 12.5in wide. Gardiner Houlgate, Corsham. Apr 05. HP: £1,400. ABP: £1,646.

Troika pottery anvil vase, Louise Jinks, 8.5in. Burstow & Hewett, Battle. Mar 04. HP: £1,400. ABP: £1,646.

Troika St Ives shallow dish, c1963/4, hieroglyphic design centre panel, imp'd trident mark, 11.75 x 7.75in. Burstow & Hewett, Battle. Mar 04. HP: £1,400. ABP: £1,646.

Pair of Derby candlestick figures, c1765, shepherd and shepherdess, 28cm, damage. Cheffins, Cambridge. Apr 04. HP: £1,400. ABP: £1,646.

Biscuit porcelain rhyton, Kangxi, (1662-1722) buffalo head, glazed in delineated patches of tones of yellow, aubergine and green, 11cm. Sworders, Stansted Mountfitchet. Nov 04. HP: £1,400. ABP: £1,646.

Early 19thC Coalport Church Gresley pattern, 7-piece part service, central floral spray, shaped reserves, gilt highlights. Gorringes, Lewes. Sep 04. HP: £1,400. ABP: £1,646.

Late 19thC French 'Pagoda' figure, seated Chinaman, head nodding, tongue oscillating, wrists flapping, painted monogram JR in underglaze blue, 11.5in. Gorringes, Lewes. Jun 05. HP: £1,400. ABP: £1,646.

Set of 3 matching William de Morgan Persian design tiles, stylised pattern of fish in a river with flowers & foliage, Sands End Pottery mark, 6in. Gorringes, Lewes. Jun 05. HP: £1,400. ABP: £1,646.

Late 18thC Derby can/saucer with Cupid being disarmed by a lady, marks in gilt/puce. Cheffins, Cambridge. Apr 05. HP: £1,400. ABP: £1,646.

19thC Royal Nymphenburg part dessert service, floral-painted decoration, pierced borders, plates 21cm dia. (16) Gorringes, Bexhill. Dec 05. HP: £1,400. ABP: £1,646.

Pair 19thC Sevres comports, lobed leaf form on dolphin stems, coloured in lilac and gold, printed mark, 8in dia. Gorringes, Lewes. Feb 07. HP: £1,400. ABP: £1,646.

430

Pair Meissen vases, painted with a named view, Dresden and Herrnskretschen, floral panels to the obverse sides, 9.5in. Gorringes, Lewes. Jun 06. HP: £1,400. ABP: £1,646.

431

Staffs greyhound, seated beside dead hare, 10.5in. long, restored leg. Gorringes, Lewes. Jul 06. HP: £1,400. ABP: £1,646.

432

Pair Royal Worcester porcelain plates, painted with fruit by R Sebright, blue/peach borders gilded with flowers, dated 1911, 9in wide, signed, mark for Townsend & Co, Newcastle-on-Tyne. Hartleys, Ilkley. Aug 06. HP: £1,400. ABP: £1,646.

433

Royal Worcester plate by R. Sebright, of fruit and foliage, gilt scroll border, 10.5in. Gorringes, Lewes. Mar 06. HP: £1,400. ABP: £1,646.

434

Cox & Son earthenware ewer, c1875, painted with stylised hares on a Minton blank, 20.5cm. Sworders, Stansted Mountfitchet. Apr 06. HP: £1,400. ABP: £1,646.

435

Royal Doulton Flambe vase by Harry Nixon, with exotic birds, prunus and peonies, monogram to base, 8in. Louis Taylor, Stoke. Sep 06. HP: £1,400. ABP: £1,646.

436

Chinese porcelain vase, 11in, neck rim repaired. Gorringes, Lewes. Oct 06. HP: £1,400. ABP: £1,646.

> Prices quoted are actual hammer prices (HP) and the Approximate Buyer's Price (ABP) includes an average premium of 15% + VAT.

437

19thC pair Copeland porcelain figural comports, Moorish male and female, 27.5in. Andrew Hartley, Ilkley, W Yorks. Feb 06. HP: £1,400. ABP: £1,646.

438

Bretby figure, boy playing a whistle, marked 877B, seated on a pedestal, cream glaze, 48.5in high. Hartleys, Ilkley. Dec 06. HP: £1,400. ABP: £1,646.

Hammer: £1,400 - £1,300

439

Sang-de-boeuf glazed table lamp, with ormolu mount, 32in. Gorringes, Lewes. Feb 07. HP: £1,400. ABP: £1,646.

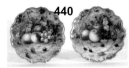

440

Pair Royal Worcester porcelain plates by Lockyer, with fruit, 1921 date mark, 8.75in wide. A. Hartley, Ilkley. Aug 04. HP: £1,350. ABP: £1,587.

441

Pair Royal Worcester vases, gilt side handles, with sheep in a Highland Scene, signed E Barker, 6.25in. Ibbett Mosely, Sevenoaks. Nov 05. HP: £1,350. ABP: £1,587.

442

Early Royal Doulton figure of 'Reggie Bunnykins', 3.5in, D.6025, printed mark to base, imp'd No. 8313. Canterbury Auction Galleries, Kent. Dec 05. HP: £1,350. ABP: £1,587.

443

Clarice Cliff Bizarre tea service with green band and square enclosing house with orange roof with trees. (32) Ewbank, Send, Surrey. Dec 05. HP: £1,350. ABP: £1,587.

444

Beswick grazing shire horse palomino gloss, No. 1050. Louis Taylor, Stoke. Dec 06. HP: £1,350. ABP: £1,587.

445

Minton majolica teapot/cover, c1879, aesthetic taste, moulded panels of 'Three Friends', 15cm high, large crack to base. Sworders, Stansted Mountfitchet. Feb 04. HP: £1,300. ABP: £1,529.

446

Moorcroft vase, 34cm high. Eastbourne Auction Rooms, Sussex. Feb 04. HP: £1,300. ABP: £1,529.

447

Pair Japanese blue/white porcelain wall plates, with carp, peonies & prunus blossom, 21.5in. Gorringes, Lewes. Mar 04. HP: £1,300. ABP: £1,529.

448

Beswick eleven piece hunting group. Huntsman 1501, 8.25in, huntswoman 1730, 8.25in, 2 boys on ponies 1500, 2 girls on ponies 1499, 5.5in, four hounds and a fox. Halls Fine Art, Shrewsbury. Jun 04. HP: £1,300. ABP: £1,529.

Hammer: £1,300

449

Chelsea porcelain sauce boat, 'red anchor' period, 1752-56, moulded & painted, unmarked, 6in long. Gorringes, Lewes. Jul 04. HP: £1,300. ABP: £1,529.

450

Montelupo maiolica dish, c1700, painted with striding soldier in a landscape, 31cm. Sworders, Stansted Mountfitchet. Jul 04. HP: £1,300. ABP: £1,529.

451

Pair of Royal Doulton vases, by Eliza Simmance, with Art Nouveau floral designs with triangular flowerheads in shades of blue, green and ochre, 18.5in. Gorringes, Lewes. Dec 04. HP: £1,300. ABP: £1,529.

452

Wedgwood Fairyland octagonal lustre bowl. Gorringes, Bexhill. Sep 04. HP: £1,300. ABP: £1,529.

453

Barr, Flight & Barr Worcester garniture. Gorringes, Bexhill. Sep 04. HP: £1,300. ABP: £1,529.

454

18thC Worcester blue/white wall pocket, moulded with cattle in landscape, painters mark, 8.5in. Gorringes, Lewes. Sep 04. HP: £1,300. ABP: £1,529.

455

Satsuma meiping vase, Meiji period, painted with 2 panels, figures in a garden, domestic objects, gilded turquoise ground, imp'd mark, 8.25in. Gorringes, Lewes. Apr 05. HP: £1,300. ABP: £1,529.

> The numbering system acts as a reader reference and links to the Analysis of each section.

456

Wedgwood 1950s garden implements pattern lemonade set, by Eric Ravillious 1938, Patt No. CMH6322, printed marks, one beaker a.f. (7) Sworders, Stansted Mountfitchet. Apr 05. HP: £1,300. ABP: £1,529.

457

Carltonware ginger jar/cover, transfer-gilded with ancient Egyptian figures, pattern No. 2708, Pharaoh handle, 12in. Gorringes, Lewes. Jun 05. HP: £1,300. ABP: £1,529.

458

Pair of Royal Crown Derby dishes, English 1906, floral study, signed 'A. Gregory', 27cm long. Rosebery's, London. Jun 05. HP: £1,300. ABP: £1,529.

459

Meissen figural salt, German 19thC, crossed swords to base, 17cm, chip. Rosebery's, London. Jun 05. HP: £1,300. ABP: £1,529.

460

Moorcroft Owlpen Manor vase. Stroud Auctions, Stroud. May 05. HP: £1,300. ABP: £1,529.

461

Doulton Lambeth stoneware vase by Mary Ann Thomson, 11.75in. Andrew Hartley, Ilkley. Aug 05. HP: £1,300. ABP: £1,529.

462

Pair Royal Worcester candelabra, modelled with children with a frog and birds nest beside trees, 1115, 19in. Gorringes, Lewes. Apr 04. HP: £1,300. ABP: £1,529.

463

Royal Doulton four-handled vase by Frank Butler, 14in. Gorringes, Lewes. Nov 05. HP: £1,300. ABP: £1,529.

464

Leeds creamware teapot, painted with a basket of fruit and flowers, c1770, 4.5in. Gorringes, Lewes. Nov 05. HP: £1,300. ABP: £1,529.

465

Large collection of Goss and other crested china including model buildings etc, 9.5cm high. Gorringes, Bexhill. Feb 06. HP: £1,300. ABP: £1,529.

466

The Swimmer HN1270, designer L.H. introduced 1928 and withdrawn 1938. Louis Taylor, Stoke. Sep 06. HP: £1,300. ABP: £1,529.

467

Royal Doulton figure 'The Lavender Woman', HN22. Louis Taylor, Stoke. Mar 06. HP: £1,300. ABP: £1,529.

468

R. Doulton 'The Huntsman', HN1815, slight restoration. Louis Taylor, Stoke. Mar 06. HP: £1,300. ABP: £1,529.

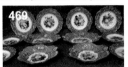

469

Early 19thC Staffs part dessert service, green borders, flowers highlighted in gilt s-scrolls, central cartouches with fruit. (12) Ewbank, Send, Surrey. Jul 06. HP: £1,300. ABP: £1,529.

470

Pair of Royal Dux porcelain figures as a carpet seller and a textiles spinner, each in pink/green Turkish dress, 16in. Hartleys, Ilkley. Oct 06. HP: £1,300. ABP: £1,529.

471

Kang Hsi famille verte wine pot, floral decoration and a similar two handled cup. Gorringes, Lewes. Feb 07. HP: £1,300. ABP: £1,529.

472

19thC Chinese vase, decorated with figures in landscape, vineous borders, 15in. Gorringes, Lewes. Feb 07. HP: £1,300. ABP: £1,529. HP: £1,300. ABP: £1,529.

473

Meissen porcelain figural group as a harlequin dancing with a lady, 19thC, 7.5in, cross swords mark. Hartleys, Ilkley. Feb 07. HP: £1,300. ABP: £1,529.

474

Bernard Moore flambe vase decorated with fish. Louis Taylor, Stoke. Mar 07. HP: £1,300. ABP: £1,529.

475

Dated hunting jug, c1825, prob. Ridgway, monogrammed and dated, 6.25in high. Halls Fine Art, Shrewsbury. Mar 04. HP: £1,250. ABP: £1,470.

476

Chinese blue/white square jar and cover, 35cm. Gorringes, Bexhill. Sep 04. HP: £1,250. ABP: £1,470.

477

Masons ironstone neopolitan ewer, unsigned, later wood base, early 19thC, 28in high. Andrew Hartley, Ilkley. Apr 05. HP: £1,250. ABP: £1,470.

Hammer: £1,300 - £1,250

478

William Moorcroft shallow bowl, Eventide pattern, hammered Tudric mount to base, 27cm dia. Clevedon Salerooms, Bristol. Jun 05. HP: £1,250. ABP: £1,470.

479

Clarice Cliff 'Sungleam Crocus' Bizarre bonjour teaset. (16) Gardiner Houlgate, Corsham. Apr 05. HP: £1,250. ABP: £1,470.

480

Pair Derby porcelain figures of Jupiter and Juno, both on scroll bases, patch marks, c1765. Bearne's, Exeter. Jun 05. HP: £1,250. ABP: £1,470.

481

Pearlware money box as a church with blue/yellow roof flanked by cherubs, inscribed John Noble, Born March 3rd 1842, 6in wide. Andrew Hartley, Ilkley. Aug 05. HP: £1,250. ABP: £1,470.

482

19thC Staffordshire pearlware pottery Wesleyan Chapel money box, old repairs. Kent Auction Galleries, Folkestone. Feb 06. HP: £1,250. ABP: £1,470.

483

Beswick pottery hunting group: huntsman 868, second version, huntswoman 1730, huntsman 1501, 2 foxes and 4 hounds. Locke & England, Leamington Spa. Mar 06. HP: £1,250. ABP: £1,470.

484

Meissen figure group of children at play. Dreweatt Neate, Godalming. Mar 06. HP: £1,250. ABP: £1,470.

485

Moorcroft Macintyre florian ware vase, squat bottle form, tube lined with poppies, 9.5in. Andrew Hartley, Ilkley. Apr 06. HP: £1,250. ABP: £1,470.

486

R. Worcester ivory porcelain figure, The Bather Surprised, imp'd T Brock, S, London, 26in high, dated 1893. Hartleys, Ilkley. Aug 06. HP: £1,250. ABP: £1,470.

Pair of William Moorcroft Macintyre vases, tube lined in florian design with flower heads and slim leaves in greens and gold, 10in high. Hartleys, Ilkley. Oct 06. HP: £1,250. ABP: £1,470.

Two Shelley Mable Lucie Atwell figures, The Bride and The Bridegroom. Louis Taylor, Stoke. Sep 05. HP: £1,240. ABP: £1,458.

Early 19thC blue/white foot-bath, transfer printed with oriental figures, pagodas and flowers, 20in wide, slightly af. Tring Market Auctions, Herts. Jul 04. HP: £1,220. ABP: £1,435.

18thC Meissen porcelain figure of a fish seller, 7.5in, weak crossed swords mark in underglaze blue to base, right hand, part of fish and bowl on ground restored. Canterbury Auction Galleries, Kent. Apr 04. HP: £1,200. ABP: £1,411.

Staffs pottery tithe group, c1820, with sign 'The New Marriage Act', 16cm high, damage. Wintertons Ltd, Lichfield. Mar 04. HP: £1,200. ABP: £1,411.

Ruskin high fired stoneware vase, dated 1903. Cotswold Auction Co, Cirencester. May 04. HP: £1,200. ABP: £1,411.

Ruskin high-fired vase, c1909, 24.5cm high, seal 'Ruskin Pottery Smethwick' 1909. Rosebery's, London. Sep 04. HP: £1,200. ABP: £1,411.

Attributed to Minton, mid 19thC garden seat designed by AWN Pugin, 49cm high. Cheffins, Cambridge. Nov 04. HP: £1,200. ABP: £1,411.

Beswick belted galloway bull, 1746B, 4.5in, restored. L. Taylor, Stoke. Mar 05. HP: £1,200. ABP: £1,411.

Early Meissen cream pot decorated in Seuter workshop of Augsburg, 3 chinoiserie scenes, applied with 3 paw feet, 4.25in, porcelain c1720, decoration c1730. Gorringes, Lewes. Jan 04. HP: £1,200. ABP: £1,411.

Early 19thC Mason's iron-stone dessert set, chicken skin textured rims printed and painted with Chinese export scrolls. (15) Cheffins, Cambridge. Feb 05. HP: £1,200. ABP: £1,411.

> The illustrations are in descending price order. The price range is indicated at the top of each page.

Beswick, Beatrix Pottery figure of Duchess, style one, designed by Graham Orwell, BP2a, 3.75in. Halls Fine Art, Shrewsbury. Apr 05. HP: £1,200. ABP: £1,411.

Martin Brothers stoneware vase, 1903, engraved by Edwin Martin with bizarre fish under a mottled green glaze, incised name, dated 10.1903, 16cm. Sworders, Stansted Mountfitchet. Apr 05. HP: £1,200. ABP: £1,411.

Royal Doulton figure, 'Lady with Rose' c1921-36, No.524, HN... hairline left shoulder, 25.5cm. Sworders, Stansted Mountfitchet. Apr 05. HP: £1,200. ABP: £1,411.

Della Robia terracotta vase, incised and painted with Art Nouveau lily heads, incised 'D.R. 735', 13.75in. Andrew Hartley, Ilkley. Jun 05. HP: £1,200. ABP: £1,411.

Royal Doulton Sung vase, by Noke, decorated with a pea-cock, No. 3858, 7.75in high. Andrew Hartley, Ilkley. Aug 05. HP: £1,200. ABP: £1,411.

Pair of Royal Dux porcelain vases with Art Nouveau maidens in pale green robes amongst large pink flower-heads, 13.5in, pink triangle mark. A. Hartley, Ilkley. Oct 05. HP: £1,200. ABP: £1,411.

Five Chinese red ware tea-pots and covers, largest 7in. Gorringes, Lewes. Jul 06. HP: £1,200. ABP: £1,411.

505

Royal Doulton figure 'London Cry', HN 752. Louis Taylor, Stoke. Mar 04. HP: £1,200. ABP: £1,411.

506

Pair Jiaqing temple urns, lids missing, & a bowl and lid, 6 character seal marks and period of Jiaqing. (1796-1820) (4) Sworders, Stansted Mountfitchet. Nov 05. HP: £1,200. ABP: £1,411.

507

Wedgwood Fairyland lustre trumpet shaped vase, 9.75in. Gorringes, Lewes. Nov 05. HP: £1,200. ABP: £1,411.

508

Moorcroft for Macintyre Florian Ware vase, painted signature, printed factory mark, 4.75in. Gorringes, Lewes. Feb 06. HP: £1,200. ABP: £1,411.

509

Wedgwood fairyland lustre bowl by Daisy Makeig-Jones, Poplar Trees pattern, interior with Woodland Elves III - Feather Hat pattern (Z4968) gold printed Portland Vase mark, 24cm dia. Cheffins, Cambridge. Feb 06. HP: £1,200. ABP: £1,411.

510

Set six Royal Crown Derby paperweights, Endangered Species Collection, certificates. L. Taylor, Stoke. Mar 06. HP: £1,200. ABP: £1,411.

511

Pair of 18thC Worcester small sauceboats, 5.25in. Gorringes, Lewes. Apr 04. HP: £1,200. ABP: £1,411.

512

Royal Doulton Titanian 'Blighty', by E W Wight, c1919, 1st WW soldier returning home, 11in. Golding Young & Co, Grantham. Feb 06. HP: £1,200. ABP: £1,411.

513

Rockingham porcelain plate, painted by Steel, red mark, and a pair of oval dishes to match, unmarked, early 19thC, 9in wide. (3) Andrew Hartley, Ilkley. Apr 06. HP: £1,200. ABP: £1,411.

514

Charles Vyse, The Daffodil Seller. Cotswold Auction Co, Cirencester. Jun 06. HP: £1,200. ABP: £1,411.

Hammer: £1,200 - £1,150

515

Pair Royal Worcester porcelain dishes, by R Sebright, dated 1911, signed, mark for Townsend & Co, Newcastle-on-Tyne, 9.75in wide. Hartleys, Ilkley. Aug 06. HP: £1,200. ABP: £1,411.

516

Moorcroft for Macintyre Florian Ware vase, tubelined, incised initials, printed mark and painted number M669 to base, c1898, 8.75in. Gorringes, Lewes. Mar 06. HP: £1,200. ABP: £1,411.

517

Troika Love Plaque by Benny Sirota, in low relief within geometric setting, painted mark Troika, St Ives, monogram of Benny Sirota, 14.75in. Gorringes, Lewes. Mar 06. HP: £1,200. ABP: £1,411.

518

Chinese ginger jar, painted with figures in underglaze blue, 8in, and two Chinese vases, 11.5in and 6.25in. Gorringes, Lewes. Oct 06. HP: £1,200. ABP: £1,411.

519

19thC pair Staffs greyhounds with a hare at their feet, 11in. Hartleys, Ilkley. Feb 07. HP: £1,200. ABP: £1,411.

520

Two Meissen models of Manx type seated cats, c1740, each wearing a bell mounted collar, workers mark of Schieffer, 27.5cm high. (AF) Rosebery's, London. Sep 04. HP: £1,150. ABP: £1,352.

521

Pearlware dessert service, possibly Davenport, c1825, some damage. (27) Sworders, Stansted Mountfitchet. Feb 05. HP: £1,150. ABP: £1,352.

522

Early 19thC Derby porcelain ice pail & matching tureens. Humberts, Bourton on the Water. Feb 05. HP: £1,150. ABP: £1,352.

523

Royal Dux (Bohemia) Art Nouveau figural bowl as a large seashell with Arum Lily and other flowers, applied and impressed pink triangle pad mark and No.914, 46cm. Marilyn Swain Auctions, Grantham. May 05. HP: £1,150. ABP: £1,352.

524

Three William De Morgan pottery tiles, c1880, two impressed different Fulham marks, each 15cm square. Sworders, Stansted Mountfitchet. Apr 05. HP: £1,150. ABP: £1,352.

Hammer: £1,150 - £1,100

525

St Ives Troika pottery vase, blue painted trident mark, monogrammed, 12.5in. Fieldings, Stourbridge. Oct 05. HP: £1,150. ABP: £1,352.

526

Pair of Sevres Bell Epoque white biscuit busts, Louis XVI, 11in, Marie Antoinette, 12.75in, printed circle mark and date code S81. (2) Dee, Atkinson & Harrison, Driffield. Nov 05. HP: £1,150. ABP: £1,352.

527

20thC Meissen porcelain clown, 12.5in, crossed swords mark, incised No. Y164 and imp'd No. 104. Canterbury Auction Galleries, Kent. Dec 05. HP: £1,150. ABP: £1,352.

528

19thC Italian maiolica vase, 34.75in, painted mark 'G.B.' to base. Canterbury Auction Galleries, Kent. Dec 05. HP: £1,150. ABP: £1,352.

529

Chinese porcelain bowl in 'Kangxi' manner, in coloured enamels with 3 dragons, interior with gilt symbol, 7.5in dia x 3.5in high, six character mark. Canterbury Auction Galleries, Kent. Oct 05. HP: £1,150. ABP: £1,352.

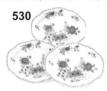

530

Set of 3 Chien Lung famille rose dessert plates, 11.75in. Gorringes, Lewes. Apr 04. HP: £1,150. ABP: £1,352.

531

Royal Dux, Art Deco figure of a naked female, clasping robe, 30cm. Locke & England, Leamington Spa. Feb 06. HP: £1,150. ABP: £1,352.

532

Royal Doulton figure 'The Princess', no number prob. HN391, undecorated, 9.5in. Louis Taylor, Stoke. Mar 06. HP: £1,150. ABP: £1,352.

533

Late 18th/early 19thC Italian maiolica plaque, Renaissance style with various warriors and horses in battle, blue crown and G mark to base, 9 x 19in. Ewbank Auctioneers, Send, Surrey. Dec 06. HP: £1,150. ABP: £1,352.

534

Royal Copenhagen bulldog, printed marks and No. 778, 30cm. Sworders, Stansted Mountfitchet. Feb 07. HP: £1,150. ABP: £1,352.

535

Early 20thC Haga pottery figure of a young girl holding a doll, printed and inscribed marks, 17.75in. Fieldings, Stourbridge. Oct 05. HP: £1,120. ABP: £1,317.

536

Satsuma pot and cover, reticulated & with painted panels. (chip to lid) Great Western Auctions, Glasgow. Aug 06. HP: £1,120. ABP: £1,317.

537

Set of 6 Royal Worcester bone china coffee cups and saucers, c1923-29, signed Jas Stinton, with 6 silver gilt and enamel coffee spoons, cased. (faults) Rupert Toovey & Co, Washington. Jan 04. HP: £1,100. ABP: £1,293.

538

Royal Doulton stoneware vase by Mark & Marshall, 7.75in wide, 4.25in high. Andrew Hartley, Ilkley. Apr 04. HP: £1,100. ABP: £1,293.

539

Moorcroft vase, tube line decorated with hibiscus, imp'd, signed to underside, 10in. Gorringes, Bexhill. Feb 04. HP: £1,100. ABP: £1,293.

540

Four Martin Brothers stoneware vases, various dates and marks, 2.25-2.75in high. Canterbury Auction Galleries, Kent. Feb 04. HP: £1,100. ABP: £1,293.

541

Troika St Ives pottery wall plaque, raised textured abstract design, 7.75 x 5.25in. Burstow & Hewett, Battle. Mar 04. HP: £1,100. ABP: £1,293.

542

Troika pottery anvil vase, Avril Bennett, 8.75in high. Burstow & Hewett, Battle. Mar 04. HP: £1,100. ABP: £1,293.

543

Sugar caster, orange roof cottage design, Clarice Cliff, Newport Pottery, England, cork stopper, 5.5in. Halls Fine Art, Shrewsbury. Jun 04. HP: £1,100. ABP: £1,293.

544

Pair blush Worcester porcelain candlesticks as a boy & girl, rustic base, No. 1125, date mark for 1892, 8.5in. Andrew Hartley, Ilkley. Aug 04. HP: £1,100. ABP: £1,293.

545

Royal Doulton stoneware vase by Hannah Barlow, scraffito decoration of grazing pigs, 28cm. Hobbs Parker, Ashford, Kent. Sep 04. HP: £1,100. ABP: £1,293.

546

Wedgwood Fairyland Lustre octagonal bowl, exterior with Dana - Castle on a Road pattern, Z 5125, interior with Fairy in a Cage pattern, wear to gilding, 9in. Gorringes, Lewes. Oct 04. HP: £1,100. ABP: £1,293.

547

Clarice Cliff 'Bonjour' shape tea set, 'Green Cowslip' pattern, Bizarre back-stamp in black. (9) Gorringes, Lewes. Oct 04. HP: £1,100. ABP: £1,293.

548

Susie Cooper for Gray's Pottery 'tete a tete' tea set, pattern 7960. (8) Gorringes, Lewes. Oct 04. HP: £1,100. ABP: £1,293.

549

Two Doulton Lambeth square terracotta plaques, by George Tinworth c1880, each incised GT, 20cm. Rosebery's, London. Sep 04. HP: £1,100. ABP: £1,293.

550

Pilkington's Royal Lancastrian lustre posy vase by William S. Mycock, c1920, with Latin inscription, 'I trust to virtue, not arms', shape No. 3178, impressed and painted marks, 7.5in. Gorringes, Lewes. Dec 04. HP: £1,100. ABP: £1,293.

> **Categories or themes can be followed through the colour coded Index which contains 1000s of cross references.**

551

Meissen porcelain figure of a young musician, 19thC, in a seated pose on a plinth base, crossed swords mark, 11.5cm. Sworders, Stansted Mountfitchet. Nov 04. HP: £1,100. ABP: £1,293.

552

Doulton Lambeth owl jar & cover, moulded with feathers and features in full detail, artist's monogram FM, 8in. Gorringes, Lewes. Sep 04. HP: £1,100. ABP: £1,293.

Hammer: £1,100

553

Moorcroft Macintyre Pansy vase, c1912, printed mark, painted signature/date, 5.5in. Gorringes, Lewes. Mar 04. HP: £1,100. ABP: £1,293.

554

Meissen figure of Harlequin holding a hat and a jug aloft, early 20thC, crossed sword mark, impressed 23, incised 3025, left hand with damage, 22.8cm. Sworders, Stansted Mountfitchet. Feb 05. HP: £1,100. ABP: £1,293.

555

Pair Imari jars/cover, 19thC, lion finials, panels of birds amidst flowering chrysanthemum & peony trees, 54cm. Rosebery's, London. Mar 05. HP: £1,100. ABP: £1,293.

556

Pair Royal Doulton vases, by Eliza Simmance, Art Nouveau floral designs with triangular flowerheads, 18.5in. Gorringes, Lewes. Mar 05. HP: £1,100. ABP: £1,293.

557

Chelsea cup/saucer, raised Anchor period, 1749-52, 'blanc de chine', trembleuse-type saucer with moulded raised anchor, saucer 4.75in. Gorringes, Lewes. Jun 05. HP: £1,100. ABP: £1,293.

558

Royal Crown Derby vase and cover, English 1911, panel of exotic birds, panel signed 'C. Harris', 24cm. Rosebery's, London. Jun 05. HP: £1,100. ABP: £1,293.

559

Clarice Cliff 'Sunray' Bizarre ginger jar base, 6.75in high. Gardiner Houlgate, Corsham. Apr 05. HP: £1,100. ABP: £1,293.

560

Lambeth Delftware ointment pot, inscribed in blue 'Thou Valle 21 hay Market', 1.5in. Cotswold Auction Company, Gloucester. Oct 05. HP: £1,100. ABP: £1,293.

561

Royal Doulton jug and 6 mugs en suite, moulded with golfing scenes, jug 9in. Gorringes, Lewes. Nov 05. HP: £1,100. ABP: £1,293.

562

William Moorcroft ' J Mackintyre Florianware vase, signed to reverse in green, 4in. Louis Taylor, Stoke on Trent. Mar 06. HP: £1,100. ABP: £1,293.

Hammer: £1,100 - £1,050

563

Doulton Lambeth wall pocket by Mark V. Marshall, 11in, damage. Gorringes, Lewes. Nov 05. HP: £1,100. ABP: £1,293.

564

Charles Vyse figure of a vegetable seller, 8.25in. Gorringes, Lewes. Nov 05. HP: £1,100. ABP: £1,293.

565

19thC Kangxi style porcelain vase, 27cm high. Lots Road Auctions, Chelsea. Feb 06. HP: £1,100. ABP: £1,293.

566

Set 10 diminishing cups, late 19thC, exteriors painted with figures in famille-rose palette, red seal marks of Tongzhi (1862-1874) 10.7 to 2.5cm. Sworders, Stansted Mountfitchet. Feb 06. HP: £1,100. ABP: £1,293.

567

Beswick pottery, huntswoman, huntsman on horses, boy & girl on ponies, 2 foxes and 8 hounds. Locke & England, Leamington Spa. Mar 06. HP: £1,100. ABP: £1,293.

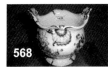

568

Continental Chelsea style cache pot, lilac shell moulded rim/handles, 6in dia. Golding Young & Co, Grantham. Feb 06. HP: £1,100. ABP: £1,293.

569

Graingers Worcester porcelain lidded vase of urn form, with birds on a gilded pale green ground, 11in. Andrew Hartley, Ilkley. Apr 06. HP: £1,100. ABP: £1,293.

> **Prices quoted are actual hammer prices (HP) and the Approximate Buyer's Price (ABP) includes an average premium of 15% + VAT.**

570

Chinese polychrome vase, of lobed baluster form with floral decoration, 13in. Gorringes, Lewes. Jun 06. HP: £1,100. ABP: £1,293.

571

Clarice Cliff Bizarre Honolulu pattern vase, c1933/1934, 9in wide. Ewbank, Send, Surrey. Jul 06. HP: £1,100. ABP: £1,293.

572

Chinese redware teapot, with moulded bamboo sides, and four other redware teapots. Gorringes, Lewes. Jul 06. HP: £1,100. ABP: £1,293.

573

19thC Chinese celadon dish, fluted interior rim and base incised with floral forms, 39cm. Locke & England, Leamington Spa. Jul 06. HP: £1,100. ABP: £1,293.

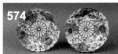

574

Pair of 18thC Worcester chinoiserie dishes, with panels of dragons and flowers, gilt painted crescent mark, 8.5in. Gorringes, Lewes. Mar 06. HP: £1,100. ABP: £1,293.

575

Chinese porcelain vase, mark & period of Guangxu (1875-1908), painted with geese below elephant head handles, four character mark of Guangxu, 19cm. Sworders, Stansted Mountfitchet. Apr 06. HP: £1,100. ABP: £1,293.

576

Wardroom plate, from HMS Discovery, manufactured by Doulton Burslem, with the expedition's penguin crest, crazing, fading & cracks, 14cm. Charterhouse Auctioneers, Sherborne. Sep 06. HP: £1,100. ABP: £1,293.

577

19thC Wedgwood creamware shell shaped 28 piece part service, each tinted in pink. Gorringes, Lewes. Dec 06. HP: £1,100. ABP: £1,293.

578

Royal Crown Derby porcelain lidded vase, domed lid with gilded bud finial, scroll foliate loop handles, floral panels by C Gresley, 10.5in high, dated 1905. Hartleys, Ilkley. Feb 07. HP: £1,100. ABP: £1,293.

579

Royal Doulton figure Meryll, slight damage. Louis Taylor, Stoke on Trent. Oct 04. HP: £1,080. ABP: £1,270.

580

Dame Lucie Rie stoneware boat/saucer, off white glaze, iron brown fleck and rim, imp'd LR seal to underside. Rosebery's, London. Mar 04. HP: £1,050. ABP: £1,235.

581

Early Wade Snow White and her 7 dwarfs. Eastbourne Auction Rooms, Sussex. Apr 04. HP: £1,050. ABP: £1,235.

582

Royal Doulton 'Old King Cole' musical Toby jug, modelled wearing a yellow crown, 15cm high. Rosebery's, London. Dec 04. HP: £1,050. ABP: £1,235.

583

Large Japanese blue and white vase, depicting warriors. Great Western Auctions, Glasgow. Jan 07. HP: £1,050. ABP: £1,235.

584

Pair Satsuma vases, Japanese late 19thC, basket weave moulded ground, 23.5in. Rosebery's, London. Sep 04. HP: £1,050. ABP: £1,235.

585

18thC Kang Hsi famille verte vase, figures in procession, cover missing, 12.5in. Dee, Atkinson & Harrison, Driffield. Nov 04. HP: £1,050. ABP: £1,235.

586

Italian polychrome albarello, with a reserve of a portrait of a lady, dated 1775, 24cm, and a waisted example painted with armorial, dated 17?2. Rosebery's, London. Dec 04. HP: £1,050. ABP: £1,235.

587

18thC Canton famille rose export porcelain bowl with armorial decoration marked Wilkes & Liberty, 10in. (f and r) Denhams, Warnham, Sussex. Jul 05. HP: £1,050. ABP: £1,235.

588

Meissen figure of Harlequin, early 20thC, crossed sword mark, imp'd 125, incised 237, painted 43, one finger lost, 18.2cm. Sworders, Stansted Mountfitchet. Feb 05. HP: £1,050. ABP: £1,235.

589

Pair of Meissen bowls held by cupids, c1860, painted and encrusted with flowers, crossed swords mark, 25cm. Sworders, Stansted Mountfitchet. Feb 05. HP: £1,050. ABP: £1,235.

590

19thC Measham Bargeware 2-spouted teapot, inscribed 'A Present from a friend 1892', sympathetic restoration to rim. 18.5cm. Marilyn Swain, Grantham. May 05. HP: £1,050. ABP: £1,235.

591

Wedgwood lustre bowl in Persian style, interior worn. Louis Taylor, Stoke. Mar 07. HP: £1,050. ABP: £1,235.

592

Pair Royal Worcester vases, painted with 'Hadley' roses, 22cm, green backstamps, F105/H, datecodes for 1910. Bearne's, Exeter. Jun 05. HP: £1,050. ABP: £1,235.

Hammer: £1050

593

Wedgwood model of the 'Portland' vase, 10.5in. Louis Taylor, Stoke. Mar 04. HP: £1,050. ABP: £1,235.

594

Doulton Lambeth vase by Florence Barlow, 10.5in. Gorringes, Lewes. Nov 05. HP: £1,050. ABP: £1,235.

595

Royal Doulton figure 'Jack Point, no number - should be HN2080, 16in. Louis Taylor, Stoke on Trent. Mar 06. HP: £1,050. ABP: £1,235.

596

Wedgwood pottery dinner service, printed in grey/blue with Travel pattern designed by Eric Ravilious, printed mark, date code for 1953, 23 pieces. Canterbury Auction Galleries, Kent. Apr 06. HP: £1,050. ABP: £1,235.

597

Canton famille rose porcelain garden seat, pierced roundels, applied beading, gilt embellished, 19in. Hartleys, Ilkley. Oct 06. HP: £1,050. ABP: £1,235.

598

One of a pair of R. Worcester chinoiserie figures. Cotswold Auction Co, Cirencester. Jun 06. HP: £1,050. ABP: £1,235.

599

William Moorcroft pottery bowl, tube lined inside and out in Spanish design, 10in wide. Hartleys, Ilkley. Dec 06. HP: £1,050. ABP: £1,235.

600

Herculaneum Pottery pearl glazed breakfast or supper set: central oval jar/cover, liner, pierced stand, 6 egg cups, salt cellar, 2 pairs of kidney-shape bowls and 3 covers, version of the Greek pattern, imp'd No 37, c1815. Bearne's, Exeter. Jun 05. HP: £1,050. ABP: £1,235.

601

19thC Italian Cantegalli maiolica vase, with pseudo coats of arm supported by cupids, caryatids, exotic birds and bold leaf scroll ornament, 17.5in, cockerel mark. Canterbury Auction Galleries, Kent. Dec 05. HP: £1,050. ABP: £1,235.

Ceramics Prices **41**

Sample Research I

Using the Index to analyse the market for a particular artist

No. 1 George Tinworth

The Index has over 4,000 cross-references in alphabetical order. This includes manufacturers, pattern and figure names and of course artists and modellers. This resource is fundamental to using this book. In addition the various sections with their hundreds of images, descriptions and prices from real sales provide an ideal browsing medium. Readers can work through the sections checking pages for a myriad of collecting areas such as animalier, human figures, inkwells, spittoons, egg-cups, plaques, tiles and so on. The research potential for almost every area of ceramic collecting is unmatched in any other work.

Here are more than 150 images of Doulton sold at auction in the last three years, about one hundred Beswick sales, sixty Carltonware sales and so on. Most of the manufacturers from the last three hundred years are represented as are many of the European factories. About two hundred and eighty are included in the Index, as are all the ceramic types such as slipware, English delft, majolica, parian, creamware etc, along with most of the leading names in the industry. A second sample research using the Index, appears on page 72. This looks closely at *Mason's Patent Ironstone China*. Further Sample Research appears on pages 102 and 132. These rely on scanning pages for examples of individual readers interest. I have chosen two popular collecting areas, that of cats and pigs.

George Tinworth.

The Index indicates eight examples of George Tinworth's work in these pages. They occur on pages 21, 32, 39, 44, 47, 60, 61 and 79. These have been placed in price order to the right and their reference numbers also indicate their positions in the Price Guide as a whole. With over 3,000 images altogether George Tinworth is clearly highly rated as even the least expensive of his examples occur in the first half of this work. His animal figure groups show superb artistry and importantly, humour. Humour in ceramics has always been with us but it prospered in the late nineteenth century and proliferated in the twentieth. This subject in itself could be a worthwhile collecting area. The sample is low but the highest price is £2,823 and the lowest £517 for sales between 2004 and 2006. The average price is £1,271 and the median or middle price about £1,150. George Tinworth is famous for his figure groups, particularly mice but also produced vases with relief-moulding, incised or sgraffito decoration, as well as plaques.

Doulton Lambeth stoneware menu holder 'Quack Doctor', by George Tinworth, 3.75in high, impressed mark, dated 1885, incised GT to rear. Canterbury Auction Galleries, Kent. Feb 04. HP: £2,400. ABP: £2,823.

Doulton Lambeth stoneware menu holder, 'Potters' by George Tinworth, imp'd mark, dated 1885, incised GT, 3.75in, damage. Canterbury Auction Galleries, Kent. Feb 04. HP: £1,400. ABP: £1,646.

Two Doulton Lambeth square terracotta plaques, by George Tinworth c1880, each incised GT, 20cm. Rosebery's, London. Sep 04. HP: £1,100. ABP: £1,293.

One of pair of early Doulton Lambeth vases by George Tinworth, 12in high. Louis Taylor, Stoke. Jun 05. HP: £1,000. ABP: £1,176.

Doulton Lambeth glazed stoneware vase by George Tinworth entitled The Waning of the Honeymoon, monogram on base, 6.5in, damage, chips. Gorringes, Lewes. Mar 04. HP: £950. ABP: £1,117.

R. Doulton glazed stoneware vase by George Tinworth, relief-moulded with rosettes, incised with leaves, powder-blue ground, dated 1877, artist's monogram at footrim, 13.5in. Gorringes, Lewes. Apr 06. HP: £700. ABP: £823.

Doulton Lambeth gilded silicon ware mouse group by George Tinworth, 4in. (chips) Louis Taylor, Stoke on Trent. Jun 04. HP: £660. ABP: £776.

Royal Doulton stoneware vase by George Tinworth, c1902, sgraffito and bead decoration, monogrammed G. T., impressed factory marks, rim restored, 31cm. Sworders, Stansted Mountfitchet. Apr 05. HP: £440. ABP: £517.

Section IV: £1,000-£500

'Better to spend £50 than 10 x £5 and better still to spend £500 than 10 x £50!
.....If you live in an old cottage you might consider terracotta.....the Burleighware story began on page 27 and continues with a further Charlotte Rhead
charger.....Charles Vyse figures work out at an average of £2,696 hammer........'

This Section has 534 images and huge diversity. It is still on the expensive side for most collectors, but should it be? Most collectibles in the market place would be best left on the shelves and it is reasonable to suggest that we should be saving our money for those extra special pieces that cross our paths only occasionally. Better to spend £50 than 10 x £5 and better still to spend £500 than 10 x £50! Of course it is even better to spend £170 and buy the Minton's *Dorothea*, worth say £450! See page 122. Rather than grouping factories and types as in previous analyses, here I will browse the Section looking for ideas and then move to other Sections to follow up clues or use the Index to pursue themes.

As Parian has been mentioned it offers a good starting point. It looks classical and would eminently suit minimalist principles in say mock-Georgian homes. Currently it is out of fashion and prices are modest. The *Veiled Bride* at **645** is too serious. **772**, a standing nude is more collectible. **922** is rather poor. At **931** is a fine Parian group, purely classical and eminently suitable at 24 inches high to occupy a grand position, and at under £800 should have investment potential. Readers can follow the Parian theme through the Index. If you live in an old cottage you might consider terracotta, but I think the 76 inch high figure at **914** would have to reside in the garden. This said we don't buy enough garden antiques and they are far better value than most of the new goods available at garden centres. For charm you could not do better than the Ming terracotta horse ridge tile at **1072** and a fair price. What a talking point! Terracotta is indexed but see **1108**. Continuing on the theme of earlier antiques and cottages and older properties, this Section contains some fine antiques. Here there is maiolica, blue and white, Iznik, Oriental, eighteenth century porcelain, Prattware and other good Staffordshire, particularly **803** and **836**. In rarity and desirability there is nothing to choose between say the Prattware lidded Toby jug at **658**, and the Ralph Wood group at **672**. Fine Oriental vases are also available in this price range. They could occupy important positions in niches or in most rooms. See **625**, **679**, **728**, **750**, **796**, **874**, etc., but don't miss the imposing maiolica at **1036** and **1129**. If your tendency and your home favours a twentieth century minimalist touch, then check out the Moorcroft flambé at **627**, the Burmontofts at **894** or the Clarice Cliff lotus jug at **904**. Check out sizes and look for a vase or jug at about 12 inches or more. Imagine for example the impact of the superb Moorcroft Sally Tuffin vase at **801**, standing at

more than 16 inches in height and as modern as you can get if your home is new. The twentieth century is superbly represented in the Section. Here is Lucie Rie, Wedgwood Fairyland, Burleighware, Pilkingtons, Burmontofts, Moorcroft, Keith Murray, Royal Dux, etc. All of these are indexed and their stories can be followed and their values analysed. Take for example Burleigh-ware. The story commenced on page 27 and continues at 44 with a further Charlotte Rhead charger in the Persian style, which fetched just £1,000 hammer. See also pages 85, 100 and 119. Or there is a Charles Vyse figure at **739** and £880 hammer. Check out Charles Vyse figures through the Index and you will find they work out at an average of £2,696 hammer.

The themes that can be related to manufacturers, categories or types are numerous and run into thousands when artists or modellers are included. I estimate at least 4000 cross-references in the Index. This does not take into account the possibilities of browsing the Sections for further collecting themes such as cats, dogs, rabbits, pigs, horses etc., or indeed mugs, jugs, egg cups, ink wells, coffee pots, cow creamers, spittoons and so on. The list is endless. There are plaques and tiles and flowerbricks and cress dishes and garden seats and garden gnomes! Let us sample some collecting areas. There are cats on pages 8, 25, 52, 59, 62, 74, 91, 95, 99, 111, 117, 129, 146 and so on, or pigs on pages 9, 55, 65, 76, 81, 86, 93, 161 etc. The Dutch delft polychrome wild boar on page 93 is delightful. With a damaged ear it fetched £320 hammer in 2005. Many collectors would have paid much more. Every animal in the Ark is repre-sented in these pages. Take mugs. Would you have had any idea that the early Worcester mug on page 8 would have fetched over £30,000? Let us go on. How about the Newhall Fidellé Duvivier mug on page 10 or the Liverpool delft mug by Sadler on page 11, averaging about £10,000 each. Even in this Section there are some outstanding pieces in the £1,000 to £500 range. On page 48 **(689)** is a rare Staffordshire saltglaze frog mug and there are other mugs at **777**, **818**, **864**, **933** and a creamware commemorative at **1023**. I am a little surprised by **864**. I know that early Queen Victoria is expensive but £882 is a surprise. Years ago I sold most of my early mugs but am beginning to form another collection and have three early Mason's patent ironstone china mugs, several early blue and white pearlware examples such as that shown on page 141, and recently I added a quite rare early Quimper mug to the collection.

Hammer: £1,000

602

Pair 19thC Dresden porcelain parakeet models, painted mark, 16.5in. (wing repaired) Gorringes, Lewes. Mar 04. HP: £1,000. ABP: £1,176.

603

19thC Meissen porcelain vase, vignette depicting 'Prince Johann's Garton Palais', 12.25in high, crossed swords mark, damage. Canterbury Auction Galleries, Kent. Apr 04. HP: £1,000. ABP: £1,176.

604

Bowl by Lucie Rie, 7cm high. Richard Winterton, Burton on Trent, Staffs. Aug 04. HP: £1,000. ABP: £1,176.

605

Majolica butter dish, c1875, handle moulded as a resting cow, marked 1811 in black to underside of stand, stand 7.5in wide. Halls Fine Art, Shrewsbury. Sep 04. HP: £1,000. ABP: £1,176.

606

Candlemas, Wedgwood Fairyland lustre vase, by Daisy Makeig-Jones, pattern No. Z5157, shape No. 2311, printed/impressed marks to base, 19cm high. Rosebery's, London. Sep 04. HP: £1,000. ABP: £1,176.

607

Pilkington's Lancastrian lustre vase by R. Joyce, with tropical fish and seaweed against ochre ground, shape No. 2922, impressed/painted marks, c1914, 6in. Gorringes, Lewes. Dec 04. HP: £1,000. ABP: £1,176.

608

Pilkington's Lancastrian lustre vase by Gordon M. Forsyth, c1907, with 2 lions rampant & scrolling foliage, shape No. 2635, impressed and painted marks, 7.75in. Gorringes, Lewes. Dec 04. HP: £1,000. ABP: £1,176.

609

Zsolnay Pecs ewer and cover, with an encircling band and all over foliate designs, gilt highlights, printed blue mark and J.J.M. initials, 19.5in. Gorringes, Lewes. Dec 04. HP: £1,000. ABP: £1,176.

610

George Jones majolica leaf dish, moulded with flowers and bullrushes, imp'd factory monogram, painted pattern No. 3395, c1875, 5.5in. Gorringes, Lewes. Sep 04. HP: £1,000. ABP: £1,176.

611

Hochst figure of a Chinaman seated on a rocky base, 6in, gilt wheel mark, c1765, tree and both wrists restored. Gorringes, Lewes. Jan 04. HP: £1,000. ABP: £1,176.

612

Burleigh Ware pottery charger by Charlotte Rhead, tube lined with Persian flowers, No.4013, 14in wide. Andrew Hartley, Ilkley. Dec 04. HP: £1,000. ABP: £1,176.

613

Early 19thC Grainger Lee and Co., Worcester miniature cabaret set with named views, painted marks, tray 19.5cm wide. Cheffins, Cambridge. Feb 05. HP: £1,000. ABP: £1,176.

614

Pair Victorian R. Worcester figural candlesticks, by Hadley, Kate Greenaway-type girl & boy beneath tree-stems, date code 1887, 9.25in. Gorringes, Lewes. Jan 05. HP: £1,000. ABP: £1,176.

615

Gold anchor Chelsea cup & saucer with sprigs & sprays of flowers within gilt rocaille waves and turquoise oeil de perdrix, gold anchor marks. Cheffins, Cambridge. Apr 05. HP: £1,000. ABP: £1,176.

616

Troika calculator plaque, early Trident mark, 20 x 30cm. Clevedon Salerooms, Bristol. Feb 05. HP: £1,000. ABP: £1,176.

617

Pair Dutch delft blue/white pedestals by Adriaen Koeks, De Grieksche A Factory, c1690, hexagonal, monogram in blue 'A K', 15.75in high, extensive damage. Halls Fine Art, Shrewsbury. Mar 05. HP: £1,000. ABP: £1,176.

618

Minton majolica vase, scroll handles, being held aloft by two mermen, 20.25in. Andrew Hartley, Ilkley. Apr 05. HP: £1,000. ABP: £1,176.

619

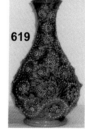

One of pair of early Doulton Lambeth vases by George Tinworth, 12in high. Louis Taylor, Stoke. Jun 05. HP: £1,000. ABP: £1,176.

620

18thC creamware teapot, entwined handle, with a Chinese view with bridge in red and black enamels, 5in. Gorringes, Lewes. Nov 05. HP: £1,000. ABP: £1,176.

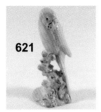

621

Beswick model of a Budgerigar. Brettells, Newport. Jul 05. HP: £1,000. ABP: £1,176.

622

R. Worcester vase, pierced rim, scroll feet, painted by Harry Stinton, highland cattle in a moorland setting, 14.5cm high, shape No G42, printed marks, date code for 1910. Bearne's, Exeter. Jun 05. HP: £1,000. ABP: £1,176.

623

Royal Doulton jug, Hannah Barlow, incised with continuous border of grazing cattle in sgraffito, incised artist's monogram, 15in. Gorringes, Lewes. Nov 05. HP: £1,000. ABP: £1,176.

624

Pair of late 19thC Meissen porcelain figures, emblematic of War and Peace, he with sword and shield, she with a basket of fruit, blue crossed swords & scratch numerals, 14in & 15in high. (faults) Diamond Mills & Co, Felixstowe. Mar 06. HP: £1,000. ABP: £1,176.

625

18th/19thC Chinese blue & white baluster vase/cover, painted with U shape motifs and prunus flowers, 24in. Gorringes, Lewes. Sep 05. HP: £1,000. ABP: £1,176.

626

Royal Doulton figure 'Verena', HN 1835. Louis Taylor, Stoke. Mar 04. HP: £1,000. ABP: £1,176.

> The numbering system acts as a reader reference and links to the Analysis of each section.

627

Moorcroft flambe orchid vase, base with monogram WM signature in blue, impressed mark 'Made in England', 13in high. Tring Market Auctions, Herts. May 04. HP: £1,000. ABP: £1,176.

628

19thC Cantonese famille rose jar/cover, two large pictorial scenes, 25in high, hardwood stand. (rim damage) Ibbett Mosely, Sevenoaks. Nov 05. HP: £1,000. ABP: £1,176.

Hammer: £1,000

629

Hugo Lonitz majolica centrepiece, as a fountain with twin columns and cherub base, 19in. Gorringes, Lewes. Nov 05. HP: £1,000. ABP: £1,176.

630

Royal Worcester porcelain miniature solitaire for one, signed Roberts?, gilded bud finials, rims & handles, black mark, coffee pot 5in high. (8) Andrew Hartley, Ilkley. Dec 05. HP: £1,000. ABP: £1,176.

631

Pair of Chinese porcelain and ormolu-mounted vases, crackle-glazed with Bacchus mounts, on scroll bases, 7in. Gorringes, Lewes. Sep 05. HP: £1,000. ABP: £1,176.

632

Berlin KPM plaque, 9in high. Kivell & Sons, Bude. Sep 05. HP: £1,000. ABP: £1,176.

633

R. Worcester double walled reticulated vase, probably by George Owen, jewelled borders, date code for 1909, 8.5cm. Sworders, Stansted Mountfitchet. Feb 06. HP: £1,000. ABP: £1,176.

634

Weiner Werkstatte Susi Singer figure, signed and impressed marks below, 11in. Gorringes, Lewes. Apr 06. HP: £1,000. ABP: £1,176.

635

Shelley figure group 'Our Pets', Lucie Mabel Attwell, printed green mark, 8.25in. Gorringes, Lewes. Apr 06. HP: £1,000. ABP: £1,176.

636

Minton Secessionist jardiniere & stand, 42in in total. Louis Taylor, Stoke. Mar 06. HP: £1,000. ABP: £1,176.

637

Moorcroft MacIntyre Pomegranate vase, c1912. Henry Adams, Chichester. Apr 06. HP: £1,000. ABP: £1,176.

638

Japanese Satsuma porcelain vase, court figures, 10in, seal mark to the base. Denhams, Warnham, Sussex. Dec 05. HP: £1,000. ABP: £1,176.

639

Beswick Beatrix Potter figure, Duchess with flowers, G.B.S, model No. 1355, produced between 1955/1967, 3in high. Golding Young & Co, Grantham. Feb 06. HP: £1,000. ABP: £1,176.

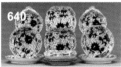

640

Early 19thC Staffordshire dessert service. Henry Adams, Chichester. Jul 06. HP: £1,000. ABP: £1,176.

641

Pair R. Worcester porcelain plates, mildly lobed form, painted with fruit by R Sebright, gilded with flowers, signed, dated 1911, mark for Townsend & Co, Newcastle-on-Tyne, 9in wide. Hartleys, Ilkley. Aug 06. HP: £1,000. ABP: £1,176.

642

Royal Doulton figure, Jester, HN45. Gorringes, Lewes. Mar 06. HP: £1,000. ABP: £1,176.

643

George Jones strawberry dish. Thos Mawer & Son, Lincoln. Sep 06. HP: £1,000. ABP: £1,176.

644

18thC Italian Maiolica drug jar, 4.5in, (chipped), and an Islamic vase, baluster form, 5in. Gorringes, Lewes. Dec 06. HP: £1,000. ABP: £1,176.

645

Copeland parian bust 'The Veiled Bride' sculptured by R Monti, c1861, 15in, imp'd marks. Hartleys, Ilkley. Dec 06. HP: £1,000. ABP: £1,176.

646

Set of 8 Meissen soup and dessert dishes, painted with insects and Deutsche Blumen in enamels, crossed swords marks in underglaze blue. Gorringes, Lewes. Feb 07. HP: £1,000. ABP: £1,176.

647

Newhall type tea canister, wrythen shape painted with a floral pattern, domed cover, 5.5in. Gorringes, Lewes. Feb 07. HP: £1,000. ABP: £1,176.

648

Moorcroft sugar shaker, hand painted in Moonlit Blue pattern, pewter top in Arts and Crafts style, c1920, impressed, blue hand painted WM initials, shape No 226, 18cm. Batemans, Stamford. Feb 07. HP: £1,000. ABP: £1,176.

649

R. Worcester figure of The Minstrel with Lester Piggott, by Bernard Winskill, printed mark, 1978, No. 9 of 150, 32.5cm, certificate. Halls Fine Art, Shrewsbury. Apr 07. HP: £1,000. ABP: £1,176.

650

R. Worcester porcelain group, Hands Across the Sea, No. 2011, depicting Uncle Sam and John Bull, 7.75in high. Andrew Hartley, Ilkley. Apr 04. HP: £980. ABP: £1,152.

> The illustrations are in descending price order. The price range is indicated at the top of each page.

651

Belleek porcelain charger, painted by Georgina Cunningham, titled 'In the Sunshine', signed verso and dated April 1879, label for Howell & James Art Pottery Exhibition, 16in wide. Andrew Hartley, Ilkley. Oct 05. HP: £980. ABP: £1,152.

652

Meissen figure of a monkey playing a piano astride another, c1870, with a music stand, right hand loss, a foot restored, 12cm. Sworders, Stansted Mountfitchet. Nov 04. HP: £980. ABP: £1,152.

653

Wedgwood & Bentley creamware 'porphyry' urn, c 1780, lacks cover, 18cm and pair of Wedgwood creamware 'porphyry' ewers, c1780, 30cm, chip, restored. Sworders, Stansted Mountfitchet. Feb 05. HP: £980. ABP: £1,152.

654

Pair of Barr, Flight & Barr cache pots, c1810, blue/grey marbled, printed mark, 15.5cm. Sworders, Stansted Mountfitchet. Feb 05. HP: £980. ABP: £1,152.

655

Lowestoft bachelor's teapot c1770, hand painted underglaze blue flowers & butterflies, painters mark to foot rim, restoration to lid, spout and rim, 9cm high. John Taylors, Louth. Mar 05. HP: £980. ABP: £1,152.

656

Chamberlain's Worcester Union dessert service, printed and overpainted in Japan pattern, approx 30 pieces. Rosebery's, London. Jun 04. HP: £980. ABP: £1,152.

657

Pair 19thC Chinese porcelain tulip vases, cinquefoil shape with 5 holes, with dragons chasing the flaming pearl, 4 character mark to base, 10in high. Diamond Mills & Co, Felixstowe. Mar 06. HP: £980. ABP: £1,152.

658

Prattware lidded Toby jug, as a seated toper, with a dog between his feet, figural moulded handle, 19thC, 10in high. Hartleys, Ilkley. Oct 06. HP: £980. ABP: £1,152.

659

Pilkingtons R. Lancastrian lustre vase, decorated with fish and seaweed, combined impressed P.L. mark & lustre lion's head, imp'd 2598, 5.5in. Maxwells, Wilmslow. Sep 04. HP: £960. ABP: £1,129.

660

Clarice Cliff 'Fantasque' pottery coffee service, Sunrise pattern within wide banded borders, 14 pieces, black printed marks to bases, and a similar sugar bowl, 3.25in dia. Canterbury Auction Galleries, Kent. Apr 06. HP: £960. ABP: £1,129.

661

19thC Meissen porcelain allegorical chariot group, 9.5in high, crossed swords mark in underglaze blue to base. Canterbury Auction Galleries, Kent. Dec 05. HP: £960. ABP: £1,129.

662

Moorcroft miniature vase, c1905, poppy design, 401753, indistinct MacIntyre factory mark, signed in green 'WM Des', 2.5in. (crazed) Halls Fine Art, Shrewsbury. Mar 04. HP: £960. ABP: £1,129.

663

Doulton Lambeth glazed stoneware vase by George Tinworth entitled The Waning of the Honeymoon, monogram on base, 6.5in, damage, chips. Gorringes, Lewes. Mar 04. HP: £950. ABP: £1,117.

664

George Jones majolica dressing table tray, c1870, impressed monogram, Reg. diamond to base, 28cm wide, minor rubbing. Sworders, Stansted Mountfitchet. Mar 04. HP: £950. ABP: £1,117.

665

Troika pottery wheel lamp base, raised Aztec designs to one side, fireplace to other, Avril Bennett, 14.5in. Burstow & Hewett, Battle. Mar 04. HP: £950. ABP: £1,117.

666

Kutani bowl, with bird and floral decoration, 21.5in. Gorringes, Lewes. Oct 04. HP: £950. ABP: £1,117.

Hammer: £980 - £950

667

Song/Ming dynasty celadon monkey, hollow figure, back opens to chamber inside, 16.5cm high. Cheffins, Cambridge. Jun 04. HP: £950. ABP: £1,117.

668

Early 19thC 'Warranted Semi China' serving plate, blue-printed, boy & two dogs at a country stile, printed banner mark, unsigned. Gorringes, Lewes. Dec 04. HP: £950. ABP: £1,117.

669

Three Palissy-style lidded and graduated jugs by Mafra of Caldas De Rainha, c1880, two with handles in the form of lizards, the other with two interlocked snakes, all on a layer of extruded clay, imp'd marks, restoration, 38cm, 34cm & 30.5cm. Sworders, Stansted Mountfitchet. Nov 04. HP: £950. ABP: £1,117.

670

Meissen group of The Good Mother, c1880, after the original model by Michel Victor Acrier, crossed swords mark, incised E69 71 40, damage, 21cm. Sworders, Stansted Mountfitchet. Nov 04. HP: £950. ABP: £1,117.

671

Set of four Samson porcelain allegorical figures, classical maidens, 19thC, 11.5in high. Andrew Hartley, Ilkley. Dec 04. HP: £950. ABP: £1,117.

672

Late 18thC Staffordshire figure group, 'The Vicar and Moses', mould 62, probably Ralph Wood of Burslem, impressed mould No. to base, 9.5in, repaired chip to corner. Gorringes, Lewes. Apr 05. HP: £950. ABP: £1,117.

673

1930s Wedgwood black basalt vase by Keith Murray, base signed in red with full signature, impressed marks, height 8in. Fieldings, West Hagley, Worcs. Jun 05. HP: £950. ABP: £1,117.

674

Collection of Chamberlains Worcester Queen's Lily pattern wares, each decorated in blue with panels of scrolling tendrils and flowers. (D) (37) Cheffins, Cambridge. Apr 05. HP: £950. ABP: £1,117.

675

Early 19thC Minton footbath, printed with Claremont pattern in blue, printed mark, 19in. Gorringes, Lewes. Jun 06. HP: £950. ABP: £1,117.

Pair Doulton, Lambeth stoneware vases by Frank Butler, 1874, 10.75in, imp'd mark, date, incised artist's monogram. Gorringes, Lewes. Oct 05. HP: £950. ABP: £1,117.

Pair of Chinese famille rose vases, painted with wild birds and chrysanthemum, 12in. Gorringes, Lewes. Oct 05. HP: £950. ABP: £1,117.

Rye Hop Ware jug, green hops & leaves, incised marks Sussex Ware, Rye, 1901, F.E. Mitchell, 10.75in. Gorringes, Lewes. Oct 05. HP: £950. ABP: £1,117.

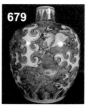

Doucai style vase, Chinese, with mythical beasts between cloud motifs, underglaze blue & polychrome enamels, 19cm. Rosebery's, London. Dec 05. HP: £950. ABP: £1,117.

Bow basket, painted with the Quail pattern in enamels, c1770, 6in. Gorringes, Lewes. Oct 06. HP: £950. ABP: £1,117.

Clarice Cliff conical sugar shaker, Café-Au-Lait pattern. Black Country, Dudley. Dec 05. HP: £950. ABP: £1,117.

Pair of Vienna vases/covers, 19thC, vase shaped bodies with twin pull up handles and pole pierced rims, with classical scenes, 26cm high. Rosebery's, London. Mar 06. HP: £950. ABP: £1,117.

Modern Coalport blue china 'Hong Kong' pattern dinner service, printed, painted and gilt in the Japan palette, approx 70 pieces. Golding Young & Co, Grantham. Feb 06. HP: £950. ABP: £1,117.

Royal Doulton figure, Lady of the Fan, HN52. Gorringes, Lewes. Mar 06. HP: £950. ABP: £1,117.

Walter Moorcroft flambe vase, tube lined in Hibiscus pattern, 8.25in high. Hartleys, Ilkley. Oct 06. HP: £950. ABP: £1,117.

19thC Austrian earthenware Staffordshire bull terrier, restoration, 21.5in. Gorringes, Lewes. Dec 06. HP: £950. ABP: £1,117.

R. Doulton figure 'St George and the Dragon', HN2856. Louis Taylor, Stoke. Mar 06. HP: £940. ABP: £1,105.

Wedgwood Keith Murray 'Bronze' vase, facsimile signature to base, 9in high. Louis Taylor, Stoke. Mar 06. HP: £940. ABP: £1,105.

Staffordshire salt glaze frog tankard, blue painted with a seated gentleman, inscribed 'W and S Peace, 1781', with stanza verso, 5in high. Andrew Hartley, Ilkley. Apr 06. HP: £940. ABP: £1,105.

Pilkingtons R. Lancastrian lustre vase, Richard Joyce, combined P.L. imp'd mark, lustre lion's head and JR monogram, imp'd 2761, 5in. Maxwells, Wilmslow. Sep 04. HP: £920. ABP: £1,082.

Prattware jug, c1800, with birds on a branch, painted in yellow, green, ochre & blue, hairline to spout, 19cm. Sworders, Stansted Mountfitchet. Feb 05. HP: £920. ABP: £1,082.

Pair Meissen children, c1870, crossed swords mark, inscribed in gold '1' and incised F31, small chips, 16cm. Sworders, Stansted Mountfitchet. Jul 05. HP: £920. ABP: £1,082.

First period Worcester porcelain pickle dish as a leaf, veined underside, with polychrome flowers, 4in wide. Andrew Hartley, Ilkley. Apr 06. HP: £920. ABP: £1,082. £920. ABP: £1,082.

Wedgwood fairyland lustre bowl, c1930, by Daisy Makeig- Jones, scratching, 27.5cm. Sworders, Stansted Mountfitchet. Apr 06. HP: £920. ABP: £1,082.

Clarice cliff 3-piece Canterbury Bells pattern tea set with matching teacup and tea plate. Gorringes, Lewes. Mar 04. HP: £900. ABP: £1,058.

696

Pair Derby botanical dessert plates, c1815, titled specimen sprays attributed to William Quaker Pegg, red crown cross batons mark, puce No. 47. Wintertons, Lichfield. Mar 04. HP: £900. ABP: £1,058.

697

Late 19thC German porcelain figure group 'Count Bruhl's Tailor', printed mark, 33cm. Locke & England, Leamington Spa. Sep 04. HP: £900. ABP: £1,058.

698

Majolica game pie dish, c1870, possibly Wedgwood, basket with a partridge on the lid, 33cm. Sworders, Stansted Mountfitchet. Nov 04. HP: £900. ABP: £1,058.

699

Satsuma squat koro, Meiji period, dog of fo finial, body with a processional scene, gilt character marks in gourd shape, handles restuck, 11cm. Sworders, Stansted Mountfitchet. Nov 04. HP: £900. ABP: £1,058.

700

Pair of Isnik tiles, late 17thC, in blue, black and green with flowers, one repaired, chips and wear, 28.2cm. Sworders, Stansted Mountfitchet. Feb 05. HP: £900. ABP: £1,058.

701

Meissen magpie, underglaze crossed swords mark, incised 62, beak restored, 53cm. Sworders, Stansted Mountfitchet. Feb 05. HP: £900. ABP: £1,058.

702

Pair of Arita dishes, 19thC, with moulded crossed carp in blue/red, underglaze blue Ken (treasure), and yellow painted 'From the Beck Coll. Sotheby. Jun. 11, 1897, Lot 740.P, 28cm. Sworders, Stansted Mountfitchet. Feb 05. HP: £900. ABP: £1,058.

> Categories or themes can be followed through the colour coded Index which contains 1000s of cross references.

703

Pair of R. Doulton stoneware vases, by Eliza Simmance, with incised/moulded stylised flowers and foliage, 13.5in. Art Union of London stamp. Gorringes, Lewes. Jan 05. HP: £900. ABP: £1,058.

704

R. Worcester Ltd Edn of 500 Figurine, base entitled Sister-Nightingale Training School St Thomas's Hospital (London) modelled by Ruth Van Ruychevett 1963, No. 327 M.A. 6.25in. Smiths of Newent, Newent. Apr 05. HP: £900. ABP: £1,058.

Hammer: £900

705

Beswick Canadian Mounted Cowboy, model No. 1377, by Mr Orwell, issued 1955-1973, 8.75in high. Halls Fine Art, Shrewsbury. Apr 05. HP: £900. ABP: £1,058.

706

Three William De Morgan tiles in Cavendish pattern, backs with imp'd circular 'DM 98' mark, 16cm square. Sworders, Stansted Mountfitchet. Apr 05. HP: £900. ABP: £1,058.

707

Moorcroft banded peacock feather vase, c1910, imp'd marks with a blue signature, 23cm. Sworders, Stansted Mountfitchet. Apr 05. HP: £900. ABP: £1,058.

708

Pair 18thC Derby plates with patt. 270 of views, 'On Loch Lomond, Scotland' & 'Near Coupar in Angus, Scotland', marks in blue, 22cm. Cheffins, Cambridge. Apr 05. HP: £900. ABP: £1,058.

709

Pair of late 19thC Chinese jars/covers painted in famille verte palette, 41cm high. (D) Cheffins, Cambridge. Apr 05. HP: £900. ABP: £1,058.

710

Beswick Beatrix Potter figure of Duchess 1355, style one, black dog holding a bunch of flowers, designed by Graham Orwell, BP2a, 3.75in. Halls Fine Art, Shrewsbury. Jul 05. HP: £900. ABP: £1,058.

711

Chinese blue/white jar, Transitional, in underglaze blue with lappets of peony on scrolls, mouth and foot with flames, 27cm. Sworders, Stansted Mountfitchet. Nov 05. HP: £900. ABP: £1,058.

712

Rare famille rose toddy ladle, c1770, petal moulded and painted with flowers within rui panels, 8cm, boxwood handle. Sworders, Stansted Mountfitchet. Nov 05. HP: £900. ABP: £1,058.

713

Pair R. Worcester vases decorated with fruit, signed W. Ricketts, 8.5in, c1926. Ibbett Mosely, Sevenoaks. Nov 05. HP: £900. ABP: £1,058.

714

Graduated set of 3 Doulton Lambeth cycling jugs, each with cycling scene, Military, Path & Road, largest 8.75in. Gorringes, Lewes. Feb 06. HP: £900. ABP: £1,058.

Hammer: £900

Large Royal Worcester blush ivory vase by E Raby. Henry Adams, Chichester. Dec 05. HP: £900. ABP: £1,058.

Pair of Coalport porcelain vases, pineapple finial on domed lid, gilded lion mask loop handles, highland landscapes by Arthur Perry, 16in. Andrew Hartley, Ilkley. Dec 05. HP: £900. ABP: £1,058.

Early R. Doulton pottery figure, 'Mother Bunnykins', 7.5in high, D.6004 - printed mark to base, impressed 8305. Canterbury Auction Galleries, Kent. Dec 05. HP: £900. ABP: £1,058.

Large Troika Wheel lamp base, moulded with an mask to one side, abstract detail to other, cream, textured ground. Gorringes, Lewes. Feb 06. HP: £900. ABP: £1,058.

Rare Arita Imari dish, c1700, with a crane swooping on a minogame, 28cm. Sworders, Stansted Mountfitchet. Feb 06. HP: £900. ABP: £1,058.

50 *Ceramics Prices*

R. Worcester floral painted plaque by E. Phillips, still life of summer flowers in a basket, signed, gilt scrolled frame, printed marks verso, date code c1915, 4in. Gorringes, Lewes. Apr 06. HP: £900. ABP: £1,058.

Large Royal Worcester urn shaped vase decorated with roses by A Shuck. Henry Adams, Chichester. Apr 06. HP: £900. ABP: £1,058.

Prices quoted are actual hammer prices (HP) and the Approximate Buyer's Price (ABP) includes an average premium of 15% + VAT.

Grainger's Worcester porcelain vase and cover by James Stinton, painted with mallard in flight, signed Jas. Stinton, model G955, date code for 1902, 14in high. Golding Young & Co, Grantham. Feb 06. HP: £900. ABP: £1,058.

Beswick pottery 'Beatrix Potter' figure - Duchess, 3.75in high, gold back stamp. Canterbury Auction Galleries, Kent. Apr 06. HP: £900. ABP: £1,058.

Victorian Mason's ironstone part dinner service, 12 setting, blue painted/enamelled in chinoiserie pattern No. 9799. (54) Hartleys, Ilkley. Aug 06. HP: £900. ABP: £1,058.

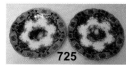

Pair R. Worcester porcelain plates, mildly lobed, painted with fruit by R Sebright, dated 1911, signed, mark for Townsend & Co, Newcastle-on-Tyne, 9in wide. Hartleys, Ilkley. Aug 06. HP: £900. ABP: £1,058.

Royal Doulton figure, Pierrette, HN644. Gorringes, Lewes. Mar 06. HP: £900. ABP: £1,058.

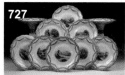

Porcelain dessert service, poss. Samuel Bourne c1835, 3 comports & 7 plates, each painted with a titled view in Ireland within gilt borders, pattern No. 124, one rubbed and indistinct. (10) Sworders, Stansted Mountfitchet. Apr 06. HP: £900. ABP: £1,058.

Pair of large Cantonese vases. Great Western Auctions, Glasgow. Sep 06. HP: £900. ABP: £1,058.

R. Doulton marked 'Noke' & 'Sung' flambe bowl, painted to interior with an exotic bird, 12in wide, No.670 to base. Hartleys, Ilkley. Oct 06. HP: £900. ABP: £1,058.

Pair of William Moorcroft florian ware vases, tube lined with butterflies and flowers, 10.75in. Hartleys, Ilkley. Oct 06. HP: £900. ABP: £1,058.

Late Meissen porcelain group, three puppies drinking from a bowl, another puppy and a cat observing, imp'd, printed cross swords marks, 11cm. Locke & England, Leamington Spa. Nov 06. HP: £900. ABP: £1,058.

Beswick Galloway bull, Silver Dunn, mould 1746C, 1962-69. Gorringes, Lewes. Feb 07. HP: £900. ABP: £1,058.

Meissen porcelain group, mid 19thC, courting couple beneath a tree and a girl picking apples, imp'd D94/34, 18 in red, blue crossed swords, chips, 26cm. Sworders, Stansted Mountfitchet. Feb 07. HP: £900. ABP: £1,058.

734

Meissen part tea/coffee service, mid 18thC, each piece painted in underglaze blue, gilt petal form roundels and puce sprays, crossed swords mark, Duhrer mark N on pot, chips. (22) Sworders, Stansted Mountfitchet. Feb 05. HP: £880. ABP: £1,035.

735

Pair of jardinières/stands, early 19thC, painted with panels of stylised flowers, one stand chipped, 17.5cm. Sworders, Stansted Mountfitchet. Feb 05. HP: £880. ABP: £1,035.

736

Beswick set of Snow White and Seven Dwarfs, slight damage to Snow White. Louis Taylor, Stoke. Mar 05. HP: £880. ABP: £1,035.

737

Early 19thC Mason's stone china dessert service in Imari colours, 19 pieces. John Taylors, Louth. Mar 05. HP: £880. ABP: £1,035.

738

Salvini Brevettato Italia early 20thC pottery vase, painted in an Art Nouveau style with the crowned head of a female bedecked with jewels, 7in high. Tring Market Auctions, Herts. Mar 05. HP: £880. ABP: £1,035.

739

Charles Vyse, The Rose Seller, blue painted CV monogram, 'Chelsea' and 1923 to underside, 22cm. Rosebery's, London. Mar 06. HP: £880. ABP: £1,035.

740

Chinese famille rose dish, 18thC, painted in colours with a nobleman in a chaise with attendants, 42cm. Rosebery's, London. Mar 06. HP: £880. ABP: £1,035.

741

Victorian Staffordshire figure, cricketer holding a bat, 35cm. Reeman Dansie, Colchester. Apr 06. HP: £880. ABP: £1,035.

742

Hans Coper and Dame Lucie Rie Art Pottery coffee service, white glazed interiors and brown glazed exteriors. 12 pieces, damage. Denhams, Warnham, Sussex. Nov 05. HP: £880. ABP: £1,035.

743

William Moorcroft flambe vase, tube lined in the Leaves and Berries design, 8.75in high. Hartleys, Ilkley. Oct 06. HP: £880. ABP: £1,035.

Hammer: £880 - £850

744

Zsolnay Pec Art Nouveau vase, metal cased with three bronzed stylistic flowers over a blue Eosin glaze, form 5569, 4.25in high. Tring Market Auctions, Herts. Mar 05. HP: £860. ABP: £1,011.

745

George Jones majolica plaque, Reg. mark for 18 Dec 1874, slight firing crack. Louis Taylor, Stoke. Mar 06. HP: £860. ABP: £1,011.

746

Doulton Lambeth stoneware three handled commemorative loving cup, inscribed 'In Commemoration of the Hoisting of the Flag of Pretoria - June 5th 1900', 10.5in high, slight damage. Louis Taylor, Stoke. Mar 06. HP: £860. ABP: £1,011.

747

Wade/Faust Lang model of a Lion Cub, impressed Faust Lang, blue printed Wade mark to paw, 4.75in. Louis Taylor, Stoke. Mar 06. HP: £860. ABP: £1,011.

748

Martin Brothers stoneware vase, dated 1902, 8.75in, firing deficiences. Louis Taylor, Stoke on Trent. Mar 06. HP: £860. ABP: £1,011.

749

Royal Doulton figure 'Pierrette', HN1391. Louis Taylor, Stoke on Trent. Mar 06. HP: £860. ABP: £1,011.

750

Pair of late 18thC Chinese vases, painted panels of figures, 11.5in high. Dee, Atkinson & Harrison, Driffield,. Mar 04. HP: £850. ABP: £999.

751

Wemyss jardiniere, decorated with daffodils, marked 'Wemyss, R.H & S', 12in dia. Gorringes, Bexhill. Mar 04. HP: £850. ABP: £999.

752

Beswick, mounted huntsman and mounted huntswoman with eight foxhounds and fox. (11) Dee, Atkinson & Harrison, Driffield. Jul 04. HP: £850. ABP: £999.

753

Extensive early 19thC Newhall tea/coffee service. Gorringes, Bexhill. Dec 04. HP: £850. ABP: £999.

Hammer: £850

754

English porcelain dessert service, 24 pieces, c1800, each painted with a different scene of rural life & arduous labours, painted pattern number, damage, restoration. Gorringes, Lewes. Jul 04. HP: £850. ABP: £999.

755

19thC Dresden group of Bacchanalian figures, putti and goat, 11in high. (s/f) Dee, Atkinson & Harrison, Driffield. Nov 04. HP: £850. ABP: £999.

756

Doulton Lambeth stoneware oil lamp by Eliza Simmance, with Hinks & Sons burner, decorated with foliate motifs and geometric ribbons in blue and green against a cream ground, c1882, 20in. Gorringes, Lewes. Dec 04. HP: £850. ABP: £999.

757

Wedgwood & Bentley green porphyry urn, c1780, with Bacchus mask handles, rare pad mark, lacks cover, 34cm. Sworders, Stansted Mountfitchet. Feb 05. HP: £850. ABP: £999.

758

The Shelley 'Animal Tea Set' after Mabel Lucie Attwell, 1930-34, teapot in the form of a duck, with cover, Regd. No. 724421, teapot 6.25in. Gorringes, Lewes. Sep 04. HP: £850. ABP: £999.

759

Pair of Rainfordware Art Nouveau glazed stoneware jardinieres, possibly retailed by Liberty & Co, unmarked 32in. Gorringes, Lewes. Sep 04. HP: £850. ABP: £999.

760

Meissen figure of the bowing Harlequin, early 20thC, crossed sword mark, imp'd 632/131 and painted 49, 15.2cm. Sworders, Stansted Mountfitchet. Feb 05. HP: £850. ABP: £999.

761

Meissen parakeet perched on a tree stump, c1900, crossed swords mark, damage. Sworders, Stansted Mountfitchet. Feb 05. HP: £850. ABP: £999.

762

Pair of late 19thC Japanese vases with large panels of geisha, children and Samurai warriors, signed on bases, 38cm high. Henry Adams, Chichester. Jun 05. HP: £850. ABP: £999.

763

Beswick Sussex cockerel, No. 1899, 7.25in high. Tring Market Auctions, Herts. Mar 05. HP: £850. ABP: £999.

764

George III shell-moulded prattware vase, relief-moulded with a portrait bust to each side, one poss. King George III, 8.5in. Gorringes, Lewes. Apr 05. HP: £850. ABP: £999.

765

Late 19thC French faience cat in style of Galle, painted with flowers against a yellow ground, 12.5in, one leg re-attached. Gorringes, Lewes. Apr 05. HP: £850. ABP: £999.

766

Worcester Hadley Ware vase, painted with egrets in a landscape by William Powell, 7.75in. Gorringes, Lewes. Jun 05. HP: £850. ABP: £999.

767

Chinese Junyao bowl, glazed in a blue-green with crimson effects, 6.75in. Gorringes, Lewes. Oct 05. HP: £850. ABP: £999.

768

Troika pottery 'Aztec' Mask, 25cm high, painted Troika with mark for Tina Doubleday, base chipped. Bearne's, Exeter. Jun 05. HP: £850. ABP: £999.

769

Set of six R. Worcester coffee cups and saucers, painted by Reginald Harry Austin, cups with pheasants perching on branches, saucers with cones and foliage in landscapes, printed marks and date code for1929, one cup cracked. Bearne's, Exeter. Jun 05. HP: £850. ABP: £999.

770

Royal Worcester Anniversary charger 16in dia. Stroud Auctions, Stroud. Jul 05. HP: £850. ABP: £999.

771

Pair of 19thC Canton vases, pierced covers, enamelled with insects, flowers and leaves, gilt handles, 8.5in, minor restoration to one vase. Gorringes, Lewes. Sep 05. HP: £850. ABP: £999.

772

Large Copeland Parian figure. Henry Adams, Chichester. Dec 05. HP: £850. ABP: £999.

773

19thC Meissen figure group, 14.5in high. Gorringes, Lewes. Apr 04. HP: £850. ABP: £999.

774

Large Wemyss jardiniere. Gorringes, Bexhill. Apr 05. HP: £850. ABP: £999.

775

Pair of Doulton Lambeth stoneware moonflasks, pierced foliate centres and incised borders, impressed factory marks and initials to base, 8in. Gorringes, Lewes. Nov 05. HP: £850. ABP: £999.

> The numbering system acts as a reader reference and links to the Analysis of each section.

776

Pair of early 19thC blue and white Chinese export tureens and covers, animal head handles, 33cm long. Rosebery's, London. Dec 05. HP: £850. ABP: £999.

777

Late 18thC creamware mug with quatrefoil centred yellow diamond rim band, body engine turned with a geometric design of cubes and coloured in chocolate slip, 14.5cm high. Cheffins, Cambridge. Feb 06. HP: £850. ABP: £999.

778

Pair of Burmantofts partie colour vases, tube lined with flowers, 16in high, mould No.2059. Andrew Hartley, Ilkley, W Yorks. Feb 06. HP: £850. ABP: £999.

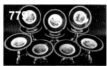

779

Graingers Worcester named view dessert service, painted with views of Scottish lochs and North of England views. (27) Rosebery's, London. Mar 06. HP: £850. ABP: £999.

780

Rookwood standard pottery vase, dated 1887, decorated by Albert Robert Valentien, imp'd marks, inscribed with initials, 47.5cm. Sworders, Stansted Mountfitchet. Apr 06. HP: £850. ABP: £999.

781

Meissen cabaret set, 'Fenced Tiger' pattern: coffee pot, creamer & sucriere, rose bud finials lids, pair of quatrefoil cups/saucers, shaped tray. Rosebery's, London. Mar 06. HP: £850. ABP: £999.

782

Royal Doulton figure, The Swimmer, HN1270. Gorringes, Lewes. Mar 06. HP: £850. ABP: £999.

Hammer: £850 - £820

783

Berlin porcelain plaque, a young girl accompanying an old lady down a church path, 19thC, 9.5 x 12in, gilt frame. Andrew Hartley, Ilkley. Jun 05. HP: £840. ABP: £988.

784

Beswick 'Knight in Armour', model 1145, 10.75in, some restoration. Louis Taylor, Stoke on Trent. Mar 05. HP: £830. ABP: £976.

785

Apothecary jar. Brettells, Newport, Shropshire. Sep 04. HP: £820. ABP: £964.

786

Meissen Hausmaler tea caddy/cover, mid 18thC, slightly ribbed form in underglaze blue, enamelled and gilt with chinoiserie figures, 11.5cm high, with a similar teapot/cover. Rosebery's, London. Sep 04. HP: £820. ABP: £964.

787

18thC Staffordshire figure of The Medici lion, tooth missing, tail f and r, 9in. Denhams, Warnham. Oct 04. HP: £820. ABP: £964.

788

Set of 4 porcelain botanical plates, English, early 19thC, painted with tulips, ground elder & other flowers, 22cm. Rosebery's, London. Dec 04. HP: £820. ABP: £964.

789

Meissen green parrot, c1870, crossed swords mark, 25cm. Sworders, Stansted Mountfitchet. Feb 05. HP: £820. ABP: £964.

790

Large Troika wheel vase by Alison Brigden, painted marks, 13in high. Gardiner Houlgate, Corsham. Apr 05. HP: £820. ABP: £964.

791

Troika globe vase by Louise Jinks, painted marks, 8in high. Gardiner Houlgate, Corsham. Apr 05. HP: £820. ABP: £964.

792

Minton blue ground dessert service, English c1900: 12 plates, 4 low & 2 comports, various maritime and inshore scenes, puce printed mark to base, pattern No. G9402, signed 'Dean'. Rosebery's, London. Dec 05. HP: £820. ABP: £964.

Hammer: £820 - £800

Jose-a-Cunha Calda De Rainha pottery Palissy style dish, c1880, with fish and an eel, imp'd oval mark, mark and inscribed no.2, 32cm. Sworders, Stansted Mountfitchet. Feb 06. HP: £820. ABP: £964.

Pair Staffordshire lion spill vase groups, 19thC, recumbent lion & lioness amongst grasses with playful cubs, 10.75in high. Halls Fine Art, Shrewsbury. Mar 06. HP: £820. ABP: £964.

Clarice Cliff 'Bizarre' pottery coffee service, Lynton shape, ribbed conical bodies, 'Coral Firs' pattern, black printed 'Bizarre' mark to bases. (15) Canterbury Auction Galleries, Kent. Feb 06. HP: £820. ABP: £964.

Oriental blue/white jar. Great Western Auctions, Glasgow. May 06. HP: £820. ABP: £964.

19thC Japanese Imari porcelain bowl, mythical beasts within gilt floral panels, 18in, slight damage. Denhams, Warnham, Sussex. May 06. HP: £820. ABP: £964.

Pair of MacIntyre Aurelian ware vases, c1897, printed & painted in gilt in an Imari palette with stylised poppies, factory brown printed mark, inscribed in enamel M414, 25cm high. Sworders, Stansted Mountfitchet. Apr 06. HP: £820. ABP: £964.

Pilkingtons Lancastrian lustre vase by Richard Joyce, swimming fish in silver on a shaded green ground, 5in high. Hartleys, Ilkley. Feb 07. HP: £820. ABP: £964.

> The illustrations are in descending price order. The price range is indicated at the top of each page.

19thC pink Sunderland lustre Masonic vase, inscribed 'Lodge No. 14 of free and easy Johns, 1830', 20cm. Boldon Auction Galleries, Tyne & Wear. Mar 06. HP: £805. ABP: £946.

Moorcroft rain forest design vase, 1992, by Sally Tuffin, Ltd Edn, No. 3 of 150, imp'd and inscribed marks, S T Des, 3/150, 13.3.1992, 42cm high. Sworders, Stansted Mountfitchet. Mar 04. HP: £800. ABP: £941.

Wedgwood and Bentley classical urn/cover, simulated Blue Palfrey design, Humphrey Palmer Hanley black basalt base, mark to base 'H Palmer Hanley', 11in high. Gorringes, Bexhill. May 04. HP: £800. ABP: £941.

Staffordshire rabbit, c1850, recumbent, enriched with gilt patches, 24cm long, some damage. Hampton & Littlewood, Exeter. Jul 04 HP: £800. ABP: £941.

Joseph Holdcroft majolica cheese stand/cover, c1870, cover glazed in cobalt blue, moulded with fish swimming, handle applied and moulded as a fish, 24cm. Sworders, Stansted Mountfitchet. Jul 04. HP: £800. ABP: £941.

Graingers Worcester porcelain cabaret set, pink rose pattern, gilt embellished. (8) Andrew Hartley, Ilkley. Oct 04. HP: £800. ABP: £941.

Swansea plate, painted with 'Billingsley' roses and other bright flowers, painted mark, 8in. Gorringes, Lewes. Dec 04. HP: £800. ABP: £941.

R. Doulton stoneware vase by Hannah Barlow, incised with a band of 5 grazing ponies, 11in high. Andrew Hartley, Ilkley. Oct 04. HP: £800. ABP: £941.

Canton hexagonal porcelain garden seat. Gorringes, Bexhill. Dec 04. HP: £800. ABP: £941.

Pair of 19thC Meissen dogs, each recumbent on hind legs, 7.5in. Gorringes, Lewes. Oct 05. HP: £800. ABP: £941.

Meissen figure group, Europa and the Bull, German, late 19thC, Europa seated upon a bull while 2 female attendants dressing the bull with a garland of flowers 22cm. Rosebery's, London. Dec 04. HP: £800. ABP: £941.

Meissen figural vase group, German, late 19thC, urn and cover supporting a fruiting vine above two figures of children, 24cm high. Rosebery's, London. Dec 04. HP: £800. ABP: £941.

812

Beswick pottery 14 piece huntsmen and hounds set, all marked. Diamond Mills & Co, Felixstowe. Dec 04. HP: £800. ABP: £941.

813

John Skeaping for Wedgwood, c1930, two deer amongst cover, finished in glazed green, with another larger group, af, impressed marks. Rosebery's, London. Mar 05. HP: £800. ABP: £941.

814

Pair of Chinese scallop shaped dishes, 7.5in. Gorringes, Lewes. Apr 04. HP: £800. ABP: £941.

815

18thC Wedgwood & Bentley black basalt twin-handled fluted urn/cover, c1780 with a frieze of scrolling acanthus leaves & figures, replacement cover, base sceptical, 14.5in. Gorringes, Lewes. Mar 05. HP: £800. ABP: £941.

816

19thC Minton majolica comport, supported by 2 putti, foot with a tambourine, vine leaves and wheatsheaf, imp'd marks, year cipher for 1867, 29.5cm high. Clevedon Salerooms, Bristol. Jun 05. HP: £800. ABP: £941.

817

Rye Sussex Pig, brown glaze, vivid iron-oxide colouring, detachable head forming drinking vessel, incised legend around the shoulder, 'Wunt be Druv', incised mark Rye within head and size 5, 8in long, rear foot re-attached. Gorringes, Lewes. Oct 05. HP: £800. ABP: £941.

818

Creamware mug, 1781, with the names of Jno. & Cathn. Little and dated, within floral cartouche, 5in. Gorringes, Lewes. Nov 05. HP: £800. ABP: £941.

819

Lambeth delftware balloon-ing plate, with an ascending hot-air balloon within formal garland border, c1785, 9in. Gorringes, Lewes. Nov 05. HP: £800. ABP: £941.

820

Two Beswick equestrian figures of huntsmen (1501), with one first version hound, (943) and 3 second version, (2262) and (2264) with a standing fox, (1440) all gloss. Bearne's, Exeter. Jun 05. HP: £800. ABP: £941.

821

Beswick model of a Bedouin Arab on Horseback, 10.25in, Connoisseur Series, no base. Louis Taylor, Stoke. Mar 06. HP: £800. ABP: £941.

Hammer: £800

822

Clarice Cliff Bizarre conical sugar sifter, Green Erin, 5.5in. Gorringes, Lewes. Nov 05. HP: £800. ABP: £941.

823

Clarice Cliff Newport Pottery Lotus jug, 8.25in. Louis Taylor, Stoke. Mar 06. HP: £800. ABP: £941.

824

Royal Doulton figure, The Moor, HN2082. Gorringes, Lewes. Mar 06. HP: £800. ABP: £941.

825

Royal Doulton figure, The Bather, HN1227. Gorringes, Lewes. Mar 06. HP: £800. ABP: £941.

826

Chinese export porcelain charger, painted with a figure standing on an island in underglaze blue, 18in. Gorringes, Lewes. Mar 06. HP: £800. ABP: £941.

827

19thC Chinese porcelain figure of an elder, bearded character wearing long floral-painted robe, holding floral offering, 17in. Gorringes, Lewes. Mar 06. HP: £800. ABP: £941.

828

Clarice Cliff vase, 'Sunray', printed marks to base and impressed shape No. 350, 8in. Gorringes, Lewes. Mar 06. HP: £800. ABP: £941.

829

Beswick black Galloway bull, model no. 1746A. Gorringes, Lewes. Oct 06. HP: £800. ABP: £941.

830

Pair of Morrisware pottery vases by George Cartlidge, with stylised flowers, yellow, green & purple on a turq-uoise ground, marked C72.1, 12in. Hartleys, Ilkley. Oct 06. HP: £800. ABP: £941.

831

Beswick Dairy Shorthorn cow, mould 1510, Champion 'Eaton Wild Eyes 91st', 1957-73. Gorringes, Lewes. Feb 07. HP: £800. ABP: £941.

Hammer: £800 - £760

Chinese celadon crackle-glazed vase, archaic squared form, 9in. Gorringes, Lewes. Dec 06. HP: £800. ABP: £941.

Late 19thC Copeland porcelain dessert service, printed marks in blue, pattern No. 7913 and 7091 in red, damage. (15) Canterbury Auction Galleries, Kent. Feb 04. HP: £780. ABP: £917.

Early Royal Doulton figure 'Butterfly', HN720, by L. Harradine, issued 1925, withdrawn 1938, restoration to left arm, script and printed marks, 16.5cm. Hampton & Littlewood, Exeter. Jul 04. HP: £780. ABP: £917.

Extensive Mason's ironstone flow blue part dinner service, printed in oriental style with flowering chrysanthemum bushes, approx 50 pieces. Rosebery's, London. Sep 04. HP: £780. ABP: £917.

19thC Staffordshire flatback figure of a standing tiger, naturalistic base, breaks to leg. John Taylors, Louth. Jul 05. HP: £780. ABP: £917.

56 *Ceramics Prices*

Dresden group, Diana & the bull with 2 female attendants, 19thC, cross swords mark in blue, slight faults, 9in high. Dee, Atkinson & Harrison, Driffield. Nov 04. HP: £780. ABP: £917.

George Jones majolica sardine dish/cover, c1875, panels of fish/foliage framed by bamboo, lid with cranes, date Reg. mark for 1875 imp'd factory marks, inscribed 3441 and 30, crane on lid reglued, 15cm dia. Sworders, Stansted Mountfitchet. Apr 05. HP: £780. ABP: £917.

> Categories or themes can be followed through the colour coded Index which contains 1000s of cross references.

Meissen figure of Harlequin, German 19th/20thC, seated playing bagpipes on a rock work base, arm replaced. 13.5cm. Rosebery's, London. Jun 05. HP: £780. ABP: £917.

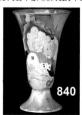

Clarice Cliff 'Newlyn' trumpet vase, shape 702, 5in. Gardiner Houlgate, Corsham. Apr 05. HP: £780. ABP: £917.

Creamware melon tureen, c1770. Richard Winterton, Burton on Trent, Staffs. Jun 05. HP: £780. ABP: £917.

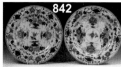

Pair of Chinese Imari dishes, c1710, underglaze blue, iron red and gilding with flowers, chips, 38.7cm. Sworders, Stansted Mountfitchet. Nov 05. HP: £780. ABP: £917.

Clarice Cliff Newport pottery hive conserve pot with bee finial, unusual design of red castle/mountain, yellow tree with green trunk and red blossoms, black and purple bushes and blue sky. Batemans, Stamford. Mar 06. HP: £780. ABP: £917.

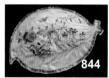

Worcester famille verte leaf moulded dish, c1756-1758, with butterfly above plants, diaper pattern border, 26cm wide. Rosebery's, London. Mar 06. HP: £780. ABP: £917.

Minton majolica garden seat, 'Indian Embossed' pattern, in blue, aubergine & mustard glazes, 44cm high. Rosebery's, London. Mar 06. HP: £780. ABP: £917.

Doulton Lambeth stoneware vase by Eliza Simmance, incised and tube lined with Art Nouveau style flowers on a green mottled ground, 10.75in. Hartleys, Ilkley. Oct 06. HP: £780. ABP: £917.

Shelley Cottage-One pattern part coffee set: 6 Queen Anne shape coffee cans/saucers, milk jug, sugar bowl and coffee pot. Charterhouse Auctioneers, Sherborne. Apr 07. HP: £780. ABP: £917.

Japanese 'Arita' blue/white porcelain charger, 'Kraak' manner, centre decorated with 2 geese within stylised borders, 19.25in, Wan Li period, rim chipped, old repairs. Canterbury Auction Galleries, Kent. Apr 07. HP: £780. ABP: £917.

Pair of late 19thC porcelain blue glazed vases, applied gilt metal floral swags, 16in, fitted as lamps. Amersham Auction Rooms, Bucks. Mar 04. HP: £770. ABP: £905.

Minton majolica basket, c1870-75, 6in x 15.25in long, damage. Louis Taylor, Stoke. Mar 06. HP: £760. ABP: £893.

851

Worcester tea bowl/saucer, unusually thinly potted, with a dragon and flaming pearls in underglaze blue, c1770, open crescent marks. Gorringes, Lewes. Jan 05. HP: £760. ABP: £893.

852

Royal Worcester porcelain group, The Picnic, No. 177 of 250 (RW 3881), two ladies seated on a rustic base, 8.5in wide. Andrew Hartley, Ilkley. Aug 05. HP: £760. ABP: £893.

853

Maw & Co pottery charger, c1870, cherub above ribbon inscribed 'Iter Ad Superos Gloria Pandet', lustre glaze, imp'd 'Maw & Co', Brosely, 56cm. Rosebery's, London. Mar 06. HP: £760. ABP: £893.

854

Clarice Cliff 'Orange Roof Cottage' pattern vase, shape No. 461. Great Western Auctions, Glasgow. Feb 07. HP: £760. ABP: £893.

855

Thirteen Ironstone plates by James Donovan of Dublin, Japan-pattern, painted mark, c1800, 8.25in, three cracked. Gorringes, Lewes. Oct 05. HP: £750. ABP: £882.

856

Clarice Cliff Bonjour shaped part teaset, 'Crocus' pattern: teapot, sugar bowl/cover, open sugar bowl, 2 cups, two saucers and side plate, black factory marks. Eastbourne Auction Rooms, Sussex. Dec 05. HP: £750. ABP: £882.

857

19thC George Jones majolica jardiniere/stand, panels of irises and flowers, conforming stand with tortoiseshell glazed base, impressed oval mark, 9.5ins high, faults. Diamond Mills & Co, Felixstowe. Dec 04. HP: £750. ABP: £882.

858

Mid Victorian George Jones majolica cheese bell/stand moulded with water lilies, bulrushes and dragonflies, 27cm high. Cheffins, Cambridge. Feb 05. HP: £750. ABP: £882.

859

Martin Brothers stoneware vase, dated 1897, incised with four dragons, incised Martin Bros/ London and Southall 6-1897, 24cm. Sworders, Stansted Mountfitchet. Apr 05. HP: £750. ABP: £882.

860

19thC Staffordshire pottery portrait group, 'Death of the Lion Queen', titled in gilt, head re-attached, 14.5in. Gorringes, Lewes. Apr 04. HP: £750. ABP: £882.

861

Early Victorian blue/white platter printed with deer in landscapes, 46.5cm wide. Cheffins, Cambridge. Apr 05. HP: £750. ABP: £882.

862

Vienna porcelain plate, biblical scene surrounded by a border of grotesques on pink and turquoise grounds, beehive mark, 37cm. Gorringes, Bexhill. Dec 05. HP: £750. ABP: £882.

863

Qianlong sang de bouf glazed stem bowl, 21cm dia. Rosebery's, London. Mar 06. HP: £750. ABP: £882.

864

Early Victorian Staffordshire royal commemorative mug, 1838, printed with 2 portraits of 'Victoria Regina' & script in puce, 3in. Gorringes, Lewes. Apr 06. HP: £750. ABP: £882.

865

Pair of Worcester Hadley porcelain candlesticks, 1886. Henry Adams, Chichester. Jul 06. HP: £750. ABP: £882.

866

Beswick, Canadian mounted cowboy, on palomino horse, model no. 1377. Gorringes, Lewes. Oct 06. HP: £750. ABP: £882.

867

Whieldon Pottery figure of a musician, in a tricorn hat. (a.f.) Charterhouse Auctioneers, Sherborne. Oct 06. HP: £750. ABP: £882.

868

Pair Staffordshire liver and white comforter spaniels, holding floral baskets, 7.5in. Gorringes, Lewes. Oct 04. HP: £750. ABP: £882.

869

Pair Moorcroft for Macintyre Florian ware vases, painted signature and printed marks to base, c1902, with repairs, 11.5in. Gorringes, Lewes. Mar 06. HP: £750. ABP: £882.

Hammer: £740 - £720

870

Meissen apple picking group, late 19thC, cross sword marks, underglaze blue, incised numerals 2229-73, 26.5cm high. Hampton & Littlewood, Exeter. Jul 04. HP: £740. ABP: £870.

871

Japanese late Satsuma porcelain vase, 8in. Denhams, Warnham, Sussex. Mar 05. HP: £740. ABP: £870.

872

19thC Italian maiolica charger, centre in colours with 'Father Time', cupid and an angel, 20in. (apparently unmarked). Canterbury Auction Galleries, Kent. Dec 05. HP: £740. ABP: £870.

873

Carlton Ware coffee set, pattern 3450 'Awakening'. Louis Taylor, Stoke. Mar 06. HP: £740. ABP: £870.

874

Pair of Dutch Delft jars, painted with birds & stylised flowers, blue enamel, domed covers, kylin handles, 24in high. Gorringes, Lewes. Oct 06. HP: £740. ABP: £870.

58 *Ceramics Prices*

875

William Moorcroft matt pottery vase, tube lined in the Cornflower design, blue on a white ground, 6.75in high. Hartleys, Ilkley. Oct 06. HP: £740. ABP: £870.

876

Chinese blue/white porcelain coffee pot, domed cover with turned finial, decorated with flowering plants, 10.25in high. Canterbury Auction Galleries, Kent. Jun 07. HP: £740. ABP: £870.

> Prices quoted are actual hammer prices (HP) and the Approximate Buyer's Price (ABP) includes an average premium of 15% + VAT.

877

Ruskin high-fired stoneware vase, mottled glaze effects in mauve, ox-blood red & sea-green, imp'd mark, date 1914, 12.75in, glue-repair, chip to rim. Gorringes, Lewes. Apr 05. HP: £730. ABP: £858.

878

Royal Dux porcelain figure, gentleman on a chariot and two rearing horses, 16in wide, pink triangle mark. Hartleys, Ilkley. Oct 06. HP: £730. ABP: £858.

879

Canton Persian market dish, dated 1878, panels of figures, flowers & butterflies, gold ground, gilt inscription/date, 39cm. Sworders, Stansted Mountfitchet. Nov 04. HP: £720. ABP: £846.

880

English Delft drug jar, c 1700, inscribed 'U:NICOTIAN:' on label, 18.5cm. Sworders, Stansted Mount-fitchet. Feb 05. HP: £720. ABP: £846.

881

French Art Deco pottery figure 'The Harlequin', c1930, cubist form, crackle glazed, harlequin imp'd, 33.5cm high, painted mark 'Primavera'. Rosebery's, London. Mar 05. HP: £720. ABP: £846.

882

Minton encaustic bread plate, c1850, designed by A. W. N. Pugin, buff coloured stone-ware inlaid in red/blue clays, border inscribed 'Waste Not Want Not', 34 cm. Sworders, Stansted Mountfitchet. Apr 05. HP: £720. ABP: £846.

883

George Jones majolica sardine dish, printed no. 1848B, 17cm long. Boldon Auction Galleries, Tyne & Wear. Sep 05. HP: £720. ABP: £846.

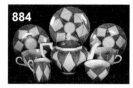

884

Clarice Cliff 'Original Bizarre' tea for two: Athens teapot/cover, side plate, milk jug, sugar basin and 2 globe cups/saucers. (8) Gardiner Houlgate, Corsham. Apr 05. HP: £720. ABP: £846.

885

Clarice Cliff 'Moselle' Bizarre vase, shape 342, 8in. Gardiner Houlgate, Corsham. Apr 05. HP: £720. ABP: £846.

886

Pair of Chinese blue/white porcelain garden seats, pierced top/sides decorated with shaped reserves, 12in dia x 18.5in. Canterbury Auction Galleries, Kent. Oct 05. HP: £720. ABP: £846.

887

Pair of Wedgwood blue Jasperware portrait minia-tures, black frames, imp'd mark. Boldon Auction Galleries, Tyne & Wear. Mar 06. HP: £720. ABP: £846.

888

Ruskin Chinese influence bowl with mottled red glaze and green speckle, three feet, impressed 'Ruskin' England on rear of feet, 20.5cm dia. Reeman Dansie, Colchester. Apr 06. HP: £720. ABP: £846.

889

Royal Doulton figure 'The Mask Seller', HN1361. Louis Taylor, Stoke on Trent. Mar 06. HP: £720. ABP: £846.

890

Troika pottery face mask, decorated by Anne Jones. (small moulding crack). Great Western Auctions, Glasgow. Aug 06. HP: £720. ABP: £846.

891

Satsuma Kinkozan vase, with flowers amongst gilded bamboo, gilded dark blue ground. Gorringes, Lewes. Oct 04. HP: £700. ABP: £823.

892

R. Doulton stoneware vase, by Hannah Barlow, early 20thC, incised with a band of ponies before mountains, 16cm high, impressed factory mark, incised artists initials. Rosebery's, London. Sep 04. HP: £700. ABP: £823.

893

Samson bowl, bronze stand, c1880, figures on terraces, 40cm dia. Sworders, Stansted Mountfitchet. Nov 04. HP: £700. ABP: £823.

894

Burmantofts Faience pottery vase, painted in Iznik style with white flowers on a blue ground, design no 68, signed L.K and numbered 347, 13.25in high. Dee, Atkinson & Harrison, Driffield. Nov 04. HP: £700. ABP: £823.

895

Early Worcester sauceboat, c1762, hexagonal form, body moulded with scrolling cartouches painted in famille rose style, geranium leaf moulded spout, 4.25in long, 2in high. Halls Fine Art, Shrewsbury. Dec 04. HP: £700. ABP: £823.

896

Meissen Turkish soldier, c1900, crossed swords mark and impressed 131 and 407, painted 62, sword sheath damaged, 22cm. Sworders, Stansted Mountfitchet. Feb 05. HP: £700. ABP: £823.

897

19thC pottery water jug by Frank Beardmore & Co, advertising Buchanan's Scotch Whisky Special Red Seal, gilding rubbed, firing crack to handle, 7.5in high. Kent Auction Galleries, Folkestone. Jul 05. HP: £700. ABP: £823.

Hammer: £720 - £700

898

Ercole Barovier, for Barovier & Toso, Murano, Tessere Ambra bowl, designed 1957, this example c1975-, engraved marks to base, 12.5cm. Rosebery's, London. Mar 05. HP: £700. ABP: £823.

899

R. Doulton handmade & decorated figure of the racehorse Desert Orchid No. DA 134, modelled by J G Tongue 1989, 11in high, No. 43 of 7,500. Smiths of Newent, Newent. Apr 05. HP: £700. ABP: £823.

900

George Jones majolica butter dish, swimming duck handle, base moulded with fish, sea-weed and coral, (ducks bill incomplete), 6in. Gorringes, Lewes. Jun 05. HP: £700. ABP: £823.

901

Belleek 'Tridacna' part tea/coffee service, Irish 20thC, characteristic form with pink and gilt rims, tray 40cm. (49) Rosebery's, London. Jun 05. HP: £700. ABP: £823.

902

Pair of early 20thC cream-ware cats, pink lustre splashed animals, green glass eyes matching plinths upon which they sit, 26.5cm high. (D) Cheffins, Cambridge. Apr 05. HP: £700. ABP: £823.

903

Pair of late 19thC Meissen figural candelabra, seasons Autumn & Winter, removable 3 light branches encrusted with flowers, crossed swords marks, 34.5cm high. (D) (4) Cheffins, Cambridge. Apr 05. HP: £700. ABP: £823.

904

Clarice Cliff 'Blue Chintz' Bizarre Lotus jug, 11.5in, minor overpainting to blue bands. Gardiner Houlgate, Corsham. Apr 05. HP: £700. ABP: £823.

905

Belleek porcelain basket with lid, woven sides, rope borders, applied roses & shamrocks, 8.5in wide, impressed mark. Andrew Hartley, Ilkley. Oct 05. HP: £700. ABP: £823.

906

Clarice Cliff Bizarre pottery coffee service for 6 settings in Sunshine pattern, coffee pot 7in. (15) Andrew Hartley, Ilkley. Oct 05. HP: £700. ABP: £823.

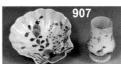

907

Lunds Bristol mustard pot, c1752, painted with exotic bird, and a Worcester famille rose pickle dish. Sworders, Stansted Mountfitchet. Nov 05. HP: £700. ABP: £823.

Hammer: £700 - £680

Doulton bone china coffee cup from the Wardroom of 'Discovery', transfer printed, vignette surrounded by the legend 'Discovery Antarctic Expedition 1901'. Mullock Madeley, Ludlow. Feb 06. HP: £700. ABP: £823.

17thC blue & white Oriental bowl, hardwood stand, seal mark to base, with Dogs of Fo, chrysanthemum leaves etc. Kent Auction Galleries, Folkestone. Feb 06. HP: £700. ABP: £823.

Beswick Sussex Cockerel No 1899, impressed and print mark. Boldon Auction Galleries, Tyne & Wear. Mar 06. HP: £700. ABP: £823.

Royal Doulton figure 'Blossom'. Louis Taylor, Stoke on Trent. Mar 06. HP: £700. ABP: £823.

19thC Staffordshire blue/white pottery 2 handled foot bath, moulded with 3 distinct bands to exterior, printed with view of a Continental town, 21 x 13 x 9.5in high, 6in crack to one side of body. Canterbury Auction Galleries, Kent. Apr 06. HP: £700. ABP: £823.

R. Doulton glazed stoneware vase by George Tinworth, relief-moulded with rosettes, incised with leaves, powder-blue ground, dated 1877, artist's monogram at footrim, 13.5in. Gorringes, Lewes. Apr 06. HP: £700. ABP: £823.

20thC terracotta figure of a lightly draped male archer, square base, moulded square plinth, 76in high. Canterbury Auction Galleries, Kent. Apr 06. HP: £700. ABP: £823.

Chinese pseudo 'Tobacco Leaf' pattern platter, 1770s, bright enamel decoration with gilding, scroll and foliate border, 41cm. Sworders, Stansted Mountfitchet. Apr 06. HP: £700. ABP: £823.

Five early 19thC Spode blue and white tea plates, 'Indian Sporting Series, hog deer at bay'. Cotswold Auction Company, Gloucester. Oct 06. HP: £700. ABP: £823.

Pair of Victorian Minton porcelain figures, in ormolu rococo candlestick mounts, 10in. Gorringes, Lewes. Dec 06. HP: £700. ABP: £823.

Beswick hunting group, Huntsman, shape 1501, leg repair, 5 hounds, and Boy on Pony, shape 1500. Gorringes, Lewes. Apr 07. HP: £700. ABP: £823.

Chinese 'Imari' meat plate, Qianlong, octagonal, painted with a peony & fence pattern 15in, with a set of 4 Chinese 'Imari' side plates, similarly painted, 9in. Gorringes, Lewes. Apr 07. HP: £700. ABP: £823.

Royal Worcester porcelain vase, painted with fruit by C Hughes, gilt embellished, 8in high. Hartleys, Ilkley. Apr 07. HP: £700. ABP: £823.

Pablo Picasso, 1881-1973, a white glazed earthenware plate, modelled with kneeling figure of the God Pan, stamped Empreinte originale de Picasso and Madoura Plein Fell, 9in. Gorringes, Lewes. Jun 07. HP: £700. ABP: £823.

Victorian Copeland parian statuette, 'Go to Sleep' girl seated with terrier, after J. Durham, pub'd by the Art Union of London, impressed marks, date code 1881, 17.75in. Gorringes, Lewes. Oct 04. HP: £680. ABP: £799.

Moorcroft 2 handled vase of Carp pattern, green background, 33cm, WM monogram etc. Boldon Auction Galleries, Tyne & Wear. Sep 04. HP: £680. ABP: £799.

The numbering system acts as a reader reference as well as linking to the Analysis of each section.

Beswick 'Seagull on a rock', model number 768, 8.5in, beak restored. Louis Taylor, Stoke on Trent. Mar 05. HP: £680. ABP: £799.

Staffordshire pearlware figure of Nelson, early 19thC, standing before a cannon, pink lustre splash base, 31cm high. Rosebery's, London. Mar 05. HP: £680. ABP: £799.

926

Pair Doulton Lambeth vases by Frank A Butler, 1884, sgraffito foliate scrolling decoration and raised floral medallions, imp'd marks F. A. B & A. O. (A. Orchin) rosette mark 1884, No. 964, 23.5cm high. Sworders, Stansted Mountfitchet. Apr 05. HP: £680. ABP: £799.

927

Royal Worcester porcelain figure of Mill Reef, by Doris Lindner, 29.5cm high, black backstamp, leather framed certificate, No. 368/500. Bearne's, Exeter. Jun 05. HP: £680. ABP: £799.

928

Imari basin, c1875, decorated in enamels and gilding with sparrows, flowers and diaper, 45.2cm. Sworders, Stansted Mountfitchet. Nov 05. HP: £680. ABP: £799.

929

Lloyds Staffordshire porcelain figure, leopard and her cub, 4.5in wide, 19thC. Andrew Hartley, Ilkley. Apr 06. HP: £680. ABP: £799.

930

Beswick figure modelled as a Canadian Mountie, on black horse, 8in high, white mark. Andrew Hartley, Ilkley. Apr 06. HP: £680. ABP: £799.

931

Victorian parian figure group of a 'kneeling angel with two embracing putto', after John Hancock c1855, 59cm high. Rosebery's, London. Mar 06. HP: £680. ABP: £799.

932

Goldscheider pottery art deco figure, lady holding her skirts in one hand and roses in the other, oval base, 12.5in high, No.7958. Hartleys, Ilkley. Jun 06. HP: £680. ABP: £799.

933

Edwardian cricket mug printed in red and white with England and Australia cricketers in cartouches, inscribed with 1905 Australia-England, 10.5cm high. Cotswold Auction Co, Gloucester. Oct 06. HP: £680. ABP: £799.

934

Pair Heubach bisque figures, lady & gentleman in Edwardian dress, holding a metal bicycle, rubber shod wheels, gilt embellished, ebonised bases, one with dome, 14.5in high. Andrew Hartley, Ilkley. Apr 05. HP: £675. ABP: £793.

Hammer: £680 - £660

935

Rare early 19thC Brameld pottery castle keep, c1820, 'Connisburgh Castle', 9.75in high. Dee, Atkinson & Harrison, Driffield. Sep 05. HP: £670. ABP: £788.

936

Doulton Lambeth gilded silicon ware mouse group by George Tinworth, 4in. (chips) Louis Taylor, Stoke on Trent. Jun 04. HP: £660. ABP: £776.

937

Pair of Clarice Cliff pottery vases, ribbed form, painted in Forest Glen pattern, 4in high. Andrew Hartley, Ilkley. Feb 05. HP: £660. ABP: £776.

938

Minton secessionist pottery charger, tube lined, white water lilies on petrol blue & purple ground, 15in, printed mark. Andrew Hartley, Ilkley. Feb 05. HP: £660. ABP: £776.

939

Beswick dairy shorthorn bull 'Ch Gwersylt Lord Oxford 74th', 5in. Louis Taylor, Stoke on Trent. Mar 05. HP: £660. ABP: £776.

940

Beswick figure of a Spanish Lipizzaner dressage horse with rider. Denhams, Warnham, Sussex. Apr 06. HP: £660. ABP: £776.

941

Goldscheider green/brown painted terracotta bust of a young woman, 27.5in high, moulded octagonal mark 'Fr. Goldscheider Wien', slight damage. Canterbury Auction Galleries, Kent. Apr 06. HP: £660. ABP: £776.

942

R. Worcester figure by Doris Linder titled 'Galloping Horses', pattern No 3466, wooden base. Great Western Auctions, Glasgow. Jul 06. HP: £660. ABP: £776.

943

Coalport Lady Anne blue bordered dinner service. (109) Ewbank Auctioneers, Send, Surrey. Dec 06. HP: £660. ABP: £776.

944

R. Dux porcelain group of a charioteer & rearing horses, gilt embellished, 16.25in wide, printed mark. Hartleys, Ilkley. Apr 07. HP: £660. ABP: £776.

Hammer: £650

945

Set of 24 R. Doulton figures 'Dicken's Characters', each bearing green printed mark, approx 11cm high. Locke & England, Leamington Spa. Sep 04. HP: £650. ABP: £764.

946

Art Deco Rosenthal porcelain figure, exotic dancer wearing snake charmer costume with snake in basket, 22cm high, factory printed marks, with similar figure. Rosebery's, London. Sep 04. HP: £650. ABP: £764.

947

Dutch Delft plate, 17thC, painted in blue/mustard with a portrait of William and initialled WR within a foliate painted fluted border, 22cm dia. Rosebery's, London. Sep 04. HP: £650. ABP: £764.

948

C.H. Brannam pottery 'comical cat', glass eyes, applied chocolate/rust/green slips on mustard ground, incised C.H. Brannam, Barum, 1911, 34cm. Bearne's, Exeter. Jun 05. HP: £650. ABP: £764.

949

Victorian blue/white pottery footbath, printed with scenes of pagodas, buildings and foliage, 44cm wide. Rosebery's, London. Sep 04. HP: £650. ABP: £764.

950

Moorcroft vase, 'Pomegranate', design, painted signature and impressed marks, 8.5in. Gorringes, Lewes. Dec 04. HP: £650. ABP: £764.

951

Kraak ware blue and white charger, 18thC, 39cm. Gorringes, Bexhill. Dec 04. HP: £650. ABP: £764.

952

English Delft drug jar, c1700, inscribed 'C. AURANT.' on a label, surmounted by cupids and a shell above tassels and swags, chip to lip, cracked, 18cm. Sworders, Stansted Mountfitchet. Feb 05. HP: £650. ABP: £764.

953

MacIntyre teapot and hot water jug. Gorringes, Bexhill. Apr 05. HP: £650. ABP: £764.

954

William Moorcroft pottery vase by Sally Tuffin, tube lined in the eagle owl design, No. 69/500, painted signature, imp'd marks, 31cm. Sworders, Stansted Mountfitchet. Apr 05. HP: £650. ABP: £764.

955

Large pair of Kutani baluster vases, decorated with dragons and shishi, 21in. Gorringes, Lewes. Jun 05. HP: £650. ABP: £764.

> The illustrations are in descending price order. The price range is indicated at the top of each page.

956

Mid Victorian Moore's tazza, oval leaf bowl, rustic stem applied with hops, amorini to one end playing a lyre and the other a cello, printed mark, 30cm high. Cheffins, Cambridge. Apr 05. HP: £650. ABP: £764.

957

Martin brothers stoneware twin handled vase decorated with flowers, brown ground, incised factory marks, 9.25in high. Gardiner Houlgate, Corsham. Apr 05. HP: £650. ABP: £764.

958

Pearlware jug, printed and painted with various cartoon people in conversation with balloon captions, inscribed, 'Bonapart Dethron'd. April 1st 1814', 13.5cm, hair crack to spout. Bearne's, Exeter. Jun 05. HP: £650. ABP: £764.

959

Spode Copeland 'Nelson Centenary 1905', Ltd. Edn. loving cup, printed/painted with roundels depicting Nelson, Britannia and H.M.S Victory, No 97 of 100, 6in high. Dee, Atkinson & Harrison, Driffield. Sep 05. HP: £650. ABP: £764.

960

Belleek basket, in the form of petals, handle as entwined stems, black-printed mark, 8.25in. Gorringes, Lewes. Nov 05. HP: £650. ABP: £764.

961

Pair of Royal Doulton vases by Eliza Simmance. Henry Adams, Chichester. Dec 05. HP: £650. ABP: £764.

962

Coalport dessert service: 8 9in plates and comport, each painted with a lake, named verso, pattern X 2289. Gorringes, Lewes. Feb 06. HP: £650. ABP: £764.

963

Mintons parian figure 'Una and the Lion', English 19thC, female nude seated on a lion, restored, with Minton figure 'Ariadne & Panther', 37cm & 36cm. Rosebery's, London. Dec 05. HP: £650. ABP: £764.

964

Chinese Famille Verte two handled vase/cover, decorated with figures & shi shi dogs, 17.5cm. Charterhouse Auctioneers, Sherborne. Feb 06. HP: £650. ABP: £764.

965

Porcelain plaque, early 20thC, painted by E Dean, signed, sheep on the fells, 22.5 x 35cm. Sworders, Stansted Mountfitchet. Feb 06. HP: £650. ABP: £764.

966

Collection of nine half dolls, 3.75in to 5.5in high, five marked foreign, restoration to hands. Kent Auction Galleries, Folkestone. Jan 06. HP: £650. ABP: £764.

967

Zsolnay Pecs ewer, painted with 2 pheasants and flowers, printed marks in blue, 14in. Gorringes, Lewes. Apr 06. HP: £650. ABP: £764.

968

Dame Lucie Rie, Art Pottery, brown glazed side handled pouring vessel and lid, 6in. Denhams, Warnham, Sussex. Nov 05. HP: £650. ABP: £764.

969

Royal Doulton figure, Butterfly, HN1456. Gorringes, Lewes. Mar 06. HP: £650. ABP: £764.

970

Chinese plate, Qianlong period, painted with female figures in a garden in underglaze blue, 10in. Gorringes, Lewes. Mar 06. HP: £650. ABP: £764.

971

Clarice Cliff 'Trees and House' pattern vase. Henry Adams, Chichester. Oct 06. HP: £650. ABP: £764.

972

Royal Copenhagen group, rock and waves, modelled as a nude couple embracing on a rock, 18.5in. Gorringes, Lewes. Feb 07. HP: £650. ABP: £764.

Hammer: £650 - £640

973

Shelley Vogue Turkish Blue Blocks pattern tea service. Charterhouse Auctioneers, Sherborne. Oct 06. HP: £650. ABP: £764.

974

Ginori wall plaque, painted with cherubs, a caryatid and flowers in renaissance style, painted mark, No. 235 - 1/52 20.75in, rivet-repaired. Gorringes, Lewes. Apr 07. HP: £650. ABP: £764.

975

Pair Worcester ivory porcelain figures, water carriers, gilded, Eastern style dress, dated 1923/4, 17in high, No.594. Hartleys, Ilkley. Apr 07. HP: £650. ABP: £764.

976

Large Royal Doulton figure of St George, HN2067, 16in, restoration to base. Gorringes, Lewes. Jun 07. HP: £650. ABP: £764.

977

Beswick 'Knight in Armour', The Earl of Warwick', 10.75in, restoration. Louis Taylor, Stoke on Trent. Jun 05. HP: £640. ABP: £752.

978

Clarice Cliff Bizarre ware charger, oval dished centre, painted with a temple, 16.25in wide, 'Biarritz' printed black mark. Andrew Hartley, Ilkley. Jun 05. HP: £640. ABP: £752.

979

Dresden porcelain plaque, c1880, lady clasping her hands and wearing a veil, velvet mounted frame, 17.5 x 12cm. Sworders, Stansted Mountfitchet. Jul 05. HP: £640. ABP: £752.

980

Beswick Huntsman, Huntswomen, five hounds and a fox (fox with chip to left ear). Boldon Auction Galleries, Tyne & Wear. Sep 05. HP: £640. ABP: £752.

981

18thC Chinese export blue/white double gourd-shaped vase, painted floral decoration, 22cm. Reeman Dansie, Colchester. Apr 06. HP: £640. ABP: £752.

982

R. Worcester porcelain teapot, leaf capped gilded loop handle, painted with peaches, grapes and blackberries by Smith, 8.25in wide, black mark. Hartleys, Ilkley. Feb 07. HP: £640. ABP: £752.

Hammer: £625 - £600

Victorian Royal Worcester majolica vase, conch shell supported by swan, 8.5in, chips. Gorringes, Lewes. Oct 06. HP: £625. ABP: £736.

Capo di Monte convex porcelain wall plaque, moulded in relief, painted with a battle scene, gilt tooled leather frame, plaque 50cm dia. Rosebery's, London. Jun 04. HP: £620. ABP: £729.

Royal Worcester porcelain Highland Bull, modelled by Doris Lindner, Ltd. Edn. No. 45, 8.5in high, certificate. Andrew Hartley, Ilkley. Jun 04. HP: £620. ABP: £729.

Pair of Staffordshire treacle glazed lions, moulded oblong base, 19thC, 12in wide. Andrew Hartley, Ilkley. Aug 04. HP: £620. ABP: £729.

Jardinière/stand, c1800, poss. Chamberlain, red classical gilt work & borders, lion mask handles, 13.7cm. Sworders, Stansted Mountfitchet. Feb 05. HP: £620. ABP: £729.

Minton majolica game pie tureen, cover and liner, 1863, in form of a basket with dead game on lid, impressed marks and date code, liner cracked 31.5cm long. Sworders, Stansted Mountfitchet. Feb 05. HP: £620. ABP: £729.

19thC English porcelain patchbox, lid decorated with Britannia and bust on plinth, inscribed 'In Memory of Nelson'. Locke & England, Leamington Spa. May 05. HP: £620. ABP: £729.

Minton dessert service. Henry Adams, Chichester. Dec 05. HP: £620. ABP: £729.

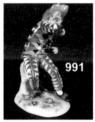

Meissen model of Harlequin, German 20thC, propped against a tree stump, base modelled with flowers. 17cm high. Rosebery's, London. Dec 05. HP: £620. ABP: £729.

Doulton Burslem Holbein-ware jardiniere, probably by Walter Nunn, 13.25in high, 'The Brothers Pet'. Louis Taylor, Stoke on Trent. Jun 06. HP: £620. ABP: £729.

Martinware stoneware four handled vase, angled faces incised with finches on flowering branches, incised mark 'R.W. Martin & Bros., London & Southall' and dated 2-85, 11in high. Canterbury Auction Galleries, Kent. Dec 05. HP: £620. ABP: £729.

Beswick figure 'Lifeguard', rider holding a flag, 9.5in high. Andrew Hartley, Ilkley. Apr 06. HP: £620. ABP: £729.

Worcester mug, printed in black by Robert Hancock, portrait of King of Prussia, trophies & figure of fame, 4.5in, printed initials RH, inscribed Worcester, dated 1757, and with anchor of Rebus for Holdship. Ewbank Auctioneers, Send, Surrey. Dec 06. HP: £620. ABP: £729.

Chinese blue/white porcelain tea caddy, silvery metal mounts/cover, with Long Eliza figures, flowerhead finial, 6.25in high. (Kangxi period) Canterbury Auction Galleries, Kent. Jun 07. HP: £620. ABP: £729.

8 19thC brown glazed stoneware tobacco jars by H.F. & S., London, labelled with names of tobaccos, japanned metal covers, 9.5in high, one cracked, some lids opening at seamed joints. Canterbury Auction Galleries, Kent. Jun 07. HP: £620. ABP: £729.

Burgess & Leigh Burleigh Ware toby jug, Winston Churchill dressed as John Bull, plinth inscribed 'Bulldogs', impressed John Bull Churchill 1940 and 'We shall defend....' etc, 11in. Louis Taylor, Stoke on Trent. Mar 06. HP: £610. ABP: £717.

Royal Worcester porcelain figure, Brahman Bull, by Doris Lindner, Ltd. Edn. No. 401, 8.5in high, certificate. Andrew Hartley, Ilkley. Jun 04. HP: £600. ABP: £705.

Pair of Royal Doulton fox hounds. Brettells, Newport, Shropshire. Sep 04. HP: £600. ABP: £705.

Canton jug/basin set, figures and garden settings against a typical ground of flowers and insects, bowl 14.75in. Gorringes, Lewes. Oct 04. HP: £600. ABP: £705.

1002

Kang Hsi 'An Hua' decorated bowl, 2 dragons chasing a pearl, M.H. Soames collection label, 5.25in. Gorringes, Lewes. Jul 04. HP: £600. ABP: £705.

1003

Collection of child's creamware, 19thC, mostly Wedgwood, some damage, approx 50 pieces. Sworders, Stansted Mountfitchet. Feb 05. HP: £600. ABP: £705.

1004

Bow sauce boat c1747, three lion mask feet, flying loop handle, painted in Kakiemon palette, diaper border, feet damaged, 21cm. Sworders, Stansted Mountfitchet. Feb 05. HP: £600. ABP: £705.

> Categories or themes can be followed through the colour coded Index which contains over 4500 cross references.

1005

Novelty TC Brown Westhead, Moore & Co, majolica desk stand, c1870, terrier's head flanked by two inkwells and pen tray, impressed motto, 11.5in. Gorringes, Lewes. Mar 05. HP: £600. ABP: £705.

1006

Worcester butterboat, painted with the 'Butterboat Formal Rose' pattern in underglaze blue, open crescent mark, 3.5in. Gorringes, Lewes. Apr 05. HP: £600. ABP: £705.

1007

Chelsea figural sweetmeat dish, Red Anchor period, 1752-56, Turk in full-length robe, 6.25in, restoration. Gorringes, Lewes. Apr 05. HP: £600. ABP: £705.

1008

Beswick dairy shorthorn cow, 'Ch Eaton Wildeyes 91st', 4.75in. slight restoration. Louis Taylor, Stoke. Mar 05. HP: £600. ABP: £705.

1009

William Morris tile, c1860/70, in Tulip and Trellis pattern, 15.5cm square. Sworders, Stansted Mountfitchet. Apr 05. HP: £600. ABP: £705.

1010

Pair of Doulton Lambeth faience vases, c1900, poppies against an orange, crimson & purple background, monograms HK & MW, No. '99' printed mark, 29cm. Sworders, Stansted Mountfitchet. Apr 05. HP: £600. ABP: £705.

1011

Pair of Royal Dux figures of a lady and gentleman, 53.5cm high, damage. Henry Adams, Chichester. Jun 05. HP: £600. ABP: £705.

Hammer: £600

1012

Bow octagonal plate painted with cherries, butterfly and insects, 22cm wide. (D) Cheffins, Cambridge. Apr 05. HP: £600. ABP: £705.

1013

Wemyss pig, 20thC, on its haunches with sponged black patches, pink detail to ears, nose and feet, 6in long. Halls Fine Art, Shrewsbury. Jul 05. HP: £600. ABP: £705.

1014

Pair of mid 19thC Meissen candlesticks, sea scroll columns supported by figures allegorical of the seasons, one with a lady, the other a man. Kent Auction Galleries, Folkestone. Jul 05. HP: £600. ABP: £705.

1015

Clarice Cliff tea set, Crocus design. Stride & Son, Chichester. Jul 05. HP: £600. ABP: £705.

1016

Doulton Lambeth charger by James Cruickshank, painted with a profile portrait of a pre-raphaelite female, 16in. Gorringes, Lewes. Sep 05. HP: £600. ABP: £705.

1017

Grainger & Co, Worcester vase, two-handled, moulded detail, painted with grazing sheep & scenic background, cover, date code 1900, 10.75in. Gorringes, Lewes. Sep 05. HP: £600. ABP: £705.

1018

Burmantofts faience vase, moulded and tube lined with persian flowers, 18in high, No.2063. Andrew Hartley, Ilkley. Oct 05. HP: £600. ABP: £705.

1019

18thC delftware flower brick, pierced top, sides with blue flowers, block feet, 5in long. Gorringes, Lewes. Nov 05. HP: £600. ABP: £705.

1020

19thC Continental Maiolica drug jug with a portrait of a lady with cartouche's and scrolling flowers, 23cm high. Boldon Auction Galleries, Tyne & Wear. Nov 05. HP: £600. ABP: £705.

1021

Pair Coalport dessert dishes, scallop shape with gilded shell handles, each painted with fruit and flowers against a gilded buff border, c1820-25, 8.5in. Gorringes, Lewes. Feb 06. HP: £600. ABP: £705.

Hammer: £600

Imari porcelain dish, flared sides, painted with a lady presenting a scroll to a warrior, 19thC, 19.5in wide. Andrew Hartley, Ilkley. Dec 05. HP: £600. ABP: £705.

18thC creamware commemorative mug, 1792, with the British merchant ship 'Brazen' in full sail, initialled AMI, dated, 5in. Gorringes, Lewes. Apr 05. HP: £600. ABP: £705.

18thC delftware cress dish, concave pierced top, painted with islands and foliage in blue in Chinese style, 8.75in. Gorringes, Lewes. Apr 05. HP: £600. ABP: £705.

Minton majolica jardiniere, turquoise glazed body with moulded fruit and vegetable ribbon tied garlands, interior pink glazed, 41cm high. Rosebery's, London. Mar 06. HP: £600. ABP: £705.

Victorian Minton majolica Lazy Susan, moulded with fleurs-de-lis and plants, revolving on domed pedestal base, top 18in. Gorringes, Lewes. Apr 06. HP: £600. ABP: £705.

Chamber pot, inside the bowl is a cartoon of Adolf Hitler and around the edge is the invitation to 'Have this on Old Nasty', side printed 'No 1 Jerry', base is musical box which plays Rule Britannia. 21.5cm dia. Wallis & Wallis, Lewes. Feb 06. HP: £600. ABP: £705.

19thC Imari vase and domed cover, painted with birds and flowers in iron-red, underglaze blue and gilt, 28.5in, neck damaged. Gorringes, Lewes. Apr 06. HP: £600. ABP: £705.

> **Prices quoted are actual hammer prices (HP) and the Approximate Buyer's Price (ABP) includes an average premium of 15% + VAT.**

Charles Brannam terracotta vase, high triangular handles, incised with fish in shades of green, 13in high, mark dated 1898. Andrew Hartley, Ilkley. Apr 06. HP: £600. ABP: £705.

18thC Ligurian wet drug jar, tin-glazed and painted with a border of rabbits and fruit in blue, 7.75in. Gorringes, Lewes. Jun 06. HP: £600. ABP: £705.

Wilkinson Ltd. character jug, Earl Kitchener of Khartoum, 10in. Gorringes, Lewes. Jun 06. HP: £600. ABP: £705.

Burmantofts faience jardiniere on stand, frilled rim, moulded with panels of sunflowers, 37.5in high, No.1947B and 1948B. Hartleys, Ilkley. Jun 06. HP: £600. ABP: £705.

Minton pottery plaque with a portrait of a young lady with startled look, gilded ground, impressed mark, 15.75in wide. Hartleys, Ilkley. Aug 06. HP: £600. ABP: £705.

Royal Doulton figure, Negligee, HN1228. Gorringes, Lewes. Mar 06. HP: £600. ABP: £705.

Beswick Jemima Puddleduck wall plaque, introduced 1967 and withdrawn 1969, 6in. Louis Taylor, Stoke. Sep 06. HP: £600. ABP: £705.

Italian maiolica wet drug jar, late 16thC, prob. Montelupo, loop and mask handle, label 'A.D.ACCETOSSA' above a yellow crest flanked with initials G C, extensively damaged, 34.5cm. Sworders, Stansted Mountfitchet. Apr 06. HP: £600. ABP: £705.

Clarice Cliff Sunray Bizarre pattern bowl, printed marks, 20.5cm. Sworders, Stansted Mountfitchet. Apr 06. HP: £600. ABP: £705.

Early Moorcroft vase, pomegranate and grape pattern, signed and dated 1912, hole drilled in centre of base, 6.5in. Gorringes, Lewes. Dec 06. HP: £600. ABP: £705.

New Hall coffee pot, painted with flower sprays, domed cover, pattern 241, 9.75in. Gorringes, Lewes. Feb 07. HP: £600. ABP: £705.

Lladro 'Country Woman' Aldeana Hebrea figurine, sculptor Alfredo Ruiz, issued 1965, 15.25in. Kent Auction Galleries, Folkestone. Feb 07. HP: £600. ABP: £705.

1041

Beswick Dairy Shorthorn bull, mould 1504, Champion 'Gwersylt Lord Oxford 74th', 1957-73. Gorringes, Lewes. Feb 07. HP: £600. ABP: £705.

1042

Set of 4 early 19thC earthen ware furniture rests, possibly Thomas Fell, Newcastle, painted with flowers against a sponged green ground, 3in high. Gorringes, Lewes. Apr 07. HP: £600. ABP: £705.

1043

Joseph Holdcroft majolica jardiniere, branch handles, moulded with swimming fish and aquatic plants against a deep-blue ground, impressed mark, 18in long, rivet-repaired. Gorringes, Lewes. Apr 07. HP: £600. ABP: £705.

1044

Clarice Cliff Moonlight pattern conical sifter, 5.5in. Gorringes, Lewes. Jun 07. HP: £600. ABP: £705.

1045

Wedgwood flower basket and cover, 2 leaf handles, glazed in green and deep brown, impressed mark, c1790, 10in. Gorringes, Lewes. Jul 04. HP: £580. ABP: £682.

1046

Garniture of 3 Royal Crown Derby vases, 1908, painted with a coloured flower spray, gilt highlights, tallest 16.5cm high. Sworders, Stansted Mountfitchet. Nov 04. HP: £580. ABP: £682.

1047

Moorcroft 'Waving Corn' geometric pattern vase, impressed factory marks and 'POTTER TO HM THE QUEEN', painted signature, 16cm high. Cheffins, Cambridge. Feb 05. HP: £580. ABP: £682.

1048

Pair Minton majolica magpies c1870, after Meissen originals, impressed marks, date code, restoration, 53cm. Sworders, Stansted Mountfitchet. Feb 05. HP: £580. ABP: £682.

1049

Beswick Connoisseur Series Arab stallion with saddle, model 2269, 9.5in. Louis Taylor, Stoke on Trent. Mar 05. HP: £580. ABP: £682.

1050

Clarice Cliff 'Applique Lucerne' Bizarre Globe cup and saucer. Gardiner Houlgate, Corsham. Apr 05. HP: £580. ABP: £682.

Hammer: £600 - £580

1051

Joseph Holdcroft majolica teapot c1880, chinaman wearing blue/yellow robes on a coconut, spout repaired, black painted 'J' to base, 5.5in. Halls Fine Art, Shrewsbury. Mar 05. HP: £580. ABP: £682.

1052

Troika Moon vase, circular flower design, signed, initialled HC for Honor Curtis, nee Perkins, 16cm, and a Troika Moon vase, circular black panels, signed, 13cm. Sworders, Stansted Mountfitchet. Apr 05. HP: £580. ABP: £682.

1053

Pair Chinese Canton garden seats, painted with birds and pink flowers, turquoise grounds, 44.5cm high. (D) Cheffins, Cambridge. Apr 05. HP: £580. ABP: £682.

1054

Famille rose dish, seal mark, period of Xianfeng, shaped/canted square dish with a dragon clutching a flaming pearl, 13cm wide. Cheffins, Cambridge. Apr 05. HP: £580. ABP: £682.

1055

Beswick set of Alice in Wonderland figures. (11) Louis Taylor, Stoke. Dec 05. HP: £580. ABP: £682.

1056

Derby porcelain stirrup cup as the head of a trout, 5in, unmarked, restored, and a late Staffordshire pottery figure of 'Jumbo', seated figure of an elephant, 6.5in high. Canterbury Auction Galleries, Kent. Oct 05. HP: £580. ABP: £682.

1057

William De Morgan ruby lustre twin handled vase, late Fulham period, painted by J.Hersey with a scene of a sea serpent and eagle in conflict, imp'd 'Sands End' mark, blue painted mark 'Fulham and JH monogram & 2275' J.H 9, 26cm. (AF) Rosebery's, London. Mar 06. HP: £580. ABP: £682.

1058

Pilkington's orange glazed ginger jar decorated with running birds by C E Cundall, impressed Made in England, 5in. Denhams, Warnham, Sussex. Sep 05. HP: £580. ABP: £682.

1059

Brantjes, Purmerend pottery vase, c1900, decorated with art nouveau stylised lilies, painted mark, No 510, 26cm. Sworders, Stansted Mountfitchet. Apr 06. HP: £580. ABP: £682.

Early Meissen figure of a lady seated at her household accounts. Cotswold Auction Company, Cirencester. Aug 04. HP: £570. ABP: £670.

Beswick figure of a Sussex Cockerel, model no 1899, by Arthur Gredington, 7in high, issued 1963-1971. Golding Young & Co, Grantham. Feb 06. HP: £570. ABP: £670.

Pair Weymss pottery candlesticks painted with black cockerels, impressed mark Weymss ware RM & S, 11.75in high. Andrew Hartley, Ilkley. Feb 05. HP: £560. ABP: £658.

Pair of Minton Seccessionist ware vases of trumpet form, slip trailed with green and yellow art nouveau scrolling on a red ground, 10in high. Andrew Hartley, Ilkley. Jun 05. HP: £560. ABP: £658.

First Period Worcester teapot (15.5cm high) and cover with matching cup/saucer in coloured enamels teapot fretted square marks, c1775, glue repair to flower knop. Bearne's, Exeter. Jun 05. HP: £560. ABP: £658.

William De Morgan Pottery tile, decorated with two large blue Persian carnations, 8.25in square. Losses. Fieldings, Stourbridge. Oct 05. HP: £560. ABP: £658.

Moorcroft Macintyre florian ware forget-me-not pattern, hot water jug & cream jug. John Taylors, Louth. Nov 05. HP: £560. ABP: £658.

> The numbering system acts as a reader reference as well as linking to the Analysis of each section.

Doulton Lambeth stoneware jug by Hannah Barlow, incised zig-zag neck and loop handle, sgraffito with hares, 8in high. Andrew Hartley, Ilkley. Dec 05. HP: £560. ABP: £658.

Early R. Doulton Bunnykins pottery figure 'Farmer Bunnykins', green smock, carrying a walking stick, 7.5in high. (D.6003, printed mark to base and impressed 8304, right ear damaged/restuck. Canterbury Auction Galleries, Kent. Dec 05. HP: £560. ABP: £658.

Early 19thC Mason's Ironstone china teaware, Chinese-style floral/fence decoration: teapot, lid and stand, tall milk jug, slop bowl, sucrier and lid and five cups. (12) Reeman Dansie, Colchester. Apr 06. HP: £560. ABP: £658.

Goldscheider Art Deco style figure of a young girl with parasol, 8in. Louis Taylor, Stoke on Trent. Mar 06. HP: £560. ABP: £658.

Dame Lucie Rie, Art Pottery side handled pouring vessel, brown glazed interior, 5in. Denhams, Warnham, Sussex. Nov 05. HP: £560. ABP: £658.

Ming green glazed terracotta ridge tile, horse sejant, 10.5in. Gorringes, Lewes. Jul 04. HP: £550. ABP: £646.

Wilkinson Ltd character jug, Edward VII, after a design by Franci Caruthers Gould, titled 'Pro Pattia', 30.5cm high. Rosebery's, London. Sep 04. HP: £550. ABP: £646.

Pair 18thC Worcester fruit baskets with underglazed blue pine-cone pattern. John Taylors, Louth. Jun 04. HP: £550. ABP: £646. .

Swansea cup/saucer painted with floral bouquets in salmon pink panels on a rich blue ground, early Victorian period. Cotswold Auction Company, Cirencester. Aug 04. HP: £550. ABP: £646.

Ruskin lustre vase, stylised thistles on a yellow ground, 12in high. Cotswold Auction Company, Cirencester. Aug 04. HP: £550. ABP: £646.

Minton majolica twin-handled vase, H 54.5cm Gorringes, Bexhill. Sep 04. HP: £550. ABP: £646.

Four Wemyss plates, early 20thC, painted with bee hive and bees, plums, gooseberries and apple, impressed marks, retailers printed mark in blue and black, T. Goode - London, 14cm dia. Hampton & Littlewood, Exeter. Jul 04. HP: £550. ABP: £646.

Macintyre 2 handled footed bowl, c1903, 'Alhambra' pattern, designed by William Moorcroft, brown printed mark, 18cm high. Rosebery's, London. Mar 05. HP: £550. ABP: £646.

Wemyss heart shaped tray with yellow chrysanthemum, a/f, impressed mark 'Wemyss Ware R.H.S.' 12in long. Tring Market Auctions, Herts. Apr 05. HP: £550. ABP: £646.

Pair of Wedgwood pottery lustre vases, yellow/blue ground with gilt enriched butterfly decoration, 8.5in high. Clarke Gammon Wellers, Guildford. Apr 05. HP: £550. ABP: £646.

Charlotte Rhead orange pattern bowl, 8.5in dia. Kivell & Sons, Bude. Dec 05. HP: £550. ABP: £646.

Pair Chamberlain's Worcester sauce tureens/covers, English early 19thC, domed cover surmounted by dolphin finial, bowl supported by three gilt dolphins, triform base, covers restored, 23cm high. Rosebery's, London. Jun 05. HP: £550. ABP: £646.

Seven small Rye items, 4 with Sussex Rustic Ware marks, 3 with additional pin-dust mark, green-glazed, 5 with applied white floral reliefs and two monochrome, and a pair of Rye green baskets, incised to bases, 'Rye 1900', baskets: 7.5cm high tallest & 9cm dia. Gorringes, Bexhill. Dec 05. HP: £550. ABP: £646.

Rare 18thC creamware pounce pot/pin stand, pierced top, flowers in mauve enamel, 2.5in Gorringes, Lewes. Apr 05. HP: £550. ABP: £646.

Troika Pottery 'Anvil' vase produced c1973-79, decorated by Avril Bennet, textured brown ground, painted mark 'Troika England', decorators monogram AB, 23.5cm high. Rosebery's, London. Mar 06. HP: £550. ABP: £646.

Pair Royal Worcester biscuit porcelain figures of chinamen, 'Le Panier' & 'L'Oiseau', by A. Azori, 32cm high, and another entitled 'Le Miroir'. Rosebery's, London. Mar 06. HP: £550. ABP: £646.

Chamberlain's Worcester armorial side plate, shield within wreath (6.5in.) and a matching plate, Kerr & Binns period, latter cracked. Gorringes, Lewes. Jun 07. HP: £550. ABP: £646.

Hammer: £550 - £540

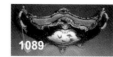

Coalport Hampton 2-handled bowl, stylized birds in landscape, gilt reserves, signed W. Waterson, early 20thC, 13in wide. Golding Young & Co, Grantham. Feb 06. HP: £550. ABP: £646.

George Jones majolica strawberry dish, moulded in four lobed sections with leaves & coloured flowers, stalk feet, PODR 1872, pair of ladles ensuite, dish 11.5in, a ladle damaged. Gorringes, Lewes. Jun 06. HP: £550. ABP: £646.

Wemyss preserve pot/cover, painted with greengages plums, impressed mark and T. Goode & Co oval stamp, 5in. Gorringes, Lewes. Jul 06. HP: £550. ABP: £646.

Morrisware vase, designed by George Cartlidge c1905, stylised thistle design, facsimile signature 29.5cm. Sworders, Stansted Mountfitchet. Apr 06. HP: £550. ABP: £646.

Beswick Hunt Group: Huntsman on Grey, Lady Rider on grey, 7 Hounds & Fox. Kent Auction Galleries, Folkestone. Mar 07. HP: £550. ABP: £646.

Goldscheider, female dancer designed by Stefan Dakon, printed in mauve and black, white-glazed, imp'd factory mark, designer's facsimile signature, restoration to one ankle, 15.5in. Gorringes, Lewes. Feb 07. HP: £550. ABP: £646.

19thC Chinese pottery vase/ cover, applied relief moulded wading bird amongst water lilies and bullrushes, dog of fo finial, moulded seal mark to base of Wang Binrong (1820-1860), 12.5in. Golding Young & Co, Grantham. Nov 06. HP: £550. ABP: £646.

Royal Worcester 'Appaloosa Stallion' by Doris Lindner No. 481, with certificate. Boldon Auction Galleries, Tyne & Wear. Sep 04. HP: £540. ABP: £635.

Crown Devon coffee set in Art Deco style, 15 pieces for six-place setting, enamelled in green, orange and black with gilding, one cup cracked, coffee pot 8in. Gorringes, Lewes. Mar 05. HP: £540. ABP: £635.

Hammer: £540 - £520

Pair Derby porcelain dwarf figures advertising Theatre Royal Haymarket, and Spike Hall, late 19thC, 7in high. Andrew Hartley, Ilkley. Jun 05. HP: £540. ABP: £635.

Beswick Pottery trotting shire horse, dappled grey, 8.5in high. Andrew Hartley, Ilkley, W Yorks. Feb 06. HP: £540. ABP: £635.

Spode bone china, Ltd. Edn. memorial vase/cover, made to commemorate the death of Sir Winston Churchill in 1965, reverse with extract from his 'We shall not flag or fail' speech, 97/125, 14in. Louis Taylor, Stoke on Trent. Mar 06. HP: £540. ABP: £635.

Pair of early 19thC Stafford-shire pottery figures, Young women, 6.5in high, one imp'd to underside '19', restoration, flaking of enamel. Canterbury Auction Galleries, Kent. Apr 06. HP: £540. ABP: £635.

William Moorcroft pottery vase, tube lined, Pomegranate design with fruit & leaves, but no berries, 4in high, imp'd No. 1645. Hartleys, Ilkley. Oct 06. HP: £540. ABP: £635.

Pair R. Worcester blush ivory porcelain vases, enamelled in colours by K. Blake with black berries & flowers, 6in high, printed marks in lilac to base, shape No. G923, date code 11.54. Canterbury Auction Galleries, Kent. Jun 07. HP: £540. ABP: £635.

Pair of Minton porcelain dishes painted by J. E. Dean, 8.25in dia. Louis Taylor, Stoke on Trent. Dec 04. HP: £530. ABP: £623.

Royal Worcester 'Stroller and Marion Coates' by Doris Lindner No 520, with certificate. Boldon Auction Galleries, Tyne & Wear. Sep 04. HP: £525. ABP: £617.

Pair Wedgwood, blue jasper-ware twin handled vases and covers, early 19thC, applied laurel wreath swags and panels of maidens dancing, socle foot, bronze square stepped bases. Rosebery's, London. Sep 04. HP: £520. ABP: £611.

Pair of William de Morgan tiles, Sands End period, c1890, painted with an amethyst flower & green trefoil leaves, impressed marks, 5.25in. Gorringes, Lewes. Dec 04. HP: £520. ABP: £611.

Austrian, painted terracotta blackamoor, late 19thC, man standing wearing loin cloth, gilt painted wooden plinth. 91cm high, restoration. Rosebery's, London. Sep 04. HP: £520. ABP: £611.

Rare biscuit porcelain figure of Li Bo, Kangxi, (1662-1722) drunken poet asleep in green robe beside a yellow glazed wine jar, restoration, 17cm. Sworders, Stansted Mountfitchet. Nov 04. HP. £520. ABP: £611.

Pair of blanc de chine dishes, quadrant section, early 18thC, impressed mark, with stands, label attached for Sidney Moss, London. Sworders, Stansted Mountfitchet. Nov 04. HP: £520. ABP: £611.

Brown Westhead & Moore parian bust of Apollo, pub'd by Art Union of London 1861, 35cm. Rosebery's, London. Dec 04. HP: £520. ABP: £611.

Chelsea silver shape dish, Red Anchor period, 1752-56, painted with flower sprays in enamels, painted mark, 8.5in. Gorringes, Lewes. Oct 06. HP: £520. ABP: £611.

Staffordshire redware coffee pot, c1765, pseudo Chinese seal mark, 23cm high. (W) (2) Cheffins, Cambridge. Feb 05. HP: £520. ABP: £611.

Royal Worcester 'Brahman Bull' by Doris Lindner no. 400 (with certificate). Boldon Auction Galleries, Tyne & Wear. Sep 04. HP: £520. ABP: £611.

Ridgway dessert service, c1835, a comport, damaged, painted with scenes within gilt and grey borders. (26) Sworders, Stansted Mountfitchet. Feb 05. HP: £520. ABP: £611.

Chinese blue/white vase, Kangxi, with Buddhist emblems and lotus, lacks lid, 29cm. Sworders, Stansted Mountfitchet. Feb 05. HP: £520. ABP: £611.

Beswick Partridge group, model No. 2064, designed by Albert Hallam, issued 1966-1975, 6in high. Halls Fine Art, Shrewsbury. Apr 05. HP: £520. ABP: £611.

Clarice Cliff for Wilkinson 'Joan Shorter-Kiddies Ware' Golliwog bowl, rim moulded in relief with a seated Golly holding spoons. Fieldings, Stourbridge. Apr 05. HP: £520. ABP: £611.

Wiltshaw & Robinson Carlton ware canted square section Egyptian pattern trumpet vase, enamelled and gilded with lotus capped columns and figures in profile, hieroglyph panels, blue soufflé ground, 9in high. Fieldings, West Hagley, Worcs. Jun 05. HP: £520. ABP: £611.

The illustrations are in descending price order. The price range is indicated at the top of each page.

Clarice Cliff 'Delecia Pansies' Fantasque Bizarre Isis vase, 10in high. Gardiner Houlgate, Corsham. Apr 05. HP: £520. ABP: £611.

Morris ware planter with purple flowers, signed George Cartlidge to base, chip to rim. Great Western Auctions, Glasgow. Sep 05. HP: £520. ABP: £611.

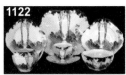

Shelley Sunrise and Tall Trees Queen Anne tea service, pattern G11678, 2 sandwich plates, milk jug, sugar basin and 12 trios. (40) Gardiner Houlgate, Corsham. Apr 05. HP: £520. ABP: £611.

Copeland 'Transvaal War' tyg. Great Western Auctions, Glasgow. Oct 05. HP: £520. ABP: £611.

19thC Pallisy-style oval dish, modelled with shells, fish and seaweed in relief on a blue ground (s/f), 12.5 x 8in. Dee, Atkinson & Harrison, Driffield. Sep 05. HP: £520. ABP: £611.

Minton Pate-sur-Pate plate, central panel a Cupid with loaded sling, pierced/gilded border, dated August 1884, 9.5in dia. Dee, Atkinson & Harrison, Driffield. Nov 05. HP: £520. ABP: £611.

Pair of Royal Crown Derby small urn vases, campana form, painted landscapes within gilt oval reserves, gilt highlights, c1898, 4.75in. Gorringes, Lewes. Feb 06. HP: £520. ABP: £611.

Hammer: £520

Doulton stoneware floral vase decorated by Frank Butler, late 19thC, buff coloured body monogrammed with stylised foliage/lappets, incised FAB and impressed factory marks, 47cm. Rosebery's, London. Mar 06. HP: £520. ABP: £611.

Royal Worcester blush ivory figure 'The Bather Suprised', 38cm. Rosebery's, London. Mar 06. HP: £520. ABP: £611.

Italian blue/white maiolica wet drug jar, 17thC, loop handle and spout, painted with figures and cherubs in landscapes and titled 'McLis Ros-pro CL', 19cm high. Rosebery's, London. Mar 06. HP: £520. ABP: £611.

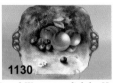

Royal Worcester dish by H. Ayrton 1931, painted with peaches and cherries against a mossy ground within two gilded scroll handles, puce printed mark and date code, 10.75in wide. Halls Fine Art, Shrewsbury. May 06. HP: £520. ABP: £611.

Goldscheider pottery art deco figure, lady in a maroon and black dress, black domed base, 13.5in high, No.6606. Hartleys, Ilkley. Jun 06. HP: £520. ABP: £611.

Beswick Tom Kitten wall plaque, introduced 1967 and withdrawn 1969, 6in. Louis Taylor, Stoke on Trent. Sep 06. HP: £520. ABP: £611.

20thC Chinese water dropper, fashioned as an open lotus leaf with character decorated stem handle, 17cm. Locke & England, Leamington Spa. Nov 06. HP: £520. ABP: £611.

Edith M Maplestone, 1878, bone china plaque painted after Sir Thomas Lawrence PRA with the infant George IV, signed and dated 30cm. Sworders, Stansted Mountfitchet. Feb 07. HP: £520. ABP: £611.

Pair Royal Worcester porcelain plates, painted with apples, peaches and grapes by Smith, gilded rims, 9in wide, black mark. Hartleys, Ilkley. Feb 07. HP: £520. ABP: £611.

Ceramics Prices 71

Sample Research II

Using the Index to analyse the market for a particular factory

No. 2 Mason's

Mason's ironstone dinner service, c1820. Sotheby's, Billingshurst. Nov 99. HP: £5,800. ABP: £6,822.

Extensive 19thC Masons Ironstone service with panels of Oriental figures in gardens. (118). Ewbank, Send. Oct 05. HP: £5,400. ABP: £6,351.

Readers are referred to **Sample Research I** on page 42 which introduces the Index and other options available when studying manufacturers, patterns, figures, artists, modellers and types and categories of ceramics.

There are at least twenty entries under Mason's in the Index. Half of these at least are services from the early period or at least preceding 1848. Only the first twelve have been illustrated here. Two of these made it into **Section 1**, averaging over £6,500 each. Services or part services here have up to 118 pieces or as few as fifteen. They still remain desirable at an astonishing average of about £71 a piece with a high of £94 and a low of £37. Victorian and later services also appear here but readers are reminded that these are not of the quality of the early Mason's PIC nor their durability being little different from a standard pottery body. These average only about £18 a piece when bought as a service and are really worth much less. Large and spectacular single items, whether ornamental or useful wares can command high sums. See the a/f footbath at **373** and the neapolitan ewer at **477**. Even a single comport at **1297** only just dipped under £500 and a pair of tureens at **1380** fetched £446. The three early jugs on page 149 and £82, as well as the set of six hydra jugs on page 98 are good value, whereas all that can be said of the late dinner/breakfast service at **1830** on page 112 is that it is an economical way of buying decorative crockery if you run a boarding house! Those interested in Mason's should learn the difference between the early pre 1848 genuine ironstone body and the later reproductions of the patterns. Marks are confusing as the originals follow through into the Morley and Ashworth periods. A list of Mason's page and image numbers follows.

Page 12-**88**, page 13-**100**, page 22-**247**, page 28-**354**, page 29-**373**, page 35-**477**, page 36-**497**, page 50-**724**, page 51-**737**, page 56-**835**, page 68-**1069**, page 82-**1297**, page 87-**1380**, page 88-**1400**,page 97-**1589**, page 98-**1595**, page 111-**1811**, page 112-**1830**, page 125-**2094** and page149-**2522**.

Mason's Ironstone dinner service, c1840, 77 pieces. Sworders, Stansted Mountfitchet. Feb 05. HP: £2,400. ABP: £2,823.

Mason's ironstone part dessert service: famille verte palette with central Chinese garden scene, printed crown & ribbon marks, c1840, two plates with damage. (25) Bearne's, Exeter. Jun 05. HP: £1,650. ABP: £1,940.

Masons patent ironstone footbath, 19thC, imari palette with scrolling flowers and foliage within 2 lamprey head handles, blue printed mark, a/f, 37.5cm wide. Halls Fine Art, Shrewsbury. Dec 06. HP: £1,600. ABP: £1,882.

Masons ironstone neopolitan ewer, unsigned, later wood base, early 19thC, 28in high. Andrew Hartley, Ilkley. Apr 05. HP: £1,250. ABP: £1,470.

Early 19thC Mason's ironstone dessert set, chicken skin textured rims printed and painted with Chinese export scrolls. (15) Cheffins, Cambridge. Feb 05. HP: £1,200. ABP: £1,411.

Victorian Mason's ironstone part dinner service, 12 setting, blue painted/enamelled in chinoiserie pattern No. 9799. (54) Hartleys, Ilkley. Aug 06. HP: £900. ABP: £1,058.

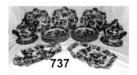

Early 19thC Mason's stone china dessert service in Imari colours, 19 pieces. John Taylors, Louth. Mar 05. HP: £880. ABP: £1,035.

Extensive Mason's ironstone flow blue part dinner service, printed in oriental style with flowering chrysanthemum bushes, approx 50 pieces. Rosebery's, London. Sep 04. HP: £780. ABP: £917.

Early 19thC Mason's Ironstone china teaware, Chinese-style floral/fence decoration: teapot, lid and stand, tall milk jug, slop bowl, sucrier and lid and five cups. (12) Reeman Dansie, Colchester. Apr 06. HP: £560. ABP: £658.

Early 19thC Masons Ironstone comport, scrolled handles, pierced support, gilded, 6.75in high. Dee, Atkinson & Harrison, Driffield. Apr 07. HP: £420. ABP: £494.

Section V: £500-£250

'Nantgarw prices are almost spiralling out of control at present.....the current Charlton book price for *Scotties* HN1281 is £1,750. A hammer price of £500 reflects the real market.....there are many homes and halls which this fine Burmantofts nautilus shell jardiniere/stand would suit to perfection..................'

Here is a mouthwatering selection which includes almost everything that the collector could wish for. Here is where I recommend collectors with a reasonable spending power should concentrate rather than buying more of the cheaper collectibles. Here, even on the first pages is a Gallé cat, Staffordshire pearlware, a good slipware dish, Wedgwood Fairyland lustre, Minton parian, paté-sur-paté, Nantgarw, Creamware, Carter Stabler Adams, Clarice Cliff, Royal Doulton and Beswick. This extends to a fine Chinese famille rose baluster vase, Royal Dux, Belleek and Troika. Note the Gallé cat is badly damaged at this price and this is the lowest price on the book for paté sur paté but probably well under-priced. The Poole vase by Mary Brown is unusual and early. Far better to go for something like this than the ubiquitous Poole from the later years. This is a good investment. I wouldn't normally advocate buying useful wares such as the cup and saucer at **1152** but this is Nantgarw which is almost spiralling out of control at present, hence the high price for a rather nondescript pair. Let us check on the Doulton in this price range. At **1146** is *Jasmine*, HN1862 and date code for 1940. At **1165** is *Scotties*, HN1281 and issued between 1928 and 1936. And at **1171** is *The Bather*, HN687 issued between 1924 and 1949. The current Charlton book prices are £1,350 for *Jasmine*, £1,750 for *Scotties* and £1,500 for *The Bather*. These prices must be taken with a pinch of salt but all of the figurines fetched £500 hammer in an open market between 2005 and 2006, so the prices must be about right. Incidentally there are a number of versions of *The Bather*. See also HN1227 back on page 55. Better in my opinion to buy at this level of the market than at the lower end which usually means extended issues and frequently much later wares.

It would be impossible to analyse all of this extensive Section at this level. In the remaining space I will comment briefly on various areas of the market. The reader of course may spend a good deal longer browsing this, one of the most important Sections in this book.

Continuing on page 75 at **1164** are two Chinese items. These look to be Ming or Transitional and of good quality, hence the price. Such pieces are real talking points in a home. The same could be said of the superb James Hadley musician at **1186**. At 32cms this could dominate a room. At **1192** is a Beswick fighting cock. Interested readers can browse the book as there are dozens of examples of these birds. Take the T'ang Dynasty camel at **1199**. This is not a lot to pay for an example from the first great period of Chinese ceramics. On the subject of Chinese ceramics the late Ming double gourd vase at **1213** is a good buy and at **1221** you can still buy Martinware at around the £500. Here is Chelsea at **1234**, and a very unusual subject for Staffordshire at **1239**. This mother and child figure should be a good investment. The same applies to a very unusual Prattware sauceboat at **1241**. What a wonderful object for use in the dining room. You can be certain no one else will ever have one or can ever find one. This is one of these rare objects that come along once in a blue moon, and worth saving for. The Burmantofts nautilus shell jardiniere/stand at **1279** is right out of its 1900 period and there are plenty of homes and halls where this fine object would display to perfection in the right setting and colours. For Yorkshire collectors again the Pratt coloured pottery horse at **1296** is another rare and desirable object. At **1302** the classical and restrained Copeland parian bust of *Winter*, by Owen Hale, though dated 1881, is a perfect ornament at over 17 inches for a modern hall of extensive size.

For the epitome of modelling expertise, don't miss **1292**, the Derby figure of *The Sailor's Lass*. If you are interested in tiles there are dozens of lots in these pages and the William de Morgan example at **1317** will be highly prized by its owner. Collectors from Sussex may be interested in the unique Brickhurst pig at **1375**. This is a substantial size at 9.5 inches and an important display object. There are some fine English delft plates in these pages. See the Bristol polychrome pair at **1359**, a further example at **1459** and a pair of Liverpool blue and white examples at **1465**. On the subject of pairs of plates and even rarer and more desirable than the English delft examples are a superb pair of Dillwyn & Co. Swansea plates at **1392**. At this price they must rate a very sound investment. Chelsea plates can be found at **1428** and **1472**, very good prices for the collector. Note the quality of the Meissen *Comedia del Arte* figure at **1436** and in total contrast, the quality and again the humour, in the Dutch Delft polychrome seated wild boar at **1497**, surely a snip despite the restored ear. There are a pair of Bow plates at **157** and only £300 hammer but I am attracted to the Doulton wall plate painted by Mary Capes at **1577**. Doulton Art Ware is in high demand, most having disappeared out of the country, mainly to the USA.

Finally £260 hammer seems reasonable for a double heart shaped Wemyss inkwell at **1657**. On the subject of art pottery note the Gateshead dish at **1660**.

Gallé faience cat, c1900, yellow glazed with green glass eyes, signed to right front paw, 32.5cm, badly damaged. Sworders, Stansted Mountfitchet. Jul 04. HP: £500. ABP: £588.

Staffordshire pearl ware bust of John Wesley, c1790. Brettells, Newport. Sep 04. HP: £500. ABP: £588.

18thC slipware baking dish, probably Sussex, trailed with a trellis design in cream slip, brown-glazed ground, 18in. Gorringes, Lewes. Oct 04. HP: £500. ABP: £588.

Royal Worcester 'H.R.H. The Duke of Edinburgh' by Doris Lindner No 624, certificate. Boldon Auction Galleries, Tyne & Wear. Sep 04. HP: £500. ABP: £588.

Henshall & Co. blue-printed meat plate, Hollywell Cottage, tree and well type with view of a country house, printed pattern name, unsigned, 20in. Gorringes, Lewes. Dec 04. HP: £500. ABP: £588.

Wedgwood Flame Fairyland lustre jardiniere, 'Big Eyes' pattern, Z 5360, printed mark, 4.5in. dia. Gorringes, Lewes. Dec 04. HP: £500. ABP: £588.

Minton Art Union of London parian figure of Solitude, semi-draped nude seated on a rock, heron beside, 1853, 20.5in. Gorringes, Lewes. Sep 04. HP: £500. ABP: £588.

English creamware botanical dessert service, c1780, boat shaped comport, pair of oval serving dishes & 8 plates, each with a botanical specimen and named to reverse. Rosebery's, London. Dec 04. HP: £500. ABP: £588.

George Jones pate-sur-pate vase, gilt borders & handles, girl seated within a cavern, green-glazed ground, imp'd mark, 8in. Gorringes, Lewes. Jan 05. HP: £500. ABP: £588.

R. Worcester bowl painted by R. Sebright, interior design of fruit and leaves, 7in. Gorringes, Lewes. Jun 05. HP: £500. ABP: £588.

Royal Doulton porcelain figure 'Jasmine', 7.5in high, HN1862, date code for 1940. Canterbury Auction Galleries, Kent. Apr 05. HP: £500. ABP: £588.

Clarice Cliff Bizarre Persian baluster vase. Great Western Auctions, Glasgow. May 05. HP: £500. ABP: £588.

> Categories or themes can be followed through the colour coded Index which contains over 4500 cross references.

Doulton Lambeth stoneware jug by Frank A Butler, FAB monogram to base, 19cm. Henry Adams, Chichester. Jun 05. HP: £500. ABP: £588.

Leeds creamware chintz pattern coffee pot and cover, English c1775, bands of floral & geometric decoration in tones of yellow, purple, black and iron red, imp'd triangle to base. 22.5cm high. Rosebery's, London. Jun 05. HP: £500. ABP: £588.

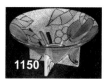

Clarice Cliff 'Apples Café au Lait' Bizarre bowl, shape 383, 9.25in dia. Gardiner Houlgate, Corsham. Apr 05. HP: £500. ABP: £588.

Carter Stabler Adams, Poole Pottery vase c1921-1934, shape 911, with pattern EP by Mary Brown, imp'd mark, shape number & artist's mono-gram, 8.25in high. Halls Fine Art, Shrewsbury. Jul 05. HP: £500. ABP: £588.

Nantgarw porcelain cup and saucer enamelled with loose sprays of roses, tulips and other flowers, gilt rims, c1820, rubbing to rim of cup. Bearne's, Exeter. Jun 05. HP: £500. ABP: £588.

Early 19thC English porce-lain teapot, bullet-shape with wishbone handle, with flower sprays in mid-18thC style, 4.25in high. Gorringes, Lewes. Sep 05. HP: £500. ABP: £588.

Beswick huntsman, in red jacket on horseback and a huntswoman in black jacket, 8.5in. Gorringes, Lewes. Feb 06. HP: £500. ABP: £588.

Chinese famille rose baluster vase, 19thC, painted with peony growing from rockwork, chips, 34.8cm. Sworders, Stansted Mountfitchet. Nov 05. HP: £500. ABP: £588.

Chinese blue/meat dish, mid 18thC, painted with a figure in a garden, 41cm. Sworders, Stansted Mountfitchet. Nov 05. HP: £500. ABP: £588.

Hammersley dessert set, 11 plates, oval stand, painted with a named fish by A Winkle, gilded apple-green border, pattern No. 6949, plates 9in, two rivetted. Gorringes, Lewes. Nov 05. HP: £500. ABP: £588.

Victorian Copeland parian bust of Celtic maiden, 'Emid', signed F.M. Miller, gilt-heightened, fluted column inscribed 'Crystal Palace Art Union', 41.5cm high. Gorringes, Bexhill. Dec 05. HP: £500. ABP: £588.

Royal Dux Bohemia figural bowl as a large seashell, one lady on edge of shell, second standing on base, applied & impressed pink triangle mark, 40cm. Brettells, Newport. Nov 05. HP: £500. ABP: £588.

19thC Booths part dinner service with green parrot on a blue tree with red and pink flowers and a blue/brown border, impressed & printed marks. (approx 58) Ewbank Auctioneers, Send, Surrey. Dec 05. HP: £500. ABP: £588.

Late 19thC Meissen porcelain group, a young man and girl, blue crossed swords and impressed numerals, 5.75in high. Diamond Mills & Co, Felixstowe. Mar 06. HP: £500. ABP: £588.

Belleek cream iridescent glazed porcelain teapot with textured scale pattern body and dragon pattern spout, three paw feet, 3.75in high, black printed First Period mark, filling instructions to interior of lid. Canterbury Auction Galleries, Kent. Feb 06. HP: £500. ABP: £588.

Royal Doulton Lambeth stoneware bust of Charles Dickens, c1912, 6.5in. Louis Taylor, Stoke on Trent. Mar 06. HP: £500. ABP: £588.

Chinese blue/white bowl with floral decoration, 6in, and a vase. Gorringes, Lewes. Oct 06. HP: £500. ABP: £588.

Hammer: £500

Royal Doulton figure group, 'Scotties', HN1281. Gorringes, Lewes. Jun 06. HP: £500. ABP: £588.

Martin Brothers salt-glazed stoneware pilgrim flask, two-handled, incised with a panel of birds, reverse with stylised leaves, incised script signature RW Martin Bros., London & Southall, 7.25in, a handle restored. Gorringes, Lewes. Jun 06. HP: £500. ABP: £588.

In manner of George Owen, Royal Worcester cup/saucer, reticulated decoration, highlighted in gilt, date mark, 1878. Ewbank Auctioneers, Send, Surrey. Jul 06. HP: £500. ABP: £588.

Clarice Cliff, pair tapering vases, red, blue and green Chintz design, No. 461. Brightwells, Leominster. Jul 06. HP: £500. ABP: £588.

Pair of famille verte plates, c1700, pastry-mould rim, centre painted with maidens, 23.6cm. Sworders, Stansted Mountfitchet. Apr 06. HP: £500. ABP: £588.

Troika wall pocket, moulded with six posy recesses, green-blue and brown against a textured ground, Cornwall mark and monogram of Jane Fitzgerald, 8.25in. Gorringes, Lewes. Mar 06. HP: £500. ABP: £588.

Royal Doulton figure, The Bather, HN687. Gorringes, Lewes. Mar 06. HP: £500. ABP: £588.

Abbeydale bone china twin handled pedestal dish, chrysanthemum pattern, Derby Imari style, printed marks, 39cm and flared vase, 18.5cm and a pair of candlesticks to match, 11cm. Sworders, Stansted Mountfitchet. Apr 06. HP: £500. ABP: £588.

Wilkinson Ltd. character jug, 'Sir Douglas Haig', Ltd. Edn. of 350, seated upon tank, designed by F. Carruthers Gould, 1917, facsimile signature, printed retailer's mark, Soane & Smith, remains of retailer's paper label, 10.5in. Gorringes, Lewes. Dec 06. HP: £500. ABP: £588.

Large Coalport 2-handled vase, cartouche of figures in castle grounds, signed J Keeling In the Garden, No. V7348A M-0161 to base in gold. Kent Auction Galleries, Folkestone. Nov 06. HP: £500. ABP: £588.

Wedgwood black basalt figure, 'Hope', loosely-robed female leaning against anchor, imp'd mark, 16.25in. Gorringes, Lewes. Feb 07. HP: £500. ABP: £588.

Clarice Cliff Bizarre pottery lotus pattern jug with ribbed body, Autumn Crocus design, 11.5in, black printed Bizarre mark to base. Canterbury Auction Galleries, Kent. Feb 07. HP: £500. ABP: £588.

18thC Chinese export chocolate pot, painted with mandarin figures in a garden setting, 'famille rose' enamels, 6.5in, cover repaired. Gorringes, Lewes. Jun 07. HP: £500. ABP: £588.

R. Worcester 'Highland Bull' by Doris Linder, No 106, certificate. Boldon Auction Galleries, Tyne & Wear. Sep 04. HP: £480. ABP: £564.

Doulton Lambeth jardiniere by Louisa E. Edwards, dated 1876, glazed stoneware incised and enamelled with flowers, incised monogram, 8.25in. Gorringes, Lewes. Dec 04. HP: £480. ABP: £564.

Paris porcelain plaque, 19thC, central panel inscribed 'Bataille De Rocroy 16 Mai 1643' signed Leber Von Schnetz, 45.5cm. Sworders, Stansted Mountfitchet. Nov 04. HP: £480. ABP: £564.

Meissen figure, 20thC, young girl placing her doll in it's pram, coloured glazes, 13cm high. Rosebery's, London. Dec 04. HP: £480. ABP: £564.

Beswick Wessex saddleback boar, 'Faracre Viscount 3rd', 2.75in. Louis Taylor, Stoke. Mar 05. HP: £480. ABP: £564.

Coalport jardinière/stand, c1800, Derby style Imari panels, gilt dolphin handles, pattern No 1227, 15.5cm. Sworders, Stansted Mountfitchet. Feb 05. HP: £480. ABP: £564.

Royal Crown Derby dish, 1918, painted with a named view of 'Loch Lomond', by C(uthbert) Gresley, signed, printed mark and date code, 27cm. Sworders, Stansted Mountfitchet. Feb 05. HP: £480. ABP: £564.

Prices quoted are actual hammer prices (HP) and the Approximate Buyer's Price (ABP) includes an average premium of 15% + VAT.

Lladro white bisque porcelain and porcelain lace bust of a veiled woman, 'White bust with veil', 14in high, wooden plinth. Canterbury Auction Galleries, Kent. Apr 05. HP: £480. ABP: £564.

James Hadley R. Worcester figure, Music, female playing the pipes and dressed in a gilt highlighted lilac robe, date code for 1894, 32cm. Clevedon Salerooms, Bristol. Jun 05. HP: £480. ABP: £564.

Newport pottery Clarice Cliff design vase with an Original Bizarre pattern formed as a band of geometric panels, 23cm high. Clevedon Salerooms, Bristol. Jun 05. HP: £480. ABP: £564.

Two Beswick figures, Queen Elizabeth on 'Imperial' and the Duke of Edinburgh on 'Alamein', Trooping the Colour 1957, 25.5cm/27cm high. (damage) Henry Adams, Chichester. Jun 05. HP: £480. ABP: £564.

Clarice Cliff Bobbins Fantasque Bizarre stepped bowl, shape 419, 6.75in dia. Gardiner Houlgate, Corsham. Apr 05. HP: £480. ABP: £564.

Royal Doulton porcelain figure entitled 'Henry VIII', H.N.3350, wood stand, and certificate. Bearne's, Exeter. Jun 05. HP: £480. ABP: £564.

Pair of Derby figural candlesticks one with Venus and Cupid, other with Mars, patch marks to base, c1765. Bearne's, Exeter. Jun 05. HP: £480. ABP: £564.

1192

Beswick fighting cock, on naturalistic base, numbered 2059, 23cm, minor chip to glaze. Locke & England, Leamington Spa. Jul 05. HP: £480. ABP: £564.

1193

Early Rye Hop Ware jug, signed F. Mitchell, Belle Vue Pottery, Rye and dated 1874, sprigged with green hops and leaves, incised marks, 7.75in. Gorringes, Lewes. Oct 05. HP: £480. ABP: £564.

1194

Moorcroft Macintyre salad bowl, EPNS moulded rim, tube lined with Art Nouveau foliage in gold on a green and blue ground, spreading foot, 10.5in wide, and a pair of servers to match, c1910. Andrew Hartley, Ilkley. Oct 05. HP: £480. ABP: £564.

1195

Wemyss pottery commemorative beaker, dated 1897, commemorating 60th year of Queen Victoria's reign, imp'd mark, printed T Goode & Co, London retailers mark, 14.9cm. Sworders, Stansted Mountfitchet. Nov 05. HP: £480. ABP: £564.

1196

Pair of Royal Doulton ewers by Eliza Simmance, with stylised leaves/flowers, in mottled blue/greys, impressed factory mark to underside, artist's initials, 28cm high. Gorringes, Bexhill. Dec 05. HP: £480. ABP: £564.

1197

Complete set of 23 Wade Vaux Breweries tankards. Boldon Auction Galleries, Tyne & Wear. Sep 05. HP: £480. ABP: £564.

1198

Pair of Royal Crown Derby 'Imari' pattern candlesticks, post war, 26.5cm. Sworders, Stansted Mountfitchet. Feb 06. HP: £480. ABP: £564.

1199

Pottery model of a recumbent bactarian camel, Tang dynasty, naturalistically modelled, traces of red pigment, ebonised wooden stand. 45cm long. Rosebery's, London. Mar 06. HP: £480. ABP: £564.

1200

Coalport, early 20thC teapot and cover, florally and gilt decorated, panels of yellow on a white ground, with three conforming cabinet cups and saucers, trumpet form with pierced scroll handle. Locke & England, Leamington Spa. Mar 06. HP: £480. ABP: £564.

Hammer: £480 - £475

1201

Royal Doulton Flambe Sung vase, 7.25in. Louis Taylor, Stoke on Trent. Mar 06. HP: £480. ABP: £564.

1202

Troika wheel lamp-stem, abstract moulded detail, blue-green textured ground, monogrammed, 14.25in. Gorringes, Lewes. Mar 06. HP: £480. ABP: £564.

1203

Beswick 'Canadian Mountie' figure and 'Indian Chief' figure. Henry Adams, Chichester. Oct 06. HP: £480. ABP: £564.

1204

Worcester transfer printed King of Prussia mug, c1760, after Robert Hancock, with battle honours and trophies, and a figure of fame, 11.6cm. Sworders, Stansted Mountfitchet. Feb 07. HP: £480. ABP: £564.

1205

Royal Worcester dish, 1940, painted with two Highland cattle, by H Stinton, signed, puce mark, No 2769, 10.5cm. Sworders, Stansted Mountfitchet. Feb 07. HP: £480. ABP: £564.

1206

Martin Brothers child's salt glaze mug, with flowers and the name Alice, 9.5cm high, Martin Bros, London Southall, 12. 1893, and a smaller mug with the name Eva, 7.5cm, dated 8. 1897. Sworders, Stansted Mountfitchet. Feb 07. HP: £480. ABP: £564.

1207

Moorcroft pomegranate pattern bowl, four applied angular supports, impressed 1881, green painted 'W Moorcroft', 23cm dia. Halls Fine Art, Shrewsbury. Apr 07. HP: £480. ABP: £564.

1208

Wemyss Earlshall Faire jug, 1914, The Rookery pattern in black, verse around the neck-rim, 'Or whiles a clan o'roosty, Craws cangle the gither', inscribed 'Earlshall Faire, A.D. 1914, painted & imp'd marks, 5.75in, handle restored. Gorringes, Lewes. Apr 07. HP: £480. ABP: £564.

1209

19thC Italian maiolica charger decorated in colours with Venus and other naked attendants, borders with cupids, mask and bold leaf scroll ornament, 18 25in dia, marked in underglaze blue 'Napoli' to base. Canterbury Auction Galleries, Kent. Apr 06. HP: £475. ABP: £558.

Hammer: £475 - £450

Slip-glaze porringer/bleeding bowl, marked in blue PNM 1686 to the handle and 2 over I R. around an image of James II, 7in. Golding Young & Co, Grantham. Nov 06. HP: £475. ABP: £558.

Six Sèvres porcelain plates, mid 19thC, later decorated depicting young courting couples, floral vignettes, bleu-céleste ground, gilt borders, factory printed/incised marks, cancellation strikes. Sworders, Stansted Mountfitchet. Nov 04. HP: £460. ABP: £541.

Clarice Cliff, 'Berries' pattern conical sugar sifter, café au lait ground, printed marks, 14cm high. Cheffins, Cambridge. Apr 05. HP: £460. ABP: £541.

Late Ming blue/white double gourd vase, with bands of medallions & flowers, pendant on ribbons from lappet bands, 20.5cm high. (D) Cheffins, Cambridge. Feb 06. HP: £460. ABP: £541.

Blue/white bowl, Jaijing, painted on exterior with Shou Lau and other immortals, on interior with a stylised pine, deer and Ling Zhi, stylised four character mark, 11.7cm George Eumorfopoulos label, No: C1569. Sworders, Stansted Mountfitchet. Nov 04. HP: £460. ABP: £541.

Beswick Connoisseur Series, Cardigan Bay, model 2340, 9.24in. Louis Taylor, Stoke on Trent Mar 05. HP: £460. ABP: £541.

Nantgarw plate, c1813-1822, lobed and painted to centre, 9.75in dia. Cotswold Auction Company, Cirencester. Aug 04. HP: £460. ABP: £541.

Carlton Ware nightingale vase. Great Western Auctions, Glasgow. Jun 05. HP: £460. ABP: £541.

Japanese Arita ware vase Gorringes, Bexhill. Apr 05. HP: £460. ABP: £541.

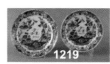

Two matching Dutch Delft plates, 1724, painted with a jardiniere & flowers, initialled PSE and dated, 8.5in. and 8in. Gorringes, Lewes. Apr 05. HP: £460. ABP: £541.

Caughley blue/white baluster jug, c1770, painted with landscape, spout with moulded mask, 17cm, and a Worcester tankard, restored, 14cm. Sworders, Stansted Mountfitchet. Feb 06. HP: £460. ABP: £541.

Martin Brothers stoneware tankard, 1880, incised with a fisherman holding his catch, possibly on the Grand Union Canal, incised to base, dated 24/3/80, 13cm. Sworders, Stansted Mountfitchet. Feb 06. HP: £460. ABP: £541.

Prattware, Sailors return and Farewell jug, c1790, moulded in relief with figures, enamelled in Pratt colours, 16cm high, and another leaf moulded Pratt jug. Rosebery's, London. Mar 06. HP: £460. ABP: £541.

Dame Lucie Rie Art Pottery pouring vessel & lid, slight chip to rim, brown glazed exterior, white interior, cypher signature on base, 8.5in. Denhams, Warnham, Sussex. Nov 05. HP: £460. ABP: £541.

Royal Doulton figure, Ladybird, HN1638. Gorringes, Lewes. Mar 06. HP: £460. ABP: £541.

Pair of black basalt portrait busts, Voltaire and Pope, attrib. to Wood & Caldwell, integral socle plinth, 9.25in, unmarked, a base repaired. Gorringes, Lewes. Oct 06. HP: £460. ABP: £541.

Staffordshire figure of Don Quixote, c1830. Brettells, Newport, Shropshire. Sep 04. HP: £450. ABP: £529.

Pair of Sitzendorf figural vases, German 19thC, flower encrusted cover, shoulder supporting two children holding floral swags over the flower encrusted mid-section, 43cm high. Rosebery's, London. Dec 04. HP: £450. ABP: £529.

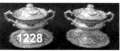

Pair of Copeland & Garrett Felspar Porcelain sauce tureens, 6.5in. Gorringes, Lewes. Nov 05. HP: £450. ABP: £529.

1229

Meissen cabinet cup/saucer, 19thC, with a portrait of Phillip Melanchton within a gilt wreath and line borders. Rosebery's, London. Dec 04. HP: £450. ABP: £529.

1230

Wedgwood black-painted earthenware portrait bust of Mercury, characterised by winged helmet,black basalt socle plinth, imp'd marks, 16.5in. Gorringes, Lewes. Mar 05. HP: £450. ABP: £529.

The numbering system acts as a reader reference as well as linking to the Analysis of each section.

1231

Late 18thC Derby can/saucer painted with pattern No 317, Cupid flying through clouds holding a torch, marks in puce. (D) Cheffins, Cambridge. Apr 05. HP: £450. ABP: £529.

1232

Soviet period ink well and cover, Russian 20thC, in the form of a bust of Lenin set upon two books and scrolled manuscript. Height 14cm. Rosebery's, London. Dec 05. HP: £450. ABP: £529.

1233

Goldscheider figural table lamp as two girls on a rock peering into a clear glass pond, signed Petri, 25in high, impressed mark to back, mould 3531,102,14. Andrew Hartley, Ilkley, W Yorks. Feb 06. HP: £450. ABP: £529.

1234

Chelsea porcelain bocage figure, shepherd playing a pipe, scroll moulded base, gilt embellishment, 18thC, red anchor mark, 9in high. Hartleys, Ilkley. Aug 06. HP: £450. ABP: £529.

1235

Pilkington's R. Lancastrian lustre vase by R. Joyce, with galleons against a blue-green ground, initialled/impressed marks, 9.25in, some damage. Gorringes, Lewes. Mar 06. HP: £450. ABP: £529.

1236

Troika disc shape lamp base, initialled E.W. inscribed Troika, Cornwall, two small firing cracks to base, 38cm high. Sworders, Stansted Mountfitchet. Apr 06. HP: £450. ABP: £529.

Hammer: £450 - £440

1237

Clarice Cliff 'Poplar' vase, shape no 461. Great Western Auctions, Glasgow. Feb 07. HP: £450. ABP: £529.

1238

Set of twelve KPM figures, months of the year, and three other Berlin figures. Gorringes, Lewes. Jun 06. HP: £450. ABP: £529.

1239

18th/19thC Staffordshire figure of a seated mother and child, 12in. Denhams, Warnham. Sep 04. HP: £440. ABP: £517.

1240

Chamberlain's Worcester bulb pot, painted with a basket of flowers and gilded, salmon-pink ground, with cover, painted mark, crack to back, 6.75in. Gorringes, Lewes. Dec 04. HP: £440. ABP: £517.

1241

Prattware sauce boat, c1800, as a duck, painted in ochre, yellow, green/blue, 20cm. Sworders, Stansted Mountfitchet. Nov 04. HP: £440. ABP: £517.

1242

Pair of Doulton Burslem vases, printed with rural Dutch views in blue, 12.5in. Gorringes, Lewes. Jul 04. HP: £440. ABP: £517.

1243

Lladro porcelain figure of a merchant explorer, possibly Christopher Columbus, blue printed mark, also 'Escul: S. vivrio?, signed and 'Decor: V. Navarra N. 203', imp'd numerals 1741, 44cm high, wooden stand. Hampton & Littlewood, Exeter. Jul 04. HP: £440. ABP: £517.

1244

Pair of Samson figures, 'The Tailor' and 'Tailor's Wife', based on the Meissen models by Eberlein, mock-Derby marks in red enamel, 6.75in. Gorringes, Lewes. Apr 05. HP: £440. ABP: £517.

1245

Royal Doulton stoneware vase by George Tinworth, c1902, sgraffito and bead decoration, monogrammed G. T., impressed factory marks, rim restored, 31cm. Sworders, Stansted Mountfitchet. Apr 05. HP: £440. ABP: £517.

Crown Devon figure 'Rio Rita', signed K. Parsons to base, No 2280. Great Western Auctions, Glasgow. Jun 05. HP: £440. ABP: £517.

1247

Moorcroft for Macintyre tobacco jar/cover, 'Spanish', screw-cover with Magdalen College crest, design against a mottled green ground, printed Macintyre mark, painted initials, c1910, 6in dia. Gorringes, Lewes. Sep 05. HP: £440. ABP: £517.

1248

Carlton china 'Felix' the cat walking with his hands behind his back, base inscribed 'Felix kept on walking', printed with Wembley British Empire Exhibition 1924 crest, 3.25in wide. Andrew Hartley, Ilkley. Oct 05. HP: £440. ABP: £517.

1249

Minton majolica shell and merman dish, 1870, swimming triton with an oar supporting the shell-form bowl on its bifid tail, rim chip, impressed marks, date code, 20.5cm. Sworders, Stansted Mountfitchet. Feb 06. HP: £440. ABP: £517.

1250

Sunderland lustre frog chamber pot, black printed, 2 humorous stanzas, figure to interior and applied frog, 19thC, 11in wide. Andrew Hartley, Ilkley, W Yorks. Feb 06. HP: £440. ABP: £517.

1251

18thC Wedgwood blue Jasper-ware portrait medallion, 'Sir John Philipson, Bart - First Lord of the Treasury', 3.5 x 2.75in, impressed mark to back, unframed. Canterbury Auction Galleries, Kent. Feb 06. HP: £440. ABP: £517.

1252

Caughley mug, printed with Chinese land and riverscape vignettes, underglaze blue, 7in. Gorringes, Lewes. Jun 05. HP: £440. ABP: £517.

1253

Royal Doulton character jug 'Mephistopheles', large, verse to base. Louis Taylor, Stoke on Trent. Mar 06. HP: £440. ABP: £517.

1254

Pair of Staffordshire mantel vases, a lurcher in pursuit of hare prey, 11in, one repaired. Gorringes, Lewes. Jun 06. HP: £440. ABP: £517.

1255

Wemyss preserve pot/cover, painted with yellow plums, painted mark, 5in. Gorringes, Lewes. Jul 06. HP: £440. ABP: £517.

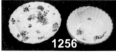

1256

Chelsea bowl and plate, Red Anchor period, 1752-56, bowl reeded, plate with shaped rim, bowl unmarked, plate with painted mark in chocolate-brown, 7in and 8.5in. Gorringes, Lewes. Oct 06. HP: £440. ABP: £517.

1257

Royal Worcester tiger figure, as two cubs, No 3318, puce mark dated 1941, 8in wide. Hartleys, Ilkley. Oct 06. HP: £440. ABP: £517.

1258

Minton Buckingham dinner and tea service. (78) Ewbank Auctioneers, Send, Surrey. Dec 06. HP: £440. ABP: £517.

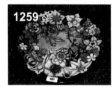

1259

Moorcroft 'Carousel' pattern charger, by Rachel Bishop, No 80 of a Ltd Edn, signed, certificate and box. Great Western Auctions, Glasgow. Feb 07. HP: £440. ABP: £517.

1260

Pair Delft polychrome plates, c1750, decorated with flowers, 22.5cm. Sworders, Stansted Mountfitchet. Feb 07. HP: £440. ABP: £517.

1261

Doulton Lambeth stoneware 'Cricketing' mug, moulded in white relief with 3 scenes of cricketers - batting, bowling, and a wicket keeper, 5in high. imp'd mark to base, 'R.B.' assistant's mark. Canterbury Auction Galleries, Kent. Apr 07. HP: £440. ABP: £517.

1262

Late 18thC pearlware bear, sponged enamelling in brown & ochre, green hollow base, 3in. high. Gorringes, Lewes. Apr 07. HP: £440. ABP: £517.

1263

Royal Worcester porcelain sugar and cream set, painted with peaches, apples/grapes by Smith and Lewis, gilt interiors, jug 4in high, black mark. Hartleys, Ilkley. Feb 07. HP: £430. ABP: £505.

1264

Fieldings Crown Devon, Eton Boating, musical tankard, 7.25in. Louis Taylor, Stoke. Sep 04. HP: £430. ABP: £505.

1265

Belleek porcelain basket with 4 strand base, trellis sides, rim applied with flower heads, encrusted handles, ropework foot, impressed 'Belleek', Co, Fermanagh, Ireland', 8.75in wide. Andrew Hartley, Ilkley. Aug 04. HP: £430. ABP: £505.

Hammer: £430 - £420

Wedgwood black jasper plaque 'cupid and psyche' white relief figures consoling psyche while cupid stands beside with his bow, imp'd mark, 13 x 18cm, framed, glazed. Hampton & Littlewood, Exeter. Jul 04. HP: £430. ABP: £505.

Moorcroft vase, 6.5in. Louis Taylor, Stoke on Trent. Dec 04. HP: £430. ABP: £505.

18thC Chinese export serving plate, painted with peonies/blossom in 'famille rose' enamels, 14.5in. Gorringes, Lewes. Oct 04. HP: £420. ABP: £494.

Aynsley salmon pink ground part dinner service, 20thC, gilt with foliate panels, 97 pieces. Rosebery's, London. Dec 04. HP: £420. ABP: £494.

Wemyss goblet, hand painted pink roses, trailing blue flora and pink ribbons, green base, 10in high. (restored) Dee, Atkinson & Harrison, Driffield. Jul 04. HP: £420. ABP: £494.

Pearlware bear baiting group, man in eastern costume with a bear on a rope, 22cm high. Rosebery's, London. Sep 04. HP: £420. ABP: £494.

Small 18thC English porcelain cream jug, cannon-ball pattern in underglaze blue, 3.5in long Gorringes, Lewes. Jul 04. HP: £420. ABP: £494.

Rye Sussex Pig, green-glazed, detachable head, incised 'Wunt be Druv', incised mark Rye & pin-dust mark, c1910, 4.75in. long. Gorringes, Lewes. Oct 05. HP: £420. ABP: £494.

> The illustrations are in descending price order. The price range is indicated at the top of each page.

Derby stirrup cup as a foxhound, painted naturalistically, gilt inscription to collar, 'Tally Ho', painted mark in puce, 5.5in. Gorringes, Lewes. Jan 05. HP: £420. ABP: £494.

Dame Lucie Rie, shaped Art Pottery white/brown glazed bowl, 5in. Denhams, Warnham, Sussex. Nov 05. HP: £420. ABP: £494.

Spode ice pail, cover & liner, c1820, with floral groups on a pale lilac/white ground, twin branch handles, twisted branch handle to cover, 28cm. Rosebery's, London. Mar 05. HP: £420. ABP: £494.

Satsuma koro/cover, white metal cover, loop ivy handles and decorated with panels of seated immortals, signed, 5in. Gorringes, Lewes. Mar 05. HP: £420. ABP: £494.

Late 19thC Cantagalli maiolica vase painted in Renaissance style with a soldier roundel, cockerel mark, 29cm high. Cheffins, Cambridge. Apr 05. HP: £420. ABP: £494.

Burmantoft nautilus shell jardiniere/stand, English c1900, shell on rockwork base, reeded column, moulded with stars, mustard yellow glaze, monogram mark to base and pattern No 816 and 1201, 142cm high. Rosebery's, London. Dec 05. HP: £420. ABP: £494.

Pair of Carltonware vases, gilded and enamelled with chinoiserie land/riverscapes, gilt kylin finials, patt. 9446, 15in. Gorringes, Lewes. Oct 05. HP: £420. ABP: £494.

Parian bust of Apollo, after the Antique. Gorringes, Bexhill. Oct 05. HP: £420. ABP: £494.

Sunderland pink lustre eel jar with lid and two looped handles 'Success to the Tars of Old England' 12cm dia. Boldon Auction Galleries, Tyne & Wear. Nov 05. HP: £420. ABP: £494.

Royal Doulton 'One of the Forty' figurine. Henry Adams, Chichester. Dec 05. HP: £420. ABP: £494.

Belleek basket/cover, mid 19thC oval twin handled form, latticework applied with roses, branch handles, 22cm dia. Rosebery's, London. Mar 06. HP: £420. ABP: £494.

Hammer: £420 - £410

1285

Martinware stoneware vase incised/decorated with thistle leaves & flowers, 9.75in high (incised mark 'R.W. Martin & Bros., London & Southall' and dated 11-1896, restoration to rim). Canterbury Auction Galleries, Kent. Dec 05. HP: £420. ABP: £494.

1286

Copeland parian figure as a classical female nude seated and clutching a gilt edged drape, base inscribed 'Crystal Palace Art Union', 18in high. Andrew Hartley, Ilkley. Apr 06. HP: £420. ABP: £494.

1287

Carltonware Guinness toucan, beside filled pint, printed with script 'My Goodness, My Guinness', 7in. Gorringes, Lewes. Jul 06. HP: £420. ABP: £494.

1288

Bow dish with gilding, attrib. to James Giles, silver shape with shell handles, gilded with flower sprays and dentil border, c1770, 12.75in. Gorringes, Lewes. Mar 06. HP: £420. ABP: £494.

1289

Clarice Cliff part tea set 'Crocus', 19 pieces including two serving plates and milk jug. Gorringes, Lewes. Mar 06. HP: £420. ABP: £494.

1290

Pair of Berlin oval porcelain portrait miniatures, 19thC, Napoleon and Josephine, both impressed '15', easel frames, 8.2cm. Sworders, Stansted Mountfitchet. Apr 06. HP: £420. ABP: £494.

Categories or themes can be followed through the colour coded Index which contains over 4500 cross references.

1291

Late 19thC Sitzendorf style Comport, pierced basket with floral encrusted decoration, tree trunk column, cavalier type gentleman and a lady collecting grapes, rococo base, 53cm. Charterhouse Auctioneers, Sherborne. Sep 06. HP: £420. ABP: £494.

1292

Derby figure, 'The Sailor's Lass', scroll base, incised shape numeral 316, 10in, restoration. Gorringes, Lewes. Oct 06. HP: £420. ABP: £494.

1293

Thomas Fell 'Warranted Winchester Measure', moulded with a floral border, imp'd mark, 1817-30, 6.25in. Gorringes, Lewes. Feb 07. HP: £420. ABP: £494.

1294

Royal Copenhagen green celadon glazed porcelain mask of 'Medusa', by Hans Hansen, 1894-1965), 10.75in high, blue printed mark to base, monogram 'HH', No. 2950. Canterbury Auction Galleries, Kent. Feb 07. HP: £420. ABP: £494.

1295

Wemyss jug, painted with two dragonflies, painted/impressed marks, 4.5in, restored crack. Gorringes, Lewes. Apr 07. HP: £420. ABP: £494.

1296

Yorkshire pottery horse, sponged enamelling in black/ochre, c1800, 5.5in high, restored. Gorringes, Lewes. Apr 07. HP: £420. ABP: £494.

1297

Early 19thC Masons Ironstone comport, scrolled handles, pierced support, gilded, 6.75in high. Dee, Atkinson & Harrison, Driffield. Apr 07. HP: £420. ABP: £494.

1298

Wemyss salad drainer/bowl, decorated with cabbage roses, 23cm dia. Great Western Auctions, Glasgow. May 05. HP: £410. ABP: £482.

1299

Beswick 'Winnie the Pooh' set. (8) Louis Taylor, Stoke. Jun 05. HP: £410. ABP: £482.

1300

Minton majolica game pie dish and cover, 7in. af. Louis Taylor, Stoke on Trent. Mar 06. HP: £410. ABP: £482.

1301

Clarice Cliff pencil holder, modelled with a Golliwog, 6.25in high, 7in long. Louis Taylor, Stoke on Trent. Mar 06. HP: £410. ABP: £482.

1302

Copeland parian bust, Winter by Owen Hale, lady with mistletoe in her hair, dated 1881, 17.25in high. Hartleys, Ilkley. Feb 07. HP: £410. ABP: £482.

1303

Chinese sang-de-boeuf footed bowl, 18.5cm dia. Gorringes, Bexhill. Dec 04. HP: £400. ABP: £470.

Early 19thC serving plate, The Beemaster, peasant carrying beehive, animal medallion border, 15.5in. Gorringes, Lewes. Dec 04. HP: £400. ABP: £470.

Clarice Cliff Summer House pattern drum preserve pot, printed marks, 10cm high. Cheffins, Cambridge. Feb 05. HP: £400. ABP: £470.

35 assorted Dutch Delft tiles, c1650-1700, decorated with flowers issuing from a vas,e fleur de lys & barred ox head corner motifs, 13.3cm square, Sworders, Stansted Mountfitchet. Feb 05. HP: £400. ABP: £470.

Royal Doulton Union Jack British Bulldog, repair to cigar. Roger Jones & Co, Colwyn Bay. Dec 04. HP: £400. ABP: £470.

Pair 19thC Derby porcelain urns, floral encrusted decoration, blue bodies, gilt feet, Derby mark (1830-1848) 7in, damage to flowers. Denhams, Warnham, West Sussex. Jan 05. HP: £400. ABP: £470.

Royal Doulton twin handled Ltd Edn mug, The Apothecary, No 125/600, by Noke, signed H. Fenton, moulded in relief, 15cm high. Rosebery's, London. Mar 05. HP: £400. ABP: £470.

Late 19thC Wedgwood blue jasper plaque, classical figures giving offerings, glazed, 62cm wide incl. frame. Rosebery's, London. Mar 05. HP: £400. ABP: £470.

Wilkinson's toby jug of Lloyd George, c1918, designed by F Carruthers Gould, holding a shell entitled 'Shell Out', in gilt decorated blue glazed uniform, signature to base, retailers mark for Soane & Smith, Oxford St, London, 26cm. Rosebery's, London. Mar 05. HP: £400. ABP: £470.

Beswick pottery figure Dulux advertising figure as an Old English Sheep dog seated with his paw on a tin of paint titled Dulux gloss finish, washed in coloured glazes, gold oval mark, 12in high. Fieldings, Stourbridge. Apr 05. HP: £400. ABP: £470.

Hammer: £400

Bow candlestick, English 18thC, fox and hen beneath flowering bocage, foliate sconce, scroll base, restored, 32cm high. Rosebery's, London. Mar 05. HP: £400. ABP: £470.

Late 19thC Burmantofts Faience ware, Anglo Persian vase by Louis Kramer, c1887, painted with flower sprays, imp'd marks and No 74, painted marks DSG.111 (798) and LK monogram, 7.5in high. Fieldings, Stourbridge. Apr 05. HP: £400. ABP: £470.

Pair 19thC Samson porcelain two handled chestnut baskets in Worcester manner, floral encrusted rustic pattern loop handles, 11.75 x 9 x 4in high, unmarked. Canterbury Auction Galleries, Kent. Apr 05. HP: £400. ABP: £470.

Michael Cardew (1901-1983) brown glazed earthenware 3-handled vase in the African manner, scratched banding, scroll ornament, 7.5in high, seal mark & seal of Winchcombe Pottery, c1940. Canterbury Auction Galleries, Kent. Apr 05. HP: £400. ABP: £470.

William Morris design tile, made by William De Morgan 'poppy' pattern, manganese pink and green, unmarked, 13cm square. Sworders, Stansted Mountfitchet. Apr 05. HP: £400. ABP: £470.

Victorian Doulton Lambeth tobacco barrel, painted with a continuous band of geese, coloured slips, brown ground, 5.25in. Gorringes, Lewes. Jun 05. HP: £400. ABP: £470.

William de Morgan Persian design red lustreware peacock tile, flower heads on a white ground, 6in. Gorringes, Lewes. Jun 05. HP: £400. ABP: £470.

Pink Sunderland lustre jug 'Have communion with faith be familiar with one etc.', 20cm high. Boldon Auction Galleries, Tyne & Wear. Jun 05. HP: £400. ABP: £470.

Pair of Bourne Denby hotwater bottles in the form of handbags, base marked RD no. 748183. Denhams, Warnham, Sussex. Jul 05. HP: £400. ABP: £470.

Ceramics Prices **83**

Pair of Derby musical bocage figures, English late 18thC, male playing bagpipes, the female a lute, 19.5cm. Rosebery's, London. Jun 05. HP: £400. ABP: £470.

Clarice Cliff Idyll Fantasque Bizarre plate, 9.5in dia. Gardiner Houlgate, Corsham. Apr 05. HP: £400. ABP: £470.

Royal Crown Derby pedestal dish, in palette 1128, 10.25in wide, 5.5in high. Halls Fine Art, Shrewsbury. Jul 05. HP: £400. ABP: £470.

Beswick pottery figure of a huntsman, dappled grey gloss horse, model No 1501, 8 hounds and a fox, damage to horse and fox. Bearne's, Exeter. Jun 05. HP: £400. ABP: £470.

Pair of Samuel Alcock vases, 'Representing the Battle between the Greeks and the Amazons found at Cumae', printed/washed in red, black ground, 8.25in. Gorringes, Lewes. Oct 05. HP: £400. ABP: £470.

English creamware masonic jug, black printed with stanza, olive branch cartouche, verso with a sun, man, compass, tools and an eye, gilded initials, 9.25in high. Andrew Hartley, Ilkley. Oct 05. HP: £400. ABP: £470.

Royal Doulton Admiral Nelson loving cup, designed by C.J. Noke and H. Fenton, issued 1935 in a Ltd Edn of 600, No 192, printed marks, 26cm. Sworders, Stansted Mountfitchet. Nov 05. HP: £400. ABP: £470.

> Prices quoted are actual hammer prices (HP) and the Approximate Buyer's Price (ABP) includes an average premium of 15% + VAT.

Kraak Wanli porcelain Kendi, 17thC, with panels of peony and lotus, rim nibbled, 19cm. Sworders, Stansted Mountfitchet. Nov 05. HP: £400. ABP: £470.

Set of four Doulton Lambeth spirit flagons, moulded shoulders, glazed in green & brown, each with stopper, 9.25in. Gorringes, Lewes. Nov 05. HP: £400. ABP: £470.

Bow porcelain figure of a sportsman with a dog, bocage to background, rococo pattern base, 11in high, unmarked, patch marks to base, restoration to musket, chipping to bocage, c1760. Canterbury Auction Galleries, Kent. Dec 05. HP: £400. ABP: £470.

Early 19thC Meissen figure of peasant girl with rake, blue under glazed mark to base and incised No 4, 5in high. Ewbank Auctioneers, Send, Surrey. Dec 05. HP: £400. ABP: £470.

Matched pair of Martin Brothers stoneware inkwells c1880s, sides incised and decorated with birds/fauna, incised marks, dates to both, 6cm high. Rosebery's, London. Mar 06. HP: £400. ABP: £470.

Collection of Royal Crown Derby miniature table and cabinet wares, each in the Imari palette. (7 pieces) Locke & England, Leamington Spa. Mar 06. HP: £400. ABP: £470.

Early 20thC Foley 'Intarsio' pottery vase, continuous band of gnomes, owl design neck and lappet border, black printed mark and No. 3015, 10.25in high. Diamond Mills & Co, Felixstowe. Mar 06. HP: £400. ABP: £470.

19thC Copeland majolica pottery centre piece in the form of two children holding an osier work oval basket, imp'd mark and 0.74 number, 10.5in high. (faults) Diamond Mills & Co, Felixstowe. Mar 06. HP: £400. ABP: £470.

First period Worcester oval lattice work blue/white basket, rope twist handles, underglaze blue crescent moon mark. 22cm long. Boldon Auction Galleries, Tyne & Wear. Mar 06. HP: £400. ABP: £470.

Late 19thC Belleek porcelain basket, naturalistically moulded rose stem handle, ornate floral encrusted mounts, intricate basket-weave decoration, impressed mark on base, 28 x 23cm. Reeman Dansie, Colchester. Apr 06. HP: £400. ABP: £470.

Pottery bust of Beethoven, hand modelled by Charles Noke, 13.5in, signed, reverse inscribed Noke & Beethoven. Louis Taylor, Stoke. Mar 06. HP: £400. ABP: £470.

Ruskin pottery vase, body with neutral marble glaze, impressed Ruskin England 1915, 10in high. Golding Young & Co, Grantham. Feb 06. HP: £400. ABP: £470.

Pair of Wemyss preserve pots with domed lids, painted with strawberries and a hive with bees, matching stands, 3in high. Andrew Hartley, Ilkley. Apr 06. HP: £400. ABP: £470.

Pair of 19thC Staffordshire pottery figures of birds, decorated in gilt, rustic pattern base, 10in high. Canterbury Auction Galleries, Kent. Apr 06. HP: £400. ABP: £470.

Late 19thC Dresden porcelain plaque painted by Henry Booker, semi-nude lady with attendant and cupid, label on reverse, 4.5 x 6in. Gorringes, Lewes. Jun 06. HP: £400. ABP: £470.

Pair of Coalport porcelain vases, domed lid, gilded cone finial, ram mask side handles, painted by M Pinter, 9.75in high. Hartleys, Ilkley. Jun 06. HP: £400. ABP: £470.

Wedgwood part tea service decorated with gilt flowers and foliage on a dark pink ground, approx 50 pieces. Rosebery's, London. Aug 06. HP: £400. ABP: £470.

R. Doulton figure, Marietta, HN1341. Gorringes, Lewes. Mar 06. HP: £400. ABP: £470.

Pair of Minton vases, 1870, designed by Christopher Dresser, tooled gilt border, imp'd marks, chips/hairline, 10.5cm. Sworders, Stansted Mountfitchet. Apr 06. HP: £400. ABP: £470.

Sally Tuffin Rainforest pattern vase, impressed and painted marks, 32cm. Sworders, Stansted Mountfitchet. Apr 06. HP: £400. ABP: £470.

Hammer: £400

Chinese Buddha, smiling seated character in turquoise gown, 10.5in. Gorringes, Lewes. Jun 06. HP: £400. ABP: £470.

Pair of Worcester Flight Barr & Barr bowls. Henry Adams, Chichester. Jul 06. HP: £400. ABP: £470.

Pair Staffordshire flat back spill vases with models of a greyhound chasing a hare. Cotswold Auction Company, Gloucester. Oct 06. HP: £400. ABP: £470.

1930s Burleighware cricket jug with a handle shaped like a batsman. Thos Mawer & Son, Lincoln. Nov 06. HP: £400. ABP: £470.

Moore Brothers, late 19thC porcelain centre piece as two cherubs carrying a lily adorned crimped rimmed shell with tinted petals and stamen, base with Greek key band, 18 x 25cm. Locke & England, Leamington Spa. Nov 06. HP: £400. ABP: £470.

Set of eight c1950s Wade nursery rhyme figures, Tinker, Taylor, Soldier, Sailor etc, 6cm to 8.5cm. Locke & England, Leamington Spa. Nov 06. HP: £400. ABP: £470.

19thC majolica teapot, attrib. to Thomas Forester, as an elephant, blue glazed cover with ribbon handle, 5.75in. Gorringes, Lewes. Dec 06. HP: £400. ABP: £470.

Chelsea figure of Mars, Gold Anchor period, 1756-69, scroll base, 8in. Gorringes, Lewes. Dec 06. HP: £400. ABP: £470.

Royal Copenhagen porcelain figure 'Slesuig', seated girl holding flowers, 4.25in high. Hartleys, Ilkley. Dec 06. HP: £400. ABP: £470.

Pair of 19thC French cornucopia vases, issuing from an eagle's head and painted and gilded with flowers, 8in. Gorringes, Lewes. Feb 07. HP: £400. ABP: £470.

Hammer: £400 - £380.

Pair Bristol delft polychrome plates, c1750, decorated with seated Chinamen, 22.5cm, minor damage. Sworders, Stansted Mountfitchet. Feb 07. HP: £400. ABP: £470.

Foley china advertising plaque, c1900, potter & lady carrying an amphora, 19.5 x 24.5cm, inscribed Depot for the Foley China, England's Finest Porcelain. Sworders, Stansted Mountfitchet. Feb 07. HP: £400. ABP: £470.

Pair Martin Brothers childrens saltglaze mugs, flower/insect decoration & names Bernard and Norman, Martin Bros, London, Southall, 12. 1893, restored, 7.5cm. Sworders, Stansted Mountfitchet. Feb 07. HP: £400. ABP: £470.

Doulton Lambeth salt glazed jug 'Marriage Day/After Marriage', c1925, designed by Harry Simeon, smiling & frowning face, half pint size, No X 8595, 12cm. Sworders, Stansted Mountfitchet. Feb 07. HP: £400. ABP: £470.

Set of 3 Minton strawberry dishes, white moulded detail, celadon ground, shape 1330, PODR 1867. Gorringes, Lewes. Jun 07. HP: £400. ABP: £470.

Kraak porcelain charger, vase of flowers within a border of fan shaped panels, rivet repair, 22in. Gorringes, Lewes. Jun 07. HP: £400. ABP: £470.

Pair of Spode spill vases, beaded rims/girdle, painted/ gilded with foliage in Imari colours, late 18th/19thC, No.967. Hartleys, Ilkley. Feb 07. HP: £390. ABP: £458.

Royal Worcester Fashionable Victorians, 12 Ltd Edn figures with certificates. Black Country Auctions, Dudley. Oct 05. HP: £385. ABP: £452.

Staffordshire pottery cottage money box, flanked by a male and female figure in ivory blue, pink and green, early/mid 19thC, 5.25in high. Andrew Hartley, Ilkley. Oct 04. HP: £380. ABP: £446.

Japanese porcelain bowl, side modelled with steps applied with ten individual figures in traditional dress, peering into a bowl, late 19th/20thC, 14in wide. Andrew Hartley, Ilkley. Oct 04. HP: £380. ABP: £446.

Palissy-style charger by Mafra of Caldas De Rainha, c1880, applied lizard, beetle, butterfly and snake, on a bed of extruded clay, impressed mark, 26.5cm. Sworders, Stansted Mountfitchet. Nov 04. HP: £380. ABP: £446.

Rare white hanging figure, mid 18thC, reclining woman holding a mirror, 14cm. Sworders, Stansted Mountfitchet. Nov 04. HP: £380. ABP: £446.

Biscuit porcelain brush washer, Kangxi, (1662-1722) in the form of a crab, hairline crack, 7.6cm. Sworders, Stansted Mountfitchet. Nov 04. HP: £380. ABP: £446.

Pair of Derby twin handled cache pots, c1820, white ground with a blue dot, gilt reserve containing a pink rose sprig, pole decorated banded borders, 15cm high. Rosebery's, London. Dec 04. HP: £380. ABP: £446.

Beswick Wessex saddleback sow, 'Merrywood Silver Wings 56th', 2.75in. Louis Taylor, Stoke on Trent. Mar 05. HP: £380. ABP: £446.

Set of 8 Tournai soft paste porcelain plates in Chelsea style, late 18thC, with butterflies within a gilt decorated spiral moulded borders, 25cm dia, and pair of conforming oval dishes and a larger example. Rosebery's, London. Mar 05. HP: £380. ABP: £446.

Unique Brickhurst Sussex pottery pig, with motto 'And you can Pook, and you can shove, But I'm a beast, as want be Druv', 9.5in. Gorringes, Lewes. Mar 05. HP: £380. ABP: £446.

Moorcroft Golden Jubilee large squat vase, by Emma Bossons, 16cm high. Henry Adams, Chichester. Jun 05. HP: £380. ABP: £446.

Clarice Cliff Idyll Bizarre bowl, 8in dia. Gardiner Houlgate, Corsham. Apr 05. HP: £380. ABP: £446.

First Period Worcester plate, scalloped form, centre enamelled in the manner of George Davis with birds in a landscape, 19cm dia, c1775. Bearne's, Exeter. Jun 05. HP: £380. ABP: £446.

Worcester, 1st period, sparrow beak jug, Chinese figures, grooved handle, c1768. A F Brock & Co Ltd, Stockport. Aug 05. HP: £380. ABP: £446.

Pair Mason's ironstone sauce tureens, 2-handled, covers & stands, printed/enamelled with a Japan pattern, 5.5in dia. Gorringes, Lewes. Sep 05. HP: £380. ABP: £446.

Pair Naples vases, campana-shape moulded and painted with numerous figures, 8.5in. Gorringes, Lewes. Oct 05. HP: £380. ABP: £446.

The numbering system acts as a reader reference as well as linking to the Analysis of each section.

Leeds pearlware figure of Neptune, crowned figure in loose-fitting robe, standing beside dolphin, imp'd mark, 7.5in. Gorringes, Lewes. Nov 05. HP: £380. ABP: £446.

Delft dish, c1770, polychrome colours, flowers and florets, nibbling, 30cm. Sworders, Stansted Mountfitchet. Feb 07. HP: £380. ABP: £446.

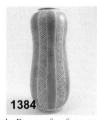

Poole Pottery freeform vase, set-pattern vertical stripes in red, blue and green, painted mark X / PKT, shape 702, 17in, neck-rim restored. Gorringes, Lewes. Feb 06. HP: £380. ABP: £446.

18thC Derby bisque figure of David Garrick, unpainted character, wearing medieval attire, incised CBD mark and model No. 21, c1770, 9.75in, damage. Gorringes, Lewes. Mar 06. HP: £380. ABP: £446.

Grainger & Co., Worcester reticulated vase, pierced with gilt rosettes, green leafage and pink anthemions, 5.75in. Gorringes, Lewes. Apr 06. HP: £380. ABP: £446.

Lenci pottery figure, lady in Continental costume with Aztec printed apron, water jar on her head, 18in high, indistinct signature to back of skirt. Andrew Hartley, Ilkley. Apr 06. HP: £380. ABP: £446.

Pair of Meissen porcelain figure groups, Man and Woman in 18thC dress, prob. 19thC, 9.5in. Louis Taylor, Stoke on Trent. Mar 06. HP: £380. ABP: £446.

German bellarmine stoneware jug, loop handle, tiger ware body incised with grotesque heads, 8.5in high. Hartleys, Ilkley. Feb 07. HP: £380. ABP: £446.

Dame Lucie Rie pottery bowl, powder blue ground, monogrammed to base, 12.8cm. Sworders, Stansted Mountfitchet. Feb 07. HP: £380. ABP: £446.

Goldscheider group of harlequin, disrobing a lady, 12.75in. Gorringes, Lewes. Apr 07. HP: £380. ABP: £446.

Pair of Dillwyn & Co., Swansea pink lustre plates, painted with a stork and a swan within pierced borders, 1811-17, 8in. Gorringes, Lewes. Apr 07. HP: £380. ABP: £446.

19thC Sevres cabinet plate, painted with the portrait bust of Me. de Bolignac, crowned gilt reserve, jewelled royal blue border, painted mark, 9.5in. Gorringes, Lewes. Apr 07. HP: £380. ABP: £446.

Fraureuth Kunstabteilung porcelain figure by A.Grath, 'Lady Godiva', white body with black and gilt detailed blanket, imp'd mark A.Grath to base, factory mark to underside, 47cm high. Rosebery's, London. Mar 06. HP: £380. ABP: £446.

Two porcelain half dolls both 5in high, first carrying a tray with breakfast items (one of chocolate girls), second doll with jointed arms by Bruno Schmidt imp'd No 3593, Germany pre-1918. Kent Auction Galleries, Folkestone. Jan 06. HP: £375. ABP: £441.

Border Fine Arts Pottery figure, The London Omnibus by R. Ayres, No 20/500, coach with driver and two horses, wooden base, 16in wide, with certificate. Hartleys, Ilkley. Oct 06. HP: £375. ABP: £441.

Hammer: £370 - £360

Pair of Rudolstadt male and female figures, he a flower & fruit encrusted tricorn hat, she a flower encrusted straw hat, 16in high. Dee, Atkinson & Harrison, Driffield. Nov 05. HP: £370. ABP: £435.

Pair Clarice Cliff Fantasque Bizarre 'Gardenia' vases. Great Western Auctions, Glasgow. Mar 07. HP: £365. ABP: £429.

Maw & Co 2-handled lustre decorated vase, white central frieze with flower and foliage design, 28.5cm high. Rosebery's, London. Sep 04. HP: £360. ABP: £423.

Early 19thC Mason's ironstone jug and bowl, gilt with butterflies on a blue ground, impressed mark, jug 22cm high. Cheffins, Cambridge. Feb 05. HP: £360. ABP: £423.

Worcester, Sir Joshua Reynolds pattern teapot/cover, c1765, restored spout, 16cm. Sworders, Stansted Mountfitchet. Feb 05. HP: £360. ABP: £423.

Montelupo maiolica dish, 18thC, painted with mounted soldier in a striped tunic, 35cm. Sworders, Stansted Mountfitchet. Feb 05. HP: £360. ABP: £423.

Beswick model of Nijinsky, with Lester Piggot up, wooden plinth base. Gorringes, Bexhill. Jun 05. HP: £360. ABP: £423.

19thC grey stoneware bear flagon/cover, possibly Denby, lift off head with grated clay details, handle behind, 8.5cm high. Cheffins, Cambridge. Apr 05. HP: £360. ABP: £423.

Italian Maiolica charger, panel with a classical scene, blue border with cherubs, monogram DA to reverse, 63cm. Charterhouse Auctioneers, Sherborne. Jun 05. HP: £360. ABP: £423.

Clarice Cliuff, Clovelly daffodil vase, shape 450, 5in high. Gardiner Houlgate, Corsham. Apr 05. HP: £360. ABP: £423.

Brannam pottery jug of squat form, strap handle, sgrafitto decorated in cream over chocolate slips with 3 oval panels of songbirds, 15cm high, incised CH Brannam, Barum Ware, N Devon, 1882, monogram for James Dewdney. Bearne's, Exeter. Jun 05. HP: £360. ABP: £423.

Royal Doulton figure, Grossmiths Tsang Ihang, HN582. Gorringes, Lewes. Nov 05. HP: £360. ABP: £423.

First Period Belleek twin-handled posy bowl, pierced-work body supporting a pair of naturalistic handles, imp'd mark to underside, 26cm wide. Gorringes, Bexhill. Dec 05. HP: £360. ABP: £423.

Beswick Dulux dog figure. Henry Adams, Chichester. Dec 05. HP: £360. ABP: £423.

R. Dux, sea maiden, figure. Henry Adams, Chichester. Dec 05. HP: £360. ABP: £423.

Leeds creamware chintz pattern coffee pot and cover, English c1775, associated domed cover, stylised floral and geometric decoration, impressed triangle to base, 22.5cm high, chips, damage to spout. Rosebery's, London. Dec 05. HP: £360. ABP: £423.

Early Moorcroft pottery vase in blue and pale green with a stylised floral design, 'Art Nouveau' manner, 4in high, base painted 'W.M. Des' in script, c1900. Canterbury Auction Galleries, Kent. Oct 05. HP: £360. ABP: £423.

Zsolnay heart shaped wall plaque, pierced floral decoration. Gorringes, Lewes. Feb 06. HP: £360. ABP: £423.

Meissen figure depicting fire, c1880, putti mixing a cup and saucer of chocolate, crossed sword mark, incised C97, loss to kettle handle and spout, 11cm. Sworders, Stansted Mountfitchet. Feb 06. HP: £360. ABP: £423.

Beswick dairy short horn bull, titled Gwersylt Lord Oxford. Thos Mawer & Son, Lincoln. Mar 06. HP: £360. ABP: £423.

1417

18thC sauce boat, c1760, poss. Worcester, enamelled in colours with flowers within rococo foliate moulded borders, 18cm long. Rosebery's, London. Mar 06. HP: £360. ABP: £423.

1418

Large Royal Albert Moonlight Rose tea/dinner service comprising of 112 various pieces. Boldon Auction Galleries, Tyne & Wear. Mar 06. HP: £360. ABP: £423.

1419

Pair Wedgwood black basalt plaques, one decorated in relief with the Three Graces, other with an angel and two classical maidens, impressed marks verso, 8.5in. Gorringes, Lewes. Apr 06. HP: £360. ABP: £423.

1420

Charlotte Rhead / Bursley Ware charger, pattern No. 1432, 14.4in. Louis Taylor, Stoke on Trent. Mar 06. HP: £360. ABP: £423.

1421

R. Doulton figure, Prudence, HN1883. Louis Taylor, Stoke. Mar 06. HP: £360. ABP: £423.

1422

Imari porcelain dish, oblong form, shaped rim, painted with a basket of flowers, foliate panel border, gilded highlights, 12.25in wide, 19thC. Andrew Hartley, Ilkley. Apr 06. HP: £360. ABP: £423.

1423

Early 19thC salt-glazed stoneware tobacco box, canted corners, moulded with rural scenes & flowers, domed cover and internal liner, 5in. Gorringes, Lewes. Jun 06. HP: £360. ABP: £423.

> The illustrations are in descending price order. The price range is indicated at the top of each page.

1424

Pair Wedgwood Black Jasper urns, 2-handled with covers, neo-classical decoration in white relief, 10in, finials detached. Gorringes, Lewes. Jun 06. HP: £360. ABP: £423.

1425

18thC Chinese armorial dish, Campbell of Inverneill in Argyle, c1780, c.f. David Sanctuary Howard, page 619, 9.5in, cracked. Gorringes, Lewes. Jun 06. HP: £360. ABP: £423.

1426

Four Royal Crown Derby seated 'Royal Cat' ornaments. Henry Adams, Chichester. Oct 06. HP: £360. ABP: £423.

Hammer: £360 - £350

1427

19thC Majolica sardine dish. (prob. George Jones) Henry Adams, Chichester. Oct 06. HP: £360. ABP: £423.

1428

Chelsea oval dish, Red Anchor period, 1752-56, with fruit and insects in enamels, painted mark in chocolate-brown, 10.25in. Gorringes, Lewes. Oct 06. HP: £360. ABP: £423.

1429

Moorcroft McIntyre rose garland pattern two handled bowl, gilt highlights, No. M2591, 7in wide overall. Gorringes, Lewes. Dec 06. HP: £360. ABP: £423.

1430

Wedgwood vase by Keith Murray, banded sides in a pale blue glaze, 11.25in high. Hartleys, Ilkley. Dec 06. HP: £360. ABP: £423.

1431

Burmantofts faience vase, Louis Kramer, painted with foliage in turquoise and blue on white ground, mottled glaze to interior, 8.25in high. Hartleys, Ilkley. Dec 06. HP: £360. ABP: £423.

1432

Castleford tea set, c1790: pot with hinged cover, sucrier/cover and jug, white pottery bodies moulded with classical motifs, chips/cracks. (4) Sworders, Stansted Mountfitchet. Feb 07. HP: £360. ABP: £423.

1433

Set of three pearlware meat dishes, blue printed with scrolling foliage/flower heads, vermiculated ground, leaf border, early 19thC, 19in wide. Hartleys, Ilkley. Apr 07. HP: £360. ABP: £423.

1434

Pair of Royal Crown Derby pink ground cups and stands, English 1939, painted with an exotic bird, floral studies within gilt borders, signed 'Mosely'. 6cm high. Rosebery's, London. Jun 05. HP: £350. ABP: £411.

1435

Clarice Cliff charger. Stride & Son, Chichester. Sep 05. HP: £350. ABP: £411.

1436

Meissen Comedia dell'Arte figure of a flower seller, German 20thC, with a basket of flowers & wearing a mask, 18cm high. Rosebery's, London. Dec 05. HP: £350. ABP: £411.

Ceramics Prices **89**

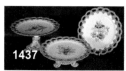

Thomas Ford botanical dessert service, English late 19thC, pierced ribbon borders, a plate AF, 23.5cm dia. (18) Rosebery's, London. Dec 05. HP: £350. ABP: £411.

Royal Worcester blush ivory figure, of a girl in country dress with a basket over her shoulder, date code for 1895, 43cm high. Rosebery's, London. Mar 06. HP: £350. ABP: £411.

George Jones majolica sardine dish, cover/stand, c1870, 4in. Louis Taylor, Stoke on Trent. Mar 06. HP: £350. ABP: £411.

18thC Worcester small teapot, decorated with an Oriental landscape and a man in a pavilion, in underglaze blue, 6in. Gorringes, Lewes. Jul 06. HP: £350. ABP: £411.

Beswick Shorthorn Bull Ch. Gwersylt Lord Oxford 74th, model No. 1504, designed by Arthur Gredlington, issued 1957-1973, 12.5cm high. Halls Fine Art, Shrewsbury. Apr 07. HP: £350. ABP: £411.

Wood & Caldwell terracotta bust of Alexander. Tring Market Auctions, Herts. Oct 04. HP: £340. ABP: £399.

Art Deco Rosenthal porcelain figure, exotic dancer, revealing costume painted in colours, base with gilt highlights, 19.5cm high, factory printed marks, with another similar. (2) Rosebery's, London. Sep 04. HP: £340. ABP: £399.

> Categories or themes can be followed through the colour coded Index which contains over 4500 cross references.

R. Doulton porcelain figure, Sibell, 6.75in high, HN1695, date code 1936. Canterbury Auction Galleries, Kent. Apr 05. HP: £340. ABP: £399.

Early 19thC Spode blue/white gravy Argyle & cover printed with baskets of flowers, printed marks, 17.5cm high. Cheffins, Cambridge. Apr 05. HP: £340. ABP: £399.

18thC Salopian blue/white mask jug printed with fisherman pattern on leaf moulded body, S mark, 23.5cm high. Cheffins, Cambridge. Apr 05. HP: £340. ABP: £399.

Pair Victorian Staffordshire models, seated spaniels with black painted decoration, 12.8in. Semley Auctioneers, Semley, Dorset. Jul 05. HP: £340. ABP: £399.

Derby, Wm. Duesbury & Co. porcelain mug, ribbed strap handle, enamelled in manner of Edward Withers, 9.5cm high, c1780, superficial scratches. Bearne's, Exeter. Jun 05. HP: £340. ABP: £399.

Worcester, 1st period, scalloped dish, mazarine blue border with gilt festoons, factory painted with bird decoration, 'W' mark in blue underglaze, c1775. A F Brock & Co Ltd, Stockport. Aug 05. HP: £340. ABP: £399.

Wemyss wash jug and basin, painted with black cockerels. (basin cracked) Gorringes, Lewes. Sep 05. HP: £340. ABP: £399.

Worcester porcelain basket, 18thC, pierced design, naturalistic handles, centred with painted scene of exotic birds in a landscape, 21cm long. Gorringes, Bexhill. Dec 05. HP: £340. ABP: £399.

Early 19thC Ridgway part tea/coffee service, painted with cartouches of black/nutbrown leaves, salmon pink ground. (40) Dee, Atkinson & Harrison, Driffield. Nov 05. HP: £340. ABP: £399.

Wedgwood black porcelain plaque, 24 x 18.5cm, scantily clad lady kneeling on plinth holding smaller female figure, gilt frame damaged. A F Brock & Co Ltd, Stockport. Nov 05. HP: £340. ABP: £399.

Leeds creamware teapot, bullet-shape, painted with a basket of fruit and flowers within floral leaf-scrolls in rust enamel, c1770, 4.5in. Gorringes, Lewes. Apr 05. HP: £340. ABP: £399.

Pair of 18thC creamware candlesticks, with corinthian columns, with flowers in blue, 10in, one restored. Gorringes, Lewes. Apr 05. HP: £340. ABP: £399.

1456

Early 19thC Sunderland pink lustre jug, printed/enamelled with a ship, figures & verse, 7in. Gorringes, Lewes. Apr 05. HP: £340. ABP: £399.

1457

Minton game pie dish, liner and cover, moulded with oak leaves against a basket ground, 13in long, dish with glue repairs. Gorringes, Lewes. Feb 06. HP: £340. ABP: £399.

1458

C.H.Brannam earthenware vase, 4 panels of flowers and birds, shades of blue/brown, initialled JD, dated 1886, 14.5in. Gorringes, Lewes. Feb 06. HP: £340. ABP: £399.

1459

Mid 18thC English Delft polychrome plate painted in blue manganese/yellow with Chinese islands pavilions and trees, 36.5cm dia. Cheffins, Cambridge. Feb 06. HP: £340. ABP: £399.

1460

Derby creamer, c1765, shell form in rococo style, 8.5cm high. Rosebery's, London. Mar 06. HP: £340. ABP: £399.

1461

Early 20thC Clarice Cliff Newport pottery sugar shaker, blue chintz pattern, black printed Fantasque mark, 5.5in high. Diamond Mills & Co, Felixstowe. Mar 06. HP: £340. ABP: £399.

1462

Beswick stocky jogging mare, model No. 855, third version, rocking horse grey, designed by Arthur Gredington, issued 1947-1962, 6in high. Halls Fine Art, Shrewsbury. Apr 06. HP: £340. ABP: £399.

1463

Beswick figure, Indian on horseback, 8.5in high, black mark, gold sticker. Andrew Hartley, Ilkley. Apr 06. HP: £340. ABP: £399.

1464

Galle-style model of a cat, painted with heart motifs in iron-red, green ground, 13in. Gorringes, Lewes. Jun 06. HP: £340. ABP: £399.

1465

Pair Liverpool Delft dishes, c1770, painted with pagoda, castle and sampans, 22.5cm. Sworders, Stansted Mountfitchet. Feb 07. HP: £340. ABP: £399.

Hammer: £340 - £330

1466

Prattware toby jug gentleman, tricorn hat, figural loop handle, early 19thC, 8in high. Hartleys, Ilkley. Jun 06. HP: £340. ABP: £399.

1467

Troika wheel vase, abstract motifs, cream textured ground, Cornwall mark, monogram FIR, 8in. Gorringes, Lewes. Mar 06. HP: £340. ABP: £399.

1468

Royal Copenhagen part dinner service, painted with blue flowers. (34) Hartleys, Ilkley. Oct 06. HP: £340. ABP: £399.

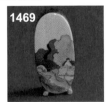

1469

Deco Clarice Cliff bizarre oval sugar shaker, with a cottage beside a river and bridge, 13cm high. Calder Valley Auctioneers, Halifax. Apr 07. HP: £340. ABP: £399.

1470

Hispano-Moresque lustre charger, deeply dished and painted with set-patterns in blue and copper lustre, 18in. Gorringes, Lewes. Oct 06. HP: £340. ABP: £399.

1471

Minton barrel-shaped garden seat, printed with leaves in blue against a wicker-effect aesthetic ground, 17.5in, restored. Gorringes, Lewes. Apr 07. HP: £340. ABP: £399.

1472

Chelsea octagonal plate, Red Anchor period, 1752-56, with flower sprays in enamels, moulded diaper border, painted mark, 8.75in. Gorringes, Lewes. Oct 06. HP: £340. ABP: £399.

1473

Derby figure group, Welsh Tailor's Wife, mother with suckling child, seated upon goat, incised numeral 62, 6in. Gorringes, Lewes. Oct 06. HP: £340. ABP: £399.

1474

R.W. Martin Brothers vase, 1889, saltglazed stoneware, incised with flowers and leaves, script signature/date, 6.5in. Gorringes, Lewes. Apr 07. HP: £340. ABP: £399.

1475

Royal Doulton Blue Children vase, 11.25in. Louis Taylor, Stoke on Trent. Mar 06. HP: £330. ABP: £388.

Hammer: £330 - £320

Carlton Ware sketching bird vase, 36cm. Great Western Auctions, Glasgow. May 05. HP: £330. ABP: £388.

Minton Secessionist jardinière decorated with tree by a river, 30cm high. Great Western Auctions, Glasgow. May 05. HP: £330. ABP: £388.

Clarice Cliff Bizarre 'Delicia Pansies' vase. Great Western Auctions, Glasgow. Sep 05. HP: £330. ABP: £388.

Dame Lucie Rie, Art Pottery charger, brown glazed interior, white glazed exterior, 10in. Denhams, Warnham, Sussex. Nov 05. HP: £330. ABP: £388.

George Jones majolica jardiniere, moulded with buttercups on a Royal blue ground, turquoise interior, 10.25in. Hartleys, Ilkley. Dec 06. HP: £330. ABP: £388.

Four Doccia florally decorated plates, gilt borders, c1780, label verso 'bought Florence Italy 1794'. Sworders, Stansted Mountfitchet. Nov 04. HP: £325. ABP: £382.

Delft blue/white bleeding bowl, inside painted with stylised plants, 2 lug handles, restored, c1720, 19.5cm. Sworders, Stansted Mountfitchet. Feb 05. HP: £320. ABP: £376.

33 assorted Dutch Delft tiles, 18thC, biblical, mythological, figural, animal/insect scenes, majority with spiders head corner motifs, 12.5cm and 13.5cm square. Sworders, Stansted Mountfitchet. Feb 05. HP: £320. ABP: £376.

Pair of Derby children with Macaroni cat & dog, c1775, naturalistic bases, 16cm high. Rosebery's, London. Mar 05. HP: £320. ABP: £376.

Pair of German porcelain seated Pug dogs, late 19thC, white with painted muzzles and bell collars, 21cm high. Rosebery's, London. Mar 05. HP: £320. ABP: £376.

William IV commemorative coronation mug, printed in black with portraits of King William and Queen Adelaide flanking a Royal crest, internally printed around the rim, pearlware glazed, 10cm high. Rosebery's, London. Mar 05. HP: £320. ABP: £376.

18thC Westerwald German stoneware jug, reeded collar, loop handle, decorated with stylized floral forms and G R imp'd crest. Locke & England, Leamington Spa. Mar 05. HP: £320. ABP: £376.

Prices quoted are actual hammer prices (HP) and the Approximate Buyer's Price (ABP) includes an average premium of 15% + VAT.

Turner & Wood parian portrait bust of Disraeli, on socle, 1880-88, impressed maker's mark, 14in. Gorringes, Lewes. Mar 05. HP: £320. ABP: £376.

Meissen portrait bust of a lady, on socle, square plinth moulded with lyre, painted mark in underglaze blue and incised numeral, 4.75in. Gorringes, Lewes. Apr 05. HP: £320. ABP: £376.

Group of 3 Beswick figures, Highland Bull, Highland Cow and Highland Calf. Clevedon Salerooms, Bristol. Jun 05. HP: £320. ABP: £376.

Wemyss teapot/cover, early 20thC, painted with cabbage roses, printed mark, spout chip, 10.5cm. Sworders, Stansted Mountfitchet. Apr 05. HP: £320. ABP: £376.

Mid-19thC salt-glazed stoneware pin-tidy, in form of a double-sided portrait bust of a lady, 4in. Gorringes, Lewes. Jun 05. HP: £320. ABP: £376.

Two Derby allegorical figures, Water & Earth, English late 18thC, fisher woman holding a net, the male as a gardener, canted square base, incised numerals to bases, 19cm. Rosebery's, London. Jun 05. HP: £320. ABP: £376.

New Hall sucrier and cover painted with the floral 1927 pattern on basket moulding, 18.5cm across the handles with an oval section sucrier and cover painted with red flowering green and gilt foliage bands, marked No.45 on the base. (4) Cheffins, Cambridge. Apr 05. HP: £320. ABP: £376.

1495

Pair of MacIntyre Alhambra jardinieres, 17cm. Charterhouse Auctioneers, Sherborne. Jun 05. HP: £320. ABP: £376.

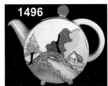

1496

Clarice Cliff 'Lorna' Bonjour teapot and cover, 6.5in high. (cover restored) Gardiner Houlgate, Corsham. Apr 05. HP: £320. ABP: £376.

1497

Dutch delft polychrome figure, seated wild boar with a panel of flowers painted on its back, 17cm high, painted with the marks of Jacobus Adriaenson Halder, one ear restuck. Bearne's, Exeter. Jun 05. HP: £320. ABP: £376.

1498

Pair of Kutani vases, c1900, shi-shi handles, cartouches painted with figures in landscapes, Kutani sei in red, 45cm. Sworders, Stansted Mountfitchet. Jul 05. HP: £320. ABP: £376.

1499

Goldscheider wall mask, female wearing blue scarf, printed mark, Goldscheider, Wien, 11in. Gorringes, Lewes. Oct 05. HP: £320. ABP: £376.

1500

Pair of 19thC Chinese porcelain parrots, feathers painted in green, perched on stumps, 7.25in. Gorringes, Lewes. Oct 05. HP: £320. ABP: £376.

1501

Marcolini Meissen silver-mounted tea canister, each side painted with a peasant figure in a field in brown enamel, shoulder with leaf festoons, silver cover with cone finial, silver scroll feet, painted crossed swords mark with star, 1774-1814, 5.75in. Gorringes, Lewes. Oct 05. HP: £320. ABP: £376.

1502

Glyn Colledge Morris ware squat bowl. Gorringes, Bexhill. Oct 05. HP: £320. ABP: £376.

1503

Two German porcelain dogs, Mopsen, c1870, each bitch on its haunches, one with pup, both restored, 21cm and 20cm. Sworders, Stansted Mountfitchet. Nov 05. HP: £320. ABP: £376.

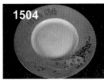

1504

Gardner charger, Russian 19thC, pale blue border, enriched with gilt Cyrillic script & floral spray, 42.5cm. Rosebery's, London. Dec 05. HP: £320. ABP: £376.

Hammer: £320

1505

18thC creamware jug, painted with the name of original owner, Elizabeth Petty Woodhall and verse in rust enamel, 5in. Gorringes, Lewes. Apr 05. HP: £320. ABP: £376.

1506

Caughley toy-size coffee cup and saucer, painted with the typical river island pattern in underglaze blue, 's' mark, c1785, 2.75in saucer. Gorringes, Lewes. Feb 06. HP: £320. ABP: £376.

1507

Royal Doulton figure of a retriever with a pheasant in its mouth. HN2529, 9in. Ewbank Auctioneers, Send, Surrey. Dec 05. HP: £320. ABP: £376.

1508

Pair of Carlton Ware ginger jars/covers, deep blue ground, gilt, chinoiserie scenes, domed covers with Fo dog finial's, 42cm high. Rosebery's, London. Feb 06. HP: £320. ABP: £376.

1509

Two Victorian Prattware oval pot lids depicting smoking scenes, oak frames. Reeman Dansie, Colchester. Apr 06. HP: £320. ABP: £376.

1510

Prattware Napoleonic commemorative jug, c1798, one side moulded in relief with a portrait bust of Admiral Duncan, other with Captain Trollope, painted in Pratt colours, 14cm high. Rosebery's, London. Mar 06. HP: £320. ABP: £376.

1511

Pair of late 19thC Samson chickens, brightly coloured cock and hen, gold anchor mark, 7.25in high. Dee, Atkinson & Harrison, Driffield. Apr 06. HP: £320. ABP: £376.

1512

Pair Royal Worcester porcelain figures, Wood Chopper and Milk Maid, base with purple R. Worcester mark, 4 dots and 1 star marked 1774. slight chip to wood chopper's hat, 7.5in. Denhams, Warnham, Sussex. Sep 05. HP: £320. ABP: £376.

1513

Burmantofts faience stick stand, tube lined with Irises, cream ground, turquoise and brown rim and foot, 24.5in high, impressed No.2026. Andrew Hartley, Ilkley. Apr 06. HP: £320. ABP: £376.

Hammer: £320 - £310

Dame Lucie Rie, Art Pottery tapering bowl, brown glazed exterior and white glazed interior, 4in. Denhams, Warnham, Sussex. Nov 05. HP: £320. ABP: £376.

Beswick mounted American Indian, mould 1391, 8.5in. Gorringes, Lewes. Jun 06. HP: £320. ABP: £376.

William De Morgan jug painted by Joe Juster, mulberry-coloured flowers and green leaves, incised painters' initials, impressed mark, c1885, 7in, handle restored. Gorringes, Lewes. Jun 06. HP: £320. ABP: £376.

Pair of Samson porcelain figure ornaments. Henry Adams, Chichester. Jul 06. HP: £320. ABP: £376.

Hispano-Moresque lustre charger, deeply-dished and painted with set-patterns in blue and copper lustre, 18in. Gorringes, Lewes. Oct 06. HP: £320. ABP: £376.

94 *Ceramics Prices*

Clarice Cliff honey pot, 'Summerhouse', cover with bee handle, 1931-33, 3.5in. Gorringes, Lewes. Oct 06. HP: £320. ABP: £376.

Worcester sauce jug, painted with flowers, underglaze blue, 7in. long. Gorringes, Lewes. Oct 06. HP: £320. ABP: £376.

Ludwigsburg figure of a violinist, seated semi-draped, on scroll base, painted mark, 6in. Gorringes, Lewes. Oct 06. HP: £320. ABP: £376.

Derby figure, 'The Dresden Shepherd', robed character on scroll base, painted by 'The Cotton Stem Painter', pad marks, 8.5in. Gorringes, Lewes. Oct 06. HP: £320. ABP: £376.

Chinese double gourd shaped porcelain vase, famille rose palette with pheasants amongst trees and rocks, 9in. Gorringes, Lewes. Dec 06. HP: £320. ABP: £376.

Troika tin mine lamp base, (May 1981), 8.5in. Gorringes, Lewes. Dec 06. HP: £320. ABP: £376.

Early Bow plate, painted with a prunus root pattern and Buddhistic symbols in underglaze blue, 9in. Gorringes, Lewes. Dec 06. HP: £320. ABP: £376.

Pair of 19thC Ansbach cups, painted with hunting scenes and gilded with leaf scrolls, saucer en suite painted with a partridge, and a gilded saucer. Gorringes, Lewes. Feb 07. HP: £320. ABP: £376.

The numbering system acts as a reader reference as well as linking to the Analysis of each section.

Royal Doulton Wandering Minstrel loving cup, moulded in relief with medieval figures around castle walls, Ltd Edn, 307/600, 5.5in high. Golding Young & Co, Grantham. Nov 06. HP: £320. ABP: £376.

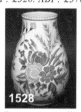

Poole Pottery vase, allover flowerheads, ZW pattern, shape 337, 10in high. George Kidner, Lymington. Jan 07. HP: £320. ABP: £376.

Carlton Ware fantasia bowl, 3 ball feet with matching flower brick. Great Western Auctions, Glasgow. Feb 07. HP: £320. ABP: £376.

Pair of Jacob Petite cornucopia vases, c1840, flowers & exotic birds, green ground, pink plinths, gilt heightening, J P mark, underglaze blue, rim restored, 23cm. Sworders, Stansted Mountfitchet. Feb 07. HP: £320. ABP: £376.

Extensive lot of Susie Cooper for Grays dinnerwares, Patt. No 7938IL: all with hand-painted floral design, gilt rims, damage. (56) Great Western Auctions, Glasgow. Jul 06. HP: £315. ABP: £370.

3 Davenport meat dishes, mid 19thC, meat plate with a well and two graduated rectangular plates, two 51cm and 45cm. (3) Sworders, Stansted Mountfitchet. Nov 05. HP: £310. ABP: £364.

Beswick pottery model of a bay showjumper with female rider clearing a log fence, naturalistic plinth, 24 x 27cm. Locke & England, Leamington Spa. Jul 05. HP: £310. ABP: £364.

Clarice Cliff Bizarre 'Forest Glen' jug. Great Western Auctions, Glasgow. Sep 05. HP: £310. ABP: £364.

Macintyre Aurelian ware tyg, tapering form painted and printed with Art Nouveau flowers in tones of red, blue and gold, 5.25in high. Hartleys, Ilkley. Oct 06. HP: £310. ABP: £364.

Carlton Ware 'Devils Copse' vase. Great Western Auctions, Glasgow. Oct 06. HP: £310. ABP: £364.

Royal Worcester porcelain plate, painted with peaches and cherries by T Lockyer, frilled/beaded gilded border, 8.75in wide. Hartleys, Ilkley. Feb 07. HP: £310. ABP: £364.

Gustavsberg Argenta twin handled pottery bowl by Wilheim Kage, mottled green ground with sea creature design, painted marks, 13.5cm high. Rosebery's, London. Sep 04. HP: £300. ABP: £352.

Two Foley Intarsio green cats, painted with brown mice, open mouths, green glass eyes, 9.5in, faults. Dee, Atkinson & Harrison, Driffield. Nov 04. HP: £300. ABP: £352.

Reissner & Kessel porcelain bust, c1905, young lady in a risqué dress, bonnet & cloak, printed R.S & K mark, 45.5cm. Sworders, Stansted Mountfitchet. Nov 04. HP: £300. ABP: £352.

Satsuma Koro, c1875, two panels in enamel and gilding of warriors and a maiden, lakeside pavillion with Shi Shi mask feet, handles and knop, signed, small chips, 17cm. Sworders, Stansted Mountfitchet. Nov 04. HP: £300. ABP: £352.

Coalport aesthetic style cabaret coffee set. Gorringes, Bexhill. Sep 04. HP: £300. ABP: £352.

Linthorpe earthenware trial plate, 28.5cm, and another plate. Gorringes, Bexhill. Dec 04. HP: £300. ABP: £352.

19thC Staffordshire pottery spaniel and puppy group, iron red, blue draped base, 6.25in high. Diamond Mills & Co, Felixstowe. Dec 04. HP: £300. ABP: £352.

Carter, Stabler & Adams Poole vase, shape No. 973, pastel browns, painted & impressed marks, 18cm high. Cheffins, Cambridge. Feb 05. HP: £300. ABP: £352.

German stoneware Bellarmine jug, c1680, with mask on the neck and a lion rampant on the belly, 21.5cm. Sworders, Stansted Mountfitchet. Feb 05. HP: £300. ABP: £352.

Pair Carl Thieme Potschappal tureens/covers, 20thC, ducks, one with beak open, printed, imp'd and painted No. 73, 24cm. Sworders, Stansted Mountfitchet. Feb 05. HP: £300. ABP: £352.

Pair of Troika square vases. Stroud Auctions, Stroud. Aug 05. HP: £300. ABP: £352.

Minton majolica game pie tureen/cover, 1870, as a basket with dead game on lid, imp'd marks, date code, cracked, 31.5cm. Sworders, Stansted Mountfitchet. Feb 05. HP: £300. ABP: £352.

Carltonware orange lustre breakfast set, 9 pieces incl. teapot and toast rack with fitted egg cruet, pattern No. 2946. Gorringes, Lewes. Jan 05. HP: £300. ABP: £352.

Italian maiolica saucer, with a Madonna and child subject and script, 'Con Pol di Casa', repaired cracks, 6in. Gorringes, Lewes. Jan 05. HP: £300. ABP: £352.

Wedgwood & Bentley black basalt oval portrait plaque, moulded in relief, profile portrait of Keppel, 11.8cm. Rosebery's, London. Mar 05. HP: £300. ABP: £352.

18thC flagon decorated with a white glaze and flowers, looped handle, 32cm. Rosebery's, London. Mar 05. HP: £300. ABP: £352.

Hammer: £300

Early 19thC pink lustre commemorative mug, 'Success to the Coal Trade', painted with ship off-shore, 4in, chipped, and a Sunderland pink lustre jug printed with a view of the Cast Iron Bridge, 4in. Gorringes, Lewes. Apr 05. HP: £300. ABP: £352.

Early 19thC Staffordshire toby jug, florid features, holding a jug of ale and clay pipe, 25cm high. Clevedon Salerooms, Bristol. Jun 05. HP: £300. ABP: £352.

Doulton Luscian ware vase Beefeater, entitled to base Tower Warder, London 1896, signed W. Nunn, 19cm high. Great Western Auctions, Glasgow. May 05. HP: £300. ABP: £352.

Gardner bisque figure group, Russian late 19thC, 2 young males, one seated on broken cart wheel, the other leaning against a tree trunk, standing figure glued, 14.5cm high. Rosebery's, London. Jun 05. HP: £300. ABP: £352.

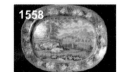

Davenport, stone-china meat platter, transfer printed in blue/white, cattle in parkland setting, floral border, c1880, 46cm. Rosebery's, London. Jun 05. HP: £300. ABP: £352.

John Dawson, Sunderland, early 19thC blue/white bowl printed with repeated scenes of a boy offering a bird's nest to lady, printed mark, 23.5cm dia. (W) Cheffins, Cambridge. Apr 05. HP: £300. ABP: £352.

Ruskin high fired jardiniere, 1925, glazed in deep red with iridescent lustre streaks, impressed Ruskin, England 1925, 7.5in high. Halls Fine Art, Shrewsbury. Jul 05. HP: £300. ABP: £352.

Royal Doulton figure Teresa, HN1682, issued 1935-1949, printed marks and inscribed number, chips to flowers and tiny chip to side base, 14.6cm high, 16.1cm. Sworders, Stansted Mountfitchet. Jul 05. HP: £300. ABP: £352.

Clarice Cliff nasturtium vase. Great Western Auctions, Glasgow. Oct 05. HP: £300. ABP: £352.

Copenhagen model of a bull, printed mark, 11.5in long. Gorringes, Lewes. Oct 05. HP: £300. ABP: £352.

Beswick model of a Staffordshire bull terrier. Louis Taylor, Stoke on Trent. Sep 05. HP: £300. ABP: £352.

Collection, Aynsley Orchard Gold and similarly transfer decorated bone china in excess of 50 pieces. Locke & England, Leamington Spa. Sep 05. HP: £300. ABP: £352.

Beswick Ayrshire bull, Champion Whitehill Mandate, brown, white & shaded gloss glaze. Locke & England, Leamington Spa. Sep 05. HP: £300. ABP: £352.

Royal Doulton pottery vase, Blue Children series, mother & child in rural landscape, 11in high, impressed Doulton Lambeth faience mark to base, blue printed Royal Doulton mark, imp'd No. L8307. Canterbury Auction Galleries, Kent. Oct 05. HP: £300. ABP: £352.

Royal Doulton 'Columbine' figurine. Henry Adams, Chichester. Dec 05. HP: £300. ABP: £352.

18thC teapot, bullet-shape with entwined handle, painted with a tortoiseshell effect, 4.5in. Gorringes, Lewes. Apr 05. HP: £300. ABP: £352.

An 18th century creamware mug, printed with verse, "A Sailor's Life...", and ship within enamelled garland, 4in. Gorringes, Lewes. Apr 05. HP: £300. ABP: £352.

Doulton Lambeth faience wall plate, painted with yellow hibiscus and leaves by Fanny Stable, signed with initials, 13.75in. Gorringes, Lewes. Feb 06. HP: £300. ABP: £352.

Daniel trio, plain edge shape, variation 'C', tea cup, coffee cup and saucer painted with fruit and flowers within gilt c-scrolls, pink ground, pattern 4562, double-scroll handles. Gorringes, Lewes. Feb 06. HP: £300. ABP: £352.

Pair Bow hexagonal plates, c1765, landscape reserves, powder blue ground, pseudo Chinese marks, chips, 16.5cm. Sworders, Stansted Mountfitchet. Feb 06. HP: £300. ABP: £352.

Pair Copeland parian portrait busts, Prince and Princess of Wales, sculpted by F M Miller imp'd marks verso 'Pub'd Feb X1 1863, Crystal Palace Art Union', socles also imp'd, 30.5cm and 30cm. Sworders, Stansted Mountfitchet. Feb 06. HP: £300. ABP: £352.

Royal Doulton Jester, damage and repairs. Lambert & Foster, Tenterden. Mar 06. HP: £300. ABP: £352.

Staffordshire flat back group of a lion resting on a killed soldier, 23cm high. Boldon Auc. Galleries, Tyne & Wear. Mar 06. HP: £300. ABP: £352.

Doulton Faience wall plate painted by Mary Capes, with flowering shrub and background hills, monogrammed and dated '78. Gorringes, Lewes. Apr 06. HP: £300. ABP: £352.

Della Robbia terracotta jug, slip decorated with leaves in cream, green and turquoise, russet ground, signed H. Pierce, 11in high. Golding Young & Co, Grantham. Feb 06. HP: £300. ABP: £352.

Dennis China Works pottery charger, designed by Sally Tuffin, with a cockerel on a pale brown ground, signed with artists initials & No.23, 14in dia. Golding Young & Co, Grantham. Feb 06. HP: £300. ABP: £352.

The illustrations are in descending price order. The price range is indicated at the top of each page.

19thC Chinese vase/cover, yellow ground and decorated in relief with butterflies and flora, moulded seal mark to base of Wang Binrong (1820-1860), 12in high. Golding Young & Co, Grantham. Feb 06. HP: £300. ABP: £352.

Royal Worcester porcelain plate, gilded and beaded rim, painted with peaches and blackberries by H Ayrton, 8.75in wide, black mark. Andrew Hartley, Ilkley. Apr 06. HP: £300. ABP: £352.

Hammer: £300

Troika slab vase of tapering form, incised with geometric patterns, blue textured ground, 6.75in high, and a similar cylindrical vase. Andrew Hartley, Ilkley. Apr 06. HP: £300. ABP: £352.

Staffordshire pottery money box as a cottage, faces in the windows, moulded foliage and central chimney, flanked by a lady and gentleman, mid 19thC, 5in high. Hartleys, Ilkley. Aug 06. HP: £300. ABP: £352.

Beswick grazing shire horse, grey, 5.5in. Hartleys, Ilkley. Aug 06. HP: £300. ABP: £352.

Persian bowl, 18th/19thC, painted with a prince in flagrante with a concubine, rim with calligraphy, 22cm, rivetted. Sworders, Stansted Mountfitchet. Apr 06. HP: £300. ABP: £352.

Worcester teapot, painted with an island pattern in underglaze blue, cover with flower handle, crescent mark, c1770, 5.5in. Gorringes, Lewes. Oct 06. HP: £300. ABP: £352.

Pair of black basalt portrait busts, Shelley & Wordsworth, attrib. to Wood & Caldwell, integral socles, stepped black marble plinths, 7.5in total height. Gorringes, Lewes. Oct 06. HP: £300. ABP: £352.

R. Lancastrian pottery vase, by William Mycock, painted with stylized trees on turquoise ground, 8.5in high. Hartleys, Ilkley. Oct 06. HP: £300. ABP: £352.

Mason's ironstone part dinner service, Imari palette, panels of flowers, foliage, scrolling borders, retailed by Thomas & Higginbotham 11 & 12 Wellington Quay Dublin, puce printed mark to bases. (20) a/f. Rosebery's, London. Oct 06. HP: £300. ABP: £352.

Early 20thC Austrian pottery standing figure, 'Blackamoor' rocky pattern base, 29in high, unmarked, imp'd No. 870 to base, basket broken/restuck. Canterbury Auction Galleries, Kent. Apr 07. HP: £300. ABP: £352.

Wemyss wash bowl & pitcher, hand painted rose decoration, painted & impressed Wemyss mark to base, 15.5in bowl dia x 5in high. Kent Auction Galleries, Folkestone. Nov 06. HP: £300. ABP: £352.

18thC Delft charger, Oriental courtier figure and attendant, 13in. Gorringes, Lewes. Dec 06. HP: £300. ABP: £352.

Bow plate, painted with wild birds, chrysanthemum and a prunus root in enamels, 9in. Gorringes, Lewes. Dec 06. HP: £300. ABP: £352.

Rudolstadt porcelain group, couple dancing, floral 18thC dress, late 19th/20thC, 17.5in high. Hartleys, Ilkley. Dec 06. HP: £300. ABP: £352.

Mason's type ironstone vase, two handled, gilded with flowers, deep blue ground, domed cover, kylin finial, 17.5in. Gorringes, Lewes. Feb 07. HP: £300. ABP: £352.

Pair of early 19thC Derby plates, painted with views, named verso, 'In Italy' and 'In Germany', gilded tangerine borders, CBD marks in red enamel, 1800-25, 8.75in. Gorringes, Lewes. Feb 07. HP: £300. ABP: £352.

Barr Flight & Barr Worcester boat shaped sucrier, two gilt handles, painted with roses, highlighted in gilt, impressed BFB mark to base, 7in wide. Ewbank Auctioneers, Send, Surrey. Dec 06. HP: £300. ABP: £352.

Categories or themes can be followed through the colour coded Index which contains over 4500 cross references.

Clarice Cliff conical sugar shaker, Fantasque pattern. Cotswold Auction Company, Gloucester. Feb 07. HP: £300. ABP: £352.

Royal Worcester plate by R. Sebright, 23cm dia. Cotswold Auction Co, Cirencester. Mar 07. HP: £300. ABP: £352.

19thC Italian 'Urbino' style maiolica charger with head of a soldier wearing ornate helmet, borders decorated with putti, mythical animals, 11.75in. Canterbury Auction Galleries, Kent. Apr 07. HP: £300. ABP: £352.

Late 18thC pottery giraffe & calf, sponged enamels in blue and ochre, recumbent, green, hollow mound base, 4.25in. high. Gorringes, Lewes. Apr 07. HP: £300. ABP: £352.

Royal Dux porcelain figure, boy collecting jugs of water, wearing green cap & trousers, 23.5in high, printed mark. Hartleys, Ilkley. Apr 07. HP: £300. ABP: £352.

R. Doulton figure, Fireside Fox, naturalistically painted, numbered HM 2634, 10in high. Fieldings, Stourbridge. Oct 05. HP: £290. ABP: £341.

Six Masons ironstone hydra jugs, painted in Imari colours, tallest 6in, and a similar, unmarked hydra jug, 5.25in. Gorringes, Lewes. Oct 05. HP: £290. ABP: £341.

Royal Doulton porcelain figure, Camille, 6.5in high, HN1648, tip of shoe broken. Canterbury Auction Galleries, Kent. Apr 05. HP: £290. ABP: £341.

Goldscheider polychrome pottery figure, after Lorenzl, reclining nude, 20cm high, factory marks to underside, a/f. Rosebery's, London. Sep 04. HP: £280. ABP: £329.

Italian maiolica plaque in Castelli style, late 18th/early 19thC, painted with women with a child milking a cow in a landscape, gadrooned painted border, 17 x 26cm. Rosebery's, London. Sep 04. HP: £280. ABP: £329.

Noritake coffee set, 15 pieces, 6-place setting, painted with landscapes, coloured against yellow borders. Gorringes, Lewes. Dec 04. HP: £280. ABP: £329.

Robin Welsh studio pottery vase, decorated internally and externally, imp'd mark, 28.5cm. Cheffins, Cambridge. Feb 05. HP: £280. ABP: £329.

1610

Beswick huntswoman, mould 982, one fore-leg damaged, 10.5in. Gorringes, Lewes. Jan 05. HP: £280. ABP: £329.

1611

Collection Midwinter salad wares: celery vase, 7in high, 2 spatulas, ladle and sauceboat, decorated with vegetables. Tring Market Auctions, Herts. Mar 05. HP: £280. ABP: £329.

1612

Wemyss strawberry decorated preserve pot and cover, 8.5cm high. Great Western Auctions, Glasgow. May 05. HP: £280. ABP: £329.

1613

Carltonware ginger jar/cover enamelled and gilded with a chinoiserie landscape, pattern No. 2728, 12.5in. Gorringes, Lewes. Jun 05. HP: £280. ABP: £329.

1614

Quarenton Ceramique figure of a nude boy, pulling a thorn from his foot, unpainted, moulded plinth base, 16.5in. Gorringes, Lewes. Jun 05. HP: £280. ABP: £329.

1615

Chelsea Derby sucrier/cover, ribbed body with chains of green flowers, gilt mark, 11cm and a first period Worcester sucrier/cover, gilt with lobed compartments and flower cover knop, 10.5cm dia. (D) Cheffins, Cambridge. Apr 05. HP: £280. ABP: £329.

1616

Christopher Dresser, Linthorpe 'Peruvian' bridge spouted earthenware pitcher, in streaked green and brown glazes, imp'd signature, 18cm high. Cheffins, Cambridge. Apr 05. HP: £280. ABP: £329.

1617

Clarice Cliff Orange Erin Biarritz plate. 9.25in wide. Gardiner Houlgate, Corsham. Apr 05. HP: £280. ABP: £329.

1618

Goldscheider terracotta wall mask. Gorringes, Bexhill. Jul 05. HP: £280. ABP: £329.

1619

Samuel Alcock jug and basin, c1830, both decorated on a blue ground, heightened with gilding, hand painted with rustic river scenes, jug 27cm. Sworders, Stansted Mountfitchet. Jul 05. HP: £280. ABP: £329.

1620

Boch Freres Keramis, Belgian earthenware vase designed by Charles Catteau, thickly enamelled with deer, crackled cream ground, c1925, 8.75in. Gorringes, Lewes. Oct 05. HP: £280. ABP: £329.

1621

Collection of Torquay and Devon pottery inkpots, all with incised inscriptions. Gorringes, Bexhill. Oct 05. HP: £280. ABP: £329.

1622

18thC creamware jug, entwined handle with leaf-terminals, painted with floral bouquets in puce, 5.5in. Gorringes, Lewes. Nov 05. HP: £280. ABP: £329.

1623

Royal Doulton 'Harlequin' figurine. Henry Adams, Chichester. Dec 05. HP: £280. ABP: £329.

1624

Royal Doulton Bulldog with Union Jack and a smaller similar bulldog. Brightwells, Leominster. Jan 06. HP: £280. ABP: £329.

1625

Clarice Cliff 'Taormina' pattern bowl & plate. Henry Adams, Chichester. Dec 05. HP: £280. ABP: £329.

1626

Beswick turkey, No. 1957. Great Western Auctions, Glasgow. May 06. HP: £280. ABP: £329.

1627

Mosanic Galle style seated cat painted with spots/hearts in blue on yellow ground, green glass eyes, 9.5in high. Andrew Hartley, Ilkley. Apr 06. HP: £280. ABP: £329.

1628

Joseph Holdcroft majolica jug, c1875, bear carrying a drum on its back, impressed mark 06, 24cm. Sworders, Stansted Mountfitchet. Apr 06. HP: £280. ABP: £329.

1629

Rare Bow toy-size trio, coffee cup, tea bowl and saucer painted with grapevines in underglaze blue. Gorringes, Lewes. Dec 06. HP: £280. ABP: £329.

Hammer: £280 - £260

1630

George III salt glazed stoneware mug, sprigged with traditional reliefs, silver mounted rim, 6in. Gorringes, Lewes. Dec 06. HP: £280. ABP: £329.

1631

Blue/white delft tobacco jar, 17th/18thC, shell handles, inscribed in mantled reserve 'Tabac Rappe', 25.4cm high, rim damage, cracks. Sworders, Stansted Mountfitchet. Feb 07. HP: £280. ABP: £329.

1632

Worcester 'Blind Earl' sweet meat dish, c1770, Rich Queen's pattern, fret mark, 15.5cm. Sworders, Stansted Mountfitchet. Feb 07. HP: £280. ABP: £329.

1633

Slipware lion, 18thC, recumbent, terracotta body striped yellow, 19cm. Sworders, Stansted Mountfitchet. Feb 07. HP: £280. ABP: £329.

1634

Pair of 19thC Staffordshire pottery figures, spaniels with puppies, blue/gilt decorated bases, 8.5in. Canterbury Auction Galleries, Kent. Jun 07. HP: £280. ABP: £329.

1635

Two 19thC Isnik dishes, 7in largest. Gorringes, Lewes. Dec 06. HP: £280. ABP: £329.

1636

Troika slab vase. Stroud Auctions, Stroud. Aug 05. HP: £275. ABP: £323.

1637

2 Royal Crown Derby lidded tureens. 5in high. Black Country Auctions, Dudley. Dec 05. HP: £275. ABP: £323.

1638

Carlton Ware Fantasia pattern vase. Great Western Auctions, Glasgow. Nov 06. HP: £275. ABP: £323.

1639

Doulton luscian ware vase, painted with mermaids in the sea, 19cm high. Great Western Auctions, Glasgow. May 05. HP: £270. ABP: £317.

1640

Staffordshire pottery bowl, deep form, flat rim, blue printed with flowers, 19thC, 6in high. Hartleys, Ilkley. Aug 06. HP: £270. ABP: £317.

1641

Royal Doulton figure 'June', HN1690. Great Western Auctions, Glasgow. Nov 05. HP: £270. ABP: £317.

1642

Sally Tuffin for Dennis China Works pottery vase, tubelined with 3 polar bears on tinted cobalt and turquoise ground, marked ST des number 9, OW 99c, 6in high. Fieldings, Stourbridge. Nov 05. HP: £270. ABP: £317.

1643

Pair of Burleigh ware Art Nouveau vases. Black Country Auctions, Dudley. Sep 05. HP: £270. ABP: £317.

1644

English pottery cow creamer, curved tail, with milkmaid, early 19thC, 6.5in wide. Hartleys, Ilkley. Jun 06. HP: £270. ABP: £317.

1645

Scarce pottery head, showing Old Bill, made by Wilkinson Royal Staffordshire factory. Wallis & Wallis, Lewes. Feb 06. HP: £270. ABP: £317.

1646

Rye pottery 'Hop Ware' tankard, bold relief with hops on a brown mottled glazed ground, 6in high, incised to base 'S.A.W Rye', Sussex Art Ware, flake chips. Canterbury Auction Galleries, Kent. Feb 06. HP: £270. ABP: £317.

1647

Border Fine Arts group 'Gathering the Strays'. Great Western Auctions, Glasgow. Sep 06. HP: £270. ABP: £317.

1648

Pair of Dresden blanc-de-chine figures, male & female carrying baskets, rococo moulded bases, 20in. Gorringes, Lewes. Oct 06. HP: £270. ABP: £317.

1649

Crown Devon Fieldings musical jug, printed with 'Auld Lang Syne' within portrait of Robert Burns and figural scene, 7in high. Hartleys, Ilkley. Dec 06. HP: £270. ABP: £317.

1650

Pinder Bourne & Hope dinner service in Baghdad pattern, c1850, 74 items. Dee, Atkinson & Harrison, Driffield. Nov 04. HP: £260. ABP: £305.

1651

Rare marked blanc de chine Guanyin, 18th/19thC, seated in repose, impressed double gourd mark, 9cm. Sworders, Stansted Mountfitchet. Nov 04. HP: £260. ABP: £305.

1652

Fourteen items of Newhall. Gorringes, Bexhill. Sep 04. HP: £260. ABP: £305.

1653

Linthorpe Christopher Dresser vase, 20cm high. Gorringes, Bexhill. Dec 04. HP: £260. ABP: £305.

1654

Late 18thC Vienna figure of a merman blowing a shell horn as he swims, marks in blue, 9cm high. Cheffins, Cambridge. Feb 05. HP: £260. ABP: £305.

1655

Pair Clews & Co. Chameleon Ware vases, stylised flowers in vivid enamels against a buff ground, 9.5in. Gorringes, Lewes. Jun 05. HP: £260. ABP: £305.

1656

Thomas Fell basket on stand, interlaced form, impressed marks Fell Newcastle, 11in. Gorringes, Lewes. Apr 07. HP: £260. ABP: £305.

1657

Wemyss heart shaped ink stand, painted with roses, glaze chips to rim, impressed mark 'Wemyss Ware R.H.S. and printed mark T.Goode & Co. South Audley Street, London W. 6in wide. Tring Market Auctions, Herts. Apr 05. HP: £260. ABP: £305.

1658

Royal Dux centrepiece figure, maiden in flowing robes, seated above a pool in form of a flower, pink iris surround, 27.5cm high, some damage. Henry Adams, Chichester. Jun 05. HP: £260. ABP: £305.

Prices quoted are actual hammer prices (HP) and the Approximate Buyer's Price (ABP) includes an average premium of 15% + VAT.

1659

Shelley Mabel Lucie Attwell nursery tea service: teapot & cover, milk jug & sugar bowl modelled as anthropomorphic duck, chick & rabbit respectively, teapot (damage) 18cm high, green backstamps, c1935. Bearne's, Exeter. Jun 05. HP: £260. ABP: £305.

1660

Gateshead Art Pottery dish, c1880, painted with bird in flight on mustard and yellow background, 36cm, marked The Gateshead Art Pottery J G Sowerby monogram and artists initials I L M. Boldon Auction Galleries, Tyne & Wear. Sep 05. HP: £260. ABP: £305.

Hammer: £260

1661

Holdcroft majolica teapot & cover, c1875, Chinese boy resting on a coconut, cover damaged, 13.5cm. Sworders, Stansted Mountfitchet. Jul 05. HP: £260. ABP: £305.

1662

Early 19thC Staffordshire bull, being tormented by a dog, painted naturalistically, 7in. Gorringes, Lewes. Oct 05. HP: £260. ABP: £305.

1663

C. H. Brannam owl jug and a C. H. Brannam Baron fish vase. Gorringes, Bexhill. Oct 05. HP: £260. ABP: £305.

1664

Massey Wildblood & Co pottery vase, inverted pyriform body, fruiting brambles/autumnal foliage, yellow, blue/green ground, signed E.D. Massey 1899, 36cm high. Gorringes, Bexhill. Dec 05. HP: £260. ABP: £305.

1665

Caughley mustard pot/cover, printed with flowers in underglaze blue, cover with flower knop, C mark, 3.75in. Gorringes, Lewes. Dec 06. HP: £260. ABP: £305.

1666

Daniel tea cup/saucer, C-scroll shape, painted with flowers in baskets, gilded green border, pattern 4271, cup on three floret feet. Gorringes, Lewes. Feb 06. HP: £260. ABP: £305.

1667

Belleek frog. Great Western Auctions, Glasgow. Apr 06. HP: £260. ABP: £305.

1668

Royal Doulton wall plate designed by Frank Brangwyn, incised/coloured design of grapes, vine leaves & wheat sheaf, D5034, imp'd date code 1934, 12.75in. Gorringes, Lewes. Jun 06. HP: £260. ABP: £305.

1669

Lladro figure, 20thC, court jester with puppet, enriched in colours, minor restoration, 23cm. Rosebery's, London. May 06. HP: £260. ABP: £305.

1670

Beswick figure, hunts woman wearing black coat, mounted on a dappled grey, 8.5in high. Hartleys, Ilkley. Aug 06. HP: £260. ABP: £305.

Sample Research III

Using the browsing method to analyse the market for a particular category of ceramics

No. 3 Ceramic Pigs

22

Pair Derby wild boars, bases applied flowers & enamelled details, c1755, 16.5cm wide, bases with stencilled marks 'Bt. at Dr. Wake Smarts Sale, April 1895, Lot 103, Chelsea China'. Woolley & Wallis, Salisbury. May 01. HP: £19,000. ABP: £22,348.

817

Rye Sussex Pig, detachable head forming drinking vessel, incised legend around the shoulder, 'Wunt be Druv', incised mark Rye within head and size 5, 8in long, rear foot re-attached. Gorringes, Lewes. Oct 05. HP: £800. ABP: £941.

Please refer to previous Sample Researches on pages 42 and 72 and again on page 132. Here I have browsed the pages to find ceramic pigs, a popular collecting area. There are thirteen examples ranging from a pair of Derby wild boars, c1755 at £22,348 on page 8 (**22**) to a set of five Nat West pig money banks on page 177 (**3046**) which fetched a mere £21 at the end of 2006, one of the largest bank crashes in history! The second example is a Rye Sussex pig on page 55 (**817**) and there is a further Rye example on page 81, (**1273**) both with detachable heads. The Rye average is therefore nearly £720 so take another look at these images! Our first Wemyss example is only £705 although our website database shows prices around £2,000 are not uncommon. There are three Beswick examples on pages 76, 86 and 142, the first a Wessex saddleback at £564 and a similar example on page 86 at £446. Both fetched a little over their Charlton Book prices. See *Beswick Animals, 9th Edition*. There is a fine Brickhurst Sussex pig on page 86, (**1375**) again with detachable head. Excelling all of these in my opinion is the Dutch Delft polychrome seated wild boar on page 93 (**1497**) with one ear restuck. Subscribers to *Antiques Info*, our two monthly magazine can research many more examples through our Gold Services. See page 191 for details. A list of pages covering pigs follows. Page 9-**22**, page 55-**817**, page 65-**1013**, page 76-**1182**, page 81-**1273**, page 86-**1373**, page 86-**1375**, page 93-**1497**, page 141-**2365**, page 142-**2376**, page 155-**2628**, page 161-**2754** and page 177-**3046**.
The subject also appears decoratively on ceramics. See sgraffito example on the Royal Doulton stoneware vase by Hannah Barlow on page 39 (**545**) which fetched £1,295 in September 2004. Her works achieve up to £3,000 in these pages.

1013

Wemyss pig, 20thC, sponged black patches, pink detail to ears, nose and feet, 6in long. Halls Fine Art, Shrewsbury. Jul 05. HP: £600. ABP: £705.

1182

Beswick Wessex saddleback boar, 'Faracre Viscount 3rd', 2.75in. Louis Taylor, Stoke. Mar 05. HP: £480. ABP: £564.

1273

Rye Sussex Pig, green-glazed, detachable head, incised 'Wunt be Druv', incised mark Rye & pin-dust mark, c1910, 4.75in. long. Gorringes, Lewes. Oct 05. HP: £420. ABP: £494.

1373

Beswick Wessex saddleback sow, 'Merrywood Silver Wings 56th', 2.75in. Louis Taylor, Stoke on Trent. Mar 05. HP: £380. ABP: £446.

1375

Unique Brickhurst Sussex pottery pig, with motto 'And you can Pook, and you can shove, But I'm a beast, as want be Druv', 9.5in. Gorringes, Lewes. Mar 05. HP: £380. ABP: £446.

3046

Five Wade Nat West pig money banks. Kent Auction Galleries, Folkestone. Dec 06. HP: £18. ABP: £21.

1497

Dutch delft polychrome figure, seated wild boar with a panel of flowers painted on its back, 17cm high, painted with the marks of Jacobus Adriaenson Halder, one ear restuck. Bearne's, Exeter. Jun 05. HP: £320. ABP: £376.

2365

Set of five Natwest Wade pigs. Gorringes, Bexhill. Oct 05. HP: £85. ABP: £99.

2376

Beswick model of a seated pig, No. 832 by Arthur Gredington, and a pair of Beswick pigs marked C.H Queen 40, a Shebeg pig and two others, 9.5cm high. Rosebery's, London. May 06. HP: £85. ABP: £99.

2628

Wade 'Nat West' pigs, two part sets, minus Nathaniel, two have stoppers missing. (8) A F Brock & Co Ltd, Stockport. Nov 05. HP: £60. ABP: £70.

2754

Beswick pottery boar 'Wall Champion Boy 53rd' and a sow 'Champion Wall Queen 40th', white gloss finish. Locke & England, Leamington Spa. Sep 05. HP: £50. ABP: £58.

Section VI: £250-£100

'A Wemyss tabby cat achieved £20,000 hammer at Lyon and Turnbull, Edinburgh in 2006.....I am surprised that collectors didn't push up the price of the Minton majolica lioness by a few hundred more.....The auction was apprehensive about the Daniel collection.....but they needn't have worried.....'

The Beswick glazed grouse, model 2063 has a Charlton Catalogue, 9th Edition price of £500. See **1671**. However the Royal Doulton, *Afternoon Tea*, HN1747 at **2064** and £294 including premium is very near its book price of £320. For the same price you could buy a Meissen *Comedia dell'Arte* figure. See **1684**. The Wemyss biscuit jar at **1690** is one of about thirty entries in this book. The prices for Wemyss range from the £6,116 paid on page 13 to £52 on page 164. A Wemyss tabby cat achieved £20,000 hammer at Lyon and Turnbull, Edinburgh in 2006, probably an auction record. Wemyss pigs also fetch a lot of money. Some items seem to fetch less than what I consider to be their value. The Minton's majolica lioness at **1693** is quite a significant item at 8 inches in length and I am surprised that collector's did not push this up for a few hundred more. Similarly (ignoring the incongruous jardiniere on top) the Bretby table centre at **1709** is again a significant piece and in my judgement worth more than £282. Other lightweight prices in my opinion are the eighteenth century creamware? *Toby Phillpots* at **1721** and the pair of Derby sheep at **1743**. Even though comparatively small at two inches long, they are highly desirable to Derby collectors and will surely sell on for much more if bought by the 'Trade. At **1753** is a Morris Ware vase at £270 and the final Morris Ware entry appears on page 116 at **1907** and £235. This gives the lower end of the market for this not well-known factory. Similarly Martinware is approaching its lower end with entries at **1782** and **1872**. There are twenty entries in total. Use the Index to study Martinware prices. Note again the lowish price at **1786** for a Derby mouse. This rare item has damages and can be restored, which will probably add a £100 to the price, but this is always a personal decision. I prefer to collect items as found.

Lladro appears several times in this Section. See **1773**, **1779**, **1875** etc and use the Index to find more. There are 28 examples, enough to analyse the market. Ceramic cats are frequently damaged and at **1825** is a Mosanic example with a front leg repair. See also **1817**. These are very large models at nearly 13 inches in height. See the **Sample Research** study of cats on page 102.

The blue and white Italian maiolica albarello at **1808** could and should have fetched nearer £500 but the bidding stopped at £220. Perhaps the specialist market judged it to be a later example. Check the Pilkington's Lancastrian vase at **1812**. There are about a further twenty examples altogether so the market can be analysed. This Section saw the first Eltonware at **1680** on page 104. I consider the sunflower vase, with all-over gold craquelure decoration at **1794** superior and under-valued. Eltonware rarely appears at auction and there is only one further example of a terracotta double gourd vase fetching a mere £52 on page 164. Daniel porcelain rarely appears at auction and like say, Davenport, when it does it is rarely appreciated. Coalport often shares the same fate, new collectors invariably concentrating on the twentieth century. We are fortunate that a substantial Daniel collection appeared at Gorringes, Lewes in February 2006 along with a limited amount of Coalport. The auction was apprehensive I know but they needn't have worried as prices were exceptionally good. See pages **96**, **101**, **112**, **117**, **119**, **123**, **126**, **128** and **136**. Coalport has about twenty entries in these pages, enough to analyse prices. Davenport is represented only about ten times but a dinner service fetched just under £3,000 on page 21 and a dessert service £1,352 on page 37. Davenport's output of the various ceramic types such as creamware, basalt etc is probably the most extensive of any English factory. In production by 1793 it was to survive until 1887, and was certainly one of the greatest manufacturers in the history of ceramics.

Other important lots include the caneware at **1845**, sold far too cheaply, and the Whieldon type cow-creamer at **1862**. The brown salt-glazed stoneware commemorative of *Admiral Lord Nelson* is a rare and desirable object, but nowhere near as rare as the early nineteenth century (could be earlier) bulb-pots at **1898**. They look like creamware but could be porcelain. Why does the auction miss out the important identifying keyword? In the previous Section there was a slipware lion on page 100 and the last slipware entry is at **1914** on page 116. I have mentioned parian in an earlier analysis but on page 122 at **2024** is a bargain, the Minton parian *Dorothea*, by John Bell. This should have fetched at least twice as much as it usually retails for about £400. Another example beyond my understanding is the low £140 hammer paid for a Samson of Paris *Harlequin Pierrot and a Lady* group, which again should have fetched more than double the price. Other prices seemingly on the low side is the Toby at **2163** and the Staffordshire egg basket at **2158**, Royal Copenhagen first appeared at **534** on page 38 and the factory is well represented with about fifteen entries, none more charming than *The Little Mermaid* on page 129. See **2165**. This 9 inch figure would grace any ceramic collection.

Hammer: £250

Beswick model 2063 glazed grouse. Kent Auction Galleries, Folkestone. Jun 06. HP: £250. ABP: £294.

Royal Doulton figure group, Afternoon Tea HN.1747. (1935-1981) Clevedon Salerooms, Bristol. Jun 05. HP: £250. ABP: £294.

Three Carltonware Guinness toucans, printed mark, Australian Design, 25, 21 and 16cm. Sworders, Stansted Mountfitchet. Apr 05. HP: £250. ABP: £294.

Clarice Cliff 'Le Bon Dieu' 3 piece teaset. Great Western Auctions, Glasgow. May 05. HP: £250. ABP: £294.

Elton Ware teapot. Stroud Auctions, Stroud. Jul 05. HP: £250. ABP: £294.

Pair Crown Devon Fieldings pottery vases, painted by J Coleman with pheasants, gilt highlights, 10.25in high, signed. Hartleys, Ilkley. Jun 06. HP: £250. ABP: £294.

Wade set of Snow White and the Seven Dwarfs, style two, issued 1981-1984. Halls Fine Art, Shrewsbury. Jul 05. HP: £250. ABP: £294.

Royal Doulton earthenware figure, The Fiddler, HN2171, 22.5cm. Locke & England, Leamington Spa. Jul 06. HP: £250. ABP: £294.

Beswick pottery model of a Canadian Mountie, black gloss horse, 21cm high, No. 1375. Bearne's, Exeter. Jun 05. HP: £250. ABP: £294.

Elton ware jug. Stroud Auctions, Stroud. Jul 05. HP: £250. ABP: £294.

Late 18thC Coughley porcelain sucrier, and a similar creamer decorated blue and gilt flowers. (2) Charterhouse Auctioneers, Sherborne. Feb 07. HP: £250. ABP: £294.

Clarice Cliff, Berries pattern candlestick, shape No. 310, printed and impressed marks, 8.5cm high. Cheffins, Cambridge. Feb 05. HP: £250. ABP: £294.

Minton's terracotta moon-flask, painted with butterflies and floral sprigs, neck with lug handles, impressed marks and date code 1876, 8.25in. Gorringes, Lewes. Jan 05. HP: £250. ABP: £294.

The numbering system acts as a reader reference as well as linking to the Analysis of each section.

Meissen Comedia dell'Arte figure of nursemaid, German 20thC, holding a baby and a basket, guilloche moulded base, 18.5cm. Rosebery's, London. Dec 05. HP: £250. ABP: £294.

Pair of Royal Copenhagen figures of fauns, Danish 20thC, portrayed seated upon a column playing pipes, model Nos. 456 & 433, 21cm. Rosebery's, London. Dec 04. HP: £250. ABP: £294.

Collection of 30 head (half dolls) incl. jester, monk, etc, various dates & makers. Kent Auction Galleries, Folkestone. Jan 06. HP: £250. ABP: £294.

Royal Worcester Crown Ware lustre vase. Great Western Auctions, Glasgow. Mar 06. HP: £250. ABP: £294.

Late 17thC Japanese Arita blue/white Kraak-style porcelain dish with central geese and floral reserve, segmented floral borders, fluted base with three stilt marks, 21.5cm. Reeman Dansie, Colchester. Apr 06. HP: £250. ABP: £294.

Pair of 19thC Staffordshire figure groups of Poodle and Puppy, 18cm high. Lambert & Foster, Tenterden. Aug 05. HP: £250. ABP: £294.

Late 19thC Wemyss pottery biscuit jar/lid with painted thistle decoration, impressed and painted marks, retailed by T Goode & Co, 11.5cm high. Reeman Dansie, Colchester. Apr 06. HP: £250. ABP: £294.

Early 19thC Queen Victoria commemorative charger, 'Victorian Regina', border of cornucopia/cherubs, incised Minton mark overpainted black crossed swords, 18in. Dee, Atkinson & Harrison, Driffield. Sep 06. HP: £250. ABP: £294.

Caroline Mitchell, Rye 'Mycenae' ware jug, set-pattern borders, incised script mark Mycenae, c1880-85, 4.75in. Gorringes, Lewes. Oct 05. HP: £250. ABP: £294.

Mintons majolica figure of a recumbent lioness, green glaze, moulded mark to base, 8in. Gorringes, Lewes. Jun 06. HP: £240. ABP: £282.

Staffordshire group of three spaniels with pen holders. Sandwich Auction Rooms, Kent. Apr 05. HP: £240. ABP: £282.

R. Doulton figure, Florence Nightingale, HN3144. Gorringes, Bexhill. Jun 05. HP: £240. ABP: £282.

George Jones majolica jardiniere on stand, c1875, modelled as roped staves, raised mark, minor chips, 22cm. Sworders, Stansted Mountfitchet. Apr 06. HP: £240. ABP: £282.

Clarice Cliff Bizarre Killarney Green pattern part teaset, produced only in 1935, small chip to a saucer. Henry Adams, Chichester. Jun 05. HP: £240. ABP: £282.

Clarice Cliff teapot, Umbrellas and Rain, Fantasque series, yellow, orange & blue, 5.25in. Gorringes, Lewes. Jun 05. HP: £240. ABP: £282.

Beswick figure of a standing bay horse with huntsman, base marked Beswick 9in. Denhams, Warnham. May 06. HP: £240. ABP: £282.

Meissen porcelain tea bowl/saucer painted with flowers in polychrome, exterior with a blue ground, 18thC, 5in wide. Hartleys, Ilkley. Aug 06. HP: £240. ABP: £282.

Royal Crown Derby part tea set, 14 pieces for a 4-place setting, pattern 1128. Gorringes, Lewes. Mar 06. HP: £240. ABP: £282.

Selection of Carlton china 'Lucky White Heather' animals: dog with a banjo, scottie dog in tam o'shanter, various birds and others. Rosebery's, London. Aug 06. HP: £240. ABP: £282.

Royal Doulton cabinet plate, 1921, central panel painted with trout by T Wilson within raised gilt border, mark: retailed by Davis Collamore Co. Limited, New York, 23.8cm. Sworders, Stansted Mountfitchet. Apr 06. HP: £240. ABP: £282.

Spode porcelain matchpot, beaded trumpet form enamelled with a Blue Tit in a landscape, 11.5cm high, inscribed Blue Titmouse, 1805 to base, c1815, minute glaze flake. Bearne's, Exeter. Jun 05. HP: £240. ABP: £282.

Collection of 26 Beswick Beatrix Potter figures, incl. Appley Dapply, BP2, Rebecca Puddleduck, Sally Henny Penny, Miss Moppet and Little Pig Robinson, all BP3 and remainder and The Tale of Two Bad Mice. Gorringes, Lewes. Sep 05. HP: £240. ABP: £282.

Pair R. Worcester Mansion House dwarves, 1883, after Derby originals, printed and impressed marks, date code, taller figure with hat repair, 18cm. Sworders, Stansted Mountfitchet. Jul 05. HP: £240. ABP: £282.

Pair of 19thC Chinese blue/white porcelain bottle vases, cracked ice and prunus decoration, 18in, one damaged rim. Gorringes, Lewes. Sep 05. HP: £240. ABP: £282.

Two R. Doulton figures from Edwardian string quartet series, Cello, HN3707 and First Violin, HN3704, certificates. Bearne's, Exeter. Jun 05. HP: £240. ABP: £282.

Bretby green/white glazed pottery table centre, form of 3 swans around a green glazed leafy centre, 16in dia x 8.5in high, imp'd mark to base and No. 1441B, and a Bretby green glazed leaf pattern jardinière, crimped rim, 10in dia x 7in high, imp'd mark and No. 1222C. Canterbury Auction Galleries, Kent. Dec 05. HP: £240. ABP: £282.

Hammer: £240

Pair of treacle glazed pottery bird whistles as a large bird on a perch, inverted conical base flanked by four smaller birds, marked 'W.B', 24.5cm high. Rosebery's, London. Jan 07. HP: £240. ABP: £282.

Beswick figure, Girl on jumping horse. Great Western Auctions, Glasgow. Feb 07. HP: £240. ABP: £282.

Pair of Staffordshire spaniels with puppies. Kivell & Sons, Bude. Sep 05. HP: £240. ABP: £282.

Victorian Staffordshire bone china leopard, chewing at leg of a horse, rocky base, 4in. Gorringes, Lewes. Jan 05. HP: £240. ABP: £282.

Minton Secessionist Art Nouveau twin-handled vase, blues and mauve, marked to underside Minton, printed factory No 8, 24.5cm high. Gorringes, Bexhill. Dec 05. HP: £240. ABP: £282.

Derby soup plate, painted with flowers against a gilded blue ground, 9.75in, another, Earl Ferrers-type, painted marks in red enamel, c1800-25, 8.75in. Gorringes, Lewes. Dec 06. HP: £240. ABP: £282.

Clarice Cliff Bizarre ware sugar shaker, reeded sides painted in Brookfields pattern, with a cottage in landscape, 4.75in high. Hartleys, Ilkley. Dec 06. HP: £240. ABP: £282.

Poole Pottery 'Atlantis' earthenware vase by Guy Sydenham, c1970s, mushroom form, body carved with tread like pattern, glazed in cream and green, impressed factory stamp & GS monogram, 17cm. Rosebery's, London. Mar 06. HP: £240. ABP: £282.

Copeland parian figure 'Penelophon the Beggar Maid', English 19thC, titled base, 68cm. Rosebery's, London. Dec 05. HP: £240. ABP: £282.

Pair of Chelsea style pottery plates, shaped oval forms, enriched with exotic birds with puce, red/blue plumage, one restored/faded, 27.5cm long. Rosebery's, London. Dec 05. HP: £240. ABP: £282.

Creamware spirit barrel, 1840, painted with flowers between blue/lilac borders, initialled WBG and dated. Gorringes, Lewes. Apr 05. HP: £240. ABP: £282.

18thC Staffordshire pottery Toby jug, Toby Philpots, 9in. (f) Denhams, Warnham. Oct 04. HP: £240. ABP: £282.

Meissen porcelain figure, c1860, cherub seated preparing a cup of chocolate, crossed swords mark, restoration, 10.5cm. Sworders, Stansted Mountfitchet. Nov 04. HP: £240. ABP: £282.

Belleek porcelain basket and cover, Irish 19thC, cover decorated with roses, shamrocks & thistles surrounding a handle formed from rustic branches, 31cm long. Rosebery's, London. Dec 04. HP: £240. ABP: £282.

KPM Berlin porcelain plaque, Madonna & child, impressed KPM, 17.5 x 12cm. Charterhouse Auctioneers, Sherborne. Apr 07. HP: £240. ABP: £282.

Rare Clarice Cliff Fantasque plate, 'Mountain', without cottage, 1931-32, 8in. Gorringes, Lewes. Apr 07. HP: £240. ABP: £282.

Pair of Creil creamware sauce boats, c1800, boat form, serpent handle, black line borders, 18cm wide. (2) Rosebery's, London. Mar 06. HP: £240. ABP: £282.

Zsolnay Pecs 5927 vase. Great Western Auctions, Glasgow. Mar 06. HP: £240. ABP: £282.

Royal Doulton figure 'Sir Walter Raleigh', HN2015. Louis Taylor, Stoke. Mar 06. HP: £240. ABP: £282.

1729

Herend green scale ground model of a seated Fo dog, 26cm high, & another small example. Rosebery's, London. Mar 05. HP: £240. ABP: £282.

1730

Pair of 19thC Meissen flower encrusted candle snuffers, bud finials, angular handles, 7.5cm. Rosebery's, London. Mar 05. HP: £240. ABP: £282.

1731

R. Worcester parian portrait bust of Prince Albert, after E. J. Jones, c1855, 13.75in. Gorringes, Lewes. Mar 05. HP: £240. ABP: £282.

The illustrations are in descending price order. The price range is indicated at the top of each page.

1732

Pair John Bevington porcelain lidded urns, acorn finial, gilded rams head handles, encrusted flowers, 9.5in high. Hartleys, Ilkley. Oct 06. HP: £240. ABP: £282.

1733

Wedgwood Keith Murray circular banded vase. Gorringes, Bexhill. Oct 05. HP: £240. ABP: £282.

1734

Pair of Lloyds Staffordshire porcelain musicians, lady playing a lute, gentleman playing a pipe, gilt embellishment, early 19thC, 4.75in. Andrew Hartley, Ilkley. Apr 06. HP: £230. ABP: £270.

1735

Troika pottery slab vase, incised/applied with geometric patterns, 8.75in high, mark for Penny Black. Hartleys, Ilkley. Aug 06. HP: £230. ABP: £270.

1736

Beswick pottery figure, racehorse with jockey, horse painted with No.24, 8.5in high. Hartleys, Ilkley. Aug 06. HP: £230. ABP: £270.

1737

Swansea porcelain coffee can & saucer printed/enamelled with the Parakeets in a tree pattern, saucer 14cm dia, c1820. Bearne's, Exeter. Jun 05. HP: £230. ABP: £270.

1738

Staffordshire flatback figure of a young girl with a black doll. Gorringes, Bexhill. Jul 05. HP: £230. ABP: £270.

Hammer: £240 - £230

1739

Three R. Doulton character jugs: Dick Whittington, D6375, Rip Van Winkle, D6438 and Falstaff, D6287. Gorringes, Bexhill. Feb 06. HP: £230. ABP: £270.

1740

Austrian Goldscheider figure of a lady, manufacturer's label to base, transfer black factory mark, incised artist mark and No 11 7279, 15in high. Ewbank Auctioneers, Send, Surrey. Dec 05. HP: £230. ABP: £270.

1741

Set of three Beswick flying partridges, imp'd No. 1118. John Taylors, Louth. Feb 05. HP: £230. ABP: £270.

1742

Two Clarice Cliff 'Bizarre' crayon scene plates, boats in landscape, stylized trees and haystack. John Taylors, Louth. Feb 05. HP: £230. ABP: £270.

1743

Pair of Derby sheep, c1820, each recumbent on a grassy mound base, 5cm long. (2) Rosebery's, London. Dec 04. HP: £230. ABP: £270.

1744

Unusual 18thC Crown Derby porcelain saucer dish, cold blue with two coronets above initials GD within gilt border with hidden beasts/grotesques, painted gold mark to underside, c1775-85, 6.5in. Gorringes, Lewes. Dec 06. HP: £230. ABP: £270.

1745

Blue and white meat platter, English mid 19thC, titled 'Antique Scenery, Cathedral Church of Glasgow', printed with figures by a river, the Cathedral on far bank, glaze chips, 48cm long. Rosebery's, London. Dec 05. HP: £230. ABP: £270.

1746

Three early pottery figures, Han/Tang, incl: a hog with a straw glaze, standing hog & a recumbent cow, damage, 10-25cm. (3) Sworders, Stansted Mountfitchet. Nov 04. HP: £230. ABP: £270.

1747

Pearlware plate, inscribed 'To the Memory of Queen Caroline, the Injured Queen of England'. Great Western Auctions, Glasgow. Feb 06. HP: £230. ABP: £270.

1748

Beswick sliding penguin chick, No. 2434, 3.75 x 8in. Louis Taylor, Stoke. Mar 05. HP: £230. ABP: £270.

R. Doulton figure group 'The Love Letter' HN2149. Great Western Auctions, Glasgow. Feb 06. HP: £230. ABP: £270.

Keith Murray for Wedgwood, small bomb vase, matt grey glaze, incised linear decoration, 15.5cm high, signature & factory mark to underside. Rosebery's, London. Mar 05. HP: £230. ABP: £270.

Beswick fox, mould 2348, curled tail, 12.25in. Gorringes, Lewes. Mar 05. HP: £230. ABP: £270.

Clarice Cliff crocus pattern conical sugar shaker. Great Western Auctions, Glasgow. Jan 06. HP: £230. ABP: £270.

Morris ware vase, stylised floral decoration, broken and cracked. Great Western Auctions, Glasgow. Sep 05. HP: £230. ABP: £270.

Aynsley porcelain incl. Orchard Gold coffee pot, milk jug, covered sugar bowl, side plate, 2 cake plates, biscuit barrel/lid, 2 handled urn/cover, fruit bowl with puce marks, 3 tea cups and saucers with green marks. Kent Auction Galleries, Folkestone. Aug 06. HP: £225. ABP: £264.

Flight of Beswick ducks No. 1530-1/2/3. Kent Auction Galleries, Folkestone. Aug 06. HP: £225. ABP: £264.

Moorcroft Woodside Farm bulbous vase. Great Western Auctions, Glasgow. May 07. HP: £220. ABP: £258.

Bretby terracotta vase, dark blue banded neck over a green, brown, blue/ochre streaky glaze, imp'd marks, No. 1548, 17in high. Golding Young & Co, Grantham. Feb 06. HP: £220. ABP: £258.

Beswick figure, boy on a chestnut pony, 5.5in high, black mark and gold sticker. Andrew Hartley, Ilkley. Apr 06. HP: £220. ABP: £258.

Royal Doulton porcelain figure, Tildy, seated figure of a young woman wearing a crinoline dress, 5in high, HN1576, date code for 1934. Canterbury Auction Galleries, Kent. Apr 06. HP: £220. ABP: £258.

Royal Worcester seated fox, glazed in natural colours, printed mark, initials to base, 7.25in. Gorringes, Lewes. Jun 06. HP: £220. ABP: £258.

20thC Nymphenburg porcelain group of a huntsman, on white horse with accompanying figure of a man with hunting hounds, largest 8.5in. Gorringes, Lewes. Jun 06. HP: £220. ABP: £258.

Staffordshire pottery toby jug, c1840, seated holding a jug of ale, handle repaired, 25cm. Sworders, Stansted Mountfitchet. Apr 05. HP: £220. ABP: £258.

Clarice Cliff Bizarre Ravel pattern tureen, 20cm dia. Henry Adams, Chichester. Jun 05. HP: £220. ABP: £258.

Part set of 4 Brown, Westhead tiles, French inscriptions, one cracked. Hobbs Parker, Ashford. Jun 05. HP: £220. ABP: £258.

19thC Spode blue and white basket and stand printed with floral swags, pierced with guilloche, printed mark, 23cm across handles. (W) Cheffins, Cambridge. Apr 05. HP: £220. ABP: £258.

15th/16thC English saltglaze bottle, slender neck & upper half of bellied body darker than the curve into the foot, 22.5cm high. Cheffins, Cambridge. Apr 05. HP: £220. ABP: £258.

Early 19thC quart mug, possibly Derby, painted with pattern No. 39, village river scene below gilt blue band, mark in brown, 12.5cm high. (D) Cheffins, Cambridge. Apr 05. HP: £220. ABP: £258.

Pair of Isnik style circular pottery bowls, chipped and cracked, 14in. Denhams, Warnham, Sussex. Jul 05. HP: £220. ABP: £258.

Late 18thC Derby figure representing justice, pink and green rocaille base, 33.5cm high. (R) Cheffins, Cambridge. Apr 05. HP: £220. ABP: £258.

Pair of late 19thC Chinese celadon bottle vases, glaze lightly crackled, tea coloured rims above white interiors, 30cm high. (2) Cheffins, Cambridge. Apr 05. HP: £220. ABP: £258.

18thC Worcester bell shaped mug, with a trailing flower in underglaze blue, workman's mark to base, 4.75in. Gorringes, Lewes. Jul 06. HP: £220. ABP: £258.

Pair Staffordshire porcelain dogs, dalmations with gilded collar and chain, blue bases with gilt line, 19thC, 5in high. Hartleys, Ilkley. Aug 06. HP: £220. ABP: £258.

Lladro dog, (AF) rare No. 308. Stroud Auctions, Stroud. Jul 05. HP: £220. ABP: £258.

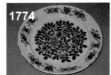

Bristol Delft charger, blue painted with flowers, 13.25in wide, mid 18thC. Hartleys, Ilkley. Aug 06. HP: £220. ABP: £258.

Beswick figure, a Canadian mountie, 8.25in high. Hartleys, Ilkley. Aug 06. HP: £220. ABP: £258.

Worcester trio, c1765, with Kakiemon style panels, heightened with gilding, seal mark. (3) Sworders, Stansted Mountfitchet. Apr 06. HP: £220. ABP: £258.

Pair of Staffordshire spaniels on cushions, c1870, black painted in parts upon yellow, turquoise/purple coloured cushions, 13cm. Sworders, Stansted Mountfitchet. Apr 06. HP: £220. ABP: £258.

Royal Doulton figure, 'Organ Grinder' HN2173, issued 1956-1965, 21.5cm. Sworders, Stansted Mountfitchet. Apr 06. HP: £220. ABP: £258.

Hammer: £220

Clarice Cliff 'Xavier' Bizarre plate, 9.25in dia. Gardiner Houlgate, Corsham. Apr 05. HP: £220. ABP: £258.

Wemyss teaware: milk jug & matching sugar bowl painted with black chickens, jug 2.5in, and pair side plates painted with fruit and leaves, 5.5in, one restored, painted marks in green enamel. Gorringes, Lewes. Sep 05. HP: £220. ABP: £258.

> Categories or themes can be followed through the colour coded Index which contains over 4500 cross references.

Meissen figure, of a boy on a push-a-long horse, 17.5cm high. Charterhouse Auctioneers, Sherborne. Feb 07. HP: £220. ABP: £258.

Martinware stoneware powder bowl/cover, incised with finches, butterflies and leaves, 4.75in dia x 2.75in high, incised mark 'Martin Bros., London & Southall', dated 27.5.84, base cracked, lid restuck. Canterbury Auction Galleries, Kent. Dec 05. HP: £220. ABP: £258.

Group of Astbury/Whieldon type wares, mid 18thC, black glazed: 2 coffee pots/covers, 2 teapots/covers, 2 jugs, various damage, restoration and losses. (10) Sworders, Stansted Mountfitchet. Feb 07. HP: £220. ABP: £258.

2 Staffordshire cow creamers, Whieldon type, mid 18thC, and a brown glazed figure of a sheep, lambs and shepherd, various damage, tallest 14cm. (3) Sworders, Stansted Mountfitchet. Feb 07. HP: £220. ABP: £258.

R. Worcester porcelain vase, pierced rim, painted with fruit by E Townsend, 3.5in high, signed. Hartleys, Ilkley. Feb 07. HP: £220. ABP: £258.

English porcelain model of a white mouse, probably Bloor Derby, c1825, iron red/puce, ears chipped, reduced tail, 10cm. Sworders, Stansted Mountfitchet. Feb 07. HP: £220. ABP: £258.

Early Zsolnay, Pecs leaf dish, cabbage leaf in green shades, impressed mark, 12.5in. Gorringes, Lewes. Dec 06. HP: £220. ABP: £258.

Two Robj, Paris figural spirit flasks, negro lady, and a Grenadier Guard, 10.5in, faults. Gorringes, Lewes. Feb 06. HP: £220. ABP: £258.

Caughley sugar box/cover, printed with Fence pattern in underglaze blue, cover with flower and leaf knop, printed C mark, c1780-90, 5.25in. Gorringes, Lewes. Feb 06. HP: £220. ABP: £258.

Majolica sardine dish/cover, c1875, prob. Joseph Holdcroft, cover with a two crossed fish knop, script 15, minute rim chip, 19cm. Sworders, Stansted Mountfitchet. Feb 06. HP: £220. ABP: £258.

Early 19thC silver resist yellow ground jug commemorative of the reformer Sir Francis Burdett, 15.5cm. Cheffins, Cambridge. Feb 05. HP: £220. ABP: £258.

Gold anchor Chelsea saucer, poss. painted by James Giles with lilac birds, 12.5cm. Cheffins, Cambridge. Feb 05. HP: £220. ABP: £258.

Early Troika St Ives D-plate, decorated in blues with abstract scraffito decoration, imp'd mark, 18.5cm wide. Cheffins, Cambridge. Feb 05. HP: £220. ABP: £258.

Sir Edmund Elton Sunflower vase, allover gold craquelure glaze, painted signature, 12.5cm high. Cheffins, Cambridge. Feb 05. HP: £220. ABP: £258.

Tang Dynasty Style, Straw glazed pottery model of an oxen, 28cm high. Rosebery's, London. Jan 06. HP: £220. ABP: £258.

Two Carlton ware pottery 'Guinness' advertising items from 'Guinness Zoo' series: 'Guinness Toucan' & 'Seal', bases worded 'My Goodness, My Guinness', 3.5 x 3.75in high. Canterbury Auction Galleries, Kent. Oct 05. HP: £220. ABP: £258.

Worcester tea bowl/saucer, ribbed shape, painted with the Hollow Rock Lily pattern in underglaze blue, crescent marks. Gorringes, Lewes. Dec 06. HP: £220. ABP: £258.

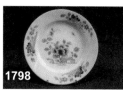

Bow plate, painted with flowers in enamels, 9in. Gorringes, Lewes. Dec 06. HP: £220. ABP: £258.

Large Lladro Figure of Dancing Girl, matt finish. Orpington Salerooms, Kent. Nov 05. HP: £220. ABP: £258.

Prices quoted are actual hammer prices (HP) and the Approximate Buyer's Price (ABP) includes an average premium of 15% + VAT.

'Majolica' teapot and cover, probably Minton & designed by Dr Christopher Dresser, c1885, printed and coloured Japanese fans and figures, bordered in turquoise/blue bamboo, enamel flakes, imp'd Rd 29637, painted 1785, 13.4cm. (2) Sworders, Stansted Mountfitchet. Nov 05. HP: £220. ABP: £258.

John Rose Coalport sauce tureen, cover/stand, c1805, boldly painted with chrysanthemum in salmon pink, white & green swags on deep blue ground gilt with oeil-deperdrix, hair crack to rim, stand 21cm. Sworders, Stansted Mountfitchet. Nov 05. HP: £220. ABP: £258.

Wemyss cabbage rose jardiniere, c1900, imp'd Wemyss Ware, R.H. & S. (for Robert Heron & Sons) firing crack to rim, 20cm high. Sworders, Stansted Mountfitchet. Nov 05. HP: £220. ABP: £258.

Copeland parian figure of a tambourine player, English 19thC, partially draped female leaning against a tree stump, 46cm high. Rosebery's, London. Dec 05. HP: £220. ABP: £258.

Meissen Comedia dell'Arte figure of the Captain, German 20thC, rim of hat chipped, 17.5cm. Rosebery's, London. Dec 05. HP: £220. ABP: £258.

18thC creamware coffee pot, printed with views of a tea party and a resting shepherd in black monochrome, 9.5in. Gorringes, Lewes. Apr 05. HP: £220. ABP: £258.

18thC English delftware fruit bowl, formal design of floral drapes in blue, green/yellow enamels, 8.75in. Gorringes, Lewes. Apr 05. HP: £220. ABP: £258.

Linthorpe Christopher Dresser vase, 20cm high. Gorringes, Bexhill. Dec 04. HP: £220. ABP: £258.

Italian blue/white tin glazed albarello, c1700, probably Savona or Naples, panel of deer in a landscape, 23cm high. Rosebery's, London. Dec 04. HP: £220. ABP: £258.

Set of 6 creamware nursery plates, with inscriptions. a.f. Charterhouse Auctioneers, Sherborne. Mar 07. HP: £220. ABP: £258.

Two early 19thC Stafford-shire pearlware figures, 'Contest', young man & two women, and a sportsman and dog with bocage, 7.5in and 8.25in high, both damaged. Canterbury Auction Galleries, Kent. Apr 07. HP: £220. ABP: £258.

Pair of Mason's ironstone jars, octagonal baluster shape, printed and enamelled with Japan pattern, domed covers, 12in, a vase cracked. Gorringes, Lewes. Apr 07. HP: £220. ABP: £258.

Pilkington Lancastrian vase designed by Gordon M Forsyth, chipped. Great Western Auctions, Glasgow. Mar 06. HP: £220. ABP: £258.

19thC Sunderland tankard, 'Jack on a Cruise' Avast there:- Back your maintopfail', 12.5cm high. Boldon Auction Galleries, Tyne & Wear. Mar 06. HP: £220. ABP: £258.

Rudolstadt figure group of two lovers, 9.75in. Gorringes, Lewes. Apr 06. HP: £220. ABP: £258.

Coalport 2 handled Gondola vase, signed E. Howard, 11.75 x 6in. Louis Taylor, Stoke on Trent. Mar 06. HP: £220. ABP: £258.

Clarice Cliff Bizarre 'Coral Firs' pattern preserve pot & cover, c1930, black pen outline landscape, 8.5cm high, printed Bizarre, Clarice Cliff and Newport marks to underside. Rosebery's, London. Mar 05. HP: £220. ABP: £258.

Hammer: £220 - £215

19thC French faience cat in style of Galle, printed with flowers against a white coat and yellow ground, green glass eyes, 13.75in, one leg re-attached. Gorringes, Lewes. Apr 05. HP: £220. ABP: £258.

Bairnsfather for Grimwades, cheese dish/cover, Sea-lions, 7.25in, and another, smaller no maker's mark, Better 'ole and Where did that one go to? Gorringes, Lewes. Oct 04. HP: £220. ABP: £258.

Royal Dux figure group of a naked female and dog. Great Western Auctions, Glasgow. Sep 06. HP: £220. ABP: £258.

Royal Worcester fox. Cotswold Auction Co, Gloucester. Oct 06. HP: £220. ABP: £258.

Early 19thC 'warty-face' Toby jug, character, 9.75in, tri-corn hat restored. Gorringes, Lewes. Oct 05. HP: £220. ABP: £258.

Caughley mask jug, moulded with cabbage leaves, printed with The Fisherman pattern in underglaze blue, S mark, 8.5in, chip to pouring lip. Gorringes, Lewes. Oct 06. HP: £220. ABP: £258.

Mosaic faience figure of a green cat, green glass eyes, hearts & motifs, 12.75in high, front leg repaired. Canterbury Auction Galleries, Kent. Apr 05. HP: £220. ABP: £258.

Beswick Huntsman, rearing horse 686 and 3 foxhounds. Boldon Auction Galleries, Tyne & Wear. Sep 05. HP: £220. ABP: £258.

Troika pottery lamp base, signed underneath. Black Country Auctions, Dudley. Sep 05. HP: £215. ABP: £252.

19thC Prattware-style money box, in the form of a house flanked by figures, 5.25in high. Dee, Atkinson & Harrison, Driffield. Apr 06. HP: £215. ABP: £252.

Early Carter Stabler Adams Poole pottery figure by Phoebe Stabler, The Bath Towel, 7.5in high, imp'd mark to base, c1922. Canterbury Auction Galleries, Kent. Jun 07. HP: £210. ABP: £247.

Minton majolica centrepiece depicting two putti. (def). Great Western Auctions, Glasgow. May 06. HP: £210. ABP: £247.

Beswick Hereford bu.., Ch. of Champions, brown/white gloss, 4.5in, cow & calf to match. Hartleys, Ilkley. Aug 06. HP: £210. ABP: £247.

Mason's Ironstone china 6 place setting dinner/breakfast service, incomplete, incl: 2 tureens, 3 jugs, sauce boat, bowls etc. blue transfer decoration, hand-painted flowers etc. Kent Auction Galleries, Folkestone. Jul 05. HP: £210. ABP: £247.

Pair of Staffordshire zebras, early 19thC, 12cm dia, with another similar of later date. (3) Rosebery's, London. Mar 06. HP: £210. ABP: £247.

First Period Worcester plate & saucer dish, silver shape, printed in blue with Pine Cone Group within diaper border, 22cm and 16cm dia, hatched and open crescent marks, c1780. Bearne's, Exeter. Jun 05. HP: £210. ABP: £247.

Doccia custard cup with ear shaped handle, domed cover and saucer enamelled en camieu with a landscape, gilt & turquoise cell border, 13cm dia saucer, cracked cover. Bearne's, Exeter. Jun 05. HP: £210. ABP: £247.

Clarice Cliff Bizarre fruit bowl, orange, yellow, purple and blue glazes, 10in dia. Ewbank, Send, Surrey. Dec 06. HP: £210. ABP: £247.

Daniel breakfast jug, painted with rural vignettes against a gilded ground, pattern 4347, 5.5in. Gorringes, Lewes. Feb 06. HP: £210. ABP: £247.

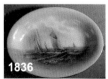

Royal Worcester, Raymond Rushton dish painted with sailing vessels in a choppy sea, sgd. R Rushton, date code for 1933, 10.5in. Ewbank, Send, Surrey. Dec 05. HP: £210. ABP: £247.

Royal Doulton figure, The Girl Evacuee, HN3203. Great Western Auctions, Glasgow. Nov 06. HP: £210. ABP: £247.

Pair of Wilton ware lustre vases, panelled sides gilded with chinoiserie landscapes, red, blue and green ground, 10.5in high. Hartleys, Ilkley. Dec 06. HP: £210. ABP: £247.

> The numbering system acts as a reader reference as well as linking to the Analysis of each section.

19thC Sunderland lustre jug, view of cast iron bridge over the river Wear, 'The loss of gold is much, the loss of time is more, but losing Christ is such a loss as no man can restore', 3.75in high. Dee, Atkinson & Harrison, Driffield. Nov 04. HP: £210. ABP: £247.

Collection of eight half dolls, 4in - 5in high, all numbered, top row 460, indistinct, 12757, 698, 13945, 13453, second row, 12775, indistinct, imp'd 'Germany 16990', 21639. Kent Auction Galleries, Folkestone. Jan 06. HP: £210. ABP: £247.

William Baron Barnstaple, signed blue glaze fish vase and a Branham blue/green glaze puzzle/rhyme jug. (2) Batemans, Stamford. Mar 06. HP: £210. ABP: £247.

Collection of blue and white spoon rests, English early 19thC, varying floral, willow, architectural and landscaped scenes,and two Chinese blue and white spoons and onion patterned Meissen cup and plate. Rosebery's, London. Mar 06. HP: £210. ABP: £247.

Beswick girl on jumping horse. Great Western Auctions, Glasgow. Feb 06. HP: £210. ABP: £247.

Wade figure of a bird, Flicker, 4.75 x 6.5in. Louis Taylor, Stoke on Trent. Mar 05. HP: £210. ABP: £247.

Wedgwood buff glazed pottery game pie dish/cover moulded in relief with dead game and fruiting vines, rabbit pattern cover, 7.5 x 5.5in, and a Copeland buff glazed pottery 'Beehive' pattern honey pot/cover, 5.5in high. Canterbury Auction Galleries, Kent. Mar 05. HP: £210. ABP: £247.

1846

R. Doulton Ltd. Edn. The Home Coming, HN3295, No. 2590, from the children of the Blitz Series, designed by A Hughes, issued 1990, 2590/9500, 7in high, certificate. Halls Fine Art, Shrewsbury. Apr 05. HP: £210. ABP: £247.

1847

Beswick Queen Elizabeth on 'Imperial', damage to ear & hat. Black Country Auctions, Dudley. Oct 05. HP: £210. ABP: £247.

1848

Portuguese Majolica dish by Caldas in the manner of Palissy, raised lizards, frogs & tortoise, 23cm, impressed marks and large number 9. Boldon Auction Galleries, Tyne & Wear. Sep 05. HP: £210. ABP: £247.

1849

Wilkinson Ltd Bizarre 'Original' pattern, bowl by Clarice Cliff. Orpington Salerooms, Kent. Sep 06. HP: £205. ABP: £241. £235.

1850

Troika pottery cache-pot, incised motifs, painted marks to base, 14.5cm. Sworders, Stansted Mountfitchet. Apr 05. HP: £200. ABP: £235.

1851

English art pottery plaque painted with a portrait of a lady, initialled verso A.A.H. dated 1883, label for Howel & James Art Pottery Exh, 14.5in. Andrew Hartley, Ilkley. Apr 06. HP: £200. ABP: £235.

1852

Royal Dux porcelain table centre, woman peering into a lily pond, 10in high, imp'd triangular mark in pink to base and No. 598, fritting to edges of lily pond and base. Canterbury Auction Galleries, Kent. Apr 06. HP: £200. ABP: £235.

1853

Maffra-Caldas wall plate, four lizards crawling upon a shredded clay ground, 10in. Gorringes, Lewes. Jun 05. HP: £200. ABP: £235.

1854

Clarice Cliff vase, Rhodanthe, U-shaped vessel on solid tri-form base, unsigned, shape 452, 8.25in. Gorringes, Lewes. Jun 05. HP: £200. ABP: £235.

1855

Caughley strainer, pierced with single handle, printed with Fisherman pattern, S mark, c1780, 3in dia. Gorringes, Lewes. Feb 06. HP: £200. ABP: £235.

Hammer: £210 - £200

1856

Chamberlain's Worcester salmon pink ground tureen & cover, English c1830, cover surmounted by a pineapple finial, base with 2 botanical studies, 25cm high. Rosebery's, London. Jun 05. HP: £200. ABP: £235.

1857

Pair 19thC Sitzendorf busts of Prince Louis Charles de Bourbon & his sister Princess Marie Zepherine, marks in blue, 10cm high. Cheffins, Cambridge. Apr 05. HP: £200. ABP: £235.

1858

George Jones majolica sardine dish, wicker basket on dished base, lid with fish and seaweed, 9.25in wide. Hartleys, Ilkley. Jun 06. HP: £200. ABP: £235.

1859

Royal Copenhagen group of three penguins, 9.25in, one beak repaired. Gorringes, Lewes. Jul 06. HP: £200. ABP: £235.

1860

Pair Ridgway sauce tureens, domed lids, acanthus leaf handles, painted with flowers on a blue ground, gilt high-lights, mid 19thC, 7.5in wide. Hartleys, Ilkley. Aug 06. HP: £200. ABP: £235.

1861

R. Worcester porcelain sauce tureen, loop handles, painted with birds/insects on a blue gilded ground, dated 1909, 7.25in long. Hartleys, Ilkley. Aug 06. HP: £200. ABP: £235.

1862

18thC Whieldon-type cow creamer, dappled brown and grey, with cover, 5.25in high, restored. Gorringes, Lewes. Sep 05. HP: £200. ABP: £235.

1863

Glyn Colledge for Denby cider set: jug and six mugs, with hunting scenes. Great Western Auctions, Glasgow. Jan 07. HP: £200. ABP: £235.

1864

Royal Doulton figure 'Rosamund' M32. Great Western Auctions, Glasgow. Jan 07. HP: £200. ABP: £235.

1865

Early 19thC Sunderland lustre? 2 handled, Po with Keep Me Clean and Use Me Well and What I See I Will Not Tell. Kent Auction Galleries, Folkestone. Feb 07. HP: £200. ABP: £235.

Hammer: £200

Royal Worcester figure, Little Blue Boy by F. Doughty, from The Nursery Rhyme Series, shape 3306, black mark to base, date for 1942-1948, 4in high. Ewbank, Send, Surrey. Dec 06. HP: £200. ABP: £235.

Royal Doulton figure, The Balloon Seller HN583, 9in high. Golding Young & Co, Grantham. Nov 06. HP: £200. ABP: £235.

Chelsea goat and bee jug, c1745/50, upper half missing, incised triangle, 9.5cm. Sworders, Stansted Mountfitchet. Feb 07. HP: £200. ABP: £235.

Three creamware soup plates, late 18thC, printed in black with exotic birds, 24cm, and one decorated in red, cracked, 24.5cm. (4) Sworders, Stansted Mountfitchet. Feb 07. HP: £200. ABP: £235.

Two oval section jugs, gilt and painted with pattern Nos. 365 & 427, 11cm high. Cheffins, Cambridge. Feb 05. HP: £200. ABP: £235.

Five Delft blue/white tiles. roundels depicting religious subjects, and ten other Delft blue and white tiles mostly depicting buildings, 5in. Canterbury Auction Galleries, Kent. Feb 07. HP: £200. ABP: £235.

Martinware stoneware miniature vase, moulded body in blue and green, 4.75in high, incised mark 'Martin Bros., London and Southall', dated 11-99, restored chip to rim. Canterbury Auction Galleries, Kent. Oct 05. HP: £200. ABP: £235.

> The illustrations are in descending price order. The price range is indicated at the top of each page.

18thC Delft blue/white octagonal baluster shaped vase, in 'Chinese' manner, moulded leaf scroll panel to front with vase of mixed flowers, 9.5in high, rim and footrim slightly chipped/fritted. Canterbury Auction Galleries, Kent. Oct 05. HP: £200. ABP: £235.

Troika pottery vase, 4.5in high. George Kidner Auctioneers, Lymington. Jan 06. HP: £200. ABP: £235.

Lladro figure of a boy with dog and barrow, 21.5cm high. Gorringes, Bexhill. Feb 06. HP: £200. ABP: £235.

19thC Wedgwood black basalt crow, glass eyes, 5in high. Ewbank Auctioneers, Send, Surrey. Dec 05. HP: £200. ABP: £235.

Midwinter Style Craft dinner service, Fashion Shape, Cannes pattern, drawings by Hugh Casson. approx 30 pieces. Kent Auction Galleries, Folkestone. Feb 06. HP: £200. ABP: £235.

Brown salt glazed stoneware flask, modelled as a bust of Admiral Lord Nelson, 20thC, 37.5cm high. Rosebery's, London. Feb 06. HP: £200. ABP: £235.

Meissen figural vase of a skater kneeling on a vase c1870, cancelled crossed sword mark, incised 2053, 15cm. Sworders, Stansted Mountfitchet. Feb 06. HP: £200. ABP: £235.

Doulton stoneware vase, c1880, with stylised flower head/floral motifs, restored rim, 54.5cm. Sworders, Stansted Mountfitchet. Feb 06. HP: £200. ABP: £235.

Samson porcelain group of Cupid administering to a seated love struck Venus, a Cupid standing nearby, 9.5in wide. Andrew Hartley, Ilkley, W Yorks. Feb 06. HP: £200. ABP: £235.

Two Beswick horse models. Gorringes, Bexhill. Dec 04. HP: £200. ABP: £235.

Chinese blue and white vase, period of Kangxi, 30cm high. Cheffins, Cambridge. Feb 05. HP: £200. ABP: £235.

Wedgwood lustre vase, with flying humming birds on a mottled blue ground designed by Daisy Makeig-Jones, patt. No. Z5294, printed/painted marks, 20cm high. Cheffins, Cambridge. Feb 05. HP: £200. ABP: £235.

1885

Clarice Cliff 'Bizarre 320' candlestick, abstract design in orange, blue and black, printed mark, 7cm high. Cheffins, Cambridge. Feb 05. HP: £200. ABP: £235.

1886

Grainger's Worcester loving cup, c1840, view of Worcester, puce ground, printed mark, 15cm. Sworders, Stansted Mountfitchet. Feb 05. HP: £200. ABP: £235.

1887

Ridgway ice cream pail/cover, c1825, 3 dolphin feet, with oriental flowers, damaged, 30cm. Sworders, Stansted Mountfitchet. Feb 05. HP: £200. ABP: £235.

1888

Bristol blue and white Delft charger, c1750, urn of flowers in centre, 33.5cm. Sworders, Stansted Mountfitchet. Feb 05. HP: £200. ABP: £235.

1889

Pair Sitzendorf figures, male and female companion, each carrying pigeon baskets, on floral-encrusted scroll bases, 9in. Gorringes, Lewes. Jan 05. HP: £200. ABP: £235.

1890

Pair Robinson & Leadbetter parian statuettes, 14.5in. Gorringes, Lewes. Nov 05. HP: £200. ABP: £235.

1891

Pair of Nymphenberg Commedia dell' Arte figures, German 20thC, man holding a monkey, the other of a woman, 16.5in. Rosebery's, London. Dec 05. HP: £200. ABP: £235.

1892

Iznik pottery bowl, Turkish, painted with stylised floral & scroll decoration, 25cm. Rosebery's, London. Dec 05. HP: £200. ABP: £235.

1893

Late 19thC Minton pottery Art Nouveau influence jardiniere, with flower heads and running tendril border, Rd. No. 616446, Minton Ltd mark, 14in high. Diamond Mills & Co, Felixstowe. Mar 06. HP: £200. ABP: £235.

1894

20thC Clarice Cliff Newport Pottery planter, hand painted with mauve/orange lattice design, orange border, gold Bizarre stamp and Corry & Co. Ltd, London, retailers mark, imp'd No. 347, 11 x 6.75in. Diamond Mills & Co, Felixstowe. Dec 04. HP: £200. ABP: £235.

Hammer Prices £200

1895

18thC pearlware chocolate stand, leaf-shape moulded with veins, painted with leaf border in green and brown, fitted dish to centre, 8.5in. Gorringes, Lewes. Apr 05. HP: £200. ABP: £235.

1896

19thC Staffordshire jug with snake head strap handle, inverted cup steadying handle to front, transfer printed with floral sprays (S/F), 12in. Dee, Atkinson & Harrison, Driffield. Nov 04. HP: £200. ABP: £235.

1897

18thC Worcester sparrow beak jug, decorated in underglaze blue with a fenced garden, hut and flying birds, 4in. Gorringes, Lewes. Dec 04. HP: £200. ABP: £235.

1898

Pair of early 19thC bulb pots, with three rural views in pink lustre, ball feet, 8.25in, one neck restored. Gorringes, Lewes. Apr 05. HP: £200. ABP: £235.

1899

Royal Dux porcelain figure, dog with a duck in his mouth, 9.5in wide, pink triangle mark. Hartleys, Ilkley. Apr 07. HP: £200. ABP: £235.

1900

Bow tureen/cover, c1760, painted with coloured flower sprays, cover with bird finial, naturalistic handles, each with a pair of female masks, various restoration, 24cm. Sworders, Stansted Mountfitchet. Nov 04. HP: £200. ABP: £235.

1901

Minton Secessionist jardiniere, c1900, stylised leaf & floral motifs, printed marks Minton Ltd, Rd No. 616446, 22cm. Sworders, Stansted Mountfitchet. Nov 04. HP: £200. ABP: £235.

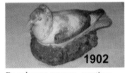

1902

Pearlware tureen, nesting dove, painted in lilac on an ochre encrusted base, early 19thC, 7in wide. Hartleys, Ilkley. Apr 07. HP: £200. ABP: £235.

1903

Bargeware teapot, 'To Commemorate the Coronation of King Edward VII June 26th 1902', 10.5in high. (cover a/f) Dee, Atkinson & Harrison, Driffield. Apr 06. HP: £200. ABP: £235.

1904

Ten various Poole pottery animals. Gorringes, Bexhill. Oct 05. HP: £200. ABP: £235.

Hammer Prices £200 - £190

1905

John Skeaping for Wedgwood, c1930, pair of deer figures, green glaze, 20cm high, imp'd marks to undersides. Rosebery's, London. Mar 05. HP: £200. ABP: £235.

1906

Pair of 18thC Wedgwood and Bentley plaques, sacrifice of Aesculapius and companion plaque, mythological scene, c1773-80, all known examples of such plaques are unmarked, 4in. Gorringes, Lewes. Mar 05. HP: £200. ABP: £235.

1907

Hancock & Sons 'Morrisware' vase designed by George Cartlidge, painted with red flowers against a mottled green-yellow ground, signed beneath, 6.75in. Gorringes, Lewes. Oct 06. HP: £200. ABP: £235.

1908

Late 18thC Prattware jug, relief-moulded/enamelled with figures and animals, chipped and cracked, 6.5in. Gorringes, Lewes. Oct 04. HP: £200. ABP: £235.

1909

19thC Staffordshire cheese cover/stand with pink glaze, fern leaves in rope twist borders, 10in high. Ewbank Auctioneers, Send, Surrey. Dec 05. HP: £195. ABP: £229.

1910

Set of 6 Royal Doulton figures from Mickey Mouse Collection. (MM1-MM6). Boldon Auction Galleries, Tyne & Wear. Sep 05. HP: £195. ABP: £229.

1911

Beswick lady's profile wall mask. Great Western Auctions, Glasgow. Apr 06. HP: £190. ABP: £223.

1912

1930s Carltonware Egyptian style blue/gilt patterned bowl, decorated with a Pharaoh, 10in. Denhams, Warnham. Oct 05. HP: £190. ABP: £223.

1913

Charles Vyse stoneware bowl, purple/blue streaky glaze, incised marks C. VYSE CHELSEA, 4in high, 6in dia. Golding Young & Co, Grantham. Feb 06. HP: £190. ABP: £223.

1914

Slipware jug, slip trailed with abstract designs in yellow on brown ground, early 19thC, 12.25in high. Andrew Hartley, Ilkley. Apr 06. HP: £190. ABP: £223.

1915

Charlotte Rhead, early 20thC earthenware charger, with yellow/orange blooms and stylized leaf forms, orange & gilt tooth border, 44.5cm dia. Locke & England, Leamington Spa. May 05. HP: £190. ABP: £223.

1916

Pair of Burmantofts faience jardinieres, swans covered in a yellow glaze, 7.75in wide. Hartleys, Ilkley. Aug 06. HP: £190. ABP: £223.

1917

Belleek nautilus vase, second period, painted with lilac shades, coral-like stem, 9in. Gorringes, Lewes. Mar 06. HP: £190. ABP: £223.

1918

Royal Worcester figure of Sunday's Child 3256, from the Days of the Week Series, modelled by Freda Doughty, B-4 Backstamp, issued 1940-1961, 4.25 high. Halls Fine Art, Shrewsbury. Jul 05. HP: £190. ABP: £223.

1919

Moorcroft, a Liberty & Co bowl, having twin loop side handles and decorated with frieze roundels on an olive green ground, 20.5cm dia. Locke & England, Leamington Spa. Feb 06. HP: £190. ABP: £223.

1920

Pair of Lambeth stoneware eagles, signed A. G. Hopkins, 1928, 20cm high. Gorringes, Bexhill. Feb 06. HP: £190. ABP: £223.

1921

Rogers blue/white transfer printed meat plate, c1820, figure on a camel, imp'd '16' & 'Rogers', 42.5cm. Sworders, Stansted Mountfitchet. Nov 05. HP: £190. ABP: £223.

1922

18thC creamware mug, with entwined handle, painted with flowers, 5in. Gorringes, Lewes. Apr 05. HP: £190. ABP: £223.

1923

Linthorpe squat bowl, 28cm dia. Gorringes, Bexhill. Dec 04. HP: £190. ABP: £223.

Categories or themes can be followed through the colour coded Index which contains over 4500 cross references.

1924

Clarice Cliff wall mask. Gorringes, Bexhill. Dec 04. HP: £190. ABP: £223.

1925

Early 19thC Maling lustre plaque, inscription 'Thou God See'st me' beneath an eye, 7in. Gorringes, Lewes. Oct 04. HP: £190. ABP: £223.

1926

Pair of late 19th/early 20thC Staffordshire pottery figures of lions, glass eyes, 11.5in high. Canterbury Auction Galleries, Kent. Jun 07. HP: £180. ABP: £211.

1927

19thC Spode blue and white pottery 2 handled soup tureen, cover and stand, printed with 'Tower' pattern, stand 17 x 12.25in, imp'd mark to base, chips restored to lid. Canterbury Auction Galleries, Kent. Jun 07. HP: £180. ABP: £211.

1928

J & M P Bells wall plaque in Constantinople pattern. Great Western Auctions, Glasgow. Apr 06. HP: £180. ABP: £211.

1929

Pair of late 19thC Staffordshire models of Dalmatians, 13cm high. (D) Cheffins, Cambridge. Apr 05. HP: £180. ABP: £211.

1930

19thC Daniel's Coalport jug, painted with flowers, gilt gadrooned rim, 22cm high. Cheffins, Cambridge. Apr 05. HP: £180. ABP: £211.

1931

Late 18thC Caughley chestnut bowl. Henry Adams, Chichester. Jul 06. HP: £180. ABP: £211.

1932

Longwy faience cache-pot, c1880, enamelled with chrys-anthemums on crackled glaze, gilt bronze pierced mounts, elephant head feet, cracked, imp'd and painted marks, 30cm dia. Sworders, Stansted Mountfitchet. Apr 06. HP: £180. ABP: £211.

1933

Two Beatrix Potter figures, Simpkin and Ginger, brown backstamps (BP3 B), boxed. Bearne's, Exeter. Jun 05. HP: £180. ABP: £211.

1934

Bow porcelain figure, monk seated in cowl reading the bible, 11cm high, c1755, loss to cape. Bearne's, Exeter. Jun 05. HP: £180. ABP: £211.

1935

Early 19thC pink lustre cow creamer/cover, 5.5in. high, restored. Gorringes, Lewes. Sep 05. HP: £180. ABP: £211.

Hammer: £180

1936

Cadborough Pottery, Rye, birth plate, type-impressed inscription reading: Matilda Turner, born November 10th 1853, 18.2cm, and 6 handled beaker, inscribed S/R/W/ Rye, 8.5cm. Sworders, Stansted Mountfitchet. Feb 07. HP: £180. ABP: £211.

1937

Daniel plate, C-scroll shape, central basket of flowers and 3 gilded panels with flowers, pattern 4271, 1827-28, 9in. Gorringes, Lewes. Feb 06. HP: £180. ABP: £211.

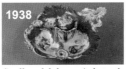

1938

Coalbrookdale pen/inkstand, rococo shape, pierced and gilded handle, tulip well with cover, script mark in blue, c1820-30, well re-attached 7.75in. Gorringes, Lewes. Feb 06. HP: £180. ABP: £211.

1939

Caughley jug, mask spout, printed pine-cone pattern in underglaze blue, indistinct printed S mark, c1780, handle with restored cracks, 6.5in. Gorringes, Lewes. Feb 06. HP: £180. ABP: £211.

1940

Pair of Compton Pottery Art Deco bookends. Gorringes, Bexhill. Oct 05. HP: £180. ABP: £211.

1941

R. Lancastrian vase, banded with gulls in flight, signed Mycott, 9.25in high. Dee, Atkinson & Harrison, Driffield. Feb 06. HP: £180. ABP: £211.

1942

Sunderland pink lustre frog mug with printed verse. Lambert & Foster, Tenterden. Jan 05. HP: £180. ABP: £211.

1943

Lorna Bailey prototype figurine, dancer with split skirt, 13/12/01 to base. Kent Auction Galleries, Folkestone. Sep 06. HP: £180. ABP: £211.

1944

Rye posy vase, 'Sussex Rustic Ware', oak tree-stem with green-glazed acorns and oak leaves, incised SRW mark, 4in. Gorringes, Lewes. Oct 05. HP: £180. ABP: £211.

1945

Scott & Co., Sunderland pink lustre fruit bowl, printed with The Great Eastern Steam-Ship, view of Sunderland Bridge & arms of The Crimea, c1850, imp'd mark Scott, 10.5in. Gorringes, Lewes. Oct 04. HP: £180. ABP: £211.

Hammer: £170

1946

Minton, late 19thC porcelain pot pourri, florally decorated pierced lid & body enclosing liner, three scrolled gilt feet, 12cm dia. Locke & England, Leamington Spa. Feb 06. HP: £170. ABP: £199.

1947

Beswick model by Arthur Gredington, 'Boy on a Horse', palomino colourway, slight chip to ear, 14cm high. Gorringes, Bexhill. Feb 06. HP: £170. ABP: £199.

1948

Pair of Sunderland splash lustre wall plaques, shell and scroll moulded borders, entitled 'Praise Ye The Lord' within a printed/overpainted wreath border surmounted by an angel, 24cm wide. (2) Rosebery's, London. Mar 06. HP: £170. ABP: £199.

1949

Small pair of Staffordshire black and gilt spaniels, 22cm high. Boldon Auction Galleries, Tyne & Wear. Mar 06. HP: £170. ABP: £199.

1950

Troika Wheel vase, geometric designs painted by Louise Jinks, textured ground, 1976-81, 6.5in. Gorringes, Lewes. Apr 06. HP: £170. ABP: £199.

118 *Ceramics Prices*

1951

Late 19thC Belleek porcelain trefoil-shaped basket, floral encrusted mounts, impressed mark on base, 12cm. Reeman Dansie, Colchester. Apr 06. HP: £170. ABP: £199.

1952

Late 19thC Italian maiolica 2 handled vase, two mythical beast scroll handles, painted animal & coat of arms, blue cockerel mark to base, 26cm. Reeman Dansie, Colchester. Apr 06. HP: £170. ABP: £199.

> Prices quoted are actual hammer prices (HP) and the Approximate Buyer's Price (ABP) includes an average premium of 15% + VAT.

1953

Copeland Parianware figure, Reading Girl by P. Macdowell, young woman with open book, 13.5in high, imp'd mark, date code for 1873. Canterbury Auction Galleries, Kent. Feb 06. HP: £170. ABP: £199.

1954

Early 18thC Delft blue/white drug jar, decorative cartouche flanked by stags and worded 'Nervin', 7in high, footrim chipped, glaze to rim flaking, c1725. Canterbury Auction Galleries, Kent. Feb 06. HP: £170. ABP: £199.

1955

Linthorpe dish, designed by Christopher Dresser, fluted form, streaky green glazes, imp'd marks for Henry Tooth, model No. 436, 6in dia. Golding Young & Co, Grantham. Feb 06. HP: £170. ABP: £199.

1956

18thC 'Liverpool' creamware coffee pot/cover printed in black, style of Robert Hancock, view of young lovers in a garden scene, moulded flower-head finial, 9in, unmarked, spout reduced at tip, minor restoration. Canterbury Auction Galleries, Kent. Apr 06. HP: £170. ABP: £199.

1957

Early 19thC Walton pottery figure, Young man holding a serpent, moulded base, 7.5in high, imp'd mark to reverse, restoration to right hand and bocage. Canterbury Auction Galleries, Kent. Apr 06. HP: £170. ABP: £199.

1958

19thC Scottish polychrome/spongeware pottery shallow dish decorated with stylised leaves and flowers, 11in dia, a polychrome decorated bowl & cover, and six other items of similar ware. Canterbury Auction Galleries, Kent. Apr 06. HP: £170. ABP: £199.

1959

Susie Cooper jug, 'The Homestead', painted with a red-roof cottage and landscape, 5.5in. Gorringes, Lewes. Jun 06. HP: £170. ABP: £199.

1960

Chamberlains Worcester porcelain plate, painted with crests within a border of floral posies, early 19thC, 10in wide, and an English porcelain plate painted with a view of Westmoreland. (2) Hartleys, Ilkley. Aug 06. HP: £170. ABP: £199.

1961

Shelley lustre bowl, by Walter Slater with stylised flowers and highlighted with gilt, gilt mark and facsimile signature, 32cm. Sworders, Stansted Mountfitchet. Apr 06. HP: £170. ABP: £199.

1962

Pair of Crown Devon pottery bookends, shaped triangular form, abstract design in black, yellow and orange, 7.5in high. Hartleys, Ilkley. Oct 06. HP: £170. ABP: £199.

1963

Ashby Guild pottery lidded jar, lid with curling handle, streaked blue glaze, 11.25in high, impressed mark. Hartleys, Ilkley. Dec 06. HP: £170. ABP: £199.

1964

19thC Meissen porcelain bowl, oval landscape reserves, 17cm dia. Reeman Dansie, Colchester. Apr 06. HP: £170. ABP: £199.

1965

Thomas Cartier (1879-1943), terracotta figure group of two dogs and sleeping youth, signed & dated 1913, 62cm wide. Rosebery's, London. Jan 07. HP: £170. ABP: £199.

1966

Doulton faience vase by Isobel Lewis, painted with chrysanthemums and a butterfly, turquoise ground, 11in high. Hartleys, Ilkley. Feb 07. HP: £170. ABP: £199.

1967

Cantagalli blue/white maiolica vase/cover, c1900, with figures in classical landscape, 17cm high, socle cracked. Sworders, Stansted Mountfitchet. Feb 07. HP: £170. ABP: £199.

1968

Pair of Minton porcelain figures, Pry and a Boot Black, c1835, 19cm and 19.3cm. Sworders, Stansted Mountfitchet. Feb 07. HP: £170. ABP: £199.

1969

David Firth pottery vase, panelled form, painted with foliate heads within pink/blue banding, 16.75in, Brookhouse Pottery & David Firth imp'd seals. Hartleys, Ilkley. Dec 06. HP: £170. ABP: £199.

1970

Late 19thC Minton majolica leaf pattern nut dish, squirrel holding a nut, 10.25 x 7.5in, imp'd No. 1522, factory mark to base, date code for 1869, ears chipped. Canterbury Auction Galleries, Kent. Feb 07. HP: £170. ABP: £199.

1971

Clarice Cliff beehive honey-pot, 8.5cm high. Charterhouse Auctioneers, Sherborne. Mar 07. HP: £170. ABP: £199.

1972

Stoneware Studio pottery vase by Waistral Cooper, in black 'Pennant' design, 5.5in high. (apparently unmarked) Canterbury Auction Galleries, Kent. Apr 07. HP: £170. ABP: £199.

1973

Lladro figure group, Grand-father and Grandson in a fishing boat Palona, base marked 5215, wooden base. Denhams, Warnham, Sussex. Apr 06. HP: £165. ABP: £194.

Hammer: £170 - £160

1974

23 half dolls to include a Kwepie, different ages and makers, no visible numbers or marks. Kent Auction Galleries, Folkestone. Jan 06. HP: £165. ABP: £194.

1975

Daniel dessert plate, Cusped shape, applied with lilac vine reliefs, gilded/painted with central flowers, patt. 3835, 8.5in. Gorringes, Lewes. Feb 06. HP: £160. ABP: £188.

1976

Coalport loving cup, twin-scroll handles, painted with floral bouquet to each side, c1825, 4in. Gorringes, Lewes. Feb 06. HP: £160. ABP: £188.

1977

Burleigh Ware Floret Pattern coffee set. Charterhouse Auctioneers, Sherborne. Feb 06. HP: £160. ABP: £188.

1978

Victorian Staffordshire cow spill vase, pail of milk at its side, 23cm high, and a figure group entitled 'Going to Market'. Rosebery's, London. Feb 06. HP: £160. ABP: £188.

1979

Two Art Nouveau Cauldon platters. Great Western Auctions, Glasgow. Feb 06. HP: £160. ABP: £188.

1980

Six 19thC pot lids, 5 framed titles incl. Pegwell Bay 4 Shrimpers, Royal Harbour Ramsgate with 2 borders, one frame AF, all sealed in frame. Kent Auction Galleries, Folkestone. Mar 06. HP: £160. ABP: £188.

1981

Pair late 19thC Japanese Kutani vases/covers with won knop, painted landscape scenes, knot/tassled handles, 27cm. Reeman Dansie, Colchester. Apr 06. HP: £160. ABP: £188.

1982

Late Victorian Royal Crown Derby Georgian silver shaped Imari palette 3 piece teaset, red printed marks. Reeman Dansie, Colchester. Apr 06. HP: £160. ABP: £188.

1983

Three 19thC Prattware dessert plates, centres printed with views of 'The Hop Queen', 'The Truant' & 'I See You My Boy', 9.5in, one has retailer's mark of James Muggleton, 8 New Street, Birmingham to base. Canterbury Auction Galleries, Kent. Feb 06. HP: £160. ABP: £188.

Hammer: £160

Wemyss 'jazzy' ware vase. Great Western Auctions, Glasgow. May 06. HP: £160. ABP: £188.

Shelley Melody pattern teaset: 12 cups, saucers & plates, milk jug, sugar bowl, 2 cake plates and 2 preserve dishes. Great Western Auctions, Glasgow. Apr 06. HP: £160. ABP: £188.

Reginald Wells stoneware vase, neck with 2 lug handles, mottled red glaze, impressed SOON, 7in high. Golding Young & Co, Grantham. Feb 06. HP: £160. ABP: £188.

Staffordshire porcelain ram, pink oval base applied with yellow shells, early 19thC, 3.75in wide. Andrew Hartley, Ilkley. Apr 06. HP: £160. ABP: £188.

Early 19thC Staffordshire pottery figure, Elijah's Widow, Woman seated on a rustic stump with a young boy 10in high. Canterbury Auction Galleries, Kent. Apr 06. HP: £160. ABP: £188.

Wilkinson Ltd., Francis Caruthers Gould character jug of Admiral Jellicoe, initialled FCG to edge of base, printed marks, 26.5cm high, handle restored. Rosebery's, London. Aug 06. HP: £160. ABP: £188.

Davenport porcelain sucrier, domed lid with gilded finial, similar scrolled acanthus leaf handles, painted with flowers, and a Royal Crown Derby floral dish, 19thC. (2) Hartleys, Ilkley. Aug 06. HP: £160. ABP: £188.

Limoges pâte-sur-pâte plaque, moulded with a nude female dancer, indistinct signature, 5 x 7.25in, gilt frame. Hartleys, Ilkley. Aug 06. HP: £160. ABP: £188.

R. Doulton porcelain figure, 'Maisie' HN1619, wearing pink dress and bonnet, 6in high. Hartleys, Ilkley. Aug 06. HP: £160. ABP: £188.

Late 19th/early 20thC Johnson Brothers blue/white corner sink, with floral decoration, 24in. Gorringes, Lewes. Mar 06. HP: £160. ABP: £188.

Satsuma vase, late 19thC, painted with warriors in gilt & enamels, 18cm. Sworders, Stansted Mountfitchet. Apr 06. HP: £160. ABP: £188.

Shelley Blue Iris pattern tea set. Lambert & Foster, Tenterden. Sep 06. HP: £160. ABP: £188.

Lorna Bailey prototype figurine, signed, paintress initials SB dated 3/1/02, dancer with outstretched arms. Kent Auction Galleries, Folkestone. Sep 06. HP: £160. ABP: £188.

Worcester tea cup/saucer, floral painted with a version of the Kempthorne pattern. Gorringes, Lewes. Oct 06. HP: £160. ABP: £188.

Set of 4 Prattware pomadore lids, 'A letter from the Diggings', 'Uncle Toby', 'The Shrimpers' and 'Tam O' Shanter and Souter Johnny', 4.25in wide, ebonised frames. Hartleys, Ilkley. Oct 06. HP: £160. ABP: £188.

Burmantofts faience vase, incised with stylised flower-heads, 15.5in high. Hartleys, Ilkley. Oct 06. HP: £160. ABP: £188.

Pair of Staffordshire lions, glass eyes, 25cm high, and a pair of figures of Jackals, pale crackled glaze, 17cm high. (4) Rosebery's, London. Oct 06. HP: £160. ABP: £188.

Extensive Aynsley dinner service decorated in red and gilt scrolling bands, over 100 items. Rosebery's, London. Oct 06. HP: £160. ABP: £188.

Pair of Clarice Cliff Bizarre stepped, square candlesticks orange/yellow fruit, 4in high and a Clarice Cliff preserve pot base, 2.5in high. Ewbank Auctioneers, Send, Surrey. Dec 06. HP: £160. ABP: £188.

2003

Set of six Mintons porcelain botanical dessert plates, each enamelled and painted with differing specimens, gilt borders, 9in dia. Golding Young & Co, Grantham. Nov 06. HP: £160. ABP: £188.

2004

Royal Doulton figure, Mary Jane HN1990, 7.75in high. Golding Young & Co, Grantham. Nov 06. HP: £160. ABP: £188.

2005

Guinness Toucan lampstand by Wiltshaw & Robinson Ltd, (later Carltonware) produced for Arthur Guinness, Son & Co. (Park Royal) Ltd, GA/2178 mark to base. Sandwich Auction Rooms, Kent. Oct 06. HP: £160. ABP: £188.

2006

Maling dish 'Dovecote'. Great Western Auctions, Glasgow. Feb 07. HP: £160. ABP: £188.

2007

Pottery plaque by David Sharp, head of an owl, brown, yellow & white on blue/black ground, signed, also signed verso and dated '63. 15 x 16.5in, gilt frame. Hartleys, Ilkley. Feb 07. HP: £160. ABP: £188.

2008

Qajar polychrome pottery tile, c1900, moulded in low relief, equestrian figure hunting wild boar, 21 x 21cm. Sworders, Stansted Mountfitchet. Feb 07. HP: £160. ABP: £188.

2009

Worcester chocolate cup and saucer, c1790, double ogee shape, painted in the Queen Charlotte pattern, crescent marks, 7.5cm. (2) Sworders, Stansted Mountfitchet. Feb 07. HP: £160. ABP: £188.

The numbering system acts as a reader reference as well as linking to the Analysis of each section.

2010

Pair Royal Worcester cream iridescent glazed porcelain nautilus shell pattern table centres, pink glazed interiors, coral pattern supports, shell encrusted bases, 6.5in high, imp'd marks to underside, one chipped. Canterbury Auction Galleries, Kent. Feb 07. HP: £160. ABP: £188.

2011

Garniture of early 19thC patent Ironstone china vases in 'Imari' pattern, centre vase 6in high, pair of smaller vases 5in high, imp'd mark to bases, one badly chipped. Canterbury Auction Galleries, Kent. Apr 07. HP: £160. ABP: £188.

Hammer: £160 - £150

2012

Clarice Cliff Crocus Pattern mustard pot from Wilkinson, matching Crocus Pattern Wilkinson covered sugar bowl, 3.5in dia, light glazing cracks. Kent Auction Galleries, Folkestone. Mar 07. HP: £160. ABP: £188.

2013

Beswick Suffolk Punch Ch Hasse Dainty. Great Western Auctions, Glasgow. Mar 07. HP: £160. ABP: £188.

2014

Clarice Cliff Bizarre Newport pottery bonjour shape tea pot No. 8874/9 to base. (AF) Kent Auction Galleries, Folkestone. Mar 06. HP: £155. ABP: £182.

2015

Two Staffordshire bocage figures, St Mark & St Matthew, early 19thC, restored. Gorringes, Bexhill. Feb 06. HP: £150. ABP: £176.

2016

Clarice Cliff crocus pattern bee hive honey jar and cover. Great Western Auctions, Glasgow. Jan 06. HP: £150. ABP: £176.

2017

Carlton Ware hand painted Guinness Toucan lamp, electric cables removed, lamp switch present. Kent Auction Galleries, Folkestone. Feb 06. HP: £150. ABP: £176.

2018

Small Keith Murray Bomb vase c1940, produced for Wedgewood, matt white with concentric incised rings to body, with a continental vase, inverted molded decoration, bomb vase 16cm high. Rosebery's, London. Mar 06. HP: £150. ABP: £176.

2019

Pratt Ware, c1810, Napoleonic commemorative pearlware jug, relief moulded with portraits of Lord Wellington opposed by General Hill, 16cm high. Rosebery's, London. Mar 06. HP: £150. ABP: £176.

2020

19thC Samson porcelain figure of a 'Mansion House' dwarf playing a lute, 7.75in high. Canterbury Auction Galleries, Kent. Feb 06. HP: £150. ABP: £176.

Collection of 21 half dolls, various styles & makes, some marked 'Made in Japan', 4in - 1.75in, two af. Kent Auction Galleries, Folkestone. Jan 06. HP: £150. ABP: £176.

Royal Doulton figure, Sweet and Twenty HN1589. Great Western Auctions, Glasgow. Mar 06. HP: £150. ABP: £176.

19thC Sevres plate, painted with lovers in a garden, gilded blue ground, 9.5in. Gorringes, Lewes. Apr 06. HP: £150. ABP: £176.

Minton parian figure, 'Dorothea' by John Bell, PODR 1847, 13.75in. Gorringes, Lewes. Apr 06. HP: £150. ABP: £176.

Antique Chinese blue/white porcelain bottle vase with floral/bamboo decoration, 6 character mark to base, 27cm. Reeman Dansie, Colchester. Apr 06. HP: £150. ABP: £176.

Early 19thC Staffordshire blue/white pottery meat plate by John and Richard Riley, Nile Street and Hill Works, Burslem, printed with 'Scene after Claude Lorraine', 17 x 13.75in, printed mark in blue to base, c1820. Canterbury Auction Galleries, Kent. Feb 06. HP: £150. ABP: £176.

Clarice Cliff crocus pattern jug. Great Western Auctions, Glasgow. May 06. HP: £150. ABP: £176.

The illustrations are in descending price order. The price range is indicated at the top of each page.

Upchurch pottery vase, slightly ribbed body with purple and green iridescent glaze, incised mark in script, 15in high. Golding Young & Co, Grantham. Feb 06. HP: £150. ABP: £176.

Kevin Francis figure of Clarice Cliff, designed by John Michael for Peggy Davies, Ltd Edn No. 337/900, 9in high, certificate. Golding Young & Co, Grantham. Feb 06. HP: £150. ABP: £176.

Hochst bottle vase, embellished with bird of prey and exotic bird in relief, 8in high. Golding Young & Co, Grantham. Feb 06. HP: £150. ABP: £176.

Carltonware novelty teapot as an early bi-plane, 'Lucy May', green-glazed with RAF roundels, pilot cover, mould 1544, 6.5in wingspan. Gorringes, Lewes. Jun 06. HP: £150. ABP: £176.

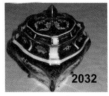

Royal Crown Derby lidded urn, pointed finial, painted with Imari panels, dated 1937, 4in high. Hartleys, Ilkley. Aug 06. HP: £150. ABP: £176.

Royal Dux porcelain figure, rustic female water carrier pouring a drink, 16.75in high. Hartleys, Ilkley. Aug 06. HP: £150. ABP: £176.

Derby porcelain sauce tureen on stand, panelled oval form, gilded lion mask loop handles, with landscapes 'In Westmoreland' & 'In Cumberland', late 18th/19thC, 8.5in wide. Hartleys, Ilkley. Aug 06. HP: £150. ABP: £176.

Three Poole pottery vases, a cylindrical flared rim vase, 23cm, tapering plant pot, 16cm and a small bluebird vase, 12cm, stylised floral designs, imp'd, painted and incised marks. (3) Sworders, Stansted Mountfitchet. Apr 06. HP: £150. ABP: £176.

Walter Awlson glazed pottery figure of a seated girl. Great Western Auctions, Glasgow. Aug 06. HP: £150. ABP: £176.

Pair Royal Worcester Hadley figures of Dutch fisherfolk, No. 1202, the man def. Great Western Auctions, Glasgow. Sep 06. HP: £150. ABP: £176.

Troika wheel vase, abstract motifs to each side, two-tone blue against textured ground, decorated by Marilyn Pascoe, c1968-74. Gorringes, Lewes. Oct 06. HP: £150. ABP: £176.

Derby porcelain figure as David Garrick striding forth with a feathered hat at his feet, late 18th/19thC, 12in high. Hartleys, Ilkley. Oct 06. HP: £150. ABP: £176.

2040

Royal Dux figure, Turkish water carrier, wearing green tunic, 17in, pink triangle mark. Hartleys, Ilkley. Dec 06. HP: £150. ABP: £176.

2041

Rogers blue/white meat plate with imp'd mark and non-matching Spode drainer with printed mark, each with figures in Far Eastern landscapes, drainer 48.5cm wide. (2) Rosebery's, London. Jan 07. HP: £150. ABP: £176.

2042

Pearlware toilet jug, shaped rim and loop handle, blue printed with unusual village scene pattern, early 19thC, 8.5in high. Hartleys, Ilkley. Feb 07. HP: £150. ABP: £176.

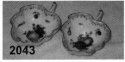

2043

Pair Meissen pickle dishes, leaf form, squared loop handle, fruit/insects within gilded rim, late 19th/20thC, 4.25in long, cross swords mark. Hartleys, Ilkley. Feb 07. HP: £150. ABP: £176.

2044

R. Doulton figure, Maureen, HN 1770, 7.5in. Golding Young & Co, Grantham. Nov 06. HP: £150. ABP: £176.

2045

Wilton ware lustre vase, gilded with a chinoiserie landscape in yellows, purples and greens, 13.5in high. Hartleys, Ilkley. Feb 07. HP: £150. ABP: £176.

2046

Pair of late 19thC Stafford-shire pottery figures, Duke & Duchess of Cambridge, on horseback, 14in high, front legs of horses cracked and restoration. Canterbury Auction Galleries, Kent. Feb 07. HP: £150. ABP: £176.

2047

Mintons porcelain armorial soup plate for use on the Royal Yacht, royal blue/gilt with oval crest of St. George and the Dragon surrounded by garter, 10in dia, printed red mark to base, retailed by T. Goode & Co, London. Canterbury Auction Galleries, Kent. Feb 07. HP: £150. ABP: £176.

2048

Staffordshire blue/white pottery W.C. pan, The Rapidus, exterior/interior transfer printed with convolvulus and stylised borders, 17 x 14 x 16in high, bowl/base cracked in several places, mahogany toilet seat. Canterbury Auction Galleries, Kent. Feb 07. HP: £150. ABP: £176.

Hammer: £150 - £140

2049

Lladro dog musicians, one singing, two playing guitar & one playing bongos, blue Lladro mark to base, other incised marks. Kent Auction Galleries, Folkestone. Dec 06. HP: £150. ABP: £176.

2050

Staffordshire farmyard group, 2 musicians seated beneath bocage, with sheep, calf and swan, 9in high, early 19thC. Hartleys, Ilkley. Feb 07. HP: £150. ABP: £176.

2051

Pottery plaque decorated in relief with bust of Richard Cobden, surrounded by a laurel wreath and painted with flowers. Great Western Auctions, Glasgow. Mar 07. HP: £150. ABP: £176.

2052

Pair of Clarice Cliff minia-ture wall masks, one def. Great Western Auctions, Glasgow. Sep 06. HP: £145. ABP: £170.

2053

Clarice Cliff Bizarre Kelverne pattern fruit bowl, 23cm dia. Gorringes, Bexhill. Feb 06. HP: £140. ABP: £164.

2054

17thC Safavid style vase, enriched with bands of stylised floral/foliate decor-ation, faults, 22cm high. Rosebery's, London. Jan 06. HP: £140. ABP: £164.

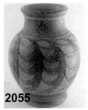

2055

Royal Lancashire, earth-enware vase with stylized floral/geometric forms in mid-blue, mottled mushroom ground, 31cm. Locke & England, Leamington Spa. Feb 06. HP: £140. ABP: £164.

2056

Daniel spill vase, shell shape with everted rim, shape 236, with wild birds and nest, on gilded shell feet, pattern 5249, 5.75in. Gorringes, Lewes. Feb 06. HP: £140. ABP: £164.

2057

Coalport teapot, cover/stand, wrythen shape painted with flower sprays and drapes in puce and pink, c1800, stand 6.25in long. Gorringes, Lewes. Feb 06. HP: £140. ABP: £164.

2058

Beswick figure, Woodpecker. Lambert & Foster, Tenterden. Mar 06. HP: £140. ABP: £164.

Crown Ducal Charlotte Rhead tubelined vase, patt. No. 6189, signed, 19cm high, 19cm dia. Gorringes, Bexhill. Feb 06. HP: £140. ABP: £164.

Royal Crown Derby loving cup, 1918, 3.5in high. Dee, Atkinson & Harrison, Driffield. Feb 06. HP: £140. ABP: £164.

Royal Worcester figure 'May' from months of year series, by F.G. Doughty, and another figure 'Friday's Child is Loving and Giving'. (2) Rosebery's, London. Mar 06. HP: £140. ABP: £164.

Sunderland lustre jug, c1820, one side printed with a view of Iron Bridge, other with an illustrated 'Sailors' Farewell', 15cm. Rosebery's, London. Mar 06. HP: £140. ABP: £164.

Pair of Gille painted biscuit porcelain figures, c1870, male and female in medieval costume, 32cm high. (2) Rosebery's, London. Mar 06. HP: £140. ABP: £164.

Aynsley China Ltd, lion figurine, Ltd Edn 22/100 to commemorate Silver Jubilee of Her Majesty Queen Elizabeth II, 23 x 14in high, certificate, signed. Kent Auction Galleries, Folkestone. Mar 06. HP: £140. ABP: £164.

Pair of Beleek figurines, boy & girl carrying basket on their shoulders, gold back stamp, 8.5in high. Kent Auction Galleries, Folkestone. Mar 06. HP: £140. ABP: £164.

Late 19thC Capodimonte porcelain ewer, classical form with satyr and rams head handle, pierced gilt maroon spout, raised mythical figure and chariot decoration, blue crowned N mark, 13in high. Diamond Mills & Co, Felixstowe. Mar 06. HP: £140. ABP: £164.

Squat Moorcroft vase, Hellebores pattern 1999, 4.25in high. Dee, Atkinson & Harrison, Driffield. Apr 06. HP: £140. ABP: £164.

Royal Doulton character jug 'Punch and Judy Man', D6590, large. Louis Taylor, Stoke on Trent. Mar 06. HP: £140. ABP: £164.

Lladro figurine, Rock Nymph, No. 1601. Sandwich Auction Rooms, Kent. May 06. HP: £140. ABP: £164.

> Categories or themes can be followed through the colour coded Index which contains over 4500 cross references.

Clarice Cliff crocus pattern 3 piece cruet. Great Western Auctions, Glasgow. May 06. HP: £140. ABP: £164.

Eugene Baudin bottle vase, blue bottle neck and yellow streaked satin matt body with loops, 7in high. Golding Young & Co, Grantham. Feb 06. HP: £140. ABP: £164.

Pair of Royal Doulton Character jugs, Stan Laurel and Oliver Hardy, by William K Harpo, No. D7009, Ltd Edn No. 1310/3500, 4in high, certificate. Golding Young & Co, Grantham. Feb 06. HP: £140. ABP: £164.

Royal Walt Disney Showcase Collection: Snow White SW9, Happy SW12, Grumpy SW11, Dopey by candlelight SW17, Bashful's melody SW18, Sneezy SW14, Doc SW10, Sleepy SW15, Bashful SW16, Snow White 6in high. Golding Young & Co, Grantham. Feb 06. HP: £140. ABP: £164.

Beswick figure of a Leghorn cockerel, model No. 1892, by Arthur Gredington, 10in high, issued 1963-1983. Golding Young & Co, Grantham. Feb 06. HP: £140. ABP: £164.

Two Beswick pottery Beatrix Potter figures, Sir Isaac Newton, 3.75in high, and Mr Jeremy Fisher Digging, 3.75in high, brown back stamps. Canterbury Auction Galleries, Kent. Apr 06. HP: £140. ABP: £164.

Collingwood Bros, Admiral Sir David Beatty, commemorative jug, printed in black with profile portrait flanked by a verse 'The surrender of the German Fleet....' opposed by an view of 'HMS Queen Elizabeth SDB' within banners, rim titled 'God Save King George V' and 'Long Live the British Navy', 15.5cm high. Rosebery's, London. May 06. HP: £140. ABP: £164.

2077

Small 18thC Whieldon ware pattern pottery jug, rustic pattern handle, 3in high, rim chipped, cracked and fritted. Canterbury Auction Galleries, Kent Apr 06. HP: £140. ABP: £164.

2078

Royal Dux porcelain group of a cow & milkmaid, pastel shades of green, brown, pink and gilt, 7.75in high, imp'd triangular mark in pink to base and No. 830. Canterbury Auction Galleries, Kent. Apr 06. HP: £140. ABP: £164.

2079

Wedgwood copy of The Portland Vase, blue jasper, moulded portrait bust beneath, 10in, rivetted. Gorringes, Lewes. Jun 06. HP: £140. ABP: £164.

2080

Victorian Staffordshire cow and milkmaid spill vase, painted in rust enamel, 8.5in. Gorringes, Lewes. Jun 06. HP: £140. ABP: £164.

2081

Pair of Worcester vases, date code for 1876, putti working on coopered barrels, enriched in gilt, 14cm high. Rosebery's, London. May 06. HP: £140. ABP: £164.

2082

Royal Crown Derby miniature coffee set: coffee pot, milk, sugar and oval tray, painted in Imari panels, 20thC, tray 7.5in wide. Hartleys, Ilkley. Aug 06. HP: £140. ABP: £164.

2083

Derby porcelain spill vase, painted with flowers within beaded and gilded borders, early 19thC, 4.5in high, possibly painted by Charles Bourne. Hartleys, Ilkley. Aug 06. HP: £140. ABP: £164.

2084

Poole pottery charger 'Eclipse' by Alan Clarke, No. 1460/1999, with certificate. Great Western Auctions, Glasgow. Jul 06. HP: £140. ABP: £164.

2085

Wemyss Pottery biscuit jar/ cover, stamped/painted marks, retailed by T Goode & Co, South Audley Street, London, 12.5cm. Sworders, Stansted Mountfitchet. Apr 06. HP: £140. ABP: £164.

2086

Beswick Study, Huntsman jumping fence. Orpington Salerooms, Kent. Sep 06. HP: £140. ABP: £164.

Hammer: £140

2087

Carlton Ware vase in Devils Copse pattern, 4.5in high. Great Western Auctions, Glasgow. Nov 06. HP: £140. ABP: £164.

2088

Four half dolls incl. lady with a fan, imp'd 8667, lady with mandolin imp'd 3721, lady with hat imp'd 5289, full figure reclining with hat & blue dress imp'd 7041, Parian Nude with hands raised to mouth imp'd 10690. (4) Kent Auction Galleries, Folkestone. Nov 06. HP: £140. ABP: £164.

2089

Boch Freres Keramis vase, post 1940, with flowers and foliage, stamped D2532 to base. Great Western Auctions, Glasgow. Jan 07. HP: £140. ABP: £164.

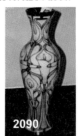

2090

Moorcroft 'Calla Lily' vase, designed by Emma Bossons. Great Western Auctions, Glasgow. Jan 07. HP: £140. ABP: £164.

2091

Twin handled Maling bowl decorated with butterflies and flowers. Great Western Auctions, Glasgow. Jan 07. HP: £140. ABP: £164.

2092

Moorcroft Wisteria vase, 6in high. Kent Auction Galleries, Folkestone. Dec 06. HP: £140. ABP: £164.

2093

Worcester Barr Flight & Barr trio with bands of peach glaze with blue/gilt foliate forms, imp'd mark to base. Ewbank Auctioneers, Send, Surrey. Dec 06. HP: £140. ABP: £164.

2094

Pair of Mason's Ironstone boxes & covers in Mandalay pattern, 14.5cm wide, and other items of china, a/f. Rosebery's, London. Jan 07. HP: £140. ABP: £164.

2095

Samson porcelain figural group, after Chelsea, harlequin Pierrot and a lady, 19thC, 10.25in high. Hartleys, Ilkley. Feb 07. HP: £140. ABP: £164.

Royal Winton Marguerite pattern tea set. Charterhouse Auctioneers, Sherborne. Feb 07. HP: £140. ABP: £164.

Six tile picture, late 19thC, riverside animals, oak frame, label verso 'given to...painted by his Great Grandfather Arthur Midgley', 67.5 x 47cm. Sworders, Stansted Mountfitchet. Feb 07. HP: £140. ABP: £164.

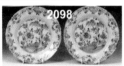

Pair Bristol Delft blue/white plates, c1770, painted with a tree, flowers, lattice fence, 23cm dia, chips. Sworders, Stansted Mountfitchet. Feb 07. HP: £140. ABP: £164.

Stevenson & Hancock figure of Billy Waters, late 19thC, titled on plinth, puce marks, 10cm, restored. Sworders, Stansted Mountfitchet. Feb 07. HP: £140. ABP: £164.

Delft polychrome dish with an Oriental figure holding a flower in each hand, bearing red mark for Adriaenus and Pieter Koeks, 35cm dia, a/f. Rosebery's, London. Apr 07. HP: £140. ABP: £164.

Crown Devon musical jug, 'Harry Lauder I Love a Lassie', 9.5in high. Dee, Atkinson & Harrison, Driffield. Jul 06. HP: £135. ABP: £158.

Wood & Sons gourd vase by Frederick Rhead, Chung pattern. Orpington Salerooms, Kent. Jan 06. HP: £130. ABP: £152.

Daniel serving plate, two-handled and pierced, painted with mixed fruit and flowers, apricot border, pattern 5666, 10.75in. Gorringes, Lewes. Feb 06. HP: £130. ABP: £152.

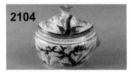

Coalport sucrier/cover, oval shape, gilded mask and ring handles, with a flowering shrub pattern, No.372, Japan colours, c1805, 6.5in long. Gorringes, Lewes. Feb 06. HP: £130. ABP: £152.

4 Hummel figures Eventide, Skier, Cinderella & Little Tailor. (TMK 5) Great Western Auctions, Glasgow. Feb 06. HP: £130. ABP: £152.

Moorcroft 'Alicante' decorated vase, c1997, sky blue ground with town scene of Alicante Spain in colours, painted factory marks and signed B A Wilkes, dated 14.11.98 to underside, 21.5cm. Rosebery's, London. Mar 06. HP: £130. ABP: £152.

Poole Pottery 'Studio' earthenware vase, by Alan White, c2000, copper green body imprinted with diagonal pattern, printed mark to underside, height 39cm. Rosebery's, London. Mar 06. HP: £130. ABP: £152.

> Prices quoted are actual hammer prices (HP) and the Approximate Buyer's Price (ABP) includes an average premium of 15% + VAT.

Gardner charger, Russian 19thC, enriched with gilt Cyrillic script and floral spray, 42.5cm. Rosebery's, London. Mar 06. HP: £130. ABP: £152.

Beswick black Labrador, recumbent on hind legs, mould 2311, 13.5in. Gorringes, Lewes. Apr 06. HP: £130. ABP: £152.

Victorian George Jones majolica-type cheese dome & base, floral & basket weave decoration, imp'd mark on base, 26cm dia. Reeman Dansie, Colchester. Apr 06. HP: £130. ABP: £152.

Late 18thC/early 19thC Pearlware miniature teapot, oval form decorated in relief depicting mother & child and girl with dog, 10cm high and 15cm wide. Reeman Dansie, Colchester. Apr 06. HP: £130. ABP: £152.

Two Burmantofts yellow glazed pottery jardinieres, as grotesque animals, each on 3 clawed feet, 8 x 5.5 x 7in high, one with imp'd factory mark, one rear leg repaired. Canterbury Auction Galleries, Kent. Feb 06. HP: £130. ABP: £152.

Early 19thC Barr Flight & Barr period Worcester porcelain part tea service, bat printed in black with reclining classical figures, cracks. (17) Canterbury Auction Galleries, Kent. Feb 06. HP: £130. ABP: £152.

Royal Worcester porcelain plate, wavy rim, painted by Johnson with Grouse, within flower gilded border, 9in wide. Hartleys, Ilkley. Oct 06. HP: £130. ABP: £152.

3 pairs of Quimper faience plates, with standing figures of a gentleman and woman in national dress within blue and yellow banded borders, 8in, 8.5in and 9.25in dia, latter pair cracked. Canterbury Auction Galleries, Kent. Feb 06. HP: £130. ABP: £152.

Ashby Potters Guild Vase, blue ground with purple and green splashes, 10in high. Golding Young & Co, Grantham. Feb 06. HP: £130. ABP: £152.

Ruskin Pottery vase, grey and blue lustre glazes, signed in script W. Howson Taylor, impressed Ruskin England 1932, 7in high. Golding Young & Co, Grantham. Feb 06. HP: £130. ABP: £152.

Royal Doulton figure 'St George', HN2051, designed by P. Davies, 8in high. Golding Young & Co, Grantham. Feb 06. HP: £130. ABP: £152.

Beswick Jersey bull and cow, Ch. Dunsley Cowboy & Ch. Newton Tinklem, 4.5in high. Hartleys, Ilkley. Aug 06. HP: £130. ABP: £152.

Susie Cooper pottery tea service, 'Kestral' shape, in pale pink and beige with banded and spotted borders, brown printed marks to bases with pattern No. 475/21, 24 pieces, cracks & chips. Canterbury Auction Galleries, Kent. Apr 06. HP: £130. ABP: £152.

19thC Staffordshire pottery figure, Dick Turpin on Black Bess, oval moulded base inscribed Dick Turpin, 11.25in high. Golding Young & Co, Grantham. Nov 06. HP: £130. ABP: £152.

Pair of Royal Doulton stoneware vases, tapering form, upper section tube lined with fruit and with a streaked blue glaze, 26cm high, with a pair of Royal Doulton Slaters patent baluster vases. (4) Rosebery's, London. May 06. HP: £130. ABP: £152.

Paragon Royal commemorative bowl & 14 plates, base printed with 'A perpetual souvenir in Paragon china to commemorate the Coronation of their Majesties King George VI & Queen Elizabeth, Crowned Westminster Abbey May 12 1937', designed by J.A. Robinson, bowl 27cm dia, 14 plates 22/24cm dia, one a/f. (15) Rosebery's, London. Aug 06. HP: £130. ABP: £152.

Hammer: £130

Victorian Prattware pot lid, 'Shakespeare's Birthplace, Stratford-on-Avon', 4in dia, framed. Golding Young & Co, Grantham. Feb 06. HP: £130. ABP: £152.

Graingers Worcester porcelain moon flask, gilded fancy loop handles, gilded with flowers on a blue ground, 7.25in high. Hartleys, Ilkley. Aug 06. HP: £130. ABP: £152.

Three Sherwin & Cotton tiles, 1870s, lady with amphora, a gentleman reading, and lady holding a lamb, imp'd marks, 30.3 x 15.2cm. (3) Sworders, Stansted Mountfitchet. Apr 06. HP: £130. ABP: £152.

Vienna porcelain twin handled bowl, 20thC, central panel printed with 2 maidens, gilt rubbed, 16cm. Sworders, Stansted Mountfitchet. Apr 06. HP: £130. ABP: £152.

Clarice Cliff Bizarre pottery fern pot, Gay Day pattern, 3.75in dia x 3.75in high, black printed mark to base. Canterbury Auction Galleries, Kent. Apr 06. HP: £130. ABP: £152.

Set of 4 1950s Wade nursery rhyme figures, 'Wynken', 'Blynken', 'Nod' and 'I've a bear behind', green printed marks, 7.5cm. Locke & England, Leamington Spa. Nov 06. HP: £130. ABP: £152.

Worcester porcelain teapot, domed lid with bud finial, blue painted in fence pattern, late 18thC, 7.5in wide, blue crescent mark. Hartleys, Ilkley. Dec 06. HP: £130. ABP: £152.

Crown Devon Fieldings musical jug, printed with 'Widdicombe Fair' moulded with gentleman and horses, 7.5in high. Hartleys, Ilkley. Dec 06. HP: £130. ABP: £152.

Pair C.H. Brannam beakers by William Baron, dated 1888, with birds amongst foliage and flowers, some def. Great Western Auctions, Glasgow. Jan 07. HP: £130. ABP: £152.

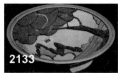

Clarice Cliff Fantasque Bizarre bowl in Limberlost pattern, shape no 454, some damage to decoration. Great Western Auctions, Glasgow. Feb 07. HP: £130. ABP: £152.

Hammer: £130 - £120

2134

R. Worcester porcelain dish, mildly frilled circular form, painted with apples and plums by Moseley, spreading foot, gilded rim, 5.75in wide. Hartleys, Ilkley. Feb 07. HP: £130. ABP: £152.

2135

Pair of 19thC Staffordshire pottery figures, greyhounds with hares in their mouths, on oval moulded bases with granitic decoration at their feet, 7.75in high. Canterbury Auction Galleries, Kent. Feb 07. HP: £130. ABP: £152.

2136

2 Royal Worcester porcelain figures, 'Reflection', ballet dancers, 5in high, No. 555 & 594 of Edn of 4500, produced for Compton & Woodhouse. Canterbury Auction Galleries, Kent. Feb 07. HP: £130. ABP: £152.

2137

Beswick black gloss Arab Xayal horse. Great Western Auctions, Glasgow. Mar 07. HP: £130. ABP: £152.

2138

Lorna Bailey ceramics, five piece frog band, harp player, cornet player, symbol player, brass player & trombone player. Kent Auction Galleries, Folkestone. Mar 06. HP: £125. ABP: £147.

2139

Late 19thC Wemyss pottery preserve jar/cover painted with blackberries, painted marks to base, 12cm. Reeman Dansie, Colchester. Apr 06. HP: £125. ABP: £147.

2140

Pair of Sitzendorf porcelain figures, young man & young woman in 18thC dress seated on rustic stumps, 7.5in high, crowned 'S' pattern mark in underglaze blue to base. Canterbury Auction Galleries, Kent. Feb 06. HP: £125. ABP: £147.

> The numbering system acts as a reader reference as well as linking to the Analysis of each section.

2141

Daniel teapot, Mayflower shape, flowers within gilt scrolls against a ground of raised pink florets, pattern 4632, 1828-29, cover repaired, knop restored. Gorringes, Lewes. Feb 06. HP: £120. ABP: £141.

2142

Royal Doulton figure 'Autumn'. Great Western Auctions, Glasgow. Jan 06. HP: £120. ABP: £141.

2143

Coalport sucrier and cover, possibly Anstice, Horton & Rose, wrythen shape gilded with flowers, leaf borders, c1800-5, 5in. Gorringes, Lewes. Feb 06. HP: £120. ABP: £141.

2144

18thC Worcester tankard, blue/white transfer decoration, apples, flowers & insects, signs of extensive restoration to body, name under handle Natt Allen. Kent Auction Galleries, Folkestone. Feb 06. HP: £120. ABP: £141.

2145

Staffordshire Inkstand caricature portrait bust of John Ridgway 19thC, 3.5in high. Halls Fine Art, Shrewsbury. Mar 06. HP: £120. ABP: £141.

2146

Troika vase. Great Western Auctions, Glasgow. Feb 06. HP: £120. ABP: £141.

2147

Goldscheider Pottery figural group c1930s, 2 foals playing, white craquelure glazed ground highlighted with turquoise, factory marks & impressed 'Melsner' to base, 23cm high. Rosebery's, London. Mar 06. HP: £120. ABP: £141.

2148

Charlotte Rhead, hand-decorated Crown Ducal vase, painted/piped floral design in blue, green, yellow & brown, shape 148, 16cm tall. (vgc) Batemans, Stamford. Mar 06. HP: £120. ABP: £141.

2149

Clarice Cliff, pair of wall pocket vases, as swallows upon nests, printed marks to reverse, 20cm high. Rosebery's, London. Mar 06. HP: £120. ABP: £141.

2150

Clarice Cliff tea-pot and milk jug, known as 'Cosy Two's, Crocus pattern. Sandwich Auction Rooms, Kent. Mar 06. HP: £120. ABP: £141.

2151

Pearlware plate inscribed 'Sprig of Shelelaigh and Shamrock So Green'. Great Western Auctions, Glasgow. Feb 06. HP: £120. ABP: £141.

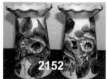

2152

Pair Wemyss cabbage rose decorated vases. (both def). Great Western Auctions, Glasgow. Mar 06. HP: £120. ABP: £141.

2153

Twenty-eight items of Goss crested china. Gorringes, Lewes. Jun 06. HP: £120. ABP: £141.

Aynsley bone china figurine 'Lady Fox', modelled by Peggy Alexander, and 'Sir Charles Fox', each dressed in hunting pink, 15.5 and 16.5cm. Locke & England, Leamington Spa. Mar 06. HP: £120. ABP: £141.

Staffordshire flat back group 'Uncle Tom', a girl standing on his right knee, 27cm high. Boldon Auction Galleries, Tyne & Wear. Mar 06. HP: £120. ABP: £141.

Royal Doulton Appaloosa horse, standing pose, 7.75in. high. Gorringes, Lewes. Apr 06. HP: £120. ABP: £141.

Wedgwood black basalt model of a cat, green glass eyes, impressed mark, 3.5in. Gorringes, Lewes. Apr 06. HP: £120. ABP: £141.

19thC Staffordshire sitting hen, 6.25in high. Dee, Atkinson & Harrison, Driffield. Apr 06. HP: £120. ABP: £141.

19thC Leeds Batavian-ware tea caddy, panels of blue/white flora, shoulder with criss-cross blue/white banding, silver cover with ribbed knop finial, mark indistinct, 4.75in high. Dee, Atkinson & Harrison, Driffield. Apr 06. HP: £120. ABP: £141.

Crown Devon Fieldings musical jug, 'Roamin in the Gloamin', moulded with figures, 8in high. Dee, Atkinson & Harrison, Driffield. Apr 06. HP: £120. ABP: £141.

Ault Pottery vase, painted in black with a nocturnal scene of owls seated on branches looking at the moon, imp'd AULT ENGLAND, 10in high. Golding Young & Co, Grantham. Feb 06. HP: £120. ABP: £141.

Royal Doulton figure 'The Mask Seller', designed by L. Harradine, HN2103, 8in high. Golding Young & Co, Grantham. Feb 06. HP: £120. ABP: £141.

Hammer: £120

19thC Staffordshire pottery 'Toby' jug, seated on barrel, worded 'Home Brewed Ale', 10.5in high, rim slightly rubbed, enamel to jacket slightly flaking. Canterbury Auction Galleries, Kent. Apr 06. HP: £120. ABP: £141.

Early 19thC Staffordshire porcelaneous figure, black & white pointer, 2.5in high x 5.5in overall, tail restored. Canterbury Auction Galleries, Kent. Apr 06. HP: £120. ABP: £141.

Royal Copenhagen figure 'The Little Mermaid', base marked 4431, 9in. Denhams, Warnham, Sussex. Jun 06. HP: £120. ABP: £141.

19thC Staffordshire pottery figure, The Duke of Wellington, wearing black coat, 13in high, enamel to coat flaking. Canterbury Auction Galleries, Kent. Apr 06. HP: £120. ABP: £141.

Worcester blue/white porcelain Cabbage Leaf pattern jug, moulded mask pattern mount, 8in high, unmarked, c1770, rim chipped, small crack to side of spout. Canterbury Auction Galleries, Kent. Apr 06. HP: £120. ABP: £141.

Mid 19thC Prattware plate with rare printed mark, c1847-60. Henry Adams, Chichester. Jul 06. HP: £120. ABP: £141.

Poole pottery earthenware charger, Delphis pattern, 36cm. Locke & England, Leamington Spa. Jul 06. HP: £120. ABP: £141.

Galle faience pierced plate, c1880, chips, 21.5cm. Sworders, Stansted Mountfitchet. Apr 06. HP: £120. ABP: £141.

Burmantofts faience jardiniere, moulded with a band of flower heads above zig-zag banding, 10.5in wide, No 1424. Hartleys, Ilkley. Oct 06. HP: £120. ABP: £141.

Foley Intarsio Bowl No. 3235, Reg. 330400, 3in high. Kent Auction Galleries, Folkestone. Nov 06. HP: £120. ABP: £141.

Pair of Royal Doulton vases, green/blue glazes and with gilt, white/blue floral decoration, 36cm high, impressed marks. Rosebery's, London. Apr 07. HP: £120. ABP: £141.

Maling ginger jar and cover. Great Western Auctions, Glasgow. Jan 07. HP: £120. ABP: £141.

Goss bisquit porcelain model of the House in Edinburgh where John Knox The Scottish Reformer Died, 24th Nov. 1572, 4in high. Golding Young & Co, Grantham. Nov 06. HP: £120. ABP: £141.

Clarice Cliff Rudyard pattern cruet set. (a.f.) Charterhouse Auctioneers, Sherborne. Mar 07. HP: £120. ABP: £141.

130 *Ceramics Prices*

Kai Nielsen figure 'Venus Kalipygos' for P. Ipsen Enke, green glaze. Great Western Auctions, Glasgow. Feb 07. HP: £120. ABP: £141.

Staffordshire porcelain figural group, shepherd and shepherdess, sheep and dog, base with gilt line embellishment, 6.5in wide. Hartleys, Ilkley. Feb 07. HP: £120. ABP: £141.

> The illustrations are in descending price order. The price range is indicated at the top of each page.

Lladro head and shoulders portrait bust of a clown, base marked 5610 Cabeza Payasito Sombrilla Copa. Denhams, Warnham, Sussex. May 06. HP: £115. ABP: £135.

19thC Staffordshire pottery spill vase figure group, two children, each with underglaze blue jackets with a panniered pony, 10in high. Golding Young & Co, Grantham. Feb 06. HP: £112. ABP: £131.

Limoges enamel plaque by R. J. Sarlandie, night time scene of figures/animals in a lane with cottages and a church, signed, damage to a corner, 9 x 6.5in. Gorringes, Lewes. Feb 06. HP: £110. ABP: £129.

Royal Doulton figure, 'The Poacher', HN2043, 16cm high. Gorringes, Bexhill. Feb 06. HP: £110. ABP: £129.

Royal Worcester model of a parrot, flower painted branch base, model No. 2054, 14cm high, and a yellow canary, model N. 2665. (2) Rosebery's, London. Mar 06. HP: £110. ABP: £129.

Aynsley vase/cover painted by T Campbell, English 20thC, scroll handles, enriched with a painted scene of Windsor Castle above a gilt scroll and motif border, 26cm high. Rosebery's, London. Mar 06. HP: £110. ABP: £129.

Troika marmalade pot, signed, LJ, 'J' with second cross through middle. Sandwich Auction Rooms, Kent. Apr 06. HP: £110. ABP: £129.

Lladro figure of two children sat upon an elephant. Great Western Auctions, Glasgow. Feb 06. HP: £110. ABP: £129.

Shelley bone china part tea set, 1930s, 20 pieces incl. teapot, sugar bowl & serving plate, printed and enamelled with a primrose pattern, milk jug cracked. Gorringes, Lewes. Apr 06. HP: £110. ABP: £129.

Clarice Cliff 'Windbells' Bizzare bowl, c1930s, in bright colours, printed marks to underside, 22cm dia, restored. Rosebery's, London. Mar 06. HP: £110. ABP: £129.

R. Doulton figure 'Collinette' HN1998. (def) Great Western Auctions, Glasgow. May 06. HP: £110. ABP: £129.

Upchurch pottery bowl, flared pedestal foot, grey streaky glaze, incised script mark, 7in dia. Golding Young & Co, Grantham. Feb 06. HP: £110. ABP: £129.

2191

Bretby two-handled vase, two integral handles, rich red flambe glaze, imp'd mask, model No. 1769, 15in high. Golding Young & Co, Grantham. Feb 06. HP: £110. ABP: £129.

2192

Maw & Co encaustic four-tile Royal Coat of Arms, VR and within crowned belt with Honi Soit Qui Mai Y Pense, 12in square, one tile is of slightly deeper dimension. Golding Young & Co, Grantham. Feb 06. HP: £110. ABP: £129.

2193

Royal Doulton figure 'The Potter', designed by C.J Noke, HN1493, 7in high. Golding Young & Co, Grantham. Feb 06. HP: £110. ABP: £129.

2194

Lladro figure group of young girl with puppies in a sledge, model No. 2234, matt coloured glazes, 35cm long. Rosebery's, London. May 06. HP: £110. ABP: £129.

2195

English treacle glaze frog mug, moulded foot, three slip ware frogs to interior, 5.75in high. Hartleys, Ilkley. Aug 06. HP: £110. ABP: £129.

2196

Pilkington's R. Lancastrian vase, c1920, uranium orange glaze, 40cm. Sworders, Stansted Mountfitchet. Apr 06. HP: £110. ABP: £129.

2197

R. Doulton figure 'Memories', HN2030. Great Western Auctions, Glasgow. Sep 06. HP: £110. ABP: £129.

2198

Royal Doulton pottery figure, Blue Beard HN2105, drawing his sword, 11in high. Hartleys, Ilkley. Dec 06. HP: £110. ABP: £129.

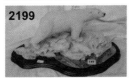

2199

Border Fine Arts figurine, Arctic Adventure, polar bear & cubs 637/850 with certificate. Kent Auction Galleries, Folkestone. Dec 06. HP: £110. ABP: £129.

2200

Beswick Beatrix Potter figure 'Pickles'. Great Western Auctions, Glasgow. Feb 07. HP: £110. ABP: £129.

Hammer: £110 - £105

2201

Leeds pottery figure of Air, late 18thC, bust length figure draped in an eagle, stepped plinth 15.5cm, and figure of Bacchus, restored, stamped. Sworders, Stansted Mountfitchet. Feb 07. HP: £110. ABP: £129.

2202

19thC Staffordshire pottery Toby jug with a jug on his knee, 9.75in high, restored hat, and a Staffordshire pottery standing figure of 'Benjamin Disraeli', 6.5in high. Canterbury Auction Galleries, Kent. Feb 07. HP: £110. ABP: £129.

2203

Beswick horse 'The Minstrel', on base. Great Western Auctions, Glasgow. Mar 07. HP: £110. ABP: £129.

2204

Lladro figure group of 2 dancing girls. Great Western Auctions, Glasgow. Mar 07. HP: £110. ABP: £129.

2205

Beswick Ayrshire cow, Ch Ikham Bessie. Great Western Auctions, Glasgow. Mar 07. HP: £105. ABP: £123.

2206

Troika pottery coffin vase signed Troika, Cornwall & SB on base. Great Western Auctions, Glasgow. Oct 06. HP: £105. ABP: £123.

2207

Moorcroft Clematis lamp base, original shade. Great Western Auctions, Glasgow. Jan 06. HP: £105. ABP: £123.

2208

Beswick Hereford Bull, 'Champion of Champions', No. 1363, brown and white gloss, 4in high. Golding Young & Co, Grantham. Feb 06. HP: £105. ABP: £123.

2209

Royal Doulton figurine 'Pretty Polly' HN2768 with signature William Harper and a Royal Doulton 'Taking Things easy' HN2677. Kent Auction Galleries, Folkestone. Jun 06. HP: £105. ABP: £123.

2210

Pair of 1950s Goebel earthenware figures, each as a child seated beneath umbrella, 12cm. Locke & England, Leamington Spa. Nov 06. HP: £105. ABP: £123.

Sample Research IV

Using the browsing method to analyse the market for a particular category of ceramics

No. 4 Ceramic Cats

Rare Delft tin glazed earthenware cat, 17thC, 5in high. Halls Fine Art, Shrewsbury. Mar 03. HP: £45,000. ABP: £52,931.

Galle faience figure of a bulldog, c1900, glass eyes, signed E Gallé, Nancy, front paw damaged. Sworders, Stansted Mountfitchet. Feb 07. HP: £2,000. ABP: £2,352.

Here the research involves browsing the pages for ceramic cats and I have located at least eighteen. The first example on page 8 is an exception at £53,000, although Wemyss tabby's have reached £20,000. The exciting thing about this beaten up old cat, dating to the later seventeenth century is that anyone could find it, even at a boot fair! On page 25 (**294**) is a Gallé bulldog. Don't mistake it for a cat as I did! There is a genuine, badly damaged Gallé cat on page 74 (**1136**) and further French faience examples on page 52 and 91. Two 'mosanic' cats appear on pages 88 and 111 and damage is a feature of most of the samples in these pages. On page 37 (**520**) is a poor image of two Meissen models of Manx cats, c1740. The damages must have been significant to have achieved only £1,150 hammer. I am amazed at the £650 hammer for a Brannam cat on page 62 (**948**) and I am not certain that this isn't a record. A Beswick *Tom Kitten* appears at **1132** on page 71 and over £600! Don't get confused witht the Arthur Gredington models worth between say £20 and £100. This is actually a *Tom Kitten* wall plaque with a Charlton Book price of £1,200, modelled by Graham Tongue. Why did it fetch only half the book price? At **1248** on page 80 is a Carlton China *Felix* which went over £500. Two Foley intarsio cats appear on page 95, and *Simpkin* and *Ginger*, two Beatrix Potter cats appear at **1933** on page 117. There is a Wedgwood basalt cat on page 129 and two Royal Crown Derby seated cat paperweights. A list of page and image numbers follows.

Late 19thC French faience cat in style of Galle, 12.5in, one leg re-attached. Gorringes, Lewes. Apr 05. HP: £850. ABP: £999.

C.H. Brannam pottery 'comical cat', glass eyes, applied chocolate/rust/green slips on mustard ground, incised C.H. Brannam, Barum, 1911, 34cm. Bearne's, Exeter. Jun 05. HP: £650. ABP: £764.

Beswick Tom Kitten wall plaque, introduced 1967 and withdrawn 1969, 6in. Louis Taylor, Stoke on Trent. Sep 06. HP: £520. ABP: £611.

Gallé faience cat, c1900, signed to right front paw, 32.5cm, badly damaged. Sworders, Stansted Mountfitchet. Jul 04. HP: £500. ABP: £588.

Carlton china 'Felix' the cat, base inscribed 'Felix kept on walking', printed with Wembley British Empire Exhibition 1924 crest, 3.25in wide. Andrew Hartley, Ilkley. Oct 05. HP: £440. ABP: £517.

Two Foley Intarsio green cats, painted with brown mice, open mouths, green glass eyes, 9.5in, faults. Dee, Atkinson & Harrison, Driffield. Nov 04. HP: £300. ABP: £352.

Mosanic Galle style seated cat painted with spots/hearts in blue on yellow ground, green glass eyes, 9.5in high. Andrew Hartley, Ilkley. Apr 06. IIP: £280. ABP: £329.

Mosanic faience figure of a green cat, green glass eyes, hearts & motifs, 12.75in high, front leg repaired. Canterbury Auction Galleries, Kent. Apr 05. HP: £220. ABP: £258.

Two Beatrix Potter figures, Simpkin and Ginger, brown backstamps (BP3 B), boxed. Bearne's, Exeter. Jun 05. HP: £180. ABP: £211.

Wedgwood black basalt model of a cat, green glass eyes, impressed mark, 3.5in. Gorringes, Lewes. Apr 06. HP: £120. ABP: £141.

'You pay a bit more for Sitzendorf or Nymphenburg, or for example Dresden, but look how much more.....Ebay has dented French faïence prices but the cow creamer must prove a good long term investment.....Would you buy T. G. Green Cornishware? .....the market has collapsed, particularly because of faking.....'

The Sitzendorf figurine at **2211** and £100 hammer and the figural comport on page 137 (**2288**) provides closure on this Thuringian (German) output which first opened its doors in 1850 and is still going today. The Index shows the first entry on page 72 at £450 hammer for a fine pair of nineteenth century figural vases. The first Crown Ducal appeared in the previous Section on page 124 with a Charlotte Rhead tube-lined vase and a further most attractive vase appeared on page 128. (**2148**) Here there are examples at **2226**, **2242** and an unusual Charlotte Rhead Edward VII Coronation jug on page 154. (**2261**) Lesser pieces appear in the £25-£30 price range. Royal Copenhagen has 14 entries, commencing with a bulldog on page 38 at £1,150 hammer. The pick of the figurines in my opinion is the final entry on page 156 (**2659**) of a seated girl sewing, at only £55 hammer. Goebel entries commence on page 131 and £105 hammer. Most other entries are in this Section with *Bathing Belle* at **2235** and a wall plaque of a woman's head at **2257**. The Goebel Norman Rockwell group, depicting a boy and a dog at **2650** is unimpressive despite the complex modelling. You pay a bit more for Sitzendorf or Nymphenburg, or for example Dresden, but look how much more you can get. See **2234** and **2239** and check out **2211**. Certainly for about a £100 or so it is worth looking around. I like the Royal Doulton figure, *The Apple Maid*, HN2160 at **2221**. The Charlton Book price is £265. See also *The Blacksmith*, HN 2782, not such good value and *Granny's Heritage*, HN2031, given a Charlton price of £500! The ubiquitous Royal Doulton continues but how about Royal Worcester? The figurine *Holland*, modelled by F. G. Doughty appears at **2281** and see also *October* at **2357** for £90 hammer.

Whilst the general market in ceramics has declined somewhat in recent years, Royal Worcester has held up well although such collecting is a long term investment. Check out Doughty using the Index. There are about six entries. I don't expect to find any spectacular bargains in this Section but it may be useful to run through the remaining pages and suggest at least what I consider good buys. On page 136 I would have considered bidding on the Staffordshire pearlware figure at **2262** or the Tang Dynasty oxen at **2265**. Consider also the Naples group at **2254**. Ebay has dented French faïence prices but the cow creamer at **2285** and only £100 must prove a good long term investment and it may even do much better in the shorter term. The blue and white drainers at **2293** are highly decorative and quite cheap

for display in the right kitchen. Alternatively I consider small pieces of Moorcroft, such as those at **2258** and **2310** a waste of money in a declining market. Don't buy small vases. They aren't worth the money they attract whilst they fail to attract the eye or display well.

Would you buy T. G. Green Cornishware? Again the market has collapsed, particularly because of faking of labels, and prices have plummeted. See **2343** and **2632**. Really good buys are the Liverpool delft plates at **2300** and a polychrome delft plate at **2360**. The blue and white pearlware tankard at **2356** is uncommon enough to attract collectors and the £90 tag is not too high. See my comments on collecting mugs on page 43. Regardless of my earlier comments on the French faïence market the quite large dog at **2397** and only £80 hammer is a real snip. £150-£200 is nearer the mark. See also the unusual Brannam boat-shaped planter at **2413**, and possibly the excellent bargain of a Royal Worcester paté-sur-paté planter at **2431**. Don't get carried away with Clarice Cliff. The water-lily bowl at **2457** is common enough and would have been a more reasonable buy at £40-£50 hammer. The pair of eighteenth century chinoiserie pearlware sauceboats at **2492** are early for this body and an excellent buy for a collector of this ceramic type. Again the blue and white cow creamer at **2533** looks early and if so is a serious bargain as they are frequently damaged or restored.

The Westerwald stoneware jug at **2551** is intriguing and looks to be early. At 9 inches it could be a tremendous bargain but more research is needed. Speculatively I would have risked twice as much. As prices approach about £50 a lot of simple art pottery is appearing, such as Upchurch for example. There looks to be some good buys here as I am certain an Upchurch collector might well pay nearer a £100 for this example at **2598**. Generally though it is not wise to buy undistinguished art pottery unless you know the market. There is far too much of it around. Pity the creamware cruet at **2664** has been restored. This is indeed a very rare item. Probably just as rare if not rarer is the blue and white pearlware hexagonal tazza at **2694** and only £50 hammer. This is one of the bargains of 2006 and again should have gone to at least £150-£200. Finally the Chinese blue and white bird feeder at **2728** is also good value as is the delftware bowl at **2755**. However if you are interested in the 1960s rather than the 1760s you would be pleased to pick up the two Carlton Ware condiment sets with their striking colours for only £50 hammer.

Hammer: £100

Sitzendorf figurine of woman carrying basket of bread and tray of cakes, 20cm high, hand painted. A F Brock & Co Ltd, Stockport. Aug 05. HP: £100. ABP: £117.

Royal Doulton figure 'The Blacksmith' HN2782. Great Western Auctions, Glasgow. Sep 05. HP: £100. ABP: £117.

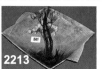

Carlton Ware 'Rabbits at Dusk' kite shaped bowl. Great Western Auctions, Glasgow. Sep 05. HP: £100. ABP: £117.

Scottish pottery figure of a goat. Great Western Auctions, Glasgow. Oct 05. HP: £100. ABP: £117.

Royal Copenhagen figure of a mermaid. Great Western Auctions, Glasgow. Oct 05. HP: £100. ABP: £117.

Meissen vase/cover, painted and encrusted with flowers, cover surmounted by figure of a girl, 17in. Gorringes, Lewes. Oct 05. HP: £100. ABP: £117.

Beswick Norman Thellwell figure 'Kick-Start'. Boldon Auction Galleries, Tyne & Wear. Sep 05. HP: £100. ABP: £117.

Crown Ducal charger in style of Charlotte Rhead, large stylised tube coloured flowers & leaves, 44cm. (6189 or 6159). Boldon Auction Galleries, Tyne & Wear. Sep 05. HP: £100. ABP: £117.

Denby-ware, tall blue/green glazed jug, strap handle, 15.25in high. Dee, Atkinson & Harrison, Driffield. Sep 05. HP: £100. ABP: £117.

Troika square vase. Great Western Auctions, Glasgow. Nov 05. HP: £100. ABP: £117.

Royal Doulton figure, The Apple Maid, HN2160. Gorringes, Bexhill. Oct 05. HP: £100. ABP: £117.

Beswick figure group 'Turtle Doves'. Great Western Auctions, Glasgow. Oct 05. HP: £100. ABP: £117.

Charlotte Rhead for Crown Ducal vase. Great Western Auctions, Glasgow. Oct 05. HP: £100. ABP: £117.

R. Doulton figure, HN1545, backstamped to underside, inscription 'Called Love, A Little Boy etc', restored. Gorringes, Bexhill. Dec 05. HP: £100. ABP: £117.

Satsuma bowl, Japanese early 20thC, interior painted with exotic birds amongst flowers/foliage, exterior similar within diaper borders, black and gold seal to base. 15.5cm dia. Rosebery's, London. Jan 06. HP: £100. ABP: £117.

Charlotte Rhead Crown Ducal vase, horizontally ribbed, tube lined with orange, green and lustre flowers, 10.25in high. Dee, Atkinson & Harrison, Driffield. Nov 05. HP: £100. ABP: £117.

Four Nankin Cargo storage jars, shouldered form with a short neck, loops moulded on the shoulder, in excavated condition, tallest 20.5cm. Rosebery's, London. Jan 06. HP: £100. ABP: £117.

Categories or themes can be followed through the colour coded Index which contains over 4500 cross references.

Marcolini Meissen plate, German late 18th/early 19thC, central vignette depicting figures standing in front of a rustic cottage, underglaze blue mark, 24.5cm. Rosebery's, London. Jan 06. HP: £100. ABP: £117.

Collection of Portmeirion 'Birds of Britain' & 'Botanic garden' pattern dinner and tea wares, English 20thC, & a graduated set of 'Botanic garden' planters and other tea wares. Rosebery's, London. Jan 06. HP: £100. ABP: £117.

2230

Daniel serving plate, Mayflower pattern, flower sprays against a moulded ground of pink florets, patt. 4632, 8.5in. Gorringes, Lewes. Feb 06. HP: £100. ABP: £117.

2231

Daniel creamer, Savoy shape, moulded/gilded with scrolls in rococo-style, pattern 8802, c1845, 6in. Gorringes, Lewes. Feb 06. HP: £100. ABP: £117.

2232

Two Royal Doulton figures, The Old Balloon Seller, HN 1315 & 'The Balloon Man', HN1954, 19cm high, 18.5cm high. Gorringes, Bexhill. Feb 06. HP: £100. ABP: £117.

2233

Early 20thC Coalport part dessert service, green & gilt with flowers and gadrooned gilt border: 2 dishes 12.5in and 6 plates 9in. Ewbank Auctioneers, Send, Surrey. Dec 05. HP: £100. ABP: £117.

2234

Pair of Dresden seated male and female figures, he with rooster & basket of flowers, she with hen & basket of corn, 4.5in high. Dee, Atkinson & Harrison, Driffield. Feb 06. HP: £100. ABP: £117.

2235

Goebel Figure No. X.S.104.B, bathing belle sitting on two books. Kent Auction Galleries, Folkestone. Feb 06. HP: £100. ABP: £117.

2236

Beswick 'Bald Eagle', No. 1018. Lambert & Foster, Tenterden. Jan 06. HP: £100. ABP: £117.

2237

Bretby jug, English c1891, raised floral/foliate spray on a moulded green and yellow ground, imp'd mark to base, model No. 957, 33cm high. Rosebery's, London. Feb 06. HP: £100. ABP: £117.

2238

Royal Doulton Maori Ware 'Kia Ora' bowl. Great Western Auctions, Glasgow. Jan 06. HP: £100. ABP: £117.

2239

Nymphenburg model of a guinea fowl, German 20thC, hand painted, imp'd model No. 769 and printed mark to base, 30cm high. Rosebery's, London. Feb 06. HP: £100. ABP: £117.

Hammer: £100

2240

R. Worcester figure 'Sleeping Doe', 1931 modelled by Eric Aumonier, printed/painted marks, 12cm. Sworders, Stansted Mountfitchet. Feb 06. HP: £100. ABP: £117.

2241

Brown-Westhead, Moore & Co pottery token for the Paris Exhibition 1878, transfer-printed in brown, 7cm dia. Sworders, Stansted Mountfitchet. Feb 06. HP: £100. ABP: £117.

2242

Two Crown Ducal urns by Charlotte Rhead, signed to base. Orpington Salerooms, Kent. Mar 06. HP: £100. ABP: £117.

2243

Royal Worcester group 'Kingfisher Alcedo Igpida and Autumn Beech', wooden base, 30cm high. Rosebery's, London. Mar 06. HP: £100. ABP: £117.

2244

Beswick Dalmatian, mould 2271, 14in. Gorringes, Lewes. Apr 06. HP: £100. ABP: £117.

2245

Pair of Staffordshire models of hounds, early 19thC, black spotted white coats, 10.5cm high. Rosebery's, London. Mar 06. HP: £100. ABP: £117.

2246

Troika pot signed SW. Sandwich Auction Rooms, Kent. Mar 06. HP: £100. ABP: £117.

2247

Lladro figure group of two ladies. Great Western Auctions, Glasgow. Feb 06. HP: £100. ABP: £117.

2248

20thC Clarice Cliff Newport pottery jug, ribbed form, 'coral firs' pattern, No. 564 black bizarre mark, 6.75in high, foot rim slightly reground. Diamond Mills & Co, Felixstowe. Mar 06. HP: £100. ABP: £117.

2249

Clarice Cliff crocus pattern preserve pot and cover. Great Western Auctions, Glasgow. May 06. HP: £100. ABP: £117.

Herend Hungary figure of 2 seated ducks 5in. Denhams, Warnham, Sussex. Mar 06. HP: £100. ABP: £117.

Royal Doulton figure, The Jester HN2016, style one, designed by C. J. Noke, issued 1949-97, 10in high. Halls Fine Art, Shrewsbury. Apr 06. HP: £100. ABP: £117.

Herend Hungary green glazed figure of a seated Labrador, 5in. Denhams, Warnham, Sussex. Mar 06. HP: £100. ABP: £117.

Pair 19thC Staffordshire pottery spaniels, 30cm high. Reeman Dansie, Colchester. Apr 06. HP: £100. ABP: £117.

Naples figure, Italian 19thC, 'Three Graces', clothing in a gold lustre glaze, 26cm high. Rosebery's, London. May 06. HP: £100. ABP: £117.

Royal Doulton Nelson commemorative mug, 'England Expects Every Man Will Do His Duty', rope-twist handle, impressed number X6424, 3.5in high. Dee, Atkinson & Harrison, Driffield. Apr 06. HP: £100. ABP: £117.

Elizabeth Mary Watt painted bowl. Great Western Auctions, Glasgow. Apr 06. HP: £100. ABP: £117.

Goebel wall plaque of a woman's head. (TMK1) Great Western Auctions, Glasgow. Apr 06. HP: £100. ABP: £117.

Moorcroft vase, base with paper label marked By Appointment To the Late Queen Mary, 4in. Denhams, Warnham, Sussex. Sep 05. HP: £100. ABP: £117.

Reginald Wells bowl, with a pink, blue and grey streaky glaze, impressed COLDRUM CHELSEA, 9in dia. Golding Young & Co, Grantham. Feb 06. HP: £100. ABP: £117.

Ashby Potters Guild vase, textured/mottled gun metal glaze, streaky russett ground, imp'd mark & artists monogram, 12in high. Golding Young & Co, Grantham. Feb 06. HP: £100. ABP: £117.

Upchurch pottery vase, ribbed form, grey/blue ground, imp'd UPCHURCH, 11in. Golding Young & Co, Grantham. Feb 06. HP: £100. ABP: £117.

> Prices quoted are actual hammer prices (HP) and the Approximate Buyer's Price (ABP) includes an average premium of 15% + VAT.

Early 19thC pearlware figure of a woman holding a violin before bocage, base moulded with 2 lambs, 6in high, some losses to bocage. Golding Young & Co, Grantham. Feb 06. HP: £100. ABP: £117.

Beswick pottery Beatrix Potter figure, Duchess, 4in high, brown back stamp. Canterbury Auction Galleries, Kent. Apr 06. HP: £100. ABP: £117.

R. Doulton porcelain figure, Sweet Anne, 7.25in high, HN1330, date code for 1938, head broken and restuck, and a Royal Doulton porcelain figure, Paisley Shawl, 6.5in high, HN1988. Canterbury Auction Galleries, Kent. Apr 06. HP: £100. ABP: £117.

Two Tang pottery models of oxen, 7.5cm long. Rosebery's, London. May 06. HP: £100. ABP: £117.

Bloor Derby 'Vale of the river Arnos' vase, English 1820/1840, acanthus scroll handles, landscape vignette view of river Arnos within a gilt border, red circular Bloor Derby mark and title inscription to base, 29cm high. Rosebery's, London. May 06. HP: £100. ABP: £117.

R. Doulton figure 'Autumn Breezes' HN 1934, and a squatting Mallard, model No. 817. Rosebery's, London. May 06. HP: £100. ABP: £117.

Set of 3 Beswick graduated wall plaques of Kingfishers, in flight, largest 8in, smallest 5in. Gorringes, Lewes. Jul 06. HP: £100. ABP: £117.

2269

English blue/white strainer, blue printed with flowers, diaper floral border, side loop handle, early 19thC, 4in wide, poss. Worcester. Hartleys, Ilkley. Aug 06. HP: £100. ABP: £117.

2270

Royal Worcester porcelain plate, painted by R Rushton with Bothwell Castle, signed, gilded rim, 10.75in wide, black mark. Hartleys, Ilkley. Aug 06. HP: £100. ABP: £117.

2271

Derby porcelain urn, serpent gilded loop handles, painted with Imari style panels, on spreading foot, early 19thC, 6.5in high. Hartleys, Ilkley. Aug 06. HP: £100. ABP: £117.

2272

Troika Pottery marmalade pot, inscribed with geometric panels, textured blue ground, 3.25in high, mark for Sue Lowe. Hartleys, Ilkley. Aug 06. HP: £100. ABP: £117.

2273

Poole Pottery Delphis charger, painted with stylised flowerheads in hues of orange, 16in wide. Hartleys, Ilkley. Aug 06. HP: £100. ABP: £117.

2274

Pair of wally dugs. Great Western Auctions, Glasgow. Jun 06. HP: £100. ABP: £117.

2275

R. Doulton figure Granny's Heritage HN2031. Great Western Auctions, Glasgow. Sep 06. HP: £100. ABP: £117.

2276

Four New Hall cups and saucers. Great Western Auctions, Glasgow. Sep 06. HP: £100. ABP: £117.

2277

W.H.Goss mode, The Tudor House, Southampton, built 1835, 8cm. Charterhouse Auctioneers, Sherborne. Sep 06. HP: £100. ABP: £117.

2278

Staffordshire pottery money box, as a hexagonal house, 3.75in high, and a similar Spongeware money box, 19thC. (2) Hartleys, Ilkley. Oct 06. HP: £100. ABP: £117.

2279

Pair of Staffordshire pottery greyhounds, 7in high. Golding Young & Co, Grantham. Nov 06. HP: £100. ABP: £117.

Hammer: £100

2280

Carltonware lidded vase, gilded finial, gilded and enamelled with a chinoiserie pagoda landscape, 14in high. Hartleys, Ilkley. Oct 06. HP: £100. ABP: £117.

2281

Royal Worcester figure Holland, modelled by F.G. Doughty. Great Western Auctions, Glasgow. Nov 06. HP: £100. ABP: £117.

2282

19thC rust-glazed infuser, four squat feet upon which rests a covered cylinder inscribed C H Holgate, Hull 1889, applied yellow flower sprigs, knop handled cover, 11.75in high. Dee, Atkinson & Harrison, Driffield. Sep 06. HP: £100. ABP: £117.

2283

Dresden flower encrusted vase, gilt scrolling handles & finial, 44cm high, a/f. Rosebery's, London. Jan 07. HP: £100. ABP: £117.

2284

Royal Crown Derby porcelain sweetmeat dish, three compartments printed in iron red with flowers, blue loop handle and rim, 8in wide, dated 1909. Hartleys, Ilkley. Dec 06. HP: £100. ABP: £117.

2285

19thC French faience cow creamer painted with flowers and foliage, underglaze blue 'L' mark to base, 12.5cm high. Rosebery's, London. Jan 07. HP: £100. ABP: £117.

2286

Royal Crown Derby Imari pattern 9 plate, imp'd to back Derby No. 8735/2. Kent Auction Galleries, Folkestone. Nov 06. HP: £100. ABP: £117.

2287

Beswick pottery figure, huntsman on his horse, 8.5in high. Hartleys, Ilkley. Dec 06. HP: £100. ABP: £117.

2288

Sitzendorf porcelain figural comport, oval pierced and flower encrusted bowl, floral column flanked by a lady seated on a chair, early 20thC, 12.75in high. Hartleys, Ilkley. Apr 07. HP: £100. ABP: £117.

Hammer: £100 - £95

2289

19thC Chinese blue/white charger, painted with central scene of flowers and foliage surrounded with banded decoration, 42cm dia. Rosebery's, London. Jan 07. HP: £100. ABP: £117.

2290

Pair Satsuma porcelain vases, gilded/painted with peacocks, hens within foliage and butterflies, late 19th/20thC, 12in high. Hartleys, Ilkley. Feb 07. HP: £100. ABP: £117.

2291

Spode porcelain scent bottle, flattened lid, gilt embellished, early 19thC, 2.25in high, No.3071. Hartleys, Ilkley. Feb 07. HP: £100. ABP: £117.

2292

Staffordshire portrait bust of George IV, c1825, simulated marble painted socle, 27cm. Sworders, Stansted Mountfitchet. Feb 07. HP: £100. ABP: £117.

2293

English blue/white drainer, possibly Copeland, transfer printed, castle and figures, 38.5cm wide, and a smaller drainer, 32.5cm wide, a/f. Rosebery's, London. Apr 07. HP: £100. ABP: £117.

2294

Beswick shire horse (large action shire) matt brown No. 2578, Spirit of Freedom matt brown No. 2689. Kent Auction Galleries, Folkestone. May 07. HP: £100. ABP: £117.

2295

Royal Doulton figure, Mirabel HN1744, hairline to parasol. Great Western Auctions, Glasgow. May 07. HP: £100. ABP: £117.

2296

Chinese blue/white porcelain spittoon, fence & peony design, 4.75in dia x 4in high, Qianlong period, small flake chip, rim crack. Canterbury Auction Galleries, Kent. Jun 07. HP: £100. ABP: £117.

2297

Set of three Beswick Friesian cows, bull, cow and calf. Ewbank, Send, Surrey. Dec 05. HP: £95. ABP: £111.

2298

Clarice Cliff wall decoration, face of woman wearing beret, pale green, broken below face and badly repaired. A F Brock & Co Ltd, Stockport. Aug 05. HP: £95. ABP: £111.

2299

Carlton Ware 'Mallards' plate, black background. Great Western Auctions, Glasgow. Sep 05. HP: £95. ABP: £111.

2300

18thC Liverpool delft plate, blue painted with river scene with trees and dwelling in the Oriental manner, 8.75in dia. Dee, Atkinson & Harrison, Driffield. Sep 05. HP: £95. ABP: £111.

2301

Art Deco stoneware bust, in the Goldscheider manner, lady with a yellow rose, 27cm high. Gorringes, Bexhill. Dec 05. HP: £95. ABP: £111.

2302

Pearlware tea caddy/cover, English 18thC, enamelled with floral & foliate sprays, 14cm. Rosebery's, London. Dec 05. HP: £95. ABP: £111.

2303

Susie Cooper table set with limed oak tray. Black Country Auctions, Dudley. Dec 05. HP: £95. ABP: £111.

2304

Beleek vase. Black Country Auctions, Dudley. Dec 05. HP: £95. ABP: £111.

2305

Pair of 18thC Lambeth Delft plates decorated in manganese in Neo-Classical manner, central paterae and floral swag borders, 9in dia, rims chipped/fritted. Canterbury Auction Galleries, Kent. Dec 05. HP: £95. ABP: £111.

2306

Quimper dish, typical male and female figure decoration, signed Henriot Quimper, 13.25 x 10.5in. Dee, Atkinson & Harrison, Driffield. Feb 06. HP: £95. ABP: £111.

2307

Beswick Palomino horse and two foals. Great Western Auctions, Glasgow. Feb 06. HP: £95. ABP: £111.

2308

Collection of Half Dolls from 4.25in to 6.5in high, Nos. incl. 10807, 15522, 14469 af, Germany, 13373, 12031, 16747, 13839, 13370 af, 13373 af. (8). Kent Auction Galleries, Folkestone. Jan 06. HP: £95. ABP: £111.

Royal Doulton figure 'Carpet Seller' HN1464. Great Western Auctions, Glasgow. Mar 06. HP: £95. ABP: £111.

Moorcroft hibiscus vase. Great Western Auctions, Glasgow. Apr 06. HP: £95. ABP: £111.

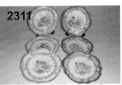

3 Limoges porcelain dessert plates, centres with playful putti within gilt floral wells, and three with yellow ground borders, Lanternier factory marks, retailed by R B Gray & Co, 8in dia. Golding Young & Co, Grantham. Feb 06. HP: £95. ABP: £111.

Set of three Beswick flying ducks, 25cm long max. (3) Rosebery's, London. May 06. HP: £95. ABP: £111.

Wemyss pottery bowl, painted with pink roses, 10.75in wide, impressed and yellow painted mark. Hartleys, Ilkley. Feb 07. HP: £95. ABP: £111.

Pair Royal Doulton Slaters patent stoneware vases, with panels of foliate relief decoration within a gilt sgraffito scroll ground, 28cm high. Rosebery's, London. May 06. HP: £95. ABP: £111.

Derby porcelain tea bowl & saucer, fluted form gilded with banding & foliate tendril, 5 .25in wide, late 18thC, purple mark, and bat printed coffee can. (2) Hartleys, Ilkley. Aug 06. HP: £95. ABP: £111.

Troika pottery marmalade pot, incised with geometric patterns, textured green ground, 4in high, mark for Jane Fitzgerald. Hartleys, Ilkley. Aug 06. HP: £95. ABP: £111.

Troika wheel vase, decorated by Tina Doubleday. Great Western Auctions, Glasgow. Sep 06. HP: £95. ABP: £111.

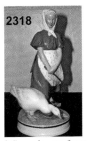

Royal Copenhagen figure of a goose girl. Great Western Auctions, Glasgow. Oct 06. HP: £95. ABP: £111.

Hammer: £95 - £90

R. Doulton porcelain figure 'Delight', woman wearing a rose dress of 18thC design, 7in high, green printed mark to base, HN1772. Canterbury Auction Galleries, Kent. Feb 07. HP: £95. ABP: £111.

Continental majolica asparagus dish, cream/blue dished centre modelled as a row of asparagus, on a bed of green and brown leaves, 15in wide. Hartleys, Ilkley. Feb 07. HP: £95. ABP: £111.

> The numbering system acts as a reader reference as well as linking to the Analysis of each section.

Pair of Minton Flo blue vases. Orpington Salerooms, Kent. Aug 06. HP: £95. ABP: £111.

19thC Staffordshire figure of Lord Beaconsfield (Disraeli), base inscribed 'Beaconsfield'. 11.5in high. Golding Young & Co, Grantham. Nov 06. HP: £95. ABP: £111.

Wedgwood lustre bowl, gilded with hoho birds to the interior, dragons to exterior, 4in wide. Hartleys, Ilkley. Feb 07. HP: £95. ABP: £111.

R. Crown Derby porcelain trinket box, pointed finial, painted in Imari colours with foliate panels, dated 1919, 4in high. Hartleys, Ilkley. Dec 06. HP: £95. ABP: £111.

Pair Chamberlain's Worcester porcelain soup plates with moulded borders, enamelled with wild roses & crest of Earl of Chesham, 10in dia, red and lilac printed mark to base. Canterbury Auction Galleries, Kent. Feb 07. HP: £95. ABP: £111.

Large Lladro figure of a clown and a ballerina. Great Western Auctions, Glasgow. Mar 07. HP: £95. ABP: £111.

St Clements pottery model of a pheasant, crackle-glazed, signed Fontinelle, 44cm long. Gorringes, Bexhill. Dec 05. HP: £90. ABP: £105.

Ceramics Prices 139

Troika cylinder vase. Stroud Auctions, Stroud. Aug 05. HP: £90. ABP: £105.

Pair late 19thC Staffordshire pottery Poodles, 9.75in high. Dee, Atkinson & Harrison, Driffield. Sep 05. HP: £90. ABP: £105.

Lladro figure group of a girl and goats. Gorringes, Bexhill. Oct 05. HP: £90. ABP: £105.

Berlin porcelain plaque, late 19thC, painted by F E Till, Dresden, signed, portrait of a boy, imp'd sceptre & KPM. Sworders, Stansted Mountfitchet. Nov 05. HP: £90. ABP: £105.

Royal Doulton figure 'The Lobster Man' HN2317. Great Western Auctions, Glasgow. Nov 05. HP: £90. ABP: £105.

Carlton Ware vert royale New Mikado 2 handled vase. Great Western Auctions, Glasgow. Nov 05. HP: £90. ABP: £105.

Davenport botanical tea service. Gorringes, Bexhill. Oct 05. HP: £90. ABP: £105.

Rosenthal porcelain dalmatian, by F. Heidenreich, 29cm long. Gorringes, Bexhill. Dec 05. HP: £90. ABP: £105.

The illustrations are in descending price order. The price range is indicated at the top of each page.

Chinese famille vert bowl & cover, opposed mask handles, red & blue iris flowers, 13cm high. Rosebery's, London. Dec 05. HP: £90. ABP: £105.

Carltonware pottery 'Guinness Zoo' advertising item, an Ostrich, base worded in red 'My Goodness - My Guinness', 4in high, printed mark in red to base. Canterbury Auction Galleries, Kent. Dec 05. HP: £90. ABP: £105.

Scent bottle, Coalport or Minton, encrusted with flowers and leaves, with stopper, c1850, several chips to flowers, 4in. Gorringes, Lewes. Feb 06. HP: £90. ABP: £105.

Late 18thC pearlware coffee pot, painted with flower sprays in bright enamels, c1780, 9.25in. Gorringes, Lewes. Feb 06. HP: £90. ABP: £105.

Three R. Doulton character jugs: The London Bobby D6744, Frankenstein's Monster D7052 (second), and Merlin D6529 (second). Gorringes, Bexhill. Feb 06. HP: £90. ABP: £105.

Five various Hummel figures, Nos. 178, 136-1, 203, 200 & 112. Gorringes, Bexhill. Feb 06. HP: £90. ABP: £105.

Capo di Monte Ltd Edn group, 'The Fortune Teller' by Roberto Braubilla, 31cm high. Gorringes, Bexhill. Feb 06. HP: £90. ABP: £105.

3 Green & Co Cornish Ware storage jars. Charterhouse Auctioneers, Sherborne. Feb 06. HP: £90. ABP: £105.

Copenhagen dog. Great Western Auctions, Glasgow. Feb 06. HP: £90. ABP: £105.

Bursley Ware 'Seed Poppy' dish. Great Western Auctions, Glasgow. Feb 06. HP: £90. ABP: £105.

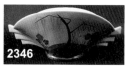

Clarice Cliff 'Opalesque Bruna' Daffodil vase, c1930s, buff ground painted with colours, printed factory mark to underside, 12cm high. Rosebery's, London. Mar 06. HP: £90. ABP: £105.

Pair of Staffordshire brown and white spaniels. 24cm high. Boldon Auction Galleries, Tyne & Wear. Mar 06. HP: £90. ABP: £105.

Troika Cornwall coffin shaped vase, monogrammed J.D. 18cm high. Boldon Auction Galleries, Tyne & Wear. Mar 06. HP: £90. ABP: £105.

R. Doulton figure Blue Beard designed by L Harradine, HN2105, 12in high. Golding Young & Co, Grantham. Feb 06. HP: £90. ABP: £105.

Moorcroft Pottery vase, c1997, orange ground decorated with flowers, painted factory marks, artists initials to underside, 21cm high. Rosebery's, London. Mar 06. HP: £90. ABP: £105.

Royal Doulton figure 'Miss Winsome' HN1666, hairline to base. Great Western Auctions, Glasgow. May 07. HP: £90. ABP: £105.

Poole Pottery vase in white earthenware design by Truda Carter & painted by Carolyn Beckwith c1980-90, 13in, spot edge pattern, signed by painter to base in black design No. 213, c1940-50. Kent Auction Galleries, Folkestone. Aug 06. HP: £90. ABP: £105.

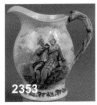

Crown Devon musical jug, 'Harry Lauder Roamin' in the Gloamin', 8in high. Dee, Atkinson & Harrison, Driffield. Jul 06. HP: £90. ABP: £105.

Three Coalport landscape plates, Laggo Maggiore, Lake of Brientz and Loch Maree, 9.5in dia. (3) Dee, Atkinson & Harrison, Driffield. Jul 06. HP: £90. ABP: £105.

Lladro figure of a standing Centor, base marked 1235, 8in. Denhams, Warnham, Sussex. May 06. HP: £90. ABP: £105.

English pottery tankard, blue printed with figures in a landscape, 19thC, 4.75in high. Hartleys, Ilkley. Oct 06. HP: £90. ABP: £105.

Royal Worcester figure 'October'. Great Western Auctions, Glasgow. Mar 07. HP: £90. ABP: £105.

Wilton ware bowl decorated with maidens by a fountain. Great Western Auctions, Glasgow. Nov 06. HP: £90. ABP: £105.

Two Beswick highland calves, in tan gloss, 3in high. Hartleys, Ilkley. Aug 06. HP: £90. ABP: £105.

18thC Delft plate, painted with Chinese figure in landscape, in blue, yellow, green and iron red, floral border, 9in dia. Golding Young & Co, Grantham. Nov 06. HP: £90. ABP: £105.

Seven pieces of Royal Winton 'Hazel' chintz, 2 toastracks, jug, cream & sugar, plate & dish. Great Western Auctions, Glasgow. Feb 07. HP: £90. ABP: £105.

1950s Poole pottery jardinière, green, yellow, mauve & red, 3 bands of horizontal rope pattern, 8.75in dia x 9in high, black printed Poole Pottery mark to base and No. 721/HYT. Canterbury Auction Galleries, Kent. Jun 07. HP: £90. ABP: £105.

Beswick pottery Great Dane 'Ruler of Oubourgh', and a Dalmatian 'Arnoldene' and a St Bernard 'Corna Garth Stroller'. Locke & England, Leamington Spa. Mar 06. HP: £88. ABP: £103.

Shelley Mode trio. Black Country Auctions, Dudley. Dec 05. HP: £86. ABP: £101.

Set of five Natwest Wade pigs. Gorringes, Bexhill. Oct 05. HP: £85. ABP: £99.

Thomas Forester & Sons jug, painted with fish by R Dean. Great Western Auctions, Glasgow. Nov 05. HP: £85. ABP: £99.

Pair of Staffordshire cottage money boxes, English 19thC, each cottage set upon grassy bank, with a cottage pastille burner, 12cm high. Rosebery's, London. Feb 06. HP: £85. ABP: £99.

Beswick pinto pony, piebald with tail hanging loose, 6.5in high. Hartleys, Ilkley. Aug 06. HP: £85. ABP: £99.

Hummel figure Crossroads. (TMK6) Great Western Auctions, Glasgow. Feb 06. HP: £85. ABP: £99.

Five pieces of Poole pottery incl. hand-painted Gazelle plate, orange Delphis dish, 26.5cm, 'Gemstones' New bud vase, 12.5cm, 2 Delphis plates, and orange Fosters similar cylindrical vase, 20cm high. (6) Batemans, Stamford. Mar 06. HP: £85. ABP: £99.

R. Doulton figure, Paisley Shawl HN1988. Great Western Auctions, Glasgow. May 06. HP: £85. ABP: £99.

Booth's 15 piece coffee service incl. coffee pot, milk jug, sugar basin, 6 demi tasse cans & saucers, 'Rajah' pattern. Kent Auction Galleries, Folkestone. Nov 06. HP: £85. ABP: £99.

Royal Doulton figure, The Orange Lady, HN1453. Denhams, Warnham, Sussex. Oct 05. HP: £85. ABP: £99.

St Ives Pottery bowl, manner of Bernard Leech, dark brown abstract decoration against a pitted grey ground, 4in high, 6in dia. Golding Young & Co, Grantham. Feb 06. HP: £85. ABP: £99.

Goebel barn owl No. CV112 and a Goebel falcon, each approx 9in. Kent Auction Galleries, Folkestone. Jun 06. HP: £85. ABP: £99.

Beswick model of a seated pig, No. 832 by Arthur Gredington, and a pair of Beswick pigs marked C.H Queen 40, a Shebeg pig and two others, 9.5cm high. Rosebery's, London. May 06. HP: £85. ABP: £99.

Beswick figure of a seated Dalmatian, base impressed Beswick England 2271, 14in high. Denhams, Warnham, Sussex. Jun 06. HP: £85. ABP: £99.

R. Crown Derby porcelain vase, painted with Imari style panels, dated 1914, 4.25in high. Hartleys, Ilkley. Aug 06. HP: £85. ABP: £99.

Carter, Stabler, Adams vase, painted with stylised floral motifs, imp'd and painted marks, 14cm. Sworders, Stansted Mountfitchet. Apr 06. HP: £85. ABP: £99.

> Categories or themes can be followed through the colour coded Index which contains over 4500 cross references.

Set of three majolica dishes as leaves with curling stalk handle, green glaze, 19thC. Hartleys, Ilkley. Oct 06. HP: £85. ABP: £99.

Burmanftofts faience jardiniere, tube lined with panels of entwined scrolls, mustard glaze, 9.7in wide, No 659. Hartleys, Ilkley. Oct 06. HP: £85. ABP: £99.

Walter Moorcroft pottery plate, tube lined in the Iris design on a green ground, 8.75in wide. Hartleys, Ilkley. Oct 06. HP: £85. ABP: £99.

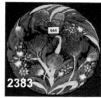

Maling plate with tulip decoration. Great Western Auctions, Glasgow. Oct 06. HP: £85. ABP: £99.

Charlotte Rhead lampbase, signed to underside. Great Western Auctions, Glasgow. Jan 07. HP: £85. ABP: £99.

Border Fine Arts, Mouse on Banana, 030, boxed. Kent Auction Galleries, Folkestone. Dec 06. HP: £85. ABP: £99.

Wade, Snow White and 6 dwarves, all def. Great Western Auctions, Glasgow. Mar 07. HP: £85. ABP: £99.

R. Doulton figure 'Fortune Teller' HN2159, printed marks, 17cm high. Rosebery's, London. Apr 07. HP: £85. ABP: £99. ABP: £99.

Art Deco pottery wall plaque by Royal Belvedere, made in Austria, signed Dakon, face with curling blond hair with dark highlights. Kent Auction Galleries, Folkestone. May 07. HP: £85. ABP: £99.

Royal Winton part coffee set with chinoiserie pattern Pekin. Black Country Auctions, Dudley. Dec 05. HP: £82. ABP: £96.

Royal Doulton figure 'Miss Demure' HN1402. Great Western Auctions, Glasgow. Jul 06. HP: £82. ABP: £96.

Beswick Aberdeen Angus bull, chip to hoof. Great Western Auctions, Glasgow. Aug 05. HP: £80. ABP: £94.

Royal Copenhagen model of a fawn holding parrot, painted No. 752, 7in. Gorringes, Lewes. Sep 05. HP: £80. ABP: £94.

Beswick Hummel designed figure, boy with pigs, mould 912. Black Country Auctions, Dudley. Oct 05. HP: £80. ABP: £94.

Staffordshire flatback lion spill vase, defective. Great Western Auctions, Glasgow. Oct 05. HP: £80. ABP: £94.

Two Royal Stanley vases, Jacobean pattern, painted with trailing fruiting vines and fruits, blue ground, 8.5in and 7in high. Dee, Atkinson & Harrison, Driffield. Sep 05. HP: £80. ABP: £94.

Graduated set of 4 William Kirkby & Co octagonal jugs, Imari palette, snake handles, c1890, 8.25in, 7.25in, 6.25in & 5.25in high. Dee, Atkinson & Harrison, Driffield. Sep 05. HP: £80. ABP: £94.

French faience type earthenware long coated dog, florally decorated, 10cm tall. Locke & England, Leamington Spa. Sep 05. HP: £80. ABP: £94.

Art Nouveau Sarreguemines jardiniere, No. 223, dated 1884, some restoration. Gorringes, Bexhill. Oct 05. HP: £80. ABP: £94.

Gouda baluster-shaped vase. Gorringes, Bexhill. Oct 05. HP: £80. ABP: £94.

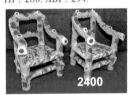

Pair of Scottish pottery chairs. Orpington Salerooms, Kent. Nov 05. HP: £80. ABP: £94.

Caughley plate, painted and gilded with chinoiserie landscape, c1770, gilder's mark to base rim, 21.8cm. Sworders, Stansted Mountfitchet. Nov 05. HP: £80. ABP: £94.

Kutani porcelain group of Ebisu and Benten, c1920, gods in colourful costume, playing drum and biwa, 32cm. Sworders, Stansted Mountfitchet. Nov 05. HP: £80. ABP: £94.

Noritake dish in green with silver decoration. Great Western Auctions, Glasgow. Nov 05. HP: £80. ABP: £94.

Two Sunderland lustre wall plaques, each decorated with a verse, 'Praise Ye The Lord' & 'Prepare To Meet Thy God', one with imp'd mark Moore & Co, 19.75cm high, 21.5cm wide. Gorringes, Bexhill. Dec 05. HP: £80. ABP: £94.

Hoi An blue/white shallow bowl, interior decorated with flowers and foliage, exterior with lappets, 24cm dia. Gorringes, Bexhill. Dec 05. HP: £80. ABP: £94.

Poole Pottery Delphis vase, shape 15, orange & yellow, large stylised design, 22.5cm and matching dish shape 91, 30.5cm. Boldon Auction Galleries, Tyne & Wear. Sep 05. HP: £80. ABP: £94.

Worcester figure, 'Mondays child is full of grace', No. 3257, girl holding a blue ribbon, 16.5cm high. Rosebery's, London. Dec 05. HP: £80. ABP: £94.

Royal Crown Derby plate, tea cup and saucer and coffee cup and saucer. Black Country Auctions, Dudley. Dec 05. HP: £80. ABP: £94.

Pair of Minton coffee cans and saucers, English c1810, painted with shells in pink, green and purple, 6cm high. Rosebery's, London. Jan 06. HP: £80. ABP: £94.

Collection of three Prattware jars/covers, English 19thC, two of shaped form, one of circular form, each with figural scenes. Rosebery's, London. Jan 06. HP: £80. ABP: £94.

Clarice Cliff fruit bowl with embossed bird design, Newport pottery stamp. Black Country Auctions, Dudley. Sep 05. HP: £80. ABP: £94.

Two Lladro figures of geisha, one in pink dress, one in blue dress, 11in high. Ewbank Auctioneers, Send, Surrey. Dec 05. HP: £80. ABP: £94.

C H Brannam pottery boat shaped planter, 1901, signed and dated, chips, 32cm. Sworders, Stansted Mountfitchet. Feb 06. HP: £80. ABP: £94.

Royal Copenhagen figure of a mother and child. Great Western Auctions, Glasgow. Feb 06. HP: £80. ABP: £94.

Beswick, Cuckoo, No. 2315, 9.75cm long. Batemans, Stamford. Mar 06. HP: £80. ABP: £94.

Moorcroft Pottery 'Anemone' pattern vase, painted in colours, green monogram, 10cm high. Rosebery's, London. Mar 06. HP: £80. ABP: £94.

Royal Doulton figurine, 'Nanny' HN2221. Sandwich Auction Rooms, Kent. Mar 06. HP: £80. ABP: £94.

Carlton ware kingfisher ginger jar and cover. Great Western Auctions, Glasgow. Feb 06. HP: £80. ABP: £94.

Pair of Staffordshire lions, one front paw supported on a ball, shaped platforms, 33cm long. Boldon Auction Galleries, Tyne & Wear. Mar 06. HP: £80. ABP: £94.

19thC Staffordshire figure of a dog, tongue out, free-standing legs, 4.5in high. (s/f) Dee, Atkinson & Harrison, Driffield. Apr 06. HP: £80. ABP: £94.

Two Myott & Sons graduated jugs. Great Western Auctions, Glasgow. Apr 06. HP: £80. ABP: £94.

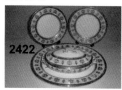

Cauldon part dinner service, borders highly gilt, Fleur de Lys and stamped scroll rims, Lambrequim borders: large oval meat plate, two oval lidded tureens and six dinner plates. Golding Young & Co, Grantham. Feb 06. HP: £80. ABP: £94.

Upchurch pottery vase, three rudimentary feet, slightly streaky glaze, incised script mark, 6in high. Golding Young & Co, Grantham. Feb 06. HP: £80. ABP: £94.

Bursley Ware Pottery bowl, octagonal form, painted with colourful poppy seed heads, 8in wide. Golding Young & Co, Grantham. Feb 06. HP: £80. ABP: £94.

19thC Parianware figure of 'The Greek Slave' after Hiram Powers, naked young woman, 12in high, unmarked, lacking chains. Canterbury Auction Galleries, Kent. Feb 06. HP: £80. ABP: £94.

Victorian Prattware pot lid, seated dog waking a sleeping child, 3in, framed. Golding Young & Co, Grantham. Feb 06. HP: £80. ABP: £94.

Goebel bird impressed CV83 another CV80 & CV81, each 7in high. Kent Auction Galleries, Folkestone. Jun 06. HP: £80. ABP: £94.

Shorter & Son spill vase as a character from the D'oyly Carte Opera. Great Western Auctions, Glasgow. May 06. HP: £80. ABP: £94.

Furstenberg porcelain enamelled vase, early 20thC, red enamelled panels highlighted with gilt, factory marks, 18cm. Rosebery's, London. May 06. HP: £80. ABP: £94.

Pair of Dresden figures of flower sellers, 20thC, flower encrusted bases, 21cm high. Rosebery's, London. May 06. HP: £80. ABP: £94.

R. Worcester pâte sur pâte planter, 1879, sides enriched with a quatrefoil peach ground panel with floral and insect studies, 11.5cm high. Rosebery's, London. May 06. HP: £80. ABP: £94.

Famille rose mug, c1780, with branch handle, painted with reserves of figures beside a river within 'C' scroll borders, 13cm high. Rosebery's, London. Aug 06. HP: £80. ABP: £94.

Staffordshire pottery spaniel, gilded collar, red markings, 19thC, 5.75in high. Hartleys, Ilkley. Aug 06. HP: £80. ABP: £94.

Pair of Royal Crown Derby porcelain coffee cans and saucers, painted with Imari style panels, dated 1927, 2.5in high. Hartleys, Ilkley. Aug 06. HP: £80. ABP: £94.

Pair Chelsea type porcelain figures, floral 18thC dress, 19thC, 9in high, red anchor mark. Hartleys, Ilkley. Aug 06. HP: £80. ABP: £94.

Royal Doulton porcelain figure 'Roseanna' HN1926, lady flanking a bowl of roses, 8.5in high. Hartleys, Ilkley. Aug 06. HP: £80. ABP: £94.

Three Carter Stabler Adams items, 2 painted with flowers, 10cm & 9.5cm and a squat pot/cover, cover with inscription RIBI, Bournemouth, 1929, 10.5cm. Sworders, Stansted Mountfitchet. Apr 06. HP: £80. ABP: £94.

Hammer: £80

Troika square vase, unknown decorator LJ. Great Western Auctions, Glasgow. Sep 06. HP: £80. ABP: £94.

R. Doulton stoneware water filter, domed lid with turned finial & moulded with flower heads, sides moulded/incised with stylised flowers on blue and turquoise ground, liner and inner lid, 16in high. Hartleys, Ilkley. Oct 06. HP: £80. ABP: £94.

Prices quoted are actual hammer prices (HP) and the Approximate Buyer's Price (ABP) includes an average premium of 15% + VAT.

Macintyre Aurelian ware jug, blue printed with Art Nouveau flowers, gilded banding, 6.5in high. Hartleys, Ilkley. Oct 06. HP: £80. ABP: £94.

19thC Japanese Imari bowl, painted with garden scenes, stylised flowers and foliage, carved hardwood stand, blue painted 6 character mark to base, 22cm dia, stand a/f. Rosebery's, London. Oct 06. HP: £80. ABP: £94.

Swatow dish, painted in iron red and green with a stylised dog of Fo amidst foliage within a foliage reserved and cross hatched border, 39cm dia. Rosebery's, London. Oct 06. HP: £80. ABP: £94.

Two Beswick pottery cows, a Guernsey and Friesan Ch. 'Claybury Leegwater', 4.5in high. Hartleys, Ilkley. Aug 06. HP: £80. ABP: £94.

Moorcroft plate, 250mm dia, decorated with fruits & birds in plum & dark blue colours. A F Brock & Co Ltd, Stockport. Oct 06. HP: £80. ABP: £94.

Victorian pottery bust, Alexander 1st of Russia, poss. Staffordshire, late 19thC, 11in high. Hartleys, Ilkley. Dec 06. HP: £80. ABP: £94.

English pottery meat plate, blue printed in the Italian scenery pattern within floral border, 19thC, 18.75in wide. Hartleys, Ilkley. Dec 06. HP: £80. ABP: £94.

Hammer: £80 - £75

2447

Wilton ware lustre bowl, painted with Oriental figures in traditional dress, 12.25in wide. Hartleys, Ilkley. Feb 07. HP: £80. ABP: £94.

2448

Doulton Lambeth stoneware vase, side tube lined with flower heads on blue ground, 7.5in high. Hartleys, Ilkley. Feb 07. HP: £80. ABP: £94.

2449

Aynsley China coffee set, in associated silver gilt mounts with cherub handles, and matched spoons, cased, af. Charterhouse Auctioneers, Sherborne. Feb 07. HP: £80. ABP: £94.

2450

Shelley Phlox pattern part tea service. Charterhouse Auctioneers, Sherborne. Apr 07. HP: £80. ABP: £94.

2451

Goldscheider figure, girl ice-skating, modelled by Claire Weiss, 22cm, af. Charterhouse Auctioneers, Sherborne. Apr 07. HP: £80. ABP: £94.

2452

Troika cube vase, textured surface, geometric decoration, with HF monogram, 8.5cm. Charterhouse Auctioneers, Sherborne. Apr 07. HP: £80. ABP: £94.

2453

Wedgwood black Jasperware bowl decorated with the dancing hours, impressed marks to base, 26cm dia. Rosebery's, London. Apr 07. HP: £80. ABP: £94.

The numbering system acts as a reader reference as well as linking to the Analysis of each section.

2454

Naples figural lamp base of a lady and gentleman taking tea, gilt scrolling base, 33cm high, af. Rosebery's, London. Apr 07. HP: £80. ABP: £94.

2455

Herend twin-handled small jardiniere with puce flower decoration, gilt highlights, printed mark to base, 14cm high. Rosebery's, London. Apr 07. HP: £80. ABP: £94.

2456

Elizabeth Mary Watt painted dish. Great Western Auctions, Glasgow. Aug 06. HP: £78. ABP: £91.

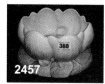

2457

Clarice Cliff bowl as a water lily, emboss mark to base 973, 8 x 5in high. Kent Auction Galleries, Folkestone. Oct 05. HP: £75. ABP: £88.

2458

Beswick Highland Bull No. 2008 gloss, horn signs of restoration. Kent Auction Galleries, Folkestone. Oct 05. HP: £75. ABP: £88.

2459

Royal Crown Derby Frog paperweight and seated cat. Boldon Auction Galleries, Tyne & Wear. Sep 05. HP: £75. ABP: £88.

2460

English pottery char dish, sides brown printed and painted with pilchards, 7.5in wide. Hartleys, Ilkley. Feb 07. HP: £75. ABP: £88.

2461

Shelley vase, trumpet-shaped horizontally ribbed, printed in 'Melody' pattern, and two similar vases, 9.75in, 6.75in & 8.5in high. Dee, Atkinson & Harrison, Driffield. Nov 05. HP: £75. ABP: £88.

2462

Pair Staffordshire spaniels, English 19thC, gilt details, enamelled features 32cm high. Rosebery's, London. Jan 06. HP: £75. ABP: £88.

2463

Large Beswick brown race-horse. Black Country Auctions, Dudley. Sep 05. HP: £75. ABP: £88.

2464

Capo di Monte Ltd Edn figure group, Thea by Roberto Beauigilla and another by Maria Angelo. Gorringes, Bexhill. Feb 06. HP: £75. ABP: £88.

2465

Earthenware jar with two crimped handles, top section covered with a yellow glaze, 8in high. Ewbank Auctioneers, Send, Surrey. Dec 05. HP: £75. ABP: £88.

2466

19thC Wedgwood green-leaf and sunflower two handled tazza, with two matching two handled shaped dishes, green flowerhead plate & Wedgwood shaped green-leaf dish. (5) Dee, Atkinson & Harrison, Driffield. Feb 06. HP: £75. ABP: £88.

2467

David Leach pottery bowl, painted with stylised ferns on a green/grey ground, 5.5in wide, impressed seal mark. Hartleys, Ilkley. Feb 07. HP: £75. ABP: £88.

David Cohen, a half-glazed raku stoneware apple plate. Batemans, Stamford. Mar 06. HP: £75. ABP: £88.

Carlton Ware Rouge Royal coffee service for 6: coffee pot, milk jug, sugar basin, 6 cups/saucers. Kent Auction Galleries, Folkestone. Mar 06. HP: £75. ABP: £88.

Royal Doulton tankard commemorating Grand National Coronation Year 1937, Royal Mail, My Prints - Flying May, imp'd to base 7119A. Kent Auction Galleries, Folkestone. Mar 06. HP: £75. ABP: £88.

Clarice Cliff Wilkinson Ltd ribbed vase, 8in, Passion Fruit Pattern, af. Kent Auction Galleries, Folkestone. May 06. HP: £75. ABP: £88.

Pilkingtons pottery vase, ribbed form, green lustre and brown glazes, 7in high. Golding Young & Co, Grantham. Feb 06. HP: £75. ABP: £88.

Castle Hedingham Pottery vase, in relief with trailing foliage between dentil and ? borders, green glaze, pink berries, 6in high. Golding Young & Co, Grantham. Feb 06. HP: £75. ABP: £88.

Mintons vase, designed by John Wadsworth, ribbed form, short conical neck, blue streaky glaze, green banding, factory mark and script signature, 7in high. Golding Young & Co, Grantham. Feb 06. HP: £75. ABP: £88.

Cambell Tile, moulded in relief, painted with a sheep & standard, 6in. Golding Young & Co, Grantham. Feb 06. HP: £75. ABP: £88.

Paragon miniature loving cups, full set of 12, plus a Leine Schloss duplicate. Kent Auction Galleries, Folkestone. Jun 06. HP: £75. ABP: £88.

Six various Pratt pot lids. Great Western Auctions, Glasgow. May 06. HP: £75. ABP: £88.

Hammer: £75

Crown Devon 'John Peel' musical jug, c1930, fox hunting scene, inscription to John Peel, handle as a fox, factory mark, 18cm high. Rosebery's, London. May 06. HP: £75. ABP: £88.

Meissen model of an owl, 20thC, in the white, 15cm high. Rosebery's, London. May 06. HP: £75. ABP: £88.

Majolica Revival picture plate by Castellani, dated 1874, with monogram T.C. Aladdins Cave Auctions, Danehill, W Sussex. Aug 06. HP: £75. ABP: £88.

Blue/white Victorian wash bowl set by Bishop & Stonier. Aladdins Cave Auctions, Danehill, W Sussex. Aug 06. HP: £75. ABP: £88.

R. Crown Derby barn owl, J Griffiths to base, imp'd K, 6in high. Kent Auction Galleries, Folkestone. Feb 07. HP: £75. ABP: £88.

Charlotte Rhead vase. Great Western Auctions, Glasgow. Aug 06. HP: £75. ABP: £88.

Brameld majolica dish of shaped oval form, scroll and wicker moulded rim, green glaze, 12.5in wide, and a crested Brameld plate. (2) Hartleys, Ilkley. Oct 06. HP: £75. ABP: £88.

Moorcroft anemone plate, 10in. Great Western Auctions, Glasgow. Nov 06. HP: £75. ABP: £88.

Mortlock treacle glazed 'Cadogan' pattern teapot in 'Chinese' manner, moulded in relief with flowers/leaves, 6.75in high, 'Cocoa' in gilt, spout restored. Canterbury Auction Galleries, Kent. Apr 06. HP: £75. ABP: £88.

Pottery figure by Marion Cole, lady in a ball gown, 9in high, incised mark to base. Hartleys, Ilkley. Feb 07. HP: £75. ABP: £88.

Ceramics Prices **147**

Pair of Beswick Highland bulls, both with def horns. Great Western Auctions, Glasgow. Feb 07. HP: £72. ABP: £84.

Royal Doulton figurine, The Orange Lady HN 1759. Lambert & Foster, Tenterden. Jun 07. HP: £70. ABP: £82.

Pair of Burmantofts faience pottery sleeve vases, moulded in relief with reeded vertical panels/starbursts, impressed marks, No. 831, 8in high. Golding Young & Co, Grantham. Feb 06. HP: £70. ABP: £82.

Linthorpe pottery wall pocket decorated with apple blossom imp'd LINTHORPE 1017, 6in high. Golding Young & Co, Grantham. Feb 06. HP: £70. ABP: £82.

Pair 18thC pearlware sauce boats, printed in blue with figural Chinese landscapes, 3.25in high. Golding Young & Co, Grantham. Nov 06. HP: £70. ABP: £82.

Baron Barnstaple wavy vase, three loop handles, green on brown scraffito body, incised Baron Barnstaple 177 to base, 6in high. Golding Young & Co, Grantham. Feb 06. HP: £70. ABP: £82.

Beswick pottery horse, Skewbald Pinto pony, 6.5in high. Hartleys, Ilkley. Aug 06. HP: £70. ABP: £82.

Upchurch pottery vase, blue running glaze over a matt grey body, incised mark, 5in high. Golding Young & Co, Grantham. Feb 06. HP: £70. ABP: £82.

Large Beswick labrador, No. 2314. Kent Auction Galleries, Folkestone. Jun 06. HP: £70. ABP: £82.

Upchurch pottery jug, lightly ribbed, loop handle, brown glaze, incised script mark, 7in high. Golding Young & Co, Grantham. Feb 06. HP: £70. ABP: £82.

Winchcombe Pottery terracotta vase, painted with a band of limited features in brown & buff, green ground, seal mark, 7in high. Golding Young & Co, Grantham. Feb 06. HP: £70. ABP: £82.

Large Beswick beagle, No. 2300. Kent Auction Galleries, Folkestone. Jun 06. HP: £70. ABP: £82.

The illustrations are in descending price order. The price range is indicated at the top of each page.

Royal Doulton figure 'Priscilla', HN1340, 20.5cm high. Rosebery's, London. Aug 06. HP: £70. ABP: £82.

Early 19thC Staffordshire pottery group, Two musicians seated under a tree with sheep, lambs and swan, 8.5in high, restored. Canterbury Auction Galleries, Kent. Apr 06. HP: £70. ABP: £82.

Royal Crown Derby porcelain vase, blue tapering neck, painted with Imari style panels, dated 1913, 5in high. Hartleys, Ilkley. Aug 06. HP: £70. ABP: £82.

Shelley (late Foley Intarsio) bottle vase, No. 3640 to base, panels of stylized leaves & strap work, 4in high, 5in dia. Kent Auction Galleries, Folkestone. Aug 06. HP: £70. ABP: £82.

Candy ware pottery vase, brown, russet/orange streaky glaze, 14in high. Golding Young & Co, Grantham. Feb 06. HP: £70. ABP: £82.

Royal Dux figure of a parrot. Great Western Auctions, Glasgow. Jul 06. HP: £70. ABP: £82.

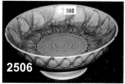

Royal Lancastrian footed bowl. Great Western Auctions, Glasgow. Jul 06. HP: £70. ABP: £82.

Moorcroft tube lined fruit & foliage jug, 5in high. Kent Auction Galleries, Folkestone. Feb 07. HP: £70. ABP: £82.

Royal Doulton figure, The Balloon Man, HN1954, 7.5in high. Golding Young & Co, Grantham. Nov 06. HP: £70. ABP: £82.

Royal Doulton figure, The Old Balloon Seller, HN1315, 7.75in high. Golding Young & Co, Grantham. Nov 06. HP: £70. ABP: £82.

18thC Delft blue dish, painted with island landscape with boats, double link border, rim with a simple lozenge band, 10.25in dia. Golding Young & Co, Grantham. Nov 06. HP: £70. ABP: £82.

Pair of Carlton Ware vases, powder blue ground with birds on branches. (1 def) Great Western Auctions, Glasgow. Feb 07. HP: £70. ABP: £82.

Two Beswick models of Babycham deer, gold printed factory mark to undersides. Gorringes, Bexhill. Dec 05. HP: £70. ABP: £82.

Samson porcelain jardinière, 2 gilt moulded/shell pattern handles, coloured enamels in 'Chinese Famille Verte' manner with birds and exotic flowers, 8.25in dia x 7.5in high. Canterbury Auction Galleries, Kent. Feb 07. HP: £70. ABP: £82.

Iznik style pottery box/cover, with a band of flowers and foliage, 11cm dia. Rosebery's, London. Jan 06. HP: £70. ABP: £82.

Royal Doulton stoneware flask, English, early 20thC, applied handle, impressed factory mark to underside, pattern No. 6027, 20.5cm. Rosebery's, London. Jan 06. HP: £70. ABP: £82.

Beswick cow, CH Newton Tinkle. Orpington Salerooms, Kent. Nov 05. HP: £70. ABP: £82.

Hammer: £70

Royal Doulton 'Kingsware' pottery spirit flask with a half-length portrait of Mr Micawber, worded Micawber - The Ever Expectant, 7in high. Canterbury Auction Galleries, Kent. Dec 05. HP: £70. ABP: £82.

Early salt glazed stoneware wine jar, incised with date 1567, 11.75in, extensive crack to body. Canterbury Auction Galleries, Kent. Oct 05. HP: £70. ABP: £82.

Aynsley cup/cover from Peter Jones Collection, hand painted by T. Abbots with cartouche of Westminster Abbey. Ltd Edn No 22/175, 9in high. Ewbank, Send, Surrey. Dec 05. HP: £70. ABP: £82.

Hummel figure 'A Letter to Santa Claus'. Great Western Auctions, Glasgow. Dec 05. HP: £70. ABP: £82.

Pair of Carlton Ware New Mikado vases. Great Western Auctions, Glasgow. Nov 05. HP: £70. ABP: £82.

Set of 3 Masons Ironstone 'Imari' graduated jugs and another similar Ironstone jug, 22cm high. (the largest) Gorringes, Bexhill. Dec 05. HP: £70. ABP: £82.

St Ives Troika abstract vase, 9cm high. Gorringes, Bexhill. Feb 06. HP: £70. ABP: £82.

Kevin Francis Ceramics 'Marilyn Monroe' figure. Henry Adams, Chichester. Dec 05. HP: £70. ABP: £82.

Carlton Ware ribbed vase painted with flowers. Great Western Auctions, Glasgow. Mar 07. HP: £70. ABP: £82.

Hammer: £70

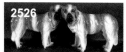

2526
Pair Staffordshire St Bernard dogs, English late 19thC, gilt collars, glass eyes, 25cm high, 33cm long. Rosebery's, London. Dec 05. HP: £70. ABP: £82.

2527
Ming Jar, blue/white floral decoration, 12cm. Charterhouse Auctioneers, Sherborne. Apr 07. HP: £70. ABP: £82.

2528
Royal Doulton figure 'Gail', HN2937. Great Western Auctions, Glasgow. Feb 06. HP: £70. ABP: £82.

2529
Beswick Donkey and a Palomino pony. Great Western Auctions, Glasgow. Feb 06. HP: £70. ABP: £82.

2530
2 Crown Staffordshire parrots, Chinese style, one glazed in yellow, other green, pierced rockwork base, 20cm high, and a Crown Staffordshire robin on a flower encrusted branch, modelled by J.T. Jones. Rosebery's, London. Mar 06. HP: £70. ABP: £82.

2531
Troika small wheel shaped vase, c1970s, textured body in colours, painted mark Troika, initials A.N, 13cm high. Rosebery's, London. Mar 06. HP: £70. ABP: £82.

2532
Macintyre 'Florian' decorated sugar bowl, c1900, green ground, blue painted flowers, brown printed mark to underside, 6.5cm high. Rosebery's, London. Mar 06. HP: £70. ABP: £82.

2533
Staffordshire Willow Pattern cow creamer. Orpington Salerooms, Kent. Mar 06. HP: £70. ABP: £82.

2534
Wiltonware 15 piece blue glazed coffee service, chinoiserie decoration: coffee pot, sugar bowl, cream jug, 6 coffee cans and 6 saucers. Denhams, Warnham, Sussex. Aug 05. HP: £70. ABP: £82.

2535
Clarice Cliff jam pot. Aladdins Cave Auction, Danehill, Sussex. Mar 06. HP: £70. ABP: £82.

2536
Coalport bone china figure 'Christmas Caroller', Ltd Edn from 1500, 20.5cm. Locke & England, Leamington Spa. Mar 06. HP: £70. ABP: £82.

2537
Victorian George Jones egg cruet, floral decoration, four hole cover, printed mark, 150cm high. Reeman Dansie, Colchester. Apr 06. HP: £70. ABP: £82.

> Categories or themes can be followed through the colour coded Index which contains over 4500 cross references.

2538
Quimper faience plate decorated in colours with standing figure of a man in national dress, 10in, similar decorated jug, 6.5in high, and another Quimper jug, 6in high. Canterbury Auction Galleries, Kent. Feb 06. HP: £70. ABP: £82.

2539
Late 19thC Staffordshire money box, twin gabled house, 5.5in high and a Staffordshire money box, twin gabled purple roofed cottage, 5in high. Dee, Atkinson & Harrison, Driffield. Apr 06. HP: £70. ABP: £82.

2540
Early Coalport jug, wrythen body, blue transfer printed, floral bouquets and moths/butterflies, copy of Caughley c1810, 5in. Dee, Atkinson & Harrison, Driffield. Apr 06. HP: £70. ABP: £82.

2541
Royal Doulton figure 'Rendezvous' HN2212. Great Western Auctions, Glasgow. Aug 06. HP: £70. ABP: £82.

2542
Pair of Delft vases, flowers and foliage, chips to tinglaze, 20cm high. Charterhouse Auctioneers, Sherborne. Sep 06. HP: £70. ABP: £82.

2543
Pair Delft twin-handled vases, painted in brown/blue with panels of flowers, octagonal bases, painted marks to bases, 17cm high, af. Rosebery's, London. Oct 06. HP: £70. ABP: £82.

2544
Pair of Carlton Ware rouge royale New Mikado vases. Great Western Auctions, Glasgow. Oct 06. HP: £70. ABP: £82.

Maling plate decorated in relief with flowers and kingfishers. Great Western Auctions, Glasgow. Oct 06. HP: £70. ABP: £82.

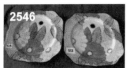

Pair of Grays pottery 'Sunbuff' plates. Great Western Auctions, Glasgow. Sep 05. HP: £70. ABP: £82.

Wedgwood butterfly box and cover. Great Western Auctions, Glasgow. Oct 05. HP: £70. ABP: £82.

Carlton Ware Spiders Web dish. Great Western Auctions, Glasgow. Oct 05. HP: £70. ABP: £82.

Royal Doulton horse with blue rug and red rosette, 20cm high. Boldon Auction Galleries, Tyne & Wear. Sep 05. HP: £70. ABP: £82.

Royal Crown Derby owl paperweight & a chipmunk. Boldon Auction Galleries, Tyne & Wear. Sep 05. HP: £70. ABP: £82.

Westerwald stoneware pitcher, G.R. cartouche, shoulder and foot with blue checkered work, neck ribbed with strap handle, 9in high. Dee, Atkinson & Harrison, Driffield. Sep 05. HP: £70. ABP: £82.

Beswick pigeon 1383, second version. Black Country Auctions, Dudley. Dec 05. HP: £68. ABP: £79.

Beswick model of a Hereford calf. Cotswold Auction Company, Cirencester. Aug 06. HP: £68. ABP: £79.

Royal Copenhagen polar bear figurine, marked Denmark No. 1137 to base, 6in high. Kent Auction Galleries, Folkestone. May 07. HP: £65. ABP: £76.

Modern Studio pottery bowl with three bands of turquoise and silver lustre decoration, 8.5in dia x 4.25in high, imp'd seal mark 'S.H.' to footrim. Canterbury Auction Galleries, Kent. Jun 07. HP: £65. ABP: £76.

Royal Worcester figure 'Little Mermaid', modelled by F.G. Doughty. Great Western Auctions, Glasgow. Apr 06. HP: £65. ABP: £76.

Wilkinson Oriflame vase, with fish/weeds in colourful lustres, printed marks, 9in high, small rim chip. Golding Young & Co, Grantham. Feb 06. HP: £65. ABP: £76.

Fell pottery meat plate, moulded with gravy channels and well, printed with a river landscape, wild rose border, c1840, 20in wide. Golding Young & Co, Grantham. Feb 06. HP: £65. ABP: £76.

Pair of Chamberlains Worcester plates. Great Western Auctions, Glasgow. Sep 05. HP: £65. ABP: £76.

Pilkingtons pottery vase, all over green mottled glaze, impressed mark darker 1909, shape No. 2651, 3in high. Golding Young & Co, Grantham. Feb 06. HP: £65. ABP: £76.

Upchurch Pottery vase, loop handles, slightly ribbed body with a khaki glaze streaked blue, incised script mark, 9in high. Golding Young & Co, Grantham. Feb 06. HP: £65. ABP: £76.

Dunmore pottery 2-handled vase, green streaky glaze over a brown and orange combed ground, 5in high. Golding Young & Co, Grantham. Feb 06. HP: £65. ABP: £76.

Minton Hollin & Co majolica frieze tile, stylized anthemion and rondel decoration, 8in square, pattern No. 145B. Golding Young & Co, Grantham. Feb 06. HP: £65. ABP: £76.

Pair of 19thC Staffordshire pottery seated spaniels, black splashes, gilt collar and chain, 12in high. Golding Young & Co, Grantham. Feb 06. HP: £65. ABP: £76.

Gouda 'Purdah' pattern platter. Great Western Auctions, Glasgow. Sep 05. HP: £65. ABP: £76.

Hammer: £65

Moorcroft 'Pansy' vase, green mark to base Moorcroft, signature BM & flag Made in England, Copyright 93, imp'd mark, 3.5in. Kent Auction Galleries, Folkestone. Aug 06. HP: £65. ABP: £76.

Royal Doulton flambé dragon, HN3552, made for the Collectors Club, 1993. Gorringes, Lewes. Feb 06. HP: £65. ABP: £76.

Royal Dux figurine blue macaw parrot, pink triangular mark to base, metallic label to side. Kent Auction Galleries, Folkestone. Dec 06. HP: £65. ABP: £76.

Royal Doulton figurine, The China Repairer, HN2943, by R. Tabbener, 1983-88. A F Brock & Co Ltd, Stockport. Aug 05. HP: £65. ABP: £76.

Moorcroft pottery vase, tube lined in the Finches design, 7.5in high. Hartleys, Ilkley. Feb 07. HP: £65. ABP: £76.

152 Ceramics Prices

Early 19thC Wedgwood black basalt teapot, moulded loop handle, slightly domed cover with turned finial, 8.5in high, impressed mark 'Wedgwood'. Canterbury Auction Galleries, Kent. Oct 05. HP: £65. ABP: £76.

Late 19thC Aesthetic movement dish decorated in Japanese manner, square panel with an iris, green seal mark on base, 12in. Ewbank Auctioneers, Send, Surrey. Dec 05. HP: £65. ABP: £76.

> Prices quoted are actual hammer prices (HP) and the Approximate Buyer's Price (ABP) includes an average premium of 15% + VAT.

Royal Staffordshire Clarice Cliff bowl formed of petals with a leaf base approx. 9 x 7in. Kent Auction Galleries, Folkestone. Feb 06. HP: £65. ABP: £76.

Pearlware figure, English 18thC, possibly Ralph Wood, reclining putto wearing a toga, 9cm high. Rosebery's, London. Feb 06. HP: £65. ABP: £76.

Carlton ware handcraft vase. Great Western Auctions, Glasgow. Oct 05. HP: £65. ABP: £76.

Crown Devon Fieldings footed bowl, stylized floral design. Great Western Auctions, Glasgow. Mar 07. HP: £65. ABP: £76.

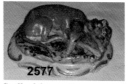

Staffordshire pottery greyhound lying on a green base, scroll moulded edge, 19thC, 4.5in wide. Hartleys, Ilkley. Apr 07. HP: £65. ABP: £76.

Maling dish. Great Western Auctions, Glasgow. Feb 06. HP: £65. ABP: £76.

Beswick Racoon on log. Great Western Auctions, Glasgow. Feb 06. HP: £65. ABP: £76.

Pair of Shelley green and orange banded vases. Great Western Auctions, Glasgow. Mar 06. HP: £65. ABP: £76.

Beswick model of a Hereford bull. Cotswold Auction Company, Cirencester. Aug 06. HP: £65. ABP: £76.

Royal Copenhagen figure of a reclining man. Great Western Auctions, Glasgow. Oct 06. HP: £65. ABP: £76.

Coalport jar/cover. Great Western Auctions, Glasgow. Oct 06. HP: £65. ABP: £76.

Lladro figure of a child and donkey. Great Western Auctions, Glasgow. Sep 05. HP: £65. ABP: £76.

Lladro figure of a young girl leaning forward, hands on her lap holding a hat. Boldon Auction Galleries, Tyne & Wear. Sep 05. HP: £65. ABP: £76.

New Hall type 12 piece part tea set, each painted with a shell, coral etc: 6 tea bowls, 3 saucers, basin, oval small plate and another circular. Boldon Auction Galleries, Tyne & Wear. Sep 05. HP: £65. ABP: £76.

Three Prattware pot lids, The Time, A False Move and The Shakespeare Room - Where He Was Born. Gorringes, Bexhill. Oct 05. HP: £65. ABP: £76.

Two Beswick Beneagles whisky decanters & contents, Barn Owl and Short Eared Owl. Great Western Auctions, Glasgow. Sep 06. HP: £64. ABP: £75.

Holyrood pottery jar, blue and green streaky glaze. 4in high. Golding Young & Co, Grantham. Feb 06. HP: £62. ABP: £72.

Wedgwood black basalt bust. 4in tall. Black Country Auctions, Dudley. Dec 05. HP: £62. ABP: £72.

Two Beswick earthenware kingfishers, models 729 1 and 2, green and blue gloss, 20 and 15cm. Locke & England, Leamington Spa. Sep 06. HP: £62. ABP: £72.

Ringtons Maling blue chintz pattern milk jug, 18.5cm. Boldon Auction Galleries, Tyne & Wear. Sep 05. HP: £62. ABP: £72.

Two Hummel figures, Stargazer and Skier, both TMK3. Great Western Auctions, Glasgow. Apr 06. HP: £60. ABP: £70.

Clarice Cliff Orange Chintz octagonal bowl. (cracked) Great Western Auctions, Glasgow. May 07. HP: £60. ABP: £70.

Bretby pottery vase, red flambé glaze, imp'd mark, No. 2215, 12in high. Golding Young & Co, Grantham. Feb 06. HP: £60. ABP: £70.

Beswick tiger 2096, gloss. Kent Auction Galleries, Folkestone. May 07. HP: £60. ABP: £70.

Maling plate, depicting a windmill. Great Western Auctions, Glasgow. Apr 06. HP: £60. ABP: £70.

Upchurch pottery vase, lightly ribbed, rudimentary handles, green/blue streaky matt glazes, incised script mark, 6in high. Golding Young & Co, Grantham. Feb 06. HP: £60. ABP: £70.

Poole pottery vase, spattered pale terracotta glaze, a matt cream ground, imp'd marks, artists initials and No. A20/5, 8in high. Golding Young & Co, Grantham. Feb 06. HP: £60. ABP: £70.

Royal Doulton porcelain figure, Boatman, HN2417, 7in high. Golding Young & Co, Grantham. Feb 06. HP: £60. ABP: £70.

Victorian Prattware pot lid, printed with travellers in a country landscape, 3in dia, another of figures & resting sheep by corn stocks, 3in dia. damaged, framed. Golding Young & Co, Grantham. Feb 06. HP: £60. ABP: £70.

Chintz Ware fruit bowl with chromed metal rim, yellow background with corn flowers & poppies, mark to base Royality Made in England, further back stamp illegible, 2261? 9 x 8in. Kent Auction Galleries, Folkestone. Jun 06. HP: £60. ABP: £70.

Carlton ware lustre bowl, gilded with butterflies, blue lustre ground, 7.5in wide. Hartleys, Ilkley. Dec 06. HP: £60. ABP: £70.

Beswick 'Charolais Bull', wood base, Connoisseur Series. Aladdins Cave Auctions, Danehill, W Sussex. Aug 06. HP: £60. ABP: £70.

Tang-style Lancotte horse, glazed in red, buff mounts, 12.25in. Gorringes, Lewes. Jul 06. HP: £60. ABP: £70.

Hammer: £60

John Maddock & Sons wash bowl, jug and soap dish in the 'Imperial' pattern and a Mason's Ironstone wash bowl and jug, a/f. Rosebery's, London. Aug 06. HP: £60. ABP: £70.

Victorian Staffordshire spill vase of a deer and gun dog, 30cm, another of huntsman and an arbour group. (3) Rosebery's. London. Aug 06. HP: £60. ABP: £70.

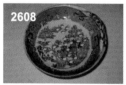

English pearlware strainer, side loop handle, blue printed in the Willow pattern, 19thC, 3.25in wide. Hartleys, Ilkley. Aug 06. HP: £60. ABP: £70.

Beswick Hereford calf, brown and white, 4.5in high. Hartleys, Ilkley. Aug 06. HP: £60. ABP: £70.

Two Beswick owl decanters for Whyte and Mackay, 16cm, and a Beswick owl, 12cm. Stride & Son, Chichester. Aug 06. HP: £60. ABP: £70.

Beswick Highland pony 'Mackionneach', dun colour. Great Western Auctions, Glasgow. Jan 07. HP: £60. ABP: £70.

Royal Worcester blush ivory figure, semi-naked maiden, c1920, 64cm high, af. Rosebery's, London. Aug 06. HP: £60. ABP: £70.

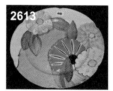

Grays pottery charger. Great Western Auctions, Glasgow. Jan 07. HP: £60. ABP: £70.

Royal Worcester porcelain bowl, sides painted with roses by M Lander, gilded rim and foot, 6.25in wide. Hartleys, Ilkley. Dec 06. HP: £60. ABP: £70.

Royal Crown Derby Gold Seal cat paperweight in Imari colours, gold button to base, original box. Kent Auction Galleries, Folkestone. Dec 06. HP: £60. ABP: £70.

Wedgwood blue jasper ware cheese dish, 9in x 5.75in high, embossed with classical figures, trees & leaves, two air holes in lid, small stains. A F Brock & Co Ltd, Stockport. Feb 07. HP: £60. ABP: £70.

Royal Doulton Elegance HN2264. Black Country Auctions, Dudley. Dec 05. HP: £60. ABP: £70.

Three Staffordshire figure groups, English 19thC, each modelled as gallant and companion, two in Scottish dress, af, tallest 38cm. Rosebery's, London. Jan 06. HP: £60. ABP: £70.

Royal Doulton character jug of Winston Churchill and a Bossons style plaster wall mask of Winston Churchill, 9.75cm & 18cm high. Gorringes, Bexhill. Feb 06. HP: £60. ABP: £70.

Clarice Cliff waterlily bowl. Great Western Auctions, Glasgow. Nov 05. HP: £60. ABP: £70.

Charlotte Rhead Crown Ducal Edward VII coronation jug 1937, 6.5in high, facsimile signature. Ewbank Auctioneers, Send, Surrey. Dec 05. HP: £60. ABP: £70.

Royal Doulton figure 'Innocence', HN2842. Ewbank, Send, Surrey. Dec 05. HP: £60. ABP: £70.

19thC Prattware oval dish 'The blind fiddler' after Sir David Wilkie, 12.25in, marked Pratt. Ewbank Auctioneers, Send, Surrey. Dec 05. HP: £60. ABP: £70.

Carlton Ware black ground plate, decorated with 3 flying mallard ducks. Great Western Auctions, Glasgow. Jan 06. HP: £60. ABP: £70.

Carlton Ware spiders web jug. Orpington Salerooms, Kent. Nov 05. HP: £60. ABP: £70.

2626

Rye Hop Ware 'Sussex Art Ware' jug, applied with green hops & leaves, incised mark to base, 9cm high. Gorringes, Bexhill. Dec 05. HP: £60. ABP: £70.

2627

French faience inkwell, heart-shaped, polychrome floral design, 12cm long. Gorringes, Bexhill. Dec 05. HP: £60. ABP: £70.

2628

Wade 'Nat West' pigs, two part sets, minus Nathaniel, two have stoppers missing. (8) A F Brock & Co Ltd, Stockport. Nov 05. HP: £60. ABP: £70.

2629

Wemyss vase, decorated with cabbage roses, painted mark to base, def. Great Western Auctions, Glasgow. Mar 07. HP: £60. ABP: £70.

2630

Lladro figure of a child in jester costume. Great Western Auctions, Glasgow. Sep 05. HP: £60. ABP: £70.

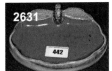

2631

Doulton dragonfly soapdish, produced for Wright's coal tar soap. Great Western Auctions, Glasgow. Mar 07. HP: £60. ABP: £70.

2632

Quantity of Cornish Kitchen Wares by T.G Green, c1950s, incl. an oil bottle, flour shaker, plates, jars and bowls etc, some damaged, all with printed marks, af. Rosebery's, London. Mar 06. HP: £60. ABP: £70.

The numbering system acts as a reader reference as well as linking to the Analysis of each section.

2633

Clarice Cliff Bizarre toast-rack, daffodil shape with painted decoration. Great Western Auctions, Glasgow. Sep 06. HP: £60. ABP: £70.

2634

Beswick polar bear. Great Western Auctions, Glasgow. Sep 06. HP: £60. ABP: £70.

2635

Poole pottery 2-handled vase with green/grey decoration. Great Western Auctions, Glasgow. Sep 05. HP: £60. ABP: £70.

Hammer: £60 - £55

2636

Royal Crown Derby vase. Great Western Auctions, Glasgow. Oct 05. HP: £60. ABP: £70.

2637

2 'Clarice Cliff' style sifters by Chelsea Works Burslem, 'Huntley Cottage' pattern, 14cm, each with different scene. Boldon Auction Galleries, Tyne & Wear. Sep 05. HP: £60. ABP: £70.

2638

Moore Bros Aesthetic style jardiniere, impressed to base, af. Gorringes, Bexhill. Oct 05. HP: £60. ABP: £70.

2639

Beswick leopard. Black Country Auctions, Dudley. Oct 05. HP: £58. ABP: £68.

2640

Carltonware teapot 'Blue Max', modelled as a bi-plane with goggled pilot. Locke & England, Leamington Spa. Nov 06. HP: £56. ABP: £65.

2641

Pair of Crown Devon vases, one def. Great Western Auctions, Glasgow. Apr 06. HP: £55. ABP: £64.

2642

Robinson & Leadbeater parian bust, Hermes after the Antique, squared inscribed base, 7.5in high. Hartleys, Ilkley. Aug 06. HP: £55. ABP: £64.

2643

Pearlware basket, oval form, fluted sides with woven band, brown rim, late 18th/19thC, 8in wide. Hartleys, Ilkley. Aug 06. HP: £55. ABP: £64.

2644

Bretby pottery vase, domed foot, blue streaky glaze, imp'd factory marks No. 2134H, 13in high. Golding Young & Co, Grantham. Feb 06. HP: £55. ABP: £64.

2645

Royal Doulton Mr. Toadflax DBH10. 1983. Black Country Auctions, Dudley. Sep 05. HP: £55. ABP: £64.

Hammer: £55

2646

Pilkington Royal Lancastrian vase, decorated by Wm. S. Mycock, painted with simple plant forms, streaky red and yellow ground, imp'd and painted marks, 6in high. Golding Young & Co, Grantham. Feb 06. HP: £55. ABP: £64.

2647

Royal Doulton miniature figurine 'Pantalettes' (M31), damage to bonnet. A F Brock & Co Ltd, Stockport. Nov 05. HP: £55. ABP: £64.

2648

Ruskin Pottery vase, pink lustre glaze, impressed RUSKIN ENGLAND 1921, 4in high. Golding Young & Co, Grantham. Feb 06. HP: £55. ABP: £64.

2649

Royal Doulton figure of Sir Winston Churchill, HN3057, modelled by Adrian Hughes, 10in high. Golding Young & Co, Grantham. Feb 06. HP: £55. ABP: £64.

2650

Goebel Norman Rockwell figure, depicting a boy and a dog No. 202. Great Western Auctions, Glasgow. Mar 07. HP: £55. ABP: £64.

2651

Susie Cooper vase, lower body moulded and incised with abstract foliage, green glaze, script signature, 5in high. Golding Young & Co, Grantham. Feb 06. HP: £55. ABP: £64.

2652

Winchcombe pottery slipware dish, decorated internally with dark brown swirls & stripes ochre ground, impressed seal marks, 9in wide. Golding Young & Co, Grantham. Feb 06. HP: £55. ABP: £64.

2653

Beswick Arthur Gredington model of a beagle Wendover Billy and a Hummel model of a spaniel. Gorringes, Bexhill. Feb 06. HP: £55. ABP: £64.

2654

Reginald Wells jar, heavily pitted grey glaze, running pink over the grey, incised initial mark and impressed Chelsea, 5in high. Golding Young & Co, Grantham. Feb 06. HP: £55. ABP: £64.

2655

Bulmer terracotta vase, slip decorated, dark brown ground, signed M E BULMER OCT 1949, 6in high. Golding Young & Co, Grantham. Feb 06. HP: £55. ABP: £64.

2656

Carlton Ware Rouge Royale vase, enamelled and gilt with a spider's web, butterflies and vegetation, 7in high. Golding Young & Co, Grantham. Feb 06. HP: £55. ABP: £64. 56. Ilkley. Aug 06. HP: £55. ABP: £64.

> The illustrations are in descending price order. The price range is indicated at the top of each page.

2657

Royal Crown Derby porcelain vase, double spouted form, scroll moulded loop handle, painted/gilded with flowers, 7.5in high. Hartleys, Ilkley. Aug 06. HP: £55. ABP: £64.

2658

Art Deco pottery vase, by Crown Devon, frilled rim, reeded body, semi circular lug handles, painted in green and cream, gilt embellished, 9in high. Hartleys, Ilkley. Aug 06. HP: £55. ABP: £64.

2659

Royal Copenhagen figure of a girl sewing. Great Western Auctions, Glasgow. Nov 05. HP: £55. ABP: £64.

2660

Carlton ware paradise bird ginger jar. Great Western Auctions, Glasgow. Oct 05. HP: £55. ABP: £64.

2661

Rye Hop Ware bowl, applied with green hops and leaves with tendrils, c1900, incised mark to base, 'Rye', af, 18cm dia. Gorringes, Bexhill. Dec 05. HP: £55. ABP: £64.

2662

Pair of Staffordshire pottery cow creamers, gilt horns and orange/brown patches, 12.5cm high. (2) Rosebery's, London. Apr 07. HP: £55. ABP: £64.

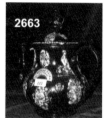

2663

Victorian Bargeware brown treacle polychrome glazed teapot, floral/bird decoration, 'A present from a friend', 33cm. Reeman Dansie, Colchester. Apr 06. HP: £55. ABP: £64.

Late 18th/early 19thC cream-ware cruet, with sugar castor and oil jar printed in black with initials 'J.C.' to one side and 'A.B.' to reverse, 8.75in high, restored. Canterbury Auction Galleries, Kent. Feb 06. HP: £55. ABP: £64.

Clarice Cliff anemone pattern dish. Great Western Auctions, Glasgow. Aug 06. HP: £55. ABP: £64.

Royal Doulton figurine 'Lady Charmian' HN 1949. Boldon Auction Galleries, Tyne & Wear. Sep 05. HP: £55. ABP: £64.

Set of 5 Royal Doulton series ware plates, Admiral D6278, Jester D 6277, Parson D6280, Doctor D6281 and Squire D6284, 26cm. Boldon Auction Galleries, Tyne & Wear. Sep 05. HP: £55. ABP: £64.

Majolica Stilton dish and cover. Gorringes, Bexhill. Oct 05. HP: £55. ABP: £64.

Early 19thC silver lustre baluster jug, 19cm. Reeman Dansie, Colchester. Apr 06. HP: £54. ABP: £63.

Poole red earthenware vase designed by Truda Carter, painted by Ruth Pavely Vase 424/Co, c1930 approx 5 x 6.5in deep. Kent Auction Galleries, Folkestone. May 07. HP: £52. ABP: £61.

Pair of 19thC Staffordshire seated lions, 3in high. S/D. Black Country Auctions, Dudley. Sep 05. HP: £52. ABP: £61.

Ringtons Maling blue chintz pattern tea pot. Boldon Auction Galleries, Tyne & Wear. Sep 05. HP: £52. ABP: £61.

Bretby pottery vase, pink metallic spatter glaze over red, impressed mark No. 1938F, 10in high. Golding Young & Co, Grantham. Feb 06. HP: £50. ABP: £58.

Border Fine Arts group of a Border Collie and puppies. Great Western Auctions, Glasgow. Apr 06. HP: £50. ABP: £58.

Ruskin pottery ginger jar and cover, crazed yellow lustre body, trailing vine decoration, imp'd mark to base, RUSKIN 11 POTTERY, 8in high. Golding Young & Co, Grantham. Feb 06. HP: £50. ABP: £58.

Rosenthal figure of a hound, 4in. Ewbank Auctioneers, Send, Surrey. Dec 05. HP: £50. ABP: £58.

Victorian Prattware pot lid, The Listener, 3in dia, framed. Golding Young & Co, Grantham. Feb 06. HP: £50. ABP: £58.

Winchcombe pottery terra-cotta jug, baluster, inscribed 'WINCHCOMBE', buff/brown slip glazes, impressed seal mark, 8in high. Golding Young & Co, Grantham. Feb 06. HP: £50. ABP: £58.

Clarice Cliff handpainted square dish, 4.75in and a Carlton Ware Australian design yellow flower plate, 6in dia, crazing throughout & some discolouration. A F Brock & Co Ltd, Stockport. Feb 07. HP: £50. ABP: £58.

Royal Doulton Titanian Ware vase, turquoise glaze, 2in high. Golding Young & Co, Grantham. Feb 06. HP: £50. ABP: £58.

Beswick charolais calf and a Palomino foal. Great Western Auctions, Glasgow. Feb 06. HP: £50. ABP: £58.

Royal Doulton figure Sheila, HN2742, 9in high. Ewbank Auctioneers, Send, Surrey. Dec 05. HP: £50. ABP: £58.

Burmantofts Faience wall plate, moulded in low relief, painted with blossom, blue ground, imp'd mark, model No. 96, 10in dia. Golding Young & Co, Grantham. Feb 06. HP: £50. ABP: £58.

Hammer: £50

2684

19thC Staffordshire pottery figure group of a cow and farm hand, moulded base, 8in high. Golding Young & Co, Grantham. Feb 06. HP: £50. ABP: £58.

2685

Pair of 19thC Staffordshire pottery spaniels, coats with iron red splashes, gilt collar and chain, 9in high, one with damaged base. Golding Young & Co, Grantham. Feb 06. HP: £50. ABP: £58.

2686

Pair of Dresden poodles. Great Western Auctions, Glasgow. Aug 05. HP: £50. ABP: £58.

2687

Beswick pottery wall face mask, Lady with a beret, model No. 277, issued between 1934 and 1954, 4in high. Golding Young & Co, Grantham. Feb 06. HP: £50. ABP: £58.

2688

Bells pottery bowl in Burns pattern. Great Western Auctions, Glasgow. Jan 07. HP: £50. ABP: £58.

2689

Royal Doulton figure of the year 1996, Belle HN3703. Kent Auction Galleries, Folkestone. Jun 06. HP: £50. ABP: £58.

2690

Samson figure, late 19thC, boy wearing a sash/garland carrying a basket of flowers, rococo scroll base. Rosebery's, London. May 06. HP: £50. ABP: £58.

> Categories or themes can be followed through the colour coded Index which contains over 4500 cross references.

2691

Staffordshire pottery figure, Scotsman, 11in high, and a spill vase with a girl, boy and goat, 19thC, 7.25in high. Hartleys, Ilkley. Aug 06. HP: £50. ABP: £58.

2692

Maling plate depicting a water wheel. Great Western Auctions, Glasgow. Jun 06. HP: £50. ABP: £58.

2693

Royal Winton summertime chintz wall pocket. Great Western Auctions, Glasgow. Jul 06. HP: £50. ABP: £58.

2694

Early 19thC blue/white pearlware tazza, printed with a family at play in a cottage garden, 8.5in wide, 3.25in high. Golding Young & Co, Grantham. Nov 06. HP: £50. ABP: £58.

2695

Beswick model, shire horse in grey dapple. Golding Young & Co, Grantham. Nov 06. HP: £50. ABP: £58.

2696

Large blue/white meat plate, central scene of deer, flower border, marked Rogers. Sandwich Auction Rooms, Kent. Dec 05. HP: £50. ABP: £58.

2697

Hereford china figure of an archer, made to commemorate the 300th anniversary of the founding of the Royal Company of Archers. Great Western Auctions, Glasgow. Jan 07. HP: £50. ABP: £58.

2698

Pair of Royal Doulton flambé penguins, 6in. Gorringes, Lewes. Feb 06. HP: £50. ABP: £58.

2699

Royal Worcester blush ivory jug, heightened in gilt, 1907, pattern No. 1094. Gorringes, Bexhill. Feb 06. HP: £50. ABP: £58.

2700

19thC Staffordshire pen holder in the form of a Grey Hound with dead hare by its feet, 5in high. Ewbank Auctioneers, Send, Surrey. Dec 05. HP: £50. ABP: £58.

2701

Royal Doulton figure, Janine HN 2461. Ewbank Auctioneers, Send, Surrey. Dec 05. HP: £50. ABP: £58.

2702

Maling Peony rose ginger jar. Great Western Auctions, Glasgow. Feb 06. HP: £50. ABP: £58.

2703

Pair Royal Worcester figure groups of boys and girls, by tree stumps, 6.25in. Ewbank Auctioneers, Send, Surrey. Dec 05. HP: £50. ABP: £58.

2704

Three early 19thC dinner plates, 9.75in dia, with a matching dish, 8.5 x 6.5in, Imari palette, with an early 19thC saucer, hand painted with a naive animal to centre within a silver lustre and red scroll work surround. (5) Dee, Atkinson & Harrison, Driffield. Feb 06. HP: £50. ABP: £58.

2705

Royal Doulton stoneware jardiniere applied with a windmill, toping and hunting scenes, 9in wide. Hartleys, Ilkley. Dec 06. HP: £50. ABP: £58.

2706

20thC Wedgwood creamware pot pourri, rope-twist handles, 8.75in high. Dee, Atkinson & Harrison, Driffield. Feb 06. HP: £50. ABP: £58.

2707

Beswick figurine, Pheasant, black circular back stamp, imp'd Beswick England 1774, 8.5 x 4.5in high. Kent Auction Galleries, Folkestone. Mar 06. HP: £50. ABP: £58.

2708

Carlton ware wall pocket, as a yellow flowerhead with bud and foliage, imp'd number 1746, 10.25in. Dee, Atkinson & Harrison, Driffield. Feb 06. HP: £50. ABP: £58.

2709

Macintyre Aurelian ware teapot, printed/painted with iron red flowers within long blue leaves, gilt embellished, 7.75in wide. Hartleys, Ilkley. Dec 06. HP: £50. ABP: £58.

2710

Clarice Cliff vase. Orpington Salerooms, Kent. Nov 05. HP: £50. ABP: £58.

2711

Clarice Cliff Bizarre plate. Orpington Salerooms, Kent. Nov 05. HP: £50. ABP: £58.

2712

Clarice Cliff cornucopia vase. Great Western Auctions, Glasgow. Nov 05. HP: £50. ABP: £58.

Hammer: £50

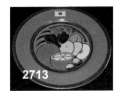

2713

Grays pottery plate, painted with fruit within banded borders. Great Western Auctions, Glasgow. Mar 07. HP: £50. ABP: £58.

2714

Beswick wall mask modelled as a young girl. Great Western Auctions, Glasgow. Mar 07. HP: £50. ABP: £58.

2715

Carlton Ware hydrangea hors d'oeuvre dish. Great Western Auctions, Glasgow. Feb 06. HP: £50. ABP: £58.

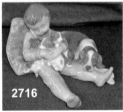

2716

Lladro figure of a sleeping boy with dog and puppies. Great Western Auctions, Glasgow. Nov 05. HP: £50. ABP: £58.

2717

Mid/late 19thC Derby miniature pot pourri, pierced lid with gilded knop and body, Imari palette, 6.5cm. Locke & England, Leamington Spa. Mar 06. HP: £50. ABP: £58.

2718

Wemyss tray, large rose design, c1910. Aladdins Cave Auction, Danehill, Sussex. Mar 06. HP: £50. ABP: £58.

2719

Royal Doulton figure 'Autumn Breezes', HN1934. Great Western Auctions, Glasgow. Feb 06. HP: £50. ABP: £58.

2720

Royal Doulton figure, Masque, HN 2330. Gorringes, Lewes. Apr 06. HP: £50. ABP: £58.

2721

Crown Devon Auld Lang Syne musical jug. Great Western Auctions, Glasgow. Aug 06. HP: £50. ABP: £58.

2722

Pair of Royal Stanley vases, decorated flowers, 25.5cm. Charterhouse Auctioneers, Sherborne. Sep 06. HP: £50. ABP: £58.

Hammer: £50

Wedgwood blue jasper-ware jardiniere, fruiting vine garlands suspended on lion mask heads, classical male and female figures, 9in dia x 8.25in high. Dee, Atkinson & Harrison, Driffield. Sep 06. HP: £50. ABP: £58.

Worcester style dish, shaped square form, painted by Moseley with peaches and grapes, signed, 4.75in wide, impressed 'W 4M7' mark. Hartleys, Ilkley. Oct 06. HP: £50. ABP: £58.

Majolica jardiniere with variously coloured bands of decoration, blue body, 35cm high, af. Rosebery's, London. Oct 06. HP: £50. ABP: £58.

Small Royal Doulton kitten licking a back paw. (2580). Boldon Auction Galleries, Tyne & Wear. Sep 05. HP: £50. ABP: £58.

Pair of Dresden porcelain hand painted woodpeckers on naturalistic bases, printed mark to bases, 28cm high, af. Rosebery's, London. Oct 06. HP: £50. ABP: £58.

19thC Chinese porcelain blue/white bird feeder, painted with 2 scrolling bands, flowers & foliage, 9.5cm wide, af. Rosebery's, London. Oct 06. HP: £50. ABP: £58.

19thC Chinese dish, centre with a dragon painted in iron red, underside painted with dragons, blue painted mark to base, 21.5cm dia, af. Rosebery's, London. Oct 06. HP: £50. ABP: £58.

Pair Royal Worcester 'Blue Dragon' jars/covers. Great Western Auctions, Glasgow. Oct 05. HP: £50. ABP: £58.

Victorian majolica rabbit. Orpington Salerooms, Kent. Sep 06. HP: £50. ABP: £58.

Carlton Ware 'New Mikado' rouge royale jar and cover. Great Western Auctions, Glasgow. Sep 05. HP: £50. ABP: £58.

Locke & Co jardiniere, hexagonal form, leaf-moulded & painted with floral sprigs, six shallow feet, 5.5in high x 6in dia. Dee, Atkinson & Harrison, Driffield. Sep 06. HP: £50. ABP: £58.

Royal Doulton 'Hilary', HN2335. Black Country Auctions, Dudley. Oct 05. HP: £50. ABP: £58.

> **Prices quoted are actual hammer prices (HP) and the Approximate Buyer's Price (ABP) includes an average premium of 15% + VAT.**

Gouda 'Purdah' jug. Great Western Auctions, Glasgow. Sep 05. HP: £50. ABP: £58.

Hummel figurine, girl with blue watering can, 6.25in high. Dee, Atkinson & Harrison, Driffield. Sep 05. HP: £50. ABP: £58.

Nao figure of a dancer. Great Western Auctions, Glasgow. Sep 05. HP: £50. ABP: £58.

1930s Shelley earthenware vase, with green/grey bands, 20.5cm. Locke & England, Leamington Spa. Sep 05. HP: £50. ABP: £58.

34 piece Minton 'Haddon Hall' part dinner and tea service. Boldon Auction Galleries, Tyne & Wear. Sep 05. HP: £50. ABP: £58.

Ringtons Maling blue chintz pattern hot water jug. Boldon Auction Galleries, Tyne & Wear. Sep 05. HP: £50. ABP: £58.

Carlton Ware dish decorated with multicoloured flowers, orange lustre background, 25.5cm (0/2298, 3478). Boldon Auction Galleries, Tyne & Wear. Sep 05. HP: £50. ABP: £58.

Boxed royal Crown Derby flat cake dish, Imari pattern, 28cm. Boldon Auction Galleries, Tyne & Wear. Sep 05. HP: £50. ABP: £58.

Clarice Cliff, Bonjour teapot and sugar bowl, concentric bands of blue/brown, printed registration mark only, No.776243. Cheffins, Cambridge. Apr 05. HP: £50. ABP: £58.

2 Carlton Ware 1960s cube condiment sets of 3 pieces on stands, one in red the other lime. Boldon Auction Galleries, Tyne & Wear. Sep 05. HP: £50. ABP: £58.

Belleek basket, encrusted with flowers, serrated rim, black Co Fermanagh mark, feet ground down, 3.5in high. Dee, Atkinson & Harrison, Driffield. Sep 05. HP: £50. ABP: £58.

Carter Stabler & Adams Poole Pottery Bowl, stylised geometric patterns, crazed, 27cm dia. Charterhouse Auctioneers, Sherborne. Jun 05. HP: £50. ABP: £58.

Sevres porcelain plate, painted with an Inn scene, imbibing seated figures, blue and gilt border, indistinctly signed, 9.5in. Dee, Atkinson & Harrison, Driffield. Sep 05. HP: £50. ABP: £58.

New Hall blue/white tea bowl and saucer, printed with crooked tree pattern. Cheffins, Cambridge. Apr 05. HP: £50. ABP: £58.

Kevin Francis Toby jug of Sandra Kuck, No. 33/600 and another, Martha Gunn No. 30/100. Gorringes, Bexhill. Jun 05. HP: £50. ABP: £58.

Late 19thC Imari charger, 12in dia. Dee, Atkinson & Harrison, Driffield. Sep 05. HP: £50. ABP: £58.

Pair of Staffordshire Pottery spill vases, 20cm. Charterhouse Auctioneers, Sherborne. Jun 05. HP: £50. ABP: £58.

Hammer: £50

Late 19thC Fairing 'Three O'Clock in the Morning', 3.5in high. Dee, Atkinson & Harrison, Driffield. Sep 05. HP: £50. ABP: £58.

18thC creamware plate, painted with a flower spray at centre, ribbed border with blue dash to rim, 9.75in. Gorringes, Lewes. Apr 05. HP: £50. ABP: £58.

Beswick pottery boar 'Wall Champion Boy 53rd' and a sow 'Champion Wall Queen 40th', white gloss finish. Locke & England, Leamington Spa. Sep 05. HP: £50. ABP: £58.

Delftware blue and white bowl. Gorringes, Bexhill. Oct 05. HP: £50. ABP: £58.

Chinese twin-handled vase and planter. Gorringes, Bexhill. Oct 05. HP: £50. ABP: £58.

Wilkinsons crocus pattern jug. Great Western Auctions, Glasgow. Oct 05. HP: £50. ABP: £58.

Pair 19thC pottery Staffordshire dogs, white glaze with gilt embellishment, glass eyes, 13in high. Dee, Atkinson & Harrison, Driffield. Sep 05. HP: £50. ABP: £58.

Doulton Lambeth stoneware miniature jug and another Doulton silicon jug, 13cm high. Gorringes, Bexhill. Jun 05. HP: £50. ABP: £58.

Royal Stanley ware biscuit ware, Jacobean pattern, with trailing fruiting vines and fruits, wicker swing handle, 6.5in high and wedge-shaped blue/white cheese dish, transfer printed exotic birds and flowers. Dee, Atkinson & Harrison, Driffield. Sep 05. HP: £50. ABP: £58.

Keith Murray for Wedgwood, conical Moonstone vase, shape No.3753, banded decoration, printed facsimile signature, 14cm high. Cheffins, Cambridge. Apr 05. HP: £50. ABP: £58.

Section VIII: Under £50

'With the HN Series alone approaching 5,000, the number of figurines in the market place must run into millions.....Chintz was a one year wonder but the toast rack at 2771 is highly decorative and useful.....This is a rare barrel-shaped body from c1780 and £100-£200 is much nearer the mark if in good condition...'

There are about 330 lots in this final Section. At under £50 hammer there will always be mixed lots and these have been eliminated from the Section as they offer no guide to values. My advice is never buy mixed lots if you are a collector, unless there is a hidden gem somewhere, and this is most unlikely. A glance at the pages here, compared to any other Section should warn the reader off. When you buy in this price range you are almost certainly, in the main, unlikely to sell on at much profit and almost certainly, you can expect little or no investment potential, even in the longer term. This said there is at least 5% of lots here which I consider worthwhile buys, but more of these later.

Let us look for the last time at Doulton figurines. We can start at *Edith*, HN2802 on page 64, which fetched £51 at auction despite having a Charlton price of £225. The list goes on: *Denise, May, Michele, Dreamweaver, Linda, Dick Turpin, Home Again, First Dance, Hilary, Christine* and so on, most made in the last twenty years or recently and many re-issued over extended periods. With the HN Series alone approaching 5,000, the number of figurines in the market place must run into millions. When I occasionally visit collectors' fairs I am staggered and amazed by the sheer numbers - death from a thousand figurines! Auction prices can in some cases average about a third to a quarter of the Charlton prices which must tell us something. Many collectors of figurines of course are buying new, and with modern production costs and taxes they are not cheap, whether produced by Doulton, Coalport, Worcester and so on. As a consequence the market is flooded because it is daily being supplied with more and more figurines! Where is it all going to end? There is now production and reproduction on a massive scale and it has completely infiltrated the lower end of the antiques and collectors' market, with disastrous consequences.

Almost as common in this price range is the lower end of the art pottery market. There are examples on page after page and most are selling only for their decorative value. Better to save until you can buy in the higher ranges and preferably at least over a £100.

Now for my suggestions for potential good buys in this price range. Chintz was a one year wonder but I think the Royal Winton chintz toast rack at **2771** is highly decorative and useful. Add the Goebel parrot, (**2769**) as an idea of course, something like the Paragon *Lady Melanie* at **2776** or a Beswick *Kingfisher*, or a Radford's butterfly ware jug, **2920** or the Charlotte Rhead Crown Ducal jug at **2962** and serve your breakfast tea from something like the Royal Winton chintz teapot at **2843** and your breakfasts or teas could be full of exciting colours and shapes. But this is not collecting as such, rather using second-hand goods to brighten up a period living space.

Collectors would be interested in the eighteenth century polychrome teapot at **2833** with chinoiserie decoration. This is a rare barrel-shaped body from c1780 and £100-£200 is much nearer the mark if in good condition. The eighteenth century delft dish or bowl is also quite rare. Plates survive in their thousands because of course they were mass produced but this bowl is worth a lot more than £47. I've a feeling the Staffordshire *Nelson* at **2906** is a reproduction but the blue and white pearlware plates with wild rose pattern at **2935** are not and at £17.50 each, a real snip.

It is a pity about the condition of the Clarice Cliff ginger jar at **2932** but I would buy it because, at getting on for 8 inches high, this will still make an important statement, say in a bedroom, and of course an important talking point. This is the real thing!

On page 171 is the last Maling entry at **2938** and this is just the the kind of Maling that has seen a price collapse. There are about a dozen Maling entries in these pages commencing at about £200. I love the pair of art deco pottery book ends at **2995**. They are genuine, absolutely right, rare and useful and well under-priced at under £30. Another delft plate, this time painted with a rare coastal scene, appears at **2997** and only £29. If damaged fair enough, but if not this is worth a £100 to the specialist collector. The four stoneware flagons at **3014** are again a snip at about £5 each and have great decorative appeal in a kitchen setting. The same applies to the stoneware jugs at **3030** and the right-hand one could be late Georgian. I would have needed a closer look at the Naples figures at **3035** but something must be amiss when they sell for only £23, and I must assume the blanc-de-chine figure at **3043** is a reproduction.

If the Welsh woman at **3044** is a reproduction then the pearlware huntsman is not. Pearlware has never been reproduced and this figure could be worth at least £100 or more. The same may be said of the pearlware bowl at **3064**. Again early bowls are uncommon and this one should have raised at least £50-£100. Check out the absurdly low price for the Victoria and George V mugs at **3055** but also consider they can be found in most retail situations and they do not fly out the door nowadays.

Moorcroft dish, Hibiscus pattern. 7in dia. Black Country Auctions, Dudley. Dec 05. HP: £48. ABP: £56.

St Ives pottery bowl, dark brown abstract motifs, faint blue lines against a neutral speckled ground, seal mark, 5in dia. Golding Young & Co, Grantham. Feb 06. HP: £48. ABP: £56.

Royal Doulton Character jug, Lord Kitchener, modelled by David Biggs, No. D7148, Ltd Edn 1136/1500, 7in high. Golding Young & Co, Grantham. Feb 06. HP: £48. ABP: £56.

Late Victorian R. Worcester porcelain white glazed figure of a monk, painted features, green printed mark, 6.5in high. Diamond Mills & Co, Felixstowe. Jun 06. HP: £48. ABP: £56.

Denby Danesby Ware pottery table ornament of rabbits on giant mushrooms, matt turquoise tinted glaze, 7in high. Golding Young & Co, Grantham. Nov 06. HP: £48. ABP: £56.

MacIntyre jug, decorated with flowers. Great Western Auctions, Glasgow. Feb 07. HP: £48. ABP: £56.

Beswick Friesian calf. Great Western Auctions, Glasgow. Mar 07. HP: £48. ABP: £56.

Goebel Parrot. Great Western Auctions, Glasgow. Feb 06. HP: £46. ABP: £54.

Noritake dish, painted with a landscape. Great Western Auctions, Glasgow. Oct 05. HP: £45. ABP: £52.

Royal Winton 'Somerset' chintz toast rack. Great Western Auctions, Glasgow. Oct 05. HP: £45. ABP: £52.

Royal Doulton, Under the Greenwood Tree series ware footed bowl. Gorringes, Bexhill. Oct 05. HP: £45. ABP: £52.

Hammer: £48 - £45

Reg Johnston studio pottery model of Falstaff. Gorringes, Bexhill. Oct 05. HP: £45. ABP: £52.

Late 19thC oval Imari dish, centre hand painted with an urn with flowers, foliate border & similar plate, 11in and 8.5in. (2) Dee, Atkinson & Harrison, Driffield. Feb 06. HP: £45. ABP: £52.

The numbering system acts as a reader reference as well as linking to the Analysis of each section.

Royal Crown Derby Imari-patterned owl, 11.5cm high. Gorringes, Bexhill. Feb 06. HP: £45. ABP: £52.

Paragon figure 'Lady Melanie'. Great Western Auctions, Glasgow. Jan 07. HP: £45. ABP: £52.

Royal Doulton, Airedale terrier (HN1023), rear right leg has been repaired. A F Brock & Co Ltd, Stockport. Nov 05. HP: £45. ABP: £52.

Corona Ware 'Cherry Ripe' jug. Great Western Auctions, Glasgow. Nov 05. HP: £45. ABP: £52.

Clarice Cliff Bamboo sandwich set. Black Country Auctions, Dudley. Dec 05. HP: £45. ABP: £52.

Pair of Doulton cauldron shaped vases, with 3 handles. Ewbank, Send, Surrey. Dec 05. HP: £45. ABP: £52.

Beswick male lion, mouth open, brown gloss, No.2089, issued 1967-1984, 14cm tall. Batemans, Stamford. Mar 06. HP: £45. ABP: £52.

Pilkington Royal Lancastrian shallow bowl, deep orange spatter glaz, yellow ground, imp'd factory mark, 3in high, 12in dia. Golding Young & Co, Grantham. Feb 06. HP: £45. ABP: £52.

Stoneware three handled tyg, English 19th/20thC, moulded with hunting and carousing figures, handles formed as greyhounds, 17.5cm high. Rosebery's, London. Jan 06. HP: £45. ABP: £52.

Elton terracotta double Gourd small vase, green streaky glaze, 3in high. Golding Young & Co, Grantham. Feb 06. HP: £45. ABP: £52.

Susie Cooper pottery vase, ribbed neck, pale green glaze, incised signature and No. 499, 9in high. Golding Young & Co, Grantham. Feb 06. HP: £45. ABP: £52.

Pair of Coalport blue-scale and gilt cabinet plates, with cartouches of exotic birds and flora, 9.25in dia. (2) Dee, Atkinson & Harrison, Driffield. Jul 06. HP: £45. ABP: £52.

Matched pair Brannam Royal Barum ware vases, deep yellow slip glazes, imp'd marks to one, 9in. Golding Young & Co, Grantham. Feb 06. HP: £45. ABP: £52.

Royal Doulton series ware plate titled 'Blood Money'. Great Western Auctions, Glasgow. Jul 06. HP: £45. ABP: £52.

Candy Ware pottery jardiniere, blue lustre mottled glaze shading to brown, 9in high, 14in dia. Golding Young & Co, Grantham. Feb 06. HP: £45. ABP: £52.

Plant Tuscan figure 'Marigold'. Great Western Auctions, Glasgow. Sep 06. HP: £45. ABP: £52.

Beswick figure of a Swish Tail Horse, first version, model No. 1182, grey gloss, by Arthur Gredington, 8in high. Golding Young & Co, Grantham. Feb 06. HP: £45. ABP: £52.

Carlton Ware Rouge Royale water jug, oval panelled form, enamelled/gilt with Chinese landscapes, 7in high. Golding Young & Co, Grantham. Feb 06. HP: £45. ABP: £52.

Victorian Prattware pot lid, 'Pegwell Bay', 4in dia, framed. Golding Young & Co, Grantham. Feb 06. HP: £45. ABP: £52.

Royal Worcester figure 'Friday's child is loving and giving', young child sitting with a robin, 15cm high, black printed mark to base. Rosebery's, London. Aug 06. HP: £45. ABP: £52.

> The illustrations are in descending price order. The price range is indicated at the top of each page.

Crown Devon two handled vase No.2551. Great Western Auctions, Glasgow. Aug 06. HP: £45. ABP: £52.

Poole charger, Aegean pattern, 13.5in. Dee, Atkinson & Harrison, Driffield. Sep 06. HP: £45. ABP: £52.

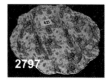

Royal Winton 'Welbeck' chintz nut dish. Great Western Auctions, Glasgow. Jan 07. HP: £45. ABP: £52.

Beswick Horse figurine, stallion, brown gloss with white glaze. Kent Auction Galleries, Folkestone. Dec 06. HP: £45. ABP: £52.

Doulton Lambeth brown glazed head of Lloyd George in the form of a stamp dampener. Great Western Auctions, Glasgow. Mar 07. HP: £45. ABP: £52.

Two Wemyss pieces, a dish with mark for R. Heron and Son and a vase with imp'd and painted mark, def. Great Western Auctions, Glasgow. Mar 07. HP: £45. ABP: £52.

Crown Devon Mattita bowl, depicting a sailing ship. Great Western Auctions, Glasgow. Sep 06. HP: £45. ABP: £52.

Royal Doulton figure, Edith, HN2957. Orpington Salerooms, Kent. Nov 05. HP: £44. ABP: £51.

2803

Royal Doulton Series ware jug, Wedlocks Joys Do Sometimes Change. Black Country Auctions, Dudley. Dec 05. HP: £44. ABP: £51.

2804

Royal Doulton 'Denise', HN2477. Black Country Auctions, Dudley. Oct 05. HP: £42. ABP: £49.

2805

Carlton Ware New Mikado vase. Great Western Auctions, Glasgow. Apr 06. HP: £42. ABP: £49.

2806

Burmantofts vase, incised with starbursts, deep yellow body, imp'd monogram, shape No. 236, 6in high. Golding Young & Co, Grantham. Feb 06. HP: £42. ABP: £49.

2807

Victorian Prattware pot lid, children by a chicken coop, 4in dia, framed. Golding Young & Co, Grantham. Feb 06. HP: £42. ABP: £49.

2808

Beswick Kingfisher No. 2371. Kent Auction Galleries, Folkestone. Nov 06. HP: £42. ABP: £49.

2809

Brannam for Liberty, green glaze jug, neck with three applied twist handles, imp'd C H BRANNAM BARUM. N. DEVON MADE FOR LIBERTY CO. 14in. Golding Young & Co, Grantham. Feb 06. HP: £42. ABP: £49.

2810

Royal Winton 'Tartans' cup and saucer. Great Western Auctions, Glasgow. Jun 06. HP: £42. ABP: £49.

2811

Candy Ware pottery vase, green streaky glaze over a buff body, 14in high. Golding Young & Co, Grantham. Feb 06. HP: £42. ABP: £49.

2812

Dunmore Pottery 2-handled vase, conical neck, body with a three-line girdle, glazed in pale blue, imp'd DUNMORE, 5in high. Golding Young & Co, Grantham. Feb 06. HP: £42. ABP: £49.

Hammer: £44 - £40

2813

R. Doulton Figurine Rupert's Silver Trumpet, RB8. Kent Auction Galleries, Folkestone. Dec 06. HP: £42. ABP: £49.

2814

St Ives stoneware coffee pot/ cover, ribbed form, dished cover, loop handles, brown streaky glaze, seal mark, 7in high. Golding Young & Co, Grantham. Feb 06. HP: £42. ABP: £49.

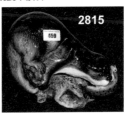

2815

Sylvac otter figure, No. 5459. Great Western Auctions, Glasgow. Mar 07. HP: £42. ABP: £49.

2816

Sarreguemines majolica basket, diced brown glazed overhead handle, moulded with lilac foxgloves & green foliage, imp'd factory marks, 11in wide. Golding Young & Co, Grantham. Feb 06. HP: £42. ABP: £49.

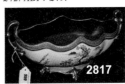

2817

Carlton Ware Gondola shape bowl with Oriental scene. Great Western Auctions, Glasgow. Feb 07. HP: £42. ABP: £49.

2818

Matched set of 3 graduated Royal Doulton stoneware jugs, applied with topers, huntsman, hounds and trees, reeded handles, 6in, 5.5in, 4.25in. Golding Young & Co, Grantham. Nov 06. HP: £42. ABP: £49.

2819

Carlton Ware handcraft candlestick. Great Western Auctions, Glasgow. Oct 05. HP: £40. ABP: £47.

2820

Royal Stanley tulip bowl. Great Western Auctions, Glasgow. Oct 05. HP: £40. ABP: £47.

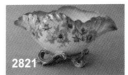

2821

Moore Bros posy bowl. Gorringes, Bexhill. Oct 05. HP: £40. ABP: £47.

2822

Crown Devon, Memphis pattern vase, designed by Colin Melbourne, bands of geometric gilding on powder blue ground, 21.5cm. Locke & England, Leamington Spa. Mar 06. HP: £40. ABP: £47.

Hammer: £40

C H Brannam of Barnstaple, green-glazed pottery lemonade set and various ramekins and dishes. Gorringes, Bexhill. Oct 05. HP: £40. ABP: £47.

Charlotte Rhead Little Boy Blue bowl. 7.5in dia. Black Country Auctions, Dudley. Dec 05. HP: £40. ABP: £47.

Pair of Wucai style Zodiac figures, Chinese 19thC, each with human body and animal head, six character mark to the reverses, faults, 15cm high. Rosebery's, London. Jan 06. HP: £40. ABP: £47.

Royal Doulton Slaters Patent jardiniere, No. 3110, signed R H, 19cm high, 23.5cm dia. Gorringes, Bexhill. Feb 06. HP: £40. ABP: £47.

Two Lladro figures of girls holding baskets of flowers, 6.5in high. Ewbank Auctioneers, Send, Surrey. Dec 05. HP: £40. ABP: £47.

Troika pottery marmalade pot c1970s, moulded textured body, abstract design, painted in greens & browns, painted 'Troika' and initials AB to underside, 9cm high. Rosebery's, London. Mar 06. HP: £40. ABP: £47.

Royal Crown Derby dish. Great Western Auctions, Glasgow. Mar 06. HP: £40. ABP: £47.

> Categories or themes can be followed through the colour coded Index which contains over 4500 cross references.

Copeland Spode pottery jar/ cover, imp'd Copeland mark, flowers & leaf decoration, 3in approx. Kent Auction Galleries, Folkestone. Mar 06. HP: £40. ABP: £47.

Ault & Tuncliffe pottery vase, pale blue and yellow streaky glaze, darker blue ground, imp'd Aultcliffe, 8in high. Golding Young & Co, Grantham. Feb 06. HP: £40. ABP: £47.

Poole pottery Ginger jar, duck egg blue speckled glaze, incised mark 6M to underside and cover, 5in high. Golding Young & Co, Grantham. Feb 06. HP: £40. ABP: £47.

18thC English teapot, female figures in Chinese manner. Locke & England, Leamington Spa. Nov 06. HP: £40. ABP: £47.

Doulton Burslem chamber pot, 'Melbourne', Rd No. 284101, c1896/97, 135mm high, 240mm in dia, blue & white with gilt trim, some gilt wearing off. A F Brock & Co Ltd, Stockport. Oct 06. HP: £40. ABP: £47.

Lilliput Lane cottages, Bow Cottage, Dial Cottage, Creel Cottage, Sunnyside, The Nutshell & Wellington Lodge, all with deeds/boxes. (6) A F Brock & Co Ltd, Stockport. Oct 06. HP: £40. ABP: £47.

Upchurch pottery vase, lightly ribbed, blue/grey matt glaze, imp'd mark, 6in high. Golding Young & Co, Grantham. Feb 06. HP: £40. ABP: £47.

19thC Staffordshire pink lustre bordered pottery plaque by Cockson & Chetwynd of Corbridge, printed in black 'God Thou Sees't Me', 6.75in dia, imp'd mark to reverse. Canterbury Auction Galleries, Kent. Oct 05. HP: £40. ABP: £47.

Dunmore Pottery pickle dish, leaf shape, loop handle, with green/brown streaky glaze, impressed DUNMORE, 2in high. Golding Young & Co, Grantham. Feb 06. HP: £40. ABP: £47.

R. Dux blue macaw figurine, pink applied triangle to base, imp'd 79. Kent Auction Galleries, Folkestone. Dec 06. HP: £40. ABP: £47.

St Ives Pottery bowl, green abstract plant forms and cream slip, seal marks for Sylvia Fox Strangways, 3in high, 5in dia. Golding Young & Co, Grantham. Feb 06. HP: £40. ABP: £47.

Burmantofts vase, frill edge neck, deep yellow ground, incised with small sun bursts, 6in high. Golding Young & Co, Grantham. Feb 06. HP: £40. ABP: £47.

2842

London School of Art pottery vase by E. Cooper, conical neck, incised with simple leaf forms and treacle glaze, 7in high. Golding Young & Co, Grantham. Feb 06. HP: £40. ABP: £47.

2843

Royal Winton Royalty chintz teapot. Great Western Auctions, Glasgow. Jun 06. HP: £40. ABP: £47.

2844

Winchcombe pottery jug, moulded neck, loop handle, brown streaky glaze, imp'd seal mark, 4in high. Golding Young & Co, Grantham. Feb 06. HP: £40. ABP: £47.

2845

Beswick kingfisher. Great Western Auctions, Glasgow. Aug 06. HP: £40. ABP: £47.

2846

Royal Doulton Romeo vase E7267. Great Western Auctions, Glasgow. Aug 06. HP: £40. ABP: £47.

2847

Naples porcelain trinket box, domed lid, gilt metal mount with shell shaped clasp, moulded and painted with figures and cherubs in relief on a gilded ground, 3.25in wide. Hartleys, Ilkley. Oct 06. HP: £40. ABP: £47.

2848

Brannam terracotta ink well, incised 'Don't forget to write', and flowers, cream ground, signed Brannam Barum 1908, 3in dia. Golding Young & Co, Grantham. Feb 06. HP: £40. ABP: £47.

2849

Vera Tollow pottery vase, moulded neck, slightly ribbed body, pink streaky glaze, 13in high. Golding Young & Co, Grantham. Feb 06. HP: £40. ABP: £47.

2850

Carlton Ware hexagonal dish, painted with shamrocks within faux panels, white ground, 9in wide. Golding Young & Co, Grantham. Feb 06. HP: £40. ABP: £47.

2851

Carlton Ware jug depicting dragonfly and waterlillies. Great Western Auctions, Glasgow. Aug 06. HP: £40. ABP: £47.

Hammer: £40

2852

Royal Doulton figure 'May' HN2746. Great Western Auctions, Glasgow. Sep 06. HP: £40. ABP: £47.

2853

Royal Doulton character jug 'Charlie Chaplin', modelled by Robert Tabbenor, Ltd Edn No. 434/3500, 4in high, with certificate. Golding Young & Co, Grantham. Feb 06. HP: £40. ABP: £47.

2854

Royal Worcester First Dance, 3629, mauve coloured dress & pink stole, 7in high. A F Brock & Co Ltd, Stockport. Feb 07. HP: £40. ABP: £47.

2855

Poole Pottery hors d'oeuvres dish, painted with floral posies, 8.5in wide, and a similar floral vase, 5.25in high. Hartleys, Ilkley. Aug 06. HP: £40. ABP: £47.

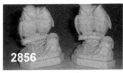

2856

Parian match striker, as two amorous owls perched on a branch, base inscribed Matchmaking, 7in high, & another example. (2) Golding Young & Co, Grantham. Feb 06. HP: £40. ABP: £47.

2857

Noritake pair of covered vases, Oriental Scenes, finials in form of roses, 8in high. Kent Auction Galleries, Folkestone. Aug 06. HP: £40. ABP: £47.

2858

R. Doulton Memories Kingsware water jug, moulded in relief with Dickens characters, 4in high. Golding Young & Co, Grantham. Feb 06. HP: £40. ABP: £47.

2859

Three pieces of Belleek china, vase of spiralling form with flared and shaped rim, 8.5cm high, cream jug, 9cm high, and a sugar bowl, 9.5cm dia, green marks to base. (3) Rosebery's, London. Apr 07. HP: £40. ABP: £47.

2860

Victorian Prattware pot lid, 'Royal Harbour, Ramsgate', 4in dia, framed. Golding Young & Co, Grantham. Feb 06. HP: £40. ABP: £47.

Hammer: £40 - £38

2861
Early 20thC Royal Doulton jardiniere, band of entwined floral swags on a mottled green ground, 20cm. Locke & England, Leamington Spa. Jul 06. HP: £40. ABP: £47.

2862
Fieldings Crown Devon musical mug, Widdicombe Fair, moulded in relief with Uncle Tom Cobley et al and painted with verse, 6in high. Golding Young & Co, Grantham. Nov 06. HP: £40. ABP: £47.

Prices quoted are actual hammer prices (HP) and the Approximate Buyer's Price (ABP) includes an average premium of 15% + VAT.

2863
18thC Delft dish, externally painted with simple Oriental landscapes, internally with a single flower, simple band rim, 10in dia. Golding Young & Co, Grantham. Nov 06. HP: £40. ABP: £47.

2864
Hummel figurines: 'Just Resting', 'Wayside Harmoney', one of girl sat in a tree, top of tree broken/repaired, and one of boy with a walking stick, all stamped Hummel, all 4in high. (4) A F Brock & Co Ltd, Stockport. Feb 07. HP: £40. ABP: £47.

2865
Longpark motto ware jug 'There would be no shadows if the sun were not shining'. Great Western Auctions, Glasgow. Mar 07. HP: £40. ABP: £47.

2866
Pearlware leaf pickle dish, blue printed with a pastoral scene, early 19thC, 5.25in wide. Hartleys, Ilkley. Apr 07. HP: £40. ABP: £47.

2867

Beswick pheasant 1774. Black Country Auctions, Dudley. Dec 05. HP: £38. ABP: £44.

2868

Royal Doulton, Mary Had A Little Lamb HN2048. Black Country Auctions, Dudley. Dec 05. HP: £38. ABP: £44.

2869

R. Doulton pottery character jug, 'Lord Nelson', 7.25in high, 6336. Canterbury Auction Galleries, Kent. Oct 05. HP: £38. ABP: £44.

2870

Wileman & Co Foley, Faience pottery vase, with yellow, brown/green streaky glazes, brown moulded ground, 5in high, incised No. 12015. Golding Young & Co, Grantham. Feb 06. HP: £38. ABP: £44.

2871

Hummel ashtray 'Happy Pastime' TM2. Great Western Auctions, Glasgow. Jun 06. HP: £38. ABP: £44.

2872

Ault pottery vase, yellow glaze, imp'd AULT ENGLAND 5, 9in high. Golding Young & Co, Grantham. Feb 06. HP: £38. ABP: £44.

2873

Satsuma bowl. Great Western Auctions, Glasgow. Feb 07. HP: £38. ABP: £44.

2874

Ricardia pottery vase, orange and red streaky textured glaze, 7in high. Golding Young & Co, Grantham. Feb 06. HP: £38. ABP: £44.

2875

Royal Venton 'Ming' Ware pottery jug, inverted waved rim, 'lava' glaze over a red and yellow mottled body, printed and impressed marks, 6in high, 9in dia. Golding Young & Co, Grantham. Feb 06. HP: £38. ABP: £44.

2876

Royal Doulton biscuit figure, the Seafarer, HN2455, 9in high. Golding Young & Co, Grantham. Feb 06. HP: £38. ABP: £44.

2877

St Ives terracotta vase, rich treacle glaze, seal mark for Sylvia Fox Strangways, 6in high. Golding Young & Co, Grantham. Feb 06. HP: £38. ABP: £44.

2878

Doulton Lambeth Impasto bottle vase, by Rosa Keen, pine cones against an ochre ground, 9in high. Golding Young & Co, Grantham. Feb 06. HP: £38. ABP: £44.

2879

Rathbone Portobello blue and white plate. Great Western Auctions, Glasgow. Mar 07. HP: £38. ABP: £44.

Troika double egg cup. Great Western Auctions, Glasgow. Aug 06. HP: £36. ABP: £42.

Royal Doulton 'Michele', HN2234. Black Country Auctions, Dudley. Oct 05. HP: £35. ABP: £41.

Large Sylvac terrier. Great Western Auctions, Glasgow. Dec 05. HP: £35. ABP: £41.

Locke and Co., Worcester, small milk jug & sugar bowl, relief floral pattern in cream and creamy pink, gilding to rims, printed mark to base of jug, c1895-1900. (2) A F Brock & Co Ltd, Stockport. Nov 05. HP: £35. ABP: £41.

Reginald Wells pottery vase, blue textured glaze, imp'd mark COLDRUM CHELSEA, 7in high, rim chip. Golding Young & Co, Grantham. Feb 06. HP: £35. ABP: £41.

Maling floral pattern bowl, with gilding, pedestal base, 10.5in dia, small dark scuff to top near rim, base marked 'Daisy, 6157'. A F Brock & Co Ltd, Stockport. Nov 05. HP: £35. ABP: £41.

Royal Venton pottery vase, red, yellow, buff and grey streaky glazes, printed and imp'd factory marks, 7in high. Golding Young & Co, Grantham. Feb 06. HP: £35. ABP: £41.

Royal Dux model of a polar bear. Gorringes, Bexhill. Oct 05. HP: £35. ABP: £41.

Hillstonia pottery vase, lightly ribbed body, orange and red with black streaks, incised HILLSTONIA ENGLAND NO121, 8in high. Golding Young & Co, Grantham. Feb 06. HP: £35. ABP: £41.

Royal. Doulton figure 'Dream-weaver' HN2283. Great Western Auctions, Glasgow. Jun 06. HP: £35. ABP: £41.

Troika earthenware vase, incise carved decorated with geometric forms, mottled green/white gloss ground 15cm, af. Locke & England, Leamington Spa. Jul 06. HP: £35. ABP: £41.

Pair of Candy Ware pottery vases, mottled black against a pink ground, 9in high. Golding Young & Co, Grantham. Feb 06. HP: £35. ABP: £41.

Winchcombe pottery dish and cover, domed cover with bun finial, brown/ochre glazes, seal mark, 5in dia. Golding Young & Co, Grantham. Feb 06. HP: £35. ABP: £41.

Beswick model of a labrador, Wendover. Gorringes, Bexhill. Oct 05. HP: £35. ABP: £41.

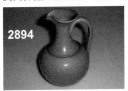

Dunmore pottery jug, flared neck, loop handle, rich yellow glaze, imp'd mark, 8in high. Golding Young & Co, Grantham. Feb 06. HP: £35. ABP: £41.

Nao Lladro figurine, Spanish couple dancing, 11in high. A F Brock & Co Ltd, Stockport. Feb 07. HP: £35. ABP: £41.

St Ives pottery bowl, brown with foliate bands against a buff ground, seal monogram for Sylvia Fox Strangways, 5in high, 6in dia. Golding Young & Co, Grantham. Feb 06. HP: £35. ABP: £41.

Meiji period Japanese Imari charger, basket pattern, 12in dia. Golding Young & Co, Grantham. Feb 06. HP: £35. ABP: £41.

Carlton Ware flower wall pocket. Great Western Auctions, Glasgow. May 06. HP: £35. ABP: £41.

Four Carlton Ware orange lustre vases, gilt rims & bases, one a/f. Rosebery's, London. Aug 06. HP: £35. ABP: £41.

Hammer: £35 - £30

Pair of Staffordshire Spaniels holding baskets of flowers in their mouths, 19.5cm high. Rosebery's, London. Oct 06. HP: £35. ABP: £41.

Four Beswick models of animals, 2 donkeys & 2 foals, printed marks. Rosebery's, London. Apr 07. HP: £35. ABP: £41.

Hummel figurines, one of a boy with rabbit, Village Boy & School Girl, all 110mm tall, latter damaged & glued at top of legs. (3) A F Brock & Co Ltd, Stockport. Oct 06. HP: £35. ABP: £41.

Pearlware plate, painted in underglaze blue with flower and leaf forms, moulded and combed border, 10in. Golding Young & Co, Grantham. Nov 06. HP: £35. ABP: £41.

Pair of Samson figures of putti seated astride goats, gilt highlighted bases, gold anchor mark to bases, 7cm high, af. Rosebery's, London. Jan 07. HP: £35. ABP: £41.

Royal Doulton Linda, by Mada M Pedley, HN 3879, 1997, 200mm tall. A F Brock & Co Ltd, Stockport. Oct 06. HP: £35. ABP: £41.

Staffordshire 'Nelson' Toby jug, in coloured glazes, 28cm high. Rosebery's, London. Apr 07. HP: £35. ABP: £41.

Staffordshire flatback of a couple and dog. Great Western Auctions, Glasgow. Sep 06. HP: £34. ABP: £39.

Coalport, Lady Alice with certificate and box. Black Country Auctions, Dudley. Oct 05. HP: £32. ABP: £37.

Pair of Hancocks Pomegranate pattern candlesticks. 6in tall. Black Country Auctions, Dudley. Dec 05. HP: £32. ABP: £37.

Victorian Staffordshire, Japanese taste, teapot/stand, Oriental figure decoration, registration marks to base. Reeman Dansie, Colchester. Apr 06. HP: £32. ABP: £37.

Pilkington Pottery small jardiniere, moulded form, streaky green glaze, imp'd mark, potting code for 1909, model No. 2817, 5in dia. Golding Young & Co, Grantham. Feb 06. HP: £32. ABP: £37.

Foley Faience terracotta vase, painted with stylized tulips against a dark green ground, incised No. 11046, 4in high, 7in dia. Golding Young & Co, Grantham. Feb 06. HP: £32. ABP: £37.

Royal Venton pottery vase, streaky glaze of turquoise, red, yellow and green, 8in high. Golding Young & Co, Grantham. Feb 06. HP: £32. ABP: £37.

St Ives Stoneware jar, heavy buff and brown streaky and mottled glazes, seal marks, 6in high. Golding Young & Co, Grantham. Feb 06. HP: £32. ABP: £37.

Candy Ware pottery vase, blue streaky glaze, 11in high. Golding Young & Co, Grantham. Feb 06. HP: £32. ABP: £37.

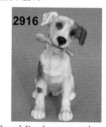

Royal Doulton, seated terrier. Gorringes, Bexhill. Oct 05. HP: £30. ABP: £35.

Aesthetic style flattened vase, 19thC. Gorringes, Bexhill. Oct 05. HP: £30. ABP: £35.

Tang pottery female standing figure, 24.3cm high, restored. Rosebery's, London. Feb 06. HP: £30. ABP: £35.

2919

Sylvac, large model of an elephant and another of her calf. Gorringes, Bexhill. Oct 05. HP: £30. ABP: £35.

2920

Radfords butterfly ware jug. Great Western Auctions, Glasgow. Nov 05. HP: £30. ABP: £35.

2921

Rye Hop Ware vase, with undulating rim, incised Rye mark, 12cm high. Gorringes, Bexhill. Dec 05. HP: £30. ABP: £35.

2922

Goss, Shakespeare's House, Rd. No. 225833. A F Brock & Co Ltd, Stockport. Nov 05. HP: £30. ABP: £35.

2923

Pilkington's R. Lancastrian lustre jar, greenish glaze, minus lid, base lightly imp'd 'P', '2889' and 'England' & with green Prince of Wales feathers, glazing faults at base and crazed. A F Brock & Co Ltd, Stockport. Nov 05. HP: £30. ABP: £35.

2924

Blanc de Chine figure, 19thC Chinese, Phu tai reclining, naturalistic base, 8cm high. Rosebery's, London. Dec 05. HP: £30. ABP: £35.

2925

Spode 2-handled urn in a presentation box, Ltd Edn. Black Country Auctions, Dudley. Dec 05. HP: £30. ABP: £35.

> The numbering system acts as a reader reference as well as linking to the Analysis of each section.

2926

Pair of Bourne Denby dogs, S/D to one tail. Black Country Auctions, Dudley. Dec 05. HP: £30. ABP: £35.

2927

Clarice Cliff Crocus pattern plate. Black Country Auctions, Dudley. Dec 05. HP: £30. ABP: £35.

2928

19thC blue/white transfer printed Willow pattern meat dish with well, 16in, and a blue/white 'Dresden' flower decorated basin, 14in dia. Ewbank, Send, Surrey. Dec 05. HP: £30. ABP: £35.

Hammer: £30

2929

Pair Staffordshire spaniels, 11.5in high. Ewbank Auctioneers, Send, Surrey. Dec 05. HP: £30. ABP: £35.

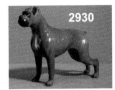

2930

Beswick bull dog, 6in high. Ewbank, Send, Surrey. Dec 05. HP: £30. ABP: £35.

2931

Dresden porcelain figure of a cherub leaning on a tree stump, German 19thC, 14.5cm high, af. Rosebery's, London. Feb 06. HP: £30. ABP: £35.

2932

Clarice Cliff 'Original Bizarre' ginger jar, c1930s, abstract pattern in colours, printed mark to underside, 18.5cm high, minus lid, af. Rosebery's, London. Mar 06. HP: £30. ABP: £35.

2933

Two 1930s Crown Devon earthenware comical puppies, one modelled as a patch eyed terrier, other forlorn looking, 10 and 13cm. Locke & England, Leamington Spa. Mar 06. HP: £30. ABP: £35.

2934

Royal Doulton character jug, 'Dick Turpin' D6528, 6in high. Golding Young & Co, Grantham. Feb 06. HP: £30. ABP: £35.

2935

Two early 19thC English blue/white wild rose pattern plates with floral and river landscape decoration, 25.5cm. Reeman Dansie, Colchester. Apr 06. HP: £30. ABP: £35.

2936

Crown Ducal lustrous bowl, iexterior orange and with water lily border, 10in dia, and a Japanese novelty condiment set in the form of a duck and two ducklings on stand. (2) Dee, Atkinson & Harrison, Driffield. Apr 06. HP: £30. ABP: £35.

2937

Royal Doulton figure 'Home Again', HN2167. Great Western Auctions, Glasgow. Apr 06. HP: £30. ABP: £35.

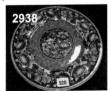

2938

Maling plate, depicting flowers. Great Western Auctions, Glasgow. Apr 06. HP: £30. ABP: £35.

2939

Two Japanese lobed dishes painted in the Imari palette with flowers/foliage, 30.5cm dia, one badly restored and a smaller similar dish, 21.5cm dia. Rosebery's, London. Oct 06. HP: £30. ABP: £35.

2940

Davenport sweetmeat server: 2 deep squared pots, gilded and painted with flowers in Imari colours, in an EPNS cagework stand, central loop handle, pad feet, early 20thC, 8in wide. Hartleys, Ilkley. Dec 06. HP: £30. ABP: £35.

2941

Susie Cooper bowl, incised with flower spray, impressed marks Susie Cooper England 1732, 8in dia, hairline/firing crack. Golding Young & Co, Grantham. Feb 06. HP: £30. ABP: £35.

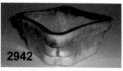

2942

Candy Ware earthenware bowl, streaky blue, purple/turquoise glazes, 8in wide. Golding Young & Co, Grantham. Feb 06. HP: £30. ABP: £35.

2943

Royal Venton pottery vase, volcanic glaze of red, greys and black, 9in high. Golding Young & Co, Grantham. Feb 06. HP: £30. ABP: £35.

2944

Burmantofts pottery jardiniere, pale lilac ground intaglio moulded with floral and foliate panels, pendant from scalloped rim, imp'd marks, No. 1085, 7in dia. Golding Young & Co, Grantham. Feb 06. HP: £30. ABP: £35.

2945

St Ives terracotta vase, brown and yellow glaze, seal mark for Sylvia Fox Strangways, 7in high. Golding Young & Co, Grantham. Feb 06. HP: £30. ABP: £35.

2946

S & E Collier terracotta vase, 3 loop handles, with a green glaze, 6in high. Golding Young & Co, Grantham. Feb 06. HP: £30. ABP: £35.

374

2947

Royal Winton tea pot for one, yellow background with flowers No. 5400, blue back stamp. Kent Auction Galleries, Folkestone. Jun 06. HP: £30. ABP: £35.

2948

Blue/white pearlware bowl, early 19thC, centrally enriched with a floral spray, outside painted in chinoiserie style, restored, 24.5cm dia. Rosebery's, London. May 06. HP: £30. ABP: £35.

2949

Spode porcelain vase, painted and gilded with a chinoiserie fence and garden in red, blue, green and gold, early 19thC, 4.75in high, No. 967 to base. Hartleys, Ilkley. Aug 06. HP: £30. ABP: £35.

2950

Leeds Pottery house with blue/grey painted roof, and foliate moulded spreading base, 4.25in high, impressed mark. Hartleys, Ilkley. Oct 06. HP: £30. ABP: £35.

The illustrations are in descending price order. The price range is indicated at the top of each page.

2951

19thC Meissen plate, moulded floral pattern, shaped rim, painted with flowers, blue crossed swords mark to base, 25cm dia. Rosebery's, London. Oct 06. HP: £30. ABP: £35.

2952

Royal Crown Derby vase, 1128, in Imari palette, 4.25in high. Kent Auction Galleries, Folkestone. Dec 06. HP: £30. ABP: £35.

2953

Coronaware 'Cremorne' vase, hand painted by Molly Hancock, 180mm tall, floral pattern on dark blue background, gilt edge & orange painted inner. A F Brock & Co Ltd, Stockport. Oct 06. HP: £30. ABP: £35.

2954

Charlotte Rhead jug by Crown Ducal, c1930s, Art Deco fruit design, pattern 5982, shape 146, 8.5in high. A F Brock & Co Ltd, Stockport. Feb 07. HP: £30. ABP: £35.

2955

Royal Doulton figurine Hilary HN2335. Kent Auction Galleries, Folkestone. Dec 06. HP: £30. ABP: £35.

2956

Royal Worcester candle snuffer, monk reading a book, black printed mark to interior, 12.5cm. Rosebery's, London. Jan 07. HP: £30. ABP: £35.

Clement Massier pottery vase, sea green streaky glaze with brown splashes, imp'd marks, 5in high. Golding Young & Co, Grantham. Feb 06. HP: £30. ABP: £35.

Minton porcelain trio: cup, saucer and plate, printed in deep blue, diving cormorants above choppy seas, pattern No. 4020, Reg. diamond for 1870. Golding Young & Co, Grantham. Nov 06. HP: £30. ABP: £35.

Royal Dux figure, elephant, with ivorine tusks, 8in high. Golding Young & Co, Grantham. Nov 06. HP: £30. ABP: £35.

Prattware pot lid and base, polychrome printed with the Albert Memorial, 4in dia. Golding Young & Co, Grantham. Nov 06. HP: £30. ABP: £35.

Royal Doulton Christine, HN 2792, 8in high. A F Brock & Co Ltd, Stockport. Feb 07. HP: £30. ABP: £35.

Charlotte Rhead jug for Crown Ducal, mottled orange and cream body, single band of geometric pattern with raised outline, raised/printed marks to base, 11.5cm high. Rosebery's, London. Apr 07. HP: £30. ABP: £35.

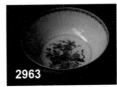

Chinese blue and white bowl, centre painted with flowers, foliage and vases, 26.5cm dia. Rosebery's, London. Aug 06. HP: £30. ABP: £35.

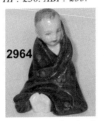

Royal Doulton, This Little Pig HN1793. Black Country Auctions, Dudley. Dec 05. HP: £28. ABP: £32.

Sampson bowl in Chinese famille rose style with panels of flowers and foliage on a red scale ground, 9in dia. Ewbank, Send, Surrey. Dec 05. HP: £28. ABP: £32.

Woods pottery jug, reeded neck and fluted body, glazed yellow with brown streaks and red highlights, 9in high. Golding Young & Co, Grantham. Feb 06. HP: £28. ABP: £32.

Hammer: £30 - £25

Rye Pottery two-handled cup, moulded rim, applied flower heads & leafage, incised mark for Sussex Rustic Ware, 3in dia. Golding Young & Co, Grantham. Feb 06. HP: £28. ABP: £32.

Royal Venton vase, painted with black, red and yellow volcanic glazes, and in relief with 'lava' glaze, 8in high. Golding Young & Co, Grantham. Feb 06. HP: £28. ABP: £32.

Staffordshire pottery model of a bull, 10in high. Golding Young & Co, Grantham. Nov 06. HP: £28. ABP: £32.

Dunmore pottery 2-handled vase, cup shape neck flanked by 2 loop handles, green and brown streaky glazes, imp'd DUNMORE, 6in high. Golding Young & Co, Grantham. Feb 06. HP: £28. ABP: £32.

St Ives vase, mottled dark blue glaze, incised initials for Sylvia Fox, Strangways, 2in high. Golding Young & Co, Grantham. Feb 06. HP: £28. ABP: £32.

Pair of 19thC Staffordshire pottery spaniels, each with separate front leg, copper lustre splashes, 9in high, cracked. Golding Young & Co, Grantham. Feb 06. HP: £28. ABP: £32.

Roger Guerin stoneware flagon, dimpled form, scroll handle, blue/brown streaky glazes, signed R Guerin, 8in high. Golding Young & Co, Grantham. Feb 06. HP: £28. ABP: £32.

Royal Doulton glazed horse 7in high. Kent Auction Galleries, Folkestone. Jun 06. HP: £26. ABP: £30.

Beswick Shetland pony. Great Western Auctions, Glasgow. Jan 07. HP: £26. ABP: £30.

Damascus border tile, 17thC style, decorated with stylized floral and foliate sprays on a blue ground, restored, 23cm long. Rosebery's, London. Feb 06. HP: £25. ABP: £29.

Hammer: £25

Macintyre match pot, cream ground, transfer printed image of 'A Gentleman in Khaki' after R. Caton Woodville 1897, printed inscription verso 'The Absent-Minded Beggar' by Rudyard Kipling, printed mark to base, 7cm high. Rosebery's, London. Apr 07. HP: £25. ABP: £29.

Royal Doulton Francine HN2422. Black Country Auctions, Dudley. Dec 05. HP: £25. ABP: £29.

Naples figure of a gentleman holding a bunch of grapes, gilt/puce highlighted scrolling base, underglaze blue mark, 17cm high, and Continental porcelain figure of a man in Tyrolean costume, 19cm high, af. (2) Rosebery's, London. Jan 07. HP: £25. ABP: £29.

Coalport Ladies of Fashion figure, 'Regina', 19cm high. Gorringes, Bexhill. Feb 06. HP: £25. ABP: £29.

174 *Ceramics Prices*

Poole pottery vase, decorated in colours with abstract panels against a red ground, yellow interior, 6in high. Golding Young & Co, Grantham. Feb 06. HP: £25. ABP: £29.

Pair of Continental porcelain stands, moulded top/base, applied with laurel festoons in relief, painted with flower heads, gilt embellished, late 19thC, 2.75in high. Hartleys, Ilkley. Apr 07. HP: £25. ABP: £29.

Categories or themes can be followed through the colour coded Index which contains over 4500 cross references.

Near pair of Delft blue/white vases, with panels painted with boats at sea framed by scrolling flowers and foliage, painted/imp'd marks, 22cm high. Rosebery's, London. Apr 07. HP: £25. ABP: £29.

Royal Venton pottery vase, colourful 'Volcanic' glazes, 10in high. Golding Young & Co, Grantham. Feb 06. HP: £25. ABP: £29.

Linthorpe vase by Henry Tooth, neck and shoulders glazed brown, green ground, imp'd mark and monogram, 2in high. Golding Young & Co, Grantham. Feb 06. HP: £25. ABP: £29.

Crown Ducal Spectria Flambé bowl, black stylized flower heads, red flambé ground, printed marks, 9in dia. Golding Young & Co, Grantham. Feb 06. HP: £25. ABP: £29.

Crown Devon Cretian pottery bowl, moulded in low relief, painted with border patterns of stylized birds and simple leaf forms, 8in dia. Golding Young & Co, Grantham. Feb 06. HP: £25. ABP: £29.

Royal Venton 'Ming' pottery vase, colourful 'Volcanic' glaze, 8in high. Golding Young & Co, Grantham. Feb 06. HP: £25. ABP: £29.

Regal Ware pottery vase, polychrome streaky glaze, printed factory mark, signed N. W. Keates, 9in. Golding Young & Co, Grantham. Feb 06. HP: £25. ABP: £29.

Delft ink stand, seated gentleman, flanked by ink pots, hat as the pen holder, red, blue and clear glazes, 24cm high, af. Rosebery's, London. Apr 07. HP: £25. ABP: £29.

Wilkinson Ambeston Ware with a marbled lustre glaze, 7in high. Golding Young & Co, Grantham. Feb 06. HP: £25. ABP: £29.

St Ives Pottery mug, capped scroll handle, pale green speckled glaze, seal mark, 4in high. Golding Young & Co, Grantham. Feb 06. HP: £25. ABP: £29.

Roger Guerin stoneware vase, moulded neck and foot rim, grey, brown and blue streaky glazes, signed R Guerin No. 917/C, 8in high. Golding Young & Co, Grantham. Feb 06. HP: £25. ABP: £29.

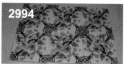

Six early 20thC tiles, printed with Christmas roses around a cruciform design, 6in square. Golding Young & Co, Grantham. Feb 06. HP: £25. ABP: £29.

2995

Pair Art Deco pottery book-ends, ochre splash vertical/horizontal books upon which sits a green dog, 5.25in high. Dee, Atkinson & Harrison, Driffield. Jul 06. HP: £25. ABP: £29.

2996

Royal Doulton Jessica, by Peggy Davies, HN 3169, 1987, 200mm tall. A F Brock & Co Ltd, Stockport. Oct 06. HP: £25. ABP: £29.

2997

Delft plate, naive coastal scene painted to well, 9.25in dia. Golding Young & Co, Grantham. Nov 06. HP: £25. ABP: £29.

2998

Royal Doulton figure 'Wendy' HN2109. Great Western Auctions, Glasgow. Nov 05. HP: £24. ABP: £28.

2999

18thC English porcelain blue/white fluted tea bowl, damage. Reeman Dansie, Colchester. Apr 06. HP: £24. ABP: £28.

3000

Carltonware Toucan jug, damaged. Black Country Auctions, Dudley. Oct 05. HP: £23. ABP: £27.

3001

Wade Heath wall charger. Black Country Auctions, Dudley. Dec 05. HP: £23. ABP: £27.

3002

Royal Doulton character jug, The Cardinal, just over 1in high. Black Country Auctions, Dudley. Dec 05. HP: £22. ABP: £25.

3003

Poole Pottery Sylvan ware bowl, flared rim, slightly ribbed body, mottled orange glaze, imp'd Poole England, incised 683, painted Sylvan Ware M72, 14in dia. Golding Young & Co, Grantham. Feb 06. HP: £22. ABP: £25.

3004

Staffordshire flatback figure group of Napoleon & Prince Albert. (defective) Great Western Auctions, Glasgow. Oct 05. HP: £20. ABP: £23.

Hammer: £25 - £20

3005

Pair of Chinese floral-decorated flower bricks. Gorringes, Bexhill. Oct 05. HP: £20. ABP: £23.

3006

R. Doulton small figurine, 'Bedtime', HN1978. A F Brock & Co Ltd, Stockport. Nov 05. HP: £20. ABP: £23.

3007

Goss, Ann Hathaway's Cottage, Shottery, Stratford-on-Avon, Rd. No. 208047. A F Brock & Co Ltd, Stockport. Nov 05. HP: £20. ABP: £23.

3008

Royal Dalton tankard, 'Old English Coaching Scenes', signed W. E. Grace, D6393. A F Brock & Co Ltd, Stockport. Nov 05. HP: £20. ABP: £23.

3009

Dunmore pottery jug, spherical form, raised neck, loop handle, turquoise glaze, imp'd DUNMORE, 5in high, minor rim chips. Golding Young & Co, Grantham. Feb 06. HP: £20. ABP: £23.

3010

Royal Doulton figure, 'Lily', HN1799, 12.5cm high. Rosebery's, London. Jan 06. HP: £20. ABP: £23.

3011

Johnson Brothers flower decorated wash basin, 17.5in. Ewbank, Send, Surrey. Dec 05. HP: £20. ABP: £23.

3012

19thC blue/white transfer printed meat dish, figures punting on a river, broad floral border, 18.5in. Ewbank Auctioneers, Send, Surrey. Dec 05. HP: £20. ABP: £23.

3013

Royal Doulton Character Jug 'Sam Weller' 5in. Ewbank, Send, Surrey. Dec 05. HP: £20. ABP: £23.

3014

Wileman & Co Foley faience vase, green, yellow/brown streaky glazes within incised abstract lines, printed mark and incised No. 12065, 7in high. Golding Young & Co, Grantham. Feb 06. HP: £20. ABP: £23.

Four large stoneware flagons, incl. three Doulton Lambeth, Edmonds Stamford 482, 'J.S. Loweth Wine Merchant Spirit, Stamford', Wellingborough, and P. Phipps & Co 4583, Northampton. (Loweth good condition, other 3 with rim chips.) Batemans, Stamford. Mar 06. HP: £20. ABP: £23.

Bough pottery toastrack. Great Western Auctions, Glasgow. Apr 06. HP: £20. ABP: £23.

W.L. Baron Pottery vase, mottled glazes, incised Baron Barnstaple, shape No. 419, 4in high. Golding Young & Co, Grantham. Feb 06. HP: £20. ABP: £23.

Pair of Chinese blue/white ginger jars/covers, painted with stylised foliage and an abstract geometric pattern, 25cm. Rosebery's, London. Oct 06. HP: £20. ABP: £23.

Royal Venton Ware pottery vase, moulded neck, colourful volcanic glazes, 5in high. Golding Young & Co, Grantham. Feb 06. HP: £20. ABP: £23.

19thC Staffordshire figure, The Prince of Wales, 44.5cm, and a Staffordshire figure of a lady holding a lute, 35cm high. Rosebery's, London. Aug 06. HP: £20. ABP: £23.

Rye Pottery oval platter, painted with black/pink star shapes over wavy lines, cream slip, 4 small feet, impressed mark, 8in wide. Golding Young & Co, Grantham. Feb 06. HP: £20. ABP: £23.

> Prices quoted are actual hammer prices (HP) and the Approximate Buyer's Price (ABP) includes an average premium of 15% + VAT.

Salopian Art Pottery vase, decorated with running brown glaze over green, 6in high. Golding Young & Co, Grantham. Feb 06. HP: £20. ABP: £23.

Lipscombe & Co., saltglazed water cistern, applied grape/vine decoration, cartouche reads 'Lipscombe & Co. Patentees 44 Queen Victoria St. Mansion House London and at Temple Bar, 40cm. Rosebery's, London. Aug 06. HP: £20. ABP: £23.

Two Carltonware Guinness promotional toucans, flying with pint glasses perched on beaks, 21 and 25cm. Locke & England, Leamington Spa. Nov 06. HP: £20. ABP: £23.

Wilkinsons Oriflame Pottery vase, with pink, purple and yellow marbled glazes, 4in high. Golding Young & Co, Grantham. Feb 06. HP: £20. ABP: £23.

Chinese blue/white tea bowl on stand, 6cm high. Rosebery's, London. Aug 06. HP: £20. ABP: £23.

Winchcombe Pottery terracotta preserve pot cover, with simple slip decoration and glazes, seal marks, 3in high. Golding Young & Co, Grantham. Feb 06. HP: £20. ABP: £23.

S & E Collier Silchester Ware terracotta jug, scroll handle, dark brown metallic glaze, imp'd mark, No. 340, 6in high, and another example, No. 439, 7in high. Golding Young & Co, Grantham. Feb 06. HP: £20. ABP: £23.

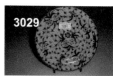

Cantagalli Plate, painted with flowerheads, leaves and sprigs, yellow ground, hatched border, painted mask and initialled T G, 8in dia. Golding Young & Co, Grantham. Feb 06. HP: £20. ABP: £23.

Doulton Lambeth jug, dark and light brown band with embossed decoration of figures drinking and hunting scenes, imp'd mark, 16.5cm, and a Doulton style jug with similar decoration, 22cm, af. (2) Rosebery's, London. Oct 06. HP: £20. ABP: £23.

Two Spode decorative plates, winter scene with people skating, holly/berry border. Kent Auction Galleries, Folkestone. Nov 06. HP: £20. ABP: £23.

Royal Crown Derby frog paperweight, Imari colours. (second) Kent Auction Galleries, Folkestone. Dec 06. HP: £20. ABP: £23.

Royal Crown Derby rabbit paperweight in blue & gilt, original box. Kent Auction Galleries, Folkestone. Dec 06. HP: £20. ABP: £23.

3034

W. H. Grindley part dinner service, to incl. 3 graduated meat plates, soup bowls, 2 vegetable dishes & covers, dinner plates and other plates, printed mark to bases. Rosebery's, London. Jan 07. HP: £20. ABP: £23.

3035

Two Naples figures, one of an old woman on crutches, 15cm high, other of a street vendor with a basket of rats on pole, 18cm, both underglaze blue mark to bases. (2) Rosebery's, London. Apr 07. HP: £20. ABP: £23.

3036

18thC Chinese bowl in the Mandarin palette, painted with panels of figures, iron red/gilt geometric decoration, 29cm dia, extensive restorations. Rosebery's, London. Jan 07. HP: £20. ABP: £23.

3037

Pair of Chinese blue/white saucer dishes painted with pomegranates and foliage, underglaze blue mark to bases, 16cm dia. Rosebery's, London. Apr 07. HP: £20. ABP: £23.

3038

19thC Chinese famille rose bowl enamelled with pomegranates, flowers & foliage, underglaze iron red mark to base, 20cm dia. Rosebery's, London. Jan 07. HP: £20. ABP: £23.

3039

Royal Doulton, The Last Waltz, HN 2315, 8in. A F Brock & Co Ltd, Stockport. Feb 07. HP: £20. ABP: £23.

3040

Nao Lladro goose figurines, 6in high. (2) A F Brock & Co Ltd, Stockport. Feb 07. HP: £20. ABP: £23.

3041

Pair of Winton Grimwade's Old Bill Expeditionary Force wall plates with cartoons after Bruce Bairnsfather, 25.5cm, printed marks, one af. Rosebery's, London. Apr 07. HP: £20. ABP: £23.

3042

Treasure of Tek Sing Chrysanthemum Dish, 150mm, No. 11598, with certificate. A F Brock & Co Ltd, Stockport. Feb 07. HP: £20. ABP: £23.

3043

Blanc de chine figure of a Chinese man seated on rock, underglaze blue & imp'd marks to base, 14.5cm high, af. Rosebery's, London. Apr 07. HP: £20. ABP: £23.

3044

Staffordshire figure, Welsh woman in costume, 23cm, & Pearlware figure of huntsman, 18cm, damaged. Rosebery's, London. Apr 07. HP: £20. ABP: £23.

3045

Wileman & Co Foley faience pottery vase, abstract incised decoration, printed factory mark, incised No. 12603, 7in high. Golding Young & Co, Grantham. Feb 06. HP: £18. ABP: £21.

3046

Five Wade Nat West pig money banks. Kent Auction Galleries, Folkestone. Dec 06. HP: £18. ABP: £21.

3047

Candy Ware pottery vase, compressed form, blue streaky glaze, 8 x 4in high. Golding Young & Co, Grantham. Feb 06. HP: £18. ABP: £21.

3048

Delft Tile, painted in blue with a view of buildings in a landscape, foliate spandrels, 5in square. Golding Young & Co, Grantham. Feb 06. HP: £18. ABP: £21.

3049

Selection of Midwinter 'Sienna' tableware: plates, lidded tureens, teapot, coffee pot, etc. Locke & England, Leamington Spa. Jul 06. HP: £16. ABP: £18.

3050

Carter Stabler Adams Ltd Poole pottery vase of ribbed globular form, imp'd mark to base, 4in high. Golding Young & Co, Grantham. Feb 06. HP: £18. ABP: £21.

3051

Coronet Ware Pottery vase, blue/yellow mottled glaze, printed factory mark, 8in high. Golding Young & Co, Grantham. Feb 06. HP: £18. ABP: £21.

3052

Winchcombe pottery terracotta lidded pot, domed cover, single handle, green/brown mottled glaze, cover with a wavy line border, seal mark, 5in high. Golding Young & Co, Grantham. Feb 06. HP: £18. ABP: £21.

3053

Beleek shell moulded teapot and cover with shamrock decoration, 8in. Ewbank Auctioneers, Send, Surrey. Dec 05. HP: £15. ABP: £17.

Hammer: £15 - £12

3054

Bourne Denby Damask Ware owl jug, in blue to greenish blue glaze, 15.5cm high. A F Brock & Co Ltd, Stockport. Nov 05. HP: £15. ABP: £17.

3055

Victoria, jubilee tankard, 1887, Rd. No. 63164 to base, slight chipping around rim and George V, silver jubilee mug. A F Brock & Co Ltd, Stockport. Nov 05. HP: £15. ABP: £17.

3056

Royal Doulton figure, Rose HN1368, 5in. Ewbank Auctioneers, Send, Surrey. Dec 05. HP: £15. ABP: £17.

3057

Royal Doulton figure Make Believe, HN2225, 7in high. Ewbank, Send, Surrey. Dec 05. HP: £15. ABP: £17.

3058

Treasure of Tek Sing Aster saucer, 120mm, No. 10641, with certificate. A F Brock & Co Ltd, Stockport. Feb 07. HP: £15. ABP: £17.

178 *Ceramics Prices*

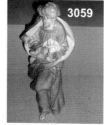

3059

Lladro figure of Christ, 13.5in high. Ewbank, Send, Surrey. Dec 05. HP: £15. ABP: £17.

3060

Roger Guerin stoneware mug, annulated neck rim and loop handle, applied figural medallion against a blue, buff and brown incised body, signed in script and No. 81A, 4in high. Golding Young & Co, Grantham. Feb 06. HP: £15. ABP: £17.

> The numbering system acts as a reader reference as well as linking to the Analysis of each section.

3061

Nowell Pottery vase, blue streaky glaze, incised C.D. Nowell, PRESTBURY, 7in high. Golding Young & Co, Grantham. Feb 06. HP: £15. ABP: £17.

3062

Wade Heath parrot jug, c1930s, hand painted with orange & brown leaves with parrot handle, crazing throughout, flaws, paint worn in places, 7in high. A F Brock & Co Ltd, Stockport. Feb 07. HP: £15. ABP: £17.

3063

William Fishley Holland Pottery jug, ribbed form, moulded loop handle, green streaky glaze, incised script signature, 8in high. Golding Young & Co, Grantham. Feb 06. HP: £15. ABP: £17.

3064

Early 19thC pearlware bowl, externally printed in blue with naive figural landscapes, internally with a vignette and floral border, 6in dia. Golding Young & Co, Grantham. Feb 06. HP: £15. ABP: £17.

3065

Treasure of Tek Sing River Scene bowl, 150mm, No. 5504, with certificate. A F Brock & Co Ltd, Stockport. Feb 07. HP: £15. ABP: £17.

3066

Pair of late 19thC Staffordshire pottery dogs, ruby coats, green collar/chains, 7.25in high. Golding Young & Co, Grantham. Nov 06. HP: £15. ABP: £17.

3067

Crown Devon Fielding's musical mug, 'On Ilkla Moor Baht'At, Tha's bin a-coortin' Mary Jane' on front with rest of rhyme on back, hairline cracks, crazing, 6in. A F Brock & Co Ltd, Stockport. Feb 07. HP: £15. ABP: £17.

3068

Royal Doulton Dinky-Do, HN 1678, 4.75in high. A F Brock & Co Ltd, Stockport. Feb 07. HP: £15. ABP: £17.

3069

Rye pottery jug, pinched spout & loop handle, stamped paint mark, 4in high. Golding Young & Co, Grantham. Feb 06. HP: £12. ABP: £14.

3070

Dunmore Pottery pate pot & cover, banded form, ball finial, pierced lug handles, imp'd DUNMORE, 3in high. Golding Young & Co, Grantham. Feb 06. HP: £12. ABP: £14.

3071

Nowell pottery vase, streaky glaze, script mark C D NOWELL Disley, 6in. Golding Young & Co, Grantham. Feb 06. HP: £12. ABP: £14.

3072

Pair of Samson armorial caddies, painted in polychrome enamels with crest amidst flowers, raised white detail, trefoil borders, 4.75in high. Golding Young & Co, Grantham. Nov 06. HP: £12. ABP: £14.

3073

W L Baron pottery cream jug, matt body with green/brown banding to neck and handles, inscribed 'Be sure your pins will find you out', incised marks Baron Barnstaple 145, 3in high. Golding Young & Co, Grantham. Feb 06. HP: £11. ABP: £12.

3074

Beswick jug, artistic pattern in blue, mauve, green, brown and yellow, incl. flowers and butterfly, 28cm high. A F Brock & Co Ltd, Stockport. Nov 05. HP: £10. ABP: £11.

3075

Royal Worcester New Arrival, baby in crib covered in pink bows, 4.75in high. A F Brock & Co Ltd, Stockport. Feb 07. HP: £10. ABP: £11.

3076

Nao Lladro figurine of lady holding flowers, & wearing a hat, one flower broken at stem & other has one petal missing, 12.75in high. A F Brock & Co Ltd, Stockport. Feb 07. HP: £10. ABP: £11.

3077

Beswick small character jug, 'Pickwick', J119. A F Brock & Co Ltd, Stockport. Nov 05. HP: £10. ABP: £11.

3078

Royal Doulton King George V Coronation 1911 plate, blue & white with gilt edge, 10.5in dia. A F Brock & Co Ltd, Stockport. Feb 07. HP: £10. ABP: £11.

3079

Fairing of zebra, Staffordshire style, smudging of paint to both sides. A F Brock & Co Ltd, Stockport. Nov 05. HP: £10. ABP: £11.

3080

Oriental style ginger jar, in multi-coloured floral/foliate pattern with two peacocks, 21cm high. A F Brock & Co Ltd, Stockport. Nov 05. HP: £10. ABP: £11.

3081

Ltd Edn plates, mainly Teddy Bear themes by Franklin Mint, six boxed. (10) A F Brock & Co Ltd, Stockport. Nov 05. HP: £10. ABP: £11.

3082

Blue/white Chinese porcelain vase, painted in deep blue with two dragons, cloud and mountain motifs, 26cm high. Rosebery's, London. Dec 05. HP: £10. ABP: £11.

3083

Dartmouth Devon potteries, a light green glazed vase, of deco design, 35cm wide also a matching wall pocket. (2) Rosebery's, London. May 06. HP: £10. ABP: £11.

3084

Carter Stabler Adams pottery dish, pouring lip, green and purple stripes on a grey slip ground, impressed mark and initials, shape T363, 5in dia. Golding Young & Co, Grantham. Feb 06. HP: £10. ABP: £11.

3085

Three Booth's meatplates. Golding Young & Co, Grantham. Nov 06. HP: £10. ABP: £11.

3086

20thC Italian pierced basket, domed cover with lemon finial, 29cm dia. Rosebery's, London. Aug 06. HP: £10. ABP: £11.

3087

Hancock's Ivory Ware jug, 160mm tall, hand painted with orange/yellow flowers, green band around top. A F Brock & Co Ltd, Stockport. Oct 06. HP: £10. ABP: £11.

3088

Rye Pottery plate, painted with flowers against a cream slip ground, printed marks, 8in dia. Golding Young & Co, Grantham. Feb 06. HP: £10. ABP: £11.

3089

Maw & Co Tile, painted with fish and seaweed, 6in square, glaze loss to corner. Golding Young & Co, Grantham. Feb 06. HP: £10. ABP: £11.

3090

Linthorpe terracotta miniature vase, brown body painted with flowers/leaves in shades of green/yellow, impressed mark and shape No. 840, 3in high, rim chips. Golding Young & Co, Grantham. Feb 06. HP: £10. ABP: £11.

3091

Set of four Minton & Co Posin floor tiles, 6in square. Golding Young & Co, Grantham. Feb 06. HP: £10. ABP: £11.

Glossary of Terms

agate ware Earthenware or stoneware imitating stratified agate. Associated with Whieldon from the 1740s and later imitations.

alabaster ware A kind of bone china with similar translucency.

albarelli Waisted maiolica drug jars mainly from Italy. There are a number of examples illustrated. See the **Index**.

amphora Two-handled ancient urn-shaped earthenware vessel for wine or oil.

armorial ware Introduced 1892 by W H Goss.

armorials Owner's coat of arms or crest decorating dinner wares etc.

Arita ware Japanese porcelain from the Hizen province. In Europe from the mid 17thC.

Astbury wares 18thC white-glazed stoneware and red earthenware particularly known for early pew-group figures.

bamboo ware From 18thC a fine stoneware suggesting strips of bamboo lashed together with cane.

bargeware Colourful earthenware suggesting canal boat painting.

basalt High quality fine stoneware from 1760s usually black and capable of decoration with encaustic colours.

bat printing Ceramics ornament developed in the early 18thC from transfer printing. A flexible sheet or bat (glue) took an impression in an oil medium from a prepared copper plate.

Bellarmines German brownish saltglazed stoneware bottles from 17thC onwards, with a relief ornament of a mask of the infamous Cardinal Bellarmine.

bianco-sopra-bianco White ornament in slight relief on tin-enamelled earthenware.

biscuit, bisque Single-fired unglazed wares.

bocage Flower or tree support behind a figure or group.

body Basic clay mix in earthenwares and stonewares. (see also paste)

bone china From 1794 (Spode) the hard-paste porcelain ingredients combined with their equivalent weight in calcined bone.

bone porcelain Soft paste porcelain strengthened with bone ash. Bow, Chelsea etc.

Bristol Pottery The white bodied earthenware with a cream coloured glaze that gradually ousted delftware.

cadogan A puzzle teapot with a handle and spout but with no lid opening.

cane ware Fine cane coloured stoneware from c1770.

cauliflower ware Cream coloured earthenware relief moulded and glaze-coloured to suggest cauliflowers, sweetcorn, pineapples etc. From 1755.

celadon ware From the Sung Dynasty, (960-1280) a porcelanous ware with a whitish body and a hard, restrained green, feldspathic glaze.

ceramic All fire-baked clay.

character jugs Popular from the late 18thC.

Chelsea-Derby (1770-84) Chelsea productions on a limited scale under William Duesbury.

china A misnomer generally attaching indiscriminately to English bone china because of its relationship to Chinese hard-paste porcelain.

china clay (kaolin) A basic ingredient of hard paste porcelain being a white refractory clay.

china stone (petuntse) The second ingredient of hard paste porcelain: a fusible, pulverised feldspathic stone derived from feldspar at different stages of decomposition.

Coalbrookdale Generic term for flower encrusted china.

combing On earthenware thick slip worked into parallel wavy lines with a notched tool.

crazing Ceramics marred by hairline cracks due to the effects of atmospheric changes on ill-matched bodies and glazes.

creamware A fine quality light-density earthenware which evolved from the 1740s.

Delftware Tin-glazed earthenware associated with Delft in Holland, with a fine white surface for painting. English delft has a small 'd'.

earthenware Opaque clay wares, porous after firing and for most purposes requiring a glaze.

Elers red ware Fine stoneware made by the Elers Brothers in England from 1688.

Elton Ware Made by Sir Edmund Elton at the Sunflower Pottery, Cleveland c1880-1920.

enamel Glass opacified and/or coloured using pigments and metal oxides for heat fusing on to ceramics

Etruria Ceramics factory, hall and village founded by Josiah Wedgwood in 1769.

faience The French name for tin-enamelled wares. Equates to delft or maiolica.

fairings Cheap novelties originally sold at fairs during the 19thC.

famille rose Chinese porcelain enamel decoration dominated by the colour pink.

famille verte Chinese porcelain enamel decoration dominated by the colour green.

feldspar porcelain Evolved by Josiah Spode II c1800 modifying the firm's bone china formula to include pure feldspar fired at a high temperature.

flambé Imitates Chinese wares in a wide range of brilliant flowing glaze colours.

glaze Glassy substances fired on to ceramic ware to make watertight, scratch resistant, etc.

granite glaze Grey-bluish mottled slip glaze used by Wedgwood from c1770.

lead glaze Application of powdered lead ore to the ware, dipped from c1750. Leadless glazes from 19thC to avoid the health hazard.

hard-paste porcelain Chinese or 'true' porcelain. English version made in Plymouth in 1768 and exploited at New Hall as a 'hybrid' hard-paste fired at a lower temperature.

Imari English name for Japanese Export porcelain made at Arita and shipped from Imari.

ironstone china A strong earthenware originally patented by C.J. Mason in 1813.

ivory porcelain Evolved from parian ware. Introduced by Worcester in 1856.

Iznik Turkish pottery made at Iznik in Istanbul.

Jackfield wares Brownish red earthenware covered in a lustrous black glaze, associated with Jackfield, Shropshire.

jasper Fine stonewares from 1774 needing no glaze. Usually in solid colour or two-tone.

jewelled porcelain Foil backed glass imitation jewels and pearls set into porcelain.

lava ware Hard-glazed ceramics ware strengthened with blast furnace slag.

Linthorpe Pottery Pioneer art pottery 1879-1890 under Henry Tooth together with art advisor Christopher Dresser.

Longton Hall Staffordshires first soft-paste porcelain factory established c1749 to 1760, directed by William Littler.

lustre wares Isnik, Espano-Moresque, maiolica etc that inspired William de Morgan and other English lustres from c1800.

maiolica The Italian equivalent to delftware or faience.

majolica A corruption of the word maiolica. Colourful relief-moulded ware in naturalistic shapes, evolved at Minton in 1851.

mocha ware Cheap tablewares imitating mocha stone.

muffle kiln Small box kiln for firing enamel colours on ceramics at temperatures from c750° to 900°C.

Nottingham stone ware Salt-glazed but given a smooth surface with glaze slip containing iron oxide. From 1690s.

Palissy ware Applied ornaments of figures, grotesques, lizards, ferns etc. in high relief.

parian A vitrified porcelain suggesting whitish Grecian marble. (Introduced from 1842 by Copeland & Garrett)

paste In porcelain, the basic material mix. (see also body)

pâte-sur-pâte Literally paste on paste to produce a cameo effect.

pearlware The light-density earthenware developed from creamware. Excellent for blue transfer printing.

porcelain A translucent paste as opposed to a non-translucent earthenware body. See bone china, bone porcelain, hard paste porcelain and soft paste porcelain etc.

pot-lids Shallow covers for earthenware pots, collected for their tranfer printed pictures.

potteries The five Staffordshire towns associated with ceramics manufacture.

pottery The general term for earthenwares and stonewares as distinct from porcelain.

Prattware Associated with Felix Pratt but made by many potters into the 1830s.

Queen's Ware Made by Wedgwood 1765 in honour of Queen Charlotte, wife of George 3rd. Generally known as creamware.

saltglaze Glassy glaze applied to stoneware by throwing salt into the kiln.

sang de boeuf An ox blood glaze using metallic compounds.

Satsuma Japanese pottery as distinct to porcelain. Popular with Victorians and imitated in Kyoto.

sgraffito Scratched or incised ceramic ornament.

scratch blue See sgraffito

slip Potters clay watered down to a creamy consistency.

slip casting Hollow ware and figures shaped by pouring slip into a revolving porous plaster mould.

slipware Earthenware ornamented with slip, i.e. a creamy watered-down clay.

smear-glaze An invisible glaze applied to domestic parian as a vapour.

soapstone Steatite, a natural mixture of china clay and magnesium silicate.

soapstone porcelain A soft-paste type containing 35-45% steatite.

soft-paste porcelain Fragile and costly glass frit type, made from 1740s until eclipsed by bone china. A 'hybrid' hard-paste porcelain intervened, lasting from 1780s to about 1813.

sprigged ornament Relief ornament shaped in separate molds and applied before firing.

Staffordshire Generically earthenware figures such as people, dogs, lambs etc originally hawked through the streets in the early 19thC.

stoneware Clay mixed with sand or flint. Fired at a higher temperature than earthenware and impervious to liquids.

terracotta Literally baked earth. A soft unglazed and porous earthenware. Usually reddish.

tortoiseshell ware In earthenware, imitating the shell, developed by Thomas Whieldon in c1750. Often known as Whieldon Ware.

transfer-printing The process of transferring a pattern from tissue paper, applied with coloured ink to an etched copper plate and hence to ceramic ware.

Whieldon Ware Either agate ware, tortoiseshell ware or green glaze or cauliflower ware.

Index

The Index is compiled from the descriptions attached to the images from 3000 plus sales from dozens of auctions nationwide. These descriptions are not edited as they represent the actual market. Occasionally certain key words such as creamware, pearlware, majolica etc do not appear in a description and in these cases the cross reference is absent from the Index. It is also possible in a very tiny number of cases that certain manufacturers may have been wrongly identified or the names of patterns or figures mistaken. Again this reflects the actual market and the difficulties of identifying and cataloguing sales.

Factories are emboldened. Names of patterns, paintings and figures are in italics.

Registered Design Information
1842 - 1980

1842 - 1867

In the first cycle the year is represented by the letter at the top of the diamond, the month by the letter on the left and the day of the month by the figure on the right. The parcel number is at the bottom of the diamond. The ring at the top enclosing Roman numerals indicates the class of goods e.g. III for glass. This cycle ends after 26 years; i.e. the number of letters in the alphabet.

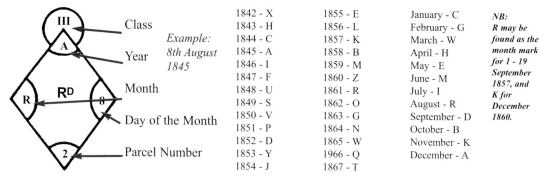

			NB:
1842 - X	1855 - E	January - C	R may be
1843 - H	1856 - L	February - G	found as the
1844 - C	1857 - K	March - W	month mark
1845 - A	1858 - B	April - H	for 1 - 19
1846 - I	1859 - M	May - E	September
1847 - F	1860 - Z	June - M	1857, and
1848 - U	1861 - R	July - I	K for
1849 - S	1862 - O	August - R	December
1850 - V	1863 - G	September - D	1860.
1851 - P	1864 - N	October - B	
1852 - D	1865 - W	November - K	
1853 - Y	1966 - Q	December - A	
1854 - J	1867 - T		

Class / Example: 8th August 1845 / Year / Month / Day of the Month / Parcel Number

1868 - 1883

In the second cycle the year of registration moves to the right of the diamond, the month to the bottom and the day of the month to the top. The parcel number appears on the left. In 1883 the Patents, Designs and Trade Marks Act merged the categories into serialised registration numbers beginning on the 1st January 1884.

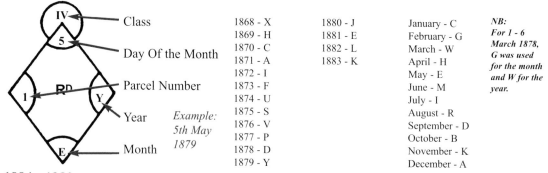

			NB:
1868 - X	1880 - J	January - C	For 1 - 6
1869 - H	1881 - E	February - G	March 1878,
1870 - C	1882 - L	March - W	G was used
1871 - A	1883 - K	April - H	for the month
1872 - I		May - E	and W for the
1873 - F		June - M	year.
1874 - U		July - I	
1875 - S		August - R	
1876 - V		September - D	
1877 - P		October - B	
1878 - D		November - K	
1879 - Y		December - A	

Class / Day Of the Month / Parcel Number / Year / Example: 5th May 1879 / Month

1884 - 1980

In 1884 the various classes of goods were amalgamated, and a single numerical series of numbers was issued to designs for goods of every category. The list below shows the approximate number at the 1st January each year. The number is prefixed with the abbreviation 'Rd. No.' starting with no 1 on the 1st January 1884.

1 = 1884	368154 = 1901	662872 = 1918	799097 = 1935	866635 = 1952	939875 = 1969
19754 = 1885	385088 = 1902	666128 = 1919	808794 = 1936	869300 = 1953	944932 = 1970
40480 = 1886	402913 = 1903	673750 = 1920	817293 = 1937	872531 = 1954	950046 = 1971
64520 = 1887	424017 = 1904	680147 = 1921	825231 = 1938	876067 = 1955	955432 = 1972
90483 = 1888	447548 = 1905	687144 = 1922	832610 = 1939	879282 = 1956	960708 = 1973
116648 = 1889	471486 = 1906	694907 = 1923	837520 = 1940	882949 = 1957	965185 = 1974
141273 = 1890	493487 = 1907	702671 = 1924	838590 = 1941	887079 = 1958	969249 = 1975
163767 = 1891	518415 = 1908	710165 = 1925	839230 = 1942	891665 = 1959	973838 = 1976
185713 = 1892	534963 = 1909	718057 = 1926	839980 = 1943	895000 = 1960	978426 = 1977
205240 = 1893	552000 = 1910	726330 = 1927	841040 = 1944	899914 = 1961	982815 = 1978
224720 = 1894	574817 = 1911	734370 = 1928	842670 = 1945	904638 = 1962	987910 = 1979
246975 = 1895	594195 = 1912	742725 = 1929	845550 = 1946	909364 = 1963	993012 = 1980
268392 = 1896	612431 = 1913	751160 = 1930	849730 = 1947	914536 = 1964	
291241 = 1897	630190 = 1914	760583 = 1931	853260 = 1948	919607 = 1965	
311658 = 1898	644935 = 1915	769670 = 1932	856999 = 1949	924510 = 1966	
331707 = 1899	653521 = 1916	779292 = 1933	860854 = 1950	929335 = 1967	
351202 = 1900	658988 = 1917	789019 = 1934	863970 = 1951	934515 = 1968	

The UKs leading antiques magazine. Provides essential market information for the dealer, collector, auctioneer and investor.

Contains multiple market led features, 1000 images and results from the latest sales, colour coded smart search diaries, and the latest collectors' news for only £21 per year.

Subscribe to *Antiques Info* today and receive all this:

Market-led Features

Each edition has multiple market-led features written by industry experts

Price Guides

1000 images and descriptions from real sales including where and when sold and hammer and buyer's prices.

Fairs and Auctions Diaries

2500 colour coded 60 day Fairs and Auctions Dates in every edition

Free Written Valuations

There is a free valuations service for subscribers to twelve editions or more.

Ask about our Gift Service, telephone:
01843 862069

Direct e-mail link to our team

Write to our experts for a quick response to your information or research needs.

Free Database Access: Become an expert on prices and values! Contains 100,000 illustrated lots from UK sales from the last seven years. Includes descriptions, hammer and buyers' prices, where and when sold. Thousands added every month. The only database in the industry which permits a category search, e.g. ceramics, silver furniture etc.

Additional Databases: 30 Day Fairs and Auctions database: searchable by region and by date. 3 other databases of Specialist Dealers, Restorers and Services plus Clubs and Societies etc. Visit *www.antiques-info.co.uk* for a courtesy preview of these *FREE* services.

For further information call **01843 862069**
visit **www.antiques-info.co.uk**
e-mail **enquiries@antiques-info.co.uk**
or ask your local newsagent to order a copy.